Leo Strauss

and the

Problem *of*

Political

Philosophy

Leo Strauss
and the
Problem *of*
Political
Philosophy

MICHAEL P. ZUCKERT *and*
CATHERINE H. ZUCKERT

THE UNIVERSITY OF CHICAGO PRESS
CHICAGO AND LONDON

MICHAEL P. ZUCKERT is a Nancy Reeves Dreux Professor of Political Science at the University of Notre Dame. CATHERINE H. ZUCKERT is a Nancy Reeves Dreux Professor of Political Science at the University of Notre Dame. Together, they are the authors of *The Truth about Leo Strauss*, also published by the Univerity of Chicago Press.

The University of Chicago Press, Chicago 60637
The University of Chicago Press, Ltd., London
© 2014 by The University of Chicago
All rights reserved. Published 2014.
Printed in the United States of America
23 22 21 20 19 18 17 16 15 14   2 3 4 5

ISBN-13: 978-0-226-13573-1 (cloth)
ISBN-13: 978-0-226-13587-8 (e-book)
DOI: 10.7208/chicago/9780226135878.001.0001

Library of Congress Cataloging-in-Publication Data
Zuckert, Michael P., 1942– author.
Leo Strauss and the problem of political philosophy /
Michael P. Zuckert and Catherine H. Zuckert.
pages ; cm
Includes bibliographical references and index.
ISBN 978-0-226-13573-1 (cloth : alkaline paper) —
ISBN 978-0-226-13587-8 (e-book)
1. Strauss, Leo—Criticism and interpretation. 2. Political
science—Philosophy. I. Zuckert, Catherine H., 1942– author.
II. Title.
JC251.S82Z835 2013
320.01—dc23

                         2013048790

This book is dedicated to
ELENA, SABINE, JAMES, AND WILLIAM

Contents

Part III. Strauss in the Twentieth Century

Acknowledgments

We would like to thank the University of Notre Dame for supporting our research for the last fifteen years. The publication of this book was made possible in part by support from the Institute for Scholarship in the Liberal Arts, College of Arts and Letters.

We also wish to thank our friends and colleagues for their encouragement and assistance. We are especially grateful to David Lewis Schaefer, who reviewed the entire manuscript carefully and made useful suggestions for ways to improve it, both substantively and stylistically. Michael Davis read the prologue and chapter 6; Harvey Mansfield, chapter 7.

John Tryneski of the University of Chicago Press encouraged us to meld together the many pieces we had written on Strauss since we published *The Truth about Leo Strauss* into one coherent statement. Rodney Powell helped us take the manuscript through the many steps to publication. And Les Harris provided us with invaluable assistance in preparing the manuscript.

Earlier versions of some of the chapters have been previously published. Chapters 4 and 12 have both been revised, but parts of them appeared earlier as "Strauss's Return to Premodern Thought" and "Straussians" in Steven B. Smith, ed., *The Cambridge Companion to Leo Strauss* (Cambridge: Cambridge University Press, 2009), 93–118, 263–86. Most of chapters 5 and 6 were previously published as "Strauss's New Reading of Plato" and "Why Leo Strauss Is Not an Aristotelian: An Exploratory Study" in J. G. York and Michael A. Peters, eds., *Leo Strauss, Education, and Political Thought* (Lanham, MD: Rowman & Littlefield Publishing Group, 2011), 74–136. A version of chapter 11 was also published as "Leo Strauss's Two Agendas for Education" in *Teaching in an Age of Ideology*, ed. John Von Heyking and Lee Trepanier (Lanham, MD: Lexington Books, 2013), 183–204. All are reprinted here with permission from the publishers.

Abbreviations

All works listed here are by Leo Strauss unless otherwise stated.

AAPL   *The Argument and the Action of Plato's "Laws"* (Chicago: University of Chicago Press, 1975).

CM   *The City and Man* (Chicago: University of Chicago Press, 1964).

ELN   *Essays on the Law of Nature*, by John Locke (Oxford: Clarendon Press, 1954).

"GN"   "German Nihilism," *Interpretation: A Journal of Political Philosophy* 26, no. 3 (1999): 353–78.

HPP   *History of Political Philosophy*, ed. Leo Strauss and Joseph Cropsey, 3rd ed. (Chicago: University of Chicago Press, 1987).

JPCM   *Jewish Philosophy and the Crisis of Modernity*, ed. Kenneth Hart Green (Albany: State University of New York Press, 1997).

LAM   *Liberalism Ancient and Modern* (New York: Basic Books, 1968).

"LER"   "Liberal Education and Responsibility," in *LAM*, 9–25.

"NCS"   "Notes on Carl Schmitt, *The Concept of the Political*," in *Carl Schmitt and Leo Strauss: The Hidden Dialogue*, by Heinrich Meier (Chicago: University of Chicago Press, 2006), 91–119.

NRH   *Natural Right and History* (Chicago: University of Chicago Press, 1953).

OT   *On Tyranny: Including the Strauss-Kojève Correspondence*, ed. Victor Gourevitch and Michael S. Roth (Chicago: University of Chicago Press, 2000).

PAW   *Persecution and the Art of Writing* (Chicago: University of Chicago Press, 1952).

"PPH"   "Political Philosophy and History," in *WIPP*, 56–77.

PPH   *The Political Philosophy of Hobbes: Its Basis and Its Genesis*, trans. Elsa M. Sinclair (Oxford: Clarendon Press, 1936).

"PR"   "Progress or Return? The Contemporary Crisis in Western Civilization," in *An Introduction to Political Philosophy: Ten Essays by Leo Strauss*, ed. Hilail Gildin (Detroit: Wayne State University Press, 1989), 249–310.

RCPR *The Rebirth of Classical Political Rationalism*, ed. Thomas Pangle (Chicago: University of Chicago Press, 1989).

SA *Socrates and Aristophanes* (Chicago: University of Chicago Press, 1966).

SCR *Spinoza's Critique of Religion*, trans. Elsa M. Sinclair (New York: Schocken Books, 1965).

SPPP *Studies in Platonic Political Philosophy*, ed. Thomas Pangle (Chicago: University of Chicago Press, 1983).

TALS *The Truth about Leo Strauss: Political Philosophy and American Democracy*, by Catherine Zuckert and Michael Zuckert (Chicago: University of Chicago Press, 2006).

"TL" "Two Lectures," *Interpretation* 22, no. 3 (1995): 301–38.

TM *Thoughts on Machiavelli* (Chicago: University of Chicago Press, 1958).

"TWM" "Three Waves of Modernity," in *An Introduction to Political Philosophy: Ten Essays by Leo Strauss*, ed. Hilail Gildin (Detroit: Wayne State University Press, 1989), 81–98.

"WILE" "What Is Liberal Education?," in *LAM*, 3–8.

"WIPP" "What Is Political Philosophy?," in *WIPP*, 9–55.

WIPP *What Is Political Philosophy? and Other Studies* (Glencoe, IL: Free Press, 1959).

Prologue

Leo Strauss was one of the preeminent political philosophers of the twentieth century. Although most of his work took the form of investigations in the history of political philosophy, his intentions were not simply those of a historian of ideas. His investigations had a philosophical and even, to a degree, a political purpose. His chief goal in both his historical and his more strictly philosophical writings was the restoration of political philosophy as a meaningful, even urgent enterprise. To that end, he delivered stinging critiques of two modern intellectual movements, positivism and historicism, that seemed to make political philosophy no longer possible. Strauss's historical inquiries led him to put forward a number of highly controversial theses about the course of Western philosophical history. He placed the beginning of political philosophy, which he presented as a new beginning for philosophy altogether, with Socrates, who, as Cicero said, "brought philosophy down from the Heavens and into the cities." Socrates founded a tradition of political philosophy that lasted, in several important variants, until Machiavelli, who revolutionized philosophy and instituted modern political philosophy, or more simply, modernity. Later thinkers subjected the tradition inaugurated by Machiavelli to very significant modifications, called by Strauss "waves" in a complex intertextual reference to Plato's *Republic*. The upshot of these modifications was the movement that Strauss called historicism, a movement that reached its fullest expression in the thinking of Friedrich Nietzsche and Martin Heidegger and that claimed to bring philosophy as previously known to an end. Strauss's philosophic activity might be understood as an effort to reestablish rationalism by showing that the death spiral of philosophy in modern times was a failure not of philosophic rationalism as such but rather of modern philosophy. That death spiral provoked him to explore premodern philosophy as an alternative, which, he argued, if understood properly, proved immune to the critique of the philosophic tradition mounted in modernity and provided the basis for the revival of rationalism.

Strauss always emphasized the importance of beginning with the surface. Following his advice we begin with the most surface observations about him: he has been hounded by controversy, both about what he thought and about its value. We thus begin by asking, why all this controversy? Three answers come to mind, all of which we shall follow out to varying degrees in this book.

The Fusion of History and Philosophy

The first answer has to do with the particular character of Strauss's work. Most of his published writing took the form of historical studies of thinkers—most often canonic thinkers—of the philosophic tradition. As a result, Strauss himself is often difficult to find in his works. One senses that he is there, but where? Do any—or all—of the thinkers he explicates speak for him? Or are his readers free to pick and choose, selecting what seems to them to comport with their intimations, or premonitions, or prejudices about Strauss? Politics often plays a role in how readers pick and choose among Strauss's various explications of texts. He is known or thought to be some sort of conservative, and how readers stand toward conservatism in many cases determines what in his studies readers hearken to.

Strauss tends to fade into the authors he is interpreting.[1] Rather than cultivating an authorial voice that stands above and outside the thinker under consideration, Strauss attempts to become a mouthpiece for the thinker, to display the inner logic of the thought by reconstructing it from the inside, so to speak. Thus he takes on the voice of major characters in Platonic dialogues, of Xenophon, of Machiavelli, of Hobbes, of Nietzsche, of Schmitt, and of many others, with all of whom Strauss cannot possibly agree—although some of his critics seem to think that he does.

We are inclined to believe that this mode of presenting his interpretations is the single largest source of the controversy we so often see concerning the content of his thought. He does seem to be voicing Thrasymachus, and Maimonides, and Locke. But Strauss does not write like this, as the ventriloquist of the canon, in order to endorse the thinkers he studies. He writes in this way in order to satisfy his interpretive standard that one must seek to understand an author as he understood himself. How better to do that than to attempt to reconstruct the thought and bring it to life as the thinker thought it?

We do not believe that Strauss leaves his readers so adrift that they are without guidance as to where he stands vis-à-vis the thinkers he studies. True, he does not usually engage in the sort of critical analysis characteristic of the modern philosophic academy. As often as not, he proceeds by setting up a dialogue among thinkers in the tradition, and allows himself to stand back and let, say, Rousseau take on Hobbes. But he does let us know what he thinks of the contest and of its winners and losers. So he considers the later modern critique of early modern political philosophy to be cogent. But it is not success alone that determines his judgment, for he argues that the early moderns, who seem to have routed the classical philosophers, did not deserve their apparent victory. If readers would pay attention to his sometimes subtle guideposts, they would find it easier to locate Strauss himself in his texts.

But there is a broader question lurking in the surface character of Strauss's corpus: Why does he devote himself to the study of the thought of others rather than turn directly to the problems of political philosophy themselves? The thinkers he lavishes attention on were not oblivious to those who preceded them in the enterprise of political philosophy, but none of them devotes the bulk of his work to textual explication, as Strauss does. Machiavelli, for example, describes in a general way all his predecessors as unhelpful utopians and addresses particular authors, like Polybius, to contest one point or another that arises in the study of politics. But Machiavelli's focus is never merely on the thought of the past. Strauss the thinker would be much easier to lay hands on if he proceeded as Machiavelli did and addressed his themes directly. It is easy, in other words, to confuse Strauss with an intellectual historian. He always had great respect for intellectual history when well done, but he clearly aspired to being something else, a political philosopher. So much of his activity as a political philosopher looks like intellectual history, because he maintained that our era calls for an unprecedented "fusion of history and philosophy." That is to say, political philosophy today can be adequately carried on only in intimate conjunction with history and historical studies. This conviction accounts for the overall character of Strauss's work, but at the same time it is deeply paradoxical, for he also drew a firm distinction between historical studies (inquiries into what this or that philosopher thought) and philosophy (inquiry into the truth of the matter). Philosophy today must both fuse with history and remain distinct from it. That paradoxical combination tends to distinguish Strauss on the one side from historicists, who accept the idea of fusion, and from political philosophers in the analytic tradition, like John Rawls, who engage in political philosophy in more or less complete independence from historical studies.[2]

We present a detailed account of that paradox in chapter 2 below. For now let us simply mention the most pressing reason for Strauss's call for this fusion of history and philosophy. Philosophy, Strauss thought for reasons we discuss in chapter 3, must begin with prephilosophic opinion, but opinion in our post-Enlightenment age is thoroughly pervaded or infected by residues of earlier philosophy. Already in the early nineteenth century Thomas Jefferson could speak of the chief concepts of Lockean political philosophy as "the common sense of the subject," a judgment that surely could not have been shared by Aristotle or Confucius or Isaiah. Moreover, it is not only Locke who has come to be part of our common opinions and concepts, but Machiavelli, Montesquieu, Marx, and many others. Strauss endorsed the Platonic image of the cave—we humans normally live in a cave defined by our opinions, the ascent from which constitutes the activity of philosophizing. But, Strauss thinks, we now live in a cave beneath the cave. Our cave is constituted by the layer upon layer of philosophically derived opinions that have become part of the atmosphere of thought we breathe. One response to this situation is the unreflective path of Rawls: he takes the consensus of opinion he finds in our cave as the necessary and sufficient starting point for constructive philosophizing. Strauss would say that Rawls only digs himself yet deeper—perhaps constructing another cave beneath the first two. Strauss follows a more radical, but slower and more tentative path. One must begin with an effort to clarify the opinions constituting our cave, and that can be done only via studies in the history of political philosophy. Such studies aim to reconnect our dead or smoldering stubs and residues of philosophic thought with their sources so that these thoughts can live for us again. Such studies can awaken us to the alternatives that lie undigested and unintegrated in our common opinions. History of philosophy, as Strauss understands it, is merely propaedeutic to philosophy proper, but a necessary propaedeutic nonetheless. (See chapter 8 below.)

Esotericism

A second reason for the elusiveness of Leo Strauss the political philosopher derives from one of his major discoveries in his studies of the history of philosophy—his rediscovery of philosophic rhetoric, or the distinction between esoteric and exoteric writing. The first political philosopher, Socrates, did not write at all, because he thought that writings say the same things to everybody, whereas the correct way of proceeding is to say different things to different people, according to what suits them. Accordingly, Socrates rarely gave speeches to large groups of listeners; he usually chose instead to engage in one-at-a-time exchanges with individuals. Philosophic writing cannot proceed as Socrates did, but, Strauss discovered, philosophers prior to the modern era did write in such a way as to capture something of the Socratic way. They wrote so that different readers could find different things in their texts. They wrote so that only the most thoughtful, persistent, and philosophically minded readers were apt to penetrate to their deepest thoughts. One reason they wrote in that way was to blunt or even conceal the degree to which philosophy was in its very nature an activity that challenged and sometimes overturned the basic opinions on which societies necessarily rest. Unlike modern or Enlightenment thinkers, premodern philosophers did not have an agenda that called for the wholesale refashioning of reigning opinion; they accepted the fact that a wholly enlightened society is not possible. Society will always rest on only more or less true opinions about matters crucial to the ongoing health or viability of society.

Many misunderstandings swirl around Strauss's notion of the necessarily unphilosophic character of society and the beliefs on which societies rest. His point is not the one often taken to be his: since the conventional views are not wholly true, they must be wholly false. Those who draw this conclusion are quick to assume that Strauss simply negates conventional views, and that he therefore must be an immoralist or nihilist. No—as he makes especially clear in his analysis of Plato's *Republic*, the reigning views are *partial* truths; the whole truth incorporates rather than simply rejects the truth contained in opinion. (See chapter 5 below.) Not entirely unlike Hegel, Strauss sees the transcended partial truths transformed, but retained in a larger, more comprehensive truth (albeit one that may consist in awareness of the enduring problems or alternatives, rather than a unifying synthesis).[3]

The Straussian philosopher may arrive at an understanding that supports in important ways the dominant opinions in a country, but along the way he intransigently challenges those opinions. Philosophers question what is taken for granted and insist on inquiring into what is held to be sacred and undeniable. Philosophy in its raw form has a natural tendency to run afoul of the keepers of authoritative opinion, and all premodern societies had such keepers. Concern with its public face is thus a self-protective garb for philosophers. Substituting "philosophy" for "learning," Strauss agreed with Alexander Pope:

> A little learning is a dangerous thing;
> Drink deep, or taste not the Pierian spring.

In Strauss's terms, this means that philosophy can be harmful not only for the philosopher but also for those who imbibe some but not all of the activity. Some individuals can be shaken in their healthy commitment to the norms of their society without going all the way to philosophy and the reorientation that it gives to a human life. A little philosophy can undermine the authority of the norms without providing anything to replace it. Since it is highly unlikely that most individuals will or can make the transition to the philosophic life and consequently highly likely that they will continue to live their lives in the realm of opinion, it is an act of moral and social responsibility to be concerned about what one says in public to those who will not "drink deeply" at "the Pierian spring."

Strauss's theory of esotericism has produced understandable controversy, both about the general theory and about the often disturbingly novel readings of the philosophers it has produced. Another kind of controversy, more relevant in our own immediate context, concerns Strauss's writings themselves. He announced the maxim that an author writes as he reads—and whether that maxim is true of all the authors in the canon or not, it would appear most likely to hold true of the person who formulated it. Thus many of the most sophisticated readers of Strauss are certain that he too engaged in esoteric writing.[4] But as many of his critics say when they challenge his application of the theory to authors like Xenophon or Locke, it is extremely difficult to pin down an esoteric writer. How can one find one's bearings in a text when one cannot take at face value what an author says? This same difficulty besets those who seek to read Strauss himself esoterically.

Strauss, of course, had a response to these worries. He does not think that "reading between the lines" can ever produce a definitive reading of a text, but he also denies that the esotericism thesis is a warrant for undisciplined and willful reading.[5] Among other things, he insists that before reading between the lines one must read what is on the lines—and take that with the utmost seriousness (*PAW*, 30–31). Unless there is reason to question what is said on the lines, that should be taken as the author's intent and meaning. Esoteric readings require actual evidence; admittedly at times that evidence is indirect and inferential, but there must be more to it than the application of a syllogism of the following sort:

A writes esoterically;

A says Y openly and on the surface;

Therefore, A must really affirm not-Y.

Unfortunately, much of the effort to read Strauss esoterically has this character. In the case of any other author it would be laughable to dismiss the many strong statements in favor of rule of law and constitutionalism Strauss makes and insist that he actually favors tyranny and even National Socialism, as some of his readers have claimed. (See chapter 9 below.) Putting aside such extreme misreadings, it is undeniable that Strauss writes, if not esoterically, then extremely subtly, a fact that contributes to the difficulty even responsible and careful scholars have in pinning him down.

We have responded to this difficulty in the following two-pronged manner. The subtleties of Strauss's texts require close attention. He constructed each essay and each book with immense care, and understanding him requires equally careful attention to each piece as a piece. Thus many of our chapters consist of close analyses of individual essays or chapters, analyses aimed at capturing his thinking at what we might call the microscopic level. In these chapters we make a point of following him as attentively as we can. But there are also parts of our book that operate macroscopically, that attempt to present the forest without losing sight of the trees. Thus, for example, in chapter 3 we present an overview of Strauss's rereading of the philosophic tradition, set off against Martin Heidegger's parallel but very different account of Western philosophy. Understanding Strauss requires this sort of bifocal view of his corpus, whereby the microscopic and macroscopic inform and check each other.

Whether we have succeeded in unraveling Strauss's thought or not, whether he engaged in full-blown esotericism or what we have elsewhere called pedagogical reserve, it is certain that he writes in a way that makes it difficult to say with certainty what the chief conclusions of his thinking are or, in many cases, what the reasoning leading to his conclusions is. In a word, Strauss's way of writing constitutes a second ground for the difficulty his readers have had in pinning down just what he does say.

Political Philosophy

The theme of Strauss's political philosophy is—political philosophy. It is Strauss's multilayered and complex understanding of political philosophy that produces most of the ambiguities in his writings that lead readers to be unsure of his meaning.

The theme of political philosophy runs throughout Strauss's work, but it rises to greatest explicitness in his set of lectures entitled "What Is Political Philosophy?," one of only two writings to explicitly raise the Socratic "what is . . . ?" question in its title. This essay, like the *Apology of Socrates* in the Platonic corpus, is the natural starting point for considering Strauss's thought.[6]

The lecture series "What Is Political Philosophy?" consists of three lectures: "The Problem of Political Philosophy," "The Classical Solution," and "The Modern Solutions." The guiding thought of the series, to judge by the titles, is "the problem of political philosophy," to which there are a number of proffered "solutions." Yet Strauss nowhere specifies in so many words what "the problem of political philosophy" is to which the classics and the moderns provided different responses.

A reader of the first lecture might be led to say that "the problem" of political philosophy is constituted by the modern challenges to political philosophy: positivism (or "science") and historicism (or "history"), "those two great powers of the modern world [that] have finally succeeded in destroying the very possibility of political philosophy" ("WIPP," 18). That inference would seem to be mistaken, however, because although Strauss speaks of both the "classical solution" and the "modern solutions" in the two later lectures, the classics and most of the moderns of whom he speaks predate the emergence of the challenges posed by positivism and historicism. The problem to which the ancient and earlier modern thinkers present solutions cannot therefore be the challenge posed by "those two great powers of the modern world."

A more promising approach to identifying "the problem of political philosophy" as Strauss understands it is to notice that he supplies not one but two different accounts of what political philosophy is in the opening pages of this essay. We might tentatively conclude that the *problem* of political philosophy concerns the relation between these different notions. Strauss's first account of political philosophy develops it as an aspect or offshoot of politics; the second develops it as an aspect or offshoot of philosophy.

"All political action," Strauss observes, "aims at either preservation or change." In general that must be true, and in the particular historical context in which Strauss was making that observation it corresponds well with the division of the political world into liberals and conservatives, the latter of which are commonly said to aim at preservation and the former to aim at change. Actions aiming at preservation and change implicitly make reference to the political good. One seeks either to preserve the good or to change to the better. "All political action has then in itself a directedness towards knowledge of the good: of the good life, or of the good society." Normally, political action tends to be incremental and not to entail an explicit formulation of anything approaching the complete political good. But human beings acting within political life may well come to formulate ever more explicit and comprehensive ideas about the political good at which their actions aim. "If men make it their explicit goal to acquire knowledge of the good life and of the good society, political philosophy emerges" ("WIPP," 10).

Political philosophy thus understood emerges directly out of political life and is implicit in the most ordinary political actions. Political philosophy comes to light as something like the completion of political life, or at least as that toward which political life itself points. Political philosophy provides the ultimate standard for improving or perfecting political life, for it explicitly articulates the state of affairs at which political action implicitly aims.

Strauss adds, however, that political philosophy "forms a part of a larger whole: of philosophy; or that political philosophy is a branch of philosophy" ("WIPP," 10). Political philosophy, on this account, emerges not from politics but from philosophy, for "philosophy is the quest for universal knowledge, for knowledge of the whole" (11). As quest for knowledge of the whole, philosophy is perforce driven to extend itself into the political realm along with all the other spheres that make up "the whole." Philosophy as Strauss understands it is the "attempt to replace opinions about the whole by knowledge of the whole" (11). Philosophy is "a treatment which both goes to the roots and is comprehensive." It goes to the roots of political life by attempting "to replace opinions about the nature of political things by knowledge of the nature of political things" (11–12).

With this formulation the "problem of political philosophy" comes to view. As an enterprise standing at the juncture of politics and philosophy, political philosophy points in two different directions and takes its bearings in two different ways. Political philosophy begins in opinion, but subjects opinion to keen dialectical examination so as to wring knowledge from it. The knowledge that emerges from philosophy drifts substantially away from the kinds of opinions that dominate political life. In the immediate sequel to his discussion of political philosophy, Strauss identifies a cognate form of political reflection that he calls "political theory." The latter consists of "comprehensive reflections on the political situation which lead up to the suggestion of broad policy. Such reflections appeal in the last resort to principles accepted by public opinion or a considerable part of it; i.e., they dogmatically assume principles which can well be questioned" ("WIPP," 13).

Political theory thus understood looks very much like the first kind of political philosophy, the kind that emerges out of and in basic continuity with political life itself. That is to say, political philosophy of that sort may fail to go "to the roots," because it may fail to challenge sufficiently the root opinions of political society. Political philosophy of the second type goes more to the roots but seems in danger of losing the intimate and guiding connection to political life itself. So far as it loses that connection, it is in danger of missing true knowledge of "political things," which are "by their nature subject to approval and disapproval, to choice and rejection, to praise and blame" ("WIPP," 12).

Since, as Strauss insists on many occasions, opinion is the element of political life, and since philosophy involves the questioning of opinion, the second sort of political philosophy is not only not directly continuous with political life but in principle at odds with, even hostile to, political life as it is lived by ordinary statesmen and citizens. This possibility results in the tension Strauss famously emphasizes between philosophy and the city. That tension leads to yet a third notion of political philosophy: political philosophy is the face philosophy shows to ordinary, nonphilosophic human existence. It is a barbered and trimmed view of philosophy, a presentation of philosophy that blunts and blurs the tension in which it stands with the opinions constitutive of society. Such blunting is in part for the sake of the philosopher and his safety, but perhaps even more for the sake of the community, because philosophy is prone to question and so (if openly expressed) undermine many of the most important opinions on which society rests. Political philosophy in this sense is more or less identical with what Strauss speaks of as the esoteric character of political philosophic texts.

Philosophy is driven into its potential conflict with society by the nature of philosophy, or of Socratic philosophy in any case. In contrast to earlier "pre-Socratic" philosophers, who sought to find the constituent elements of nature as a whole, Socrates examined the opinions of his interlocutors.

For reasons we will discuss at greater length in chapters 2, 3, and 10 below, Strauss came to see this Socratic investigation of opinions as the proper response to the quest for a non-Cartesian starting point for philosophy by three modern philosophers who greatly influenced him: Husserl, Nietzsche, and Heidegger. Political philosophy, then, in a fourth meaning stands for the proper way or approach to philosophy altogether. Political philosophy thus understood is not merely one branch of philosophy among many, but is "first philosophy."

Strauss has a rich and by no means univocal notion of political philosophy. The multiple meanings of the term as he uses it give some idea of why he considers political philosophy itself to be the central theme of his political philosophy. First, so far as political philosophy generates answers to the questions of the good life and the good society, the very questions that implicitly if not explicitly animate political life, it gives human beings valuable and much-needed guidance with regard to the politically just and good. So far as political philosophy is a constituent part of philosophy per se, it is essential, Strauss argued, that it remain alive, for philosophy is itself the good human life. If political philosophy should prove impossible, then "the city," that is, human political life, is greatly diminished, and the good or best human life is imperiled.

Just as "political philosophy" has multiple meanings within Strauss's thought, so "the problem of political philosophy" contains a number of different but connected meanings. So far as political philosophy is "first philosophy," the problem of political philosophy derives from the contestability of that approach to philosophy. That is to say, at its deepest level the problem of political philosophy concerns the validity of Socrates's "second sailing," the turn of philosophy toward opinion. So far as that turn propels philosophy out of the "ivory tower" and into the city, it provokes the problem of political philosophy Strauss most commonly addressed: the tension between philosophy as intransigent questioning and the city as based on unquestioning faith. So far as philosophy, in response to that problem, attempts to justify itself to the city, so far as it attempts to show the city that it is or can be a good citizen, helpful to the city in its concern for justice and social order by adopting the perspective of the city and developing that form of political philosophy which speaks directly to the city and its concerns in a supportive way, another dimension of the problem of political philosophy emerges: the relation between political philosophy as an offshoot of political life and political philosophy as an offshoot or core of philosophy. This aspect of the problem of political philosophy can be well characterized as the tension—or apparent tension—between Aristotelian and Socratic-Platonic political philosophy. One solution to the problem of political philosophy as conceived in the manner of the ancients affirms the philosophic life as the best life and represents the aristocratic or virtuous life as the political reflection of that life. Political philosophy in that mode is inegalitarian and makes many compromises with the perceived necessities of existence. Political philosophy of that sort is also remarkably open to being accommodated to, or even taken over by, the city in the form of the religion of the city, as occurred within Christianity. Christianity or the biblical religions more generally provided a further problem of political philosophy: How can political philosophy maintain its inner freedom of inquiry when subordinated to the highest possible authority, the divine word? One solution that emerged to that problem is the position known as Averroism, which, Strauss argued, made no concessions at the level of philosophy to revealed religion, though it made many at the level of political philosophy as the public face of philosophy. So far as this solution was perceived to be inadequate, because it consigned political life to the sway of conflicting authorities, secular and sacred, and empowered clerical authority far more than reason indicated was appropriate, the classical solution in its Platonic, Aristotelian, and Averroistic forms was rejected for a new solution in which the philosophers turned more decisively to the people and developed a different way of justifying philosophy to the city in order to free both philosophy and political life from the hold of religion. Philosophy put itself at the service of the city, or of the most common elements of the city, and promised to be useful, promised to liberate equal human beings from the shackles of inequality and restraint. It promised, most generally, to work to "relieve man's estate." Political philosophy thus became the aid and sponsor of the new natural science, which brought a new kind of knowledge, no longer contemplative and the preserve of a few, but technological at its core and capable of being pursued by almost all. Voilà, the Enlightenment.

With the emergence of modern philosophy a new dimension of the problem of political philosophy emerged: the conflict between ancients and moderns or the conflict over which solution to the problem of political philosophy has greater validity. At first the moderns attempted to ground their enterprise of relieving man's estate on a conception of nature as non-anthropomorphic, as a neutral array of forces, available for mastering, and yet as the source of norms of a certain sort for human life. As modernity progressed, it became ever clearer that this bifocal view of nature could not hold, and nature was replaced by history as a source of norms. So long as it could be said that history was progressive, this solution to the problem of political philosophy could appear viable. However, both practical and theoretical objections arose in the nineteenth century to this solution, and it soon appeared that history, now in the form of historicism, could no more supply an orientation for human life than could nature as grasped in the modern way. Thus the problem of political philosophy emerged in its most advanced or recent form: Can political philosophy remain viable or be restored? This is the moment at which Strauss takes up his philosophic task. His contribution is to attempt to demonstrate that we have come full circle: the present crisis of political philosophy propels us back to the Socratic starting point on the basis of which a new or partly restored version of political philosophy can be constructed. Thus it is no accident that the most visible part of Strauss's teaching is the call for a return to the ancients. All calls for return, he once said, are also calls for modification (*TM*, 167–73). There can be no such thing as a mere restoration. In Strauss's case he calls for a return with a particularly important modification, meant to prevent the development of the accommodation that originally led to the emergence of modernity and ultimately to "the crisis of our time." His call for return (see chapter 4 below) is a call to restore both Socratic philosophy and biblical religion in their pristine and inherently conflicting character. Rather than a synthesis, or apparent synthesis, of the two defining strands of the West, he would keep them apart and in respectful tension with each other. The failure to do that led to the break with Socratic philosophy the first time around, and he seeks to avoid an eternal return of the same. It is this array of issues that Strauss calls the theological-political problem, and it is thus easy to see why he identifies that problem (identical in important respects to the problem of political philosophy itself) as "*the* theme of [his] investigations."[7]

On Writing on Strauss—Again

Some years ago we published a book on Strauss, *The Truth about Leo Strauss*. The title was courtesy of the University of Chicago Press marketing division. We did not mean anything so presumptuous as to claim that we had captured *the* truth about Strauss in the face of the many sources of difficulty that we have just presented. But we did mean the *truth* as opposed to the many errors and silly claims that were raised about Strauss and his alleged political influence in the early 2000s, especially at the time of the Iraq

War. Much of that book had a somewhat polemical character to it, taking its bearings partly from the many things said about Strauss in the popular and scholarly presses. Fortunately, now that the theme of Strauss as alleged cause of the Iraq War and Bush foreign policy has used up its fifteen minutes of fame, attention can turn to where it always belonged—to Strauss as a thinker attempting to respond to the crisis of philosophy in the late twentieth century, in which his chief interlocutors were not foreign policy makers but thinkers such as Nietzsche and Heidegger.

This book is thus different from our earlier book. It is much less polemical and aims to be both more comprehensive and more philosophic. Its central goal is not to defend Strauss from allegations of Wilsonian Machiavellianism or philosophic tyranny, but rather to explore the many manifestations of the problem of political philosophy in Strauss's thinking. The several parts of the book are held together by the theme of "the problem of political philosophy" and by the various solutions to it posed within the tradition and by Strauss himself. In a sense, then, our book is an extended development and application of the themes Strauss explores in his most programmatic statement, his lecture series "What Is Political Philosophy?" Since "the problem of political philosophy" is so central to all aspects of Strauss's thinking, we have naturally been led to discuss many aspects of his thought that on their face may seem unconnected. Although we make no claims to present here a fully comprehensive account of Strauss's thinking, we have, following our chief topic, perforce produced a book quite comprehensive in scope.

The book is organized into three parts. Following Strauss's presentation of the problem of political philosophy, in part 1 we begin with his critiques and responses to the two forms of modern thought that threatened to make political philosophy impossible: positivism (chapter 1) and historicism (chapter 2). Part 2 deals with Strauss's novel understanding of the history of philosophy and the philosophers. In chapter 3 we present a brief overview of the new account of the history of political philosophy with which Strauss hoped to supplant the old version that formed the basis of both positivism and historicism. On the basis of that history, we show in chapter 4, Strauss argued against the characteristically modern assumption that human life and thought are essentially progressive. Instead, he urged, we ought to seek to recapture the two primary elements of Western civilization, understanding that they are essentially contradictory. In chapters 5–8 we examine more specifically the novel readings Strauss gave of several canonical political philosophers, both ancient and modern—Plato, Aristotle, Marsilius, Machiavelli, and Locke. In part 3 we then look at Strauss's thought in relation to its twentieth-century context. In chapter 9 we respond to critics who claim that Strauss formulated the basic principles of his political philosophy under the influence of Carl Schmitt by showing how and why Strauss gradually became a supporter of liberal democracy. In chapter 10 we seek to bring out the distinctive character of Strauss's response to the "theologico-political predicament" in which he found himself as a Jewish student of philosophy in Weimar Germany by contrasting it with the responses of two other similarly situated individuals, Hannah Arendt and Emil Fackenheim. In chapter 11 we examine Strauss's understanding of the activity in which he saw himself to be primarily engaged, liberal education, and show that he thought it had the same dual character as political philosophy itself. In chapter 12 we describe the different appropriations of his thought by several of his leading students. Finally, returning to the place from which we began, we conclude by highlighting some of the more controversial aspects of Strauss's thought.

The intended audience for our first book on Strauss was the reader interested in Strauss because of the swirl of controversy that followed him; we did not write primarily for those well versed in Strauss's works. We conceive of the audience for this book somewhat differently. We still aim at the general reader, but this time we also seek to speak to fellow students and scholars of Strauss. Some parts of the book may prove too detailed for the general reader and other parts too general and well known for the specialist reader. We apologize to both. We could not figure out any other way to elucidate "the problem of political philosophy" as Strauss presents it.

Part I

Positivism and Historicism

CHAPTER ONE

Introductory
Political Philosophy and Its Enemies

Like many other of the outstanding political theorists of his era Strauss was an émigré from Germany, driven into exile by the disastrous events of the 1930s in his homeland. Born a Jew in an out-of-the-way part of Germany, Strauss was of course vulnerable to the anti-Jewish Nazi regime. He left Germany just as Hitler was coming to power, traveling first to France, then to England, and, finally, to the United States, where he eventually became a citizen and established himself as one of the major political philosophers of the twentieth century.

Strauss described his family home as one deeply immersed in Jewish observance but lacking in Jewish learning. In his early years he was much engaged in the political Zionist movement, but at the same time procured a standard German secular philosophic education.[1] Two events were probably most decisive for setting him on the path that led to his mature philosophic orientation. The first was his education. He was primarily educated in the neo-Kantian tradition, the leading light of which in Strauss's younger years was the German Jewish thinker Hermann Cohen. Cohen died before Strauss reached the university. His successor as leader of the neo-Kantian movement was Ernst Cassirer. Strauss ended up writing his dissertation at the University of Hamburg under Cassirer.

Although Strauss worked under Cassirer, Cassirer does not appear to have had a major impact on him. Even as he was studying neo-Kantianism Strauss was attracted by more modern, more philosophically radical movements. He started reading Nietzsche while in gymnasium and remained in thrall to him until age thirty or so.[2] He was also exploring more formally some of the newer philosophic movements. Thus he went to Freiburg for a postdoctoral year in 1922 to study with Edmund Husserl, the founder of phenomenology. At that time he became aware of Husserl's young assistant, Martin Heidegger, who was ten years Strauss's senior. Strauss always admired Husserl, but the young Heidegger swept him away.[3] He heard the latter lecture on Aristotle and was awed by the seriousness and penetration of Heidegger as a reader of old texts and thinker of new thoughts. Strauss was apparently not present at the famous debate at Davos in 1929 between Cassirer and Heidegger, a battle of titans representing the old and the new thinking, respectively, but he was greatly impressed by reports of Heidegger's performance. At Marburg he also met Hans-Georg Gadamer and Karl Löwith, two lifelong friends.[4]

He continued to pursue his Jewish interests by affiliating with Franz Rosenzweig's Free Jewish House of Study in Frankfurt. He left that post in 1925 when he moved to the German Academy of Jewish Research in Berlin, where he began writing his first book, *Spinoza's Critique of Religion*. In 1932 he received a grant from the Rockefeller Foundation that enabled him to do research first in Paris, where he met Alexandre Kojève (with whom he subsequently published an exchange in Strauss's volume *On Tyranny*), and then in Britain, where he completed his classic study *The Political Philosophy of Hobbes*.

Three thinkers of his formative years—Nietzsche, Husserl, Heidegger—always remained important for Strauss, and elements of what he learned from them remained in his mature thought. But he did not end up a follower of any of them any more than of neo-Kantianism. The three turned out to be a springboard for an attempt by Strauss to recover earlier Greek thought. The effort was midwifed by his longtime friend Jacob Klein, who had studied with Husserl and was influenced by Heidegger, but who saw in them a possibility they had not seen in themselves—the possibility of recapturing ancient Greek thought, in Klein's case ancient mathematical thinking. Klein sought to recapture ancient thought not merely in a more historically adequate way, but as a truer grasp of the nature of mathematical reality than modern mathematics contained.[5] In the 1930s Strauss set off on a similar path—to return to ancient political philosophy. This meant breaking with two of his early philosophical guides, Nietzsche and Heidegger, whose historicism in effect decreed such a return to be impossible and unworthy.

Strauss's philosophic reorientation coincided to a considerable extent with the political disaster unfolding around him. The late 1920s made clear to all who could see, as Strauss might say, that the liberal democratic Weimar Republic established in Germany after the German defeat in World

War I was collapsing. It lurched from crisis to crisis, and the moderate liberal center seemed powerless when caught in the pincers of the communist left and the ultranationalist right, the most determined representative of which was Hitler's National Socialist Party (*LAM*, 225).

There was an uncanny and important coincidence between these two major formative forces in Strauss's life, for the philosophers to whom he was attracted, especially Nietzsche and Heidegger, were at the forefront of challenging the kind of liberal/Enlightenment thought that inspired Weimar in its noblest aspirations. From the failure of Weimar at the hands of the political extremes and the failure of Enlightenment philosophy revealed by Nietzsche and Heidegger, Strauss inferred that the liberal Enlightenment project was not viable. At first he seems to have concluded that the vacuum caused by the failure of liberalism could be filled only by a movement of the right, like Mussolini's early Fascism: in a now-infamous letter to his friend Karl Löwith Strauss wrote that only a movement of the right, not the old and now discredited appeal to "the rights of man," could fend off the "shabby" Nazis or the communists.[6] Strauss believed at the time, on the basis of the Weimar experience unfolding before his eyes and the testimony of the philosophers he most admired, that the liberal democratic experiment had proved a failure. His subsequent experience in England and the United States, and their experience in World War II, would later lead him to greatly revise his opinion, especially when, as his understanding of classical philosophy deepened, he came to see that liberal democracy, viewed in the perspective of the classics rather than the moderns, had much greater potential than he had at first believed.[7] His perspective was never the same as that of the ordinary champion of liberal democracy, but on the basis of classical political science he came to affirm it as the best regime possible for the modern world.[8]

After leaving Germany and finally settling in the United States, Strauss led a much less eventful life, at least in its externals. His first regular position was at the New School for Social Research in New York, as one of the army of émigrés employed by that haven for émigrés. He left the New School for the University of Chicago in 1947, personally recruited by its president, Robert Maynard Hutchins. Strauss spent the bulk of his remaining career at Chicago, publishing his best-known books while there, including *Natural Right and History*, *Thoughts on Machiavelli*, and *The City and Man*. He retired at the then-mandatory time in 1967, moving first to Claremont Men's College as a colleague of his former student Harry Jaffa and then to St. John's College (MD), where he was reunited with his old friend and onetime mentor Jacob Klein. His post-Chicago years were productive—he completed several studies of Xenophon and his posthumous book *The Argument and the Action of Plato's "Laws"*—but they were also years of ill health, to which he finally succumbed in 1973.

The "Crisis of Our Times"

Strauss often began his books, articles, and classroom presentations with an evocation of "the crisis of our times." By that phrase he meant, in part, the obvious political dislocations of the day—the rise of the totalitarian regimes, World War II, the Cold War, the threat of nuclear annihilation, and the bevy of other threats posed by technology. But he also meant a more strictly intellectual crisis: the dominance of positivism and historicism. These movements represented intellectual threats, in that they rendered political philosophy incredible; they also posed practical threats, in that they undermined the confidence of the West in itself and fueled a flight from rationalism, with results that became manifest in twentieth-century political life.

Positivism maintained that modern science is the highest form of knowledge and thus the model or standard for all knowledge; in its most mature form positivism announced that there is a fundamental difference between facts and values and that only factual judgments are within the competence of science. These positivist declarations meant the death of political philosophy, for "political philosophy is the attempt truly to know both the nature of political things and the right, or the good, political order" ("WIPP," 12).

Historicism rejects both claims of positivism, the paradigmatic and authoritative character of modern science and the distinction between facts and values. Historicism nonetheless also rejects the possibility of political philosophy, "because of the essentially historical character of society and of human thought" ("WIPP," 26). In this view there can be no knowledge of the truly good society, for all thought is historically bounded and cannot determine what the good society as such is.

These two doctrines provoke a practical or political crisis because they rob their adherents of the capacity to accept as a rational truth the goodness of their (or any particular) society or its aspirations and goals. Both lead to a kind of relativism, which goes beyond toleration of differences and amounts to a sense of a lack of defensible grounds for attachment to one's society, moral code, or way of life.[9] Strauss believed that he had seen the deleterious effects of this loss of confidence in moral and political truth in the ineffectual reactions of the decent democratic center to the threats posed by fanatical adherents of the left and right in Weimar Germany. As a result of the "flight from scientific reason" resulting from the doctrine that reason cannot pronounce on value questions, explicitly irrational "commitment" took the place of both reason and moderation. Strauss thus concluded that the restoration of the possibility of political philosophy was the precondition for the sober defense of liberal democratic regimes marked by rule of law and, more generally, for the support of moderate regimes. But positivism and historicism were not merely moral and political errors; they also stood in the way of the pursuit of wisdom or philosophy, which, Strauss thought, was the highest good for a human being. Positivism, with its narrowing of the sphere of rational inquiry to the scientific paradigm, and historicism, with its dogmatic insistence on the historical provenance of all thinking, prevented the kind of inquiry the awakening to philosophy requires.

Strauss's Critique of Positivism

Strauss probably gave his most thorough presentation and critique of positivism and historicism in a lecture course he offered in 1965. His presentation in this course was more historical than most of his treatments of these themes. He set out to show that both positivism and historicism depend upon claims about the history of human thought that need to be tested by an independent examination of that history.

Like most scholars, Strauss identified the specific origins of positivism in the works of Auguste Comte and Georg Simmel. He acknowledged that the Comtean position is by no means identical to current positivism, but he declared that "we cannot understand the positivism of today without having first understood Comte."[10]

Comte's "positive philosophy" consisted of an argument about the history of the development of the human mind and the necessarily comprehensive, self-reflective character of social science. In his two chief works, Strauss explained, Comte traced the intellectual development of humanity in three stages. In the first, "theological" stage, human beings thought they could answer the greatest questions and exercise unlimited control over the world by imbuing the things of the world with wills that they could influence. In the second, "metaphysical" stage, these willing beings were replaced by abstract forces or "entities." But in the third, "positive" stage, man abandoned the question of the origin and destiny of things, i.e., the *why*, and began asking merely *how* things are related.[11]

Although the theological and metaphysical approaches retained a certain practical appeal because they claimed to answer all questions, Comte thought that the victory of positive philosophy was inevitable. He observed that the human mind is powerfully disposed to unity of method. However, as a result of the metaphysical critique of religion and the development of the modern sciences—beginning with mathematics, but then extending to physics, chemistry, and biology—human beings at his time (the early nineteenth century) lived in a state of intellectual and, therefore, moral and political anarchy. The development of a comprehensive science of man was thus imperative, both theoretically and practically. This science, for which Comte coined the terms "sociology" and "positive philosophy," was not merely the last science to develop. Although it presupposes biology in the way biology presupposes chemistry and physics presupposes mathematics, Comte also recognized that his positive philosophy had to be the science of science, because he saw that science is a human activity and requires an explanation as much as any other phenomenon. He also observed that human beings cannot live together except on the basis of certain fundamental agreements, and that the critiques leveled by "metaphysical" philosophy in the seventeenth century had destroyed belief in Catholicism, i.e., the hitherto reigning belief. Science had become the only possible source of intellectual authority; but the goal and character of the science of science had not become clear until the French Revolution and its aftermath showed that humanity had a common progressive destiny.

Like our contemporary positivists, Strauss pointed out, Comte insisted that science is the only form of true knowledge. Unlike contemporary positivists, however, Comte also thought that science could discover the best form of government. His "positive philosophy" was not value free, and Comte continued to describe his investigations as "political philosophy." Comte's scientific approach did lead him to deny that there is any essential difference between human beings and animals. Like earlier modern philosophers he observed that human beings are driven primarily by their passions. But he opposed the "metaphysical," abstract notion of a "state of nature," in which individuals contract with one another to construct a government, by observing that human beings live in society with one another at all times and in all places and that these societies are not the products of intentional design so much as spontaneous growths. Comte's positivism was thus both a development from and a reaction against the preceding Enlightenment forms of modern philosophy.

Comte thought that the progressive development of the distinctively human rational faculty would gradually change the way in which human beings organize their common life. As the division of labor that constitutes society becomes greater, individuals lose a sense of the common good. Coercive authority thus becomes necessary to check the selfish, asocial passions of individuals. In earlier times the subordination of the productive classes to the rule of warriors had to be justified by theology; but with the advance of science and industry, religion could be replaced by positive philosophy and the military by captains of industry and bankers. Positive philosophers would not hold political offices, but they would tend to the spiritual development of their people by shaping public opinion and using a free press to critique the government.

Strauss concluded that Comte had vastly overestimated the power of reason. Comte's vision of an ever more pacific, prosperous, and rational future was not consonant with his own understanding of human nature as basically passionate. Although Comte acknowledged the natural right of every human being to be treated in accord with the dignity of man, his emphasis on the intellectual development of a few individuals in a system of ever greater specialization meant that human beings would become increasingly unequal. He also thought that the fate of half the human race, the female half, was biologically determined.

Strauss emphasized two differences between Comte and present-day positivism. First, for Comte positive science is simply the rationalization and universalization of common sense. For contemporary positivists, however, there is a radical difference between science and common sense.[12] Elsewhere, Strauss spoke of the social science of his day as empiricist, not just empirical, precisely because it began by rejecting the commonsense foundation of knowledge ("Epilogue," *LAM*, 210–14). The second and more practically important difference is that, unlike Comte, contemporary positivists insist that social science must be value free. This demand might appear to arise from the Is-Ought distinction, i.e., from the proposition that no statement about what ought to be can logically be derived from a statement about what is. But, Strauss pointed out, neither of the two philosophers who first announced the Is–Ought distinction (David Hume and Immanuel Kant) thought that it was therefore impossible to know the Ought. What is characteristic of contemporary positivism is the further assertion that the Ought (value) is unknowable, whereas we can have scientific knowledge of the Is (fact).

Strauss observed that while this view emerged in the last decade of the nineteenth century in Germany, it became accepted in the United States only after World War I. It was first stated in the two-volume, six-hundred-page *Einleitung in die Moralwissenschaft* (Introduction to moral science) published by Georg Simmel in 1892. "What is called 'normative science,'" Simmel explained, "is in fact only science of the normative. Science itself does not establish or prove norms, but merely explains norms and their correlations. For science always raises only causal, not teleological questions."[13] But, Strauss objected, the causal rather than teleological character of modern science cannot possibly be a sufficient reason for the view that social science must be value free. Spinoza, to take one example, was a great and outspoken enemy of all teleology, but his chief work is entitled *Ethics*. Strauss noted that it is easy to miss the revolutionary character of Simmel's claim, because Simmel announced it so matter-of-factly. Simmel could completely "break with the whole tradition of ethics in all its forms, without any apparent awareness of the immensity . . . of this change," Strauss thought, only because Simmel was writing in a nation that had been bombarded for a decade with Nietzsche's argument that no knowledge of good and evil is possible. Reading Simmel in light of Nietzsche, Strauss saw that Simmel still accepted the positivist view of the objectivity of science, but combined it with Nietzsche's view of the nonobjectivity of values. Max Weber announced the same view later with much greater passion; and, after Weber, proscribing value judgments from scientific studies became a matter of intellectual integrity.[14]

The point of the history of positivism that Strauss presented in these lectures was to show that the philosophical reasons most frequently given for the now widely accepted distinction between "facts" and "values" do not in fact justify or explain the doctrine's emergence. Even though many believe that the only genuine form of knowledge is scientific knowledge, that conviction did not prevent Comte from thinking that science could—and should—tell us about "values." Although earlier modern philosophers had emphasized the causal rather than teleological character of modern science and distinguished the Is from the Ought, neither causal analysis nor the recognition of the logical distinction between the Is and the Ought prevented these philosophers from putting forth moral arguments. The challenge to the possibility of knowing good and evil originated with Nietzsche; and Nietzsche pointed out that "truth" and "knowledge," i.e., "science" itself, are among the unjustified and unjustifiable "values." Positivists thus fail to appreciate the self-undermining character of their position. Confronting the original form of positivism in Comte thus brings to the fore the modification required to produce the fact-value distinction. As Strauss liked to emphasize, that modification undermined science itself so that the positivist fact-value distinction was from the start a nonviable combination of conflicting theses. That was the main point Strauss made in his very sophisticated treatment of Weber in *Natural Right and History*.

Strauss devoted great efforts to combating positivism for both practical/political and philosophical reasons. He took issue with the positivist dictum that the only knowledge is scientific knowledge with an argument along the lines of the position of his teacher Husserl.[15] It is impossible for scientific knowledge to be the only form of knowledge, and thus to depreciate or dismiss nonscientific "knowledge," because science itself necessarily builds upon prescientific knowledge or awareness of many kinds. According to Strauss, "Husserl had realized more profoundly than anybody else that the scientific understanding of the world, far from being the perfection of our natural understanding, is derivative from the latter in such a way as to make us oblivious of the very foundations of the scientific understanding: all philosophic understanding must start from our common understanding of the world as sensibly perceived prior to all theorizing" ("Epilogue," *LAM*, 203–23; *SPPP*, 31). That prescientific awareness or common understanding may require refinement or dialectical examination, but one can never dispense with it. Social-scientific studies do not, for example, scientifically establish that the subjects they study are human beings, but these studies take for granted that we know perfectly well the difference between human and other beings. The superstructure of the science is built on the foundation of this and much other prescientific knowledge.

Strauss was also deeply critical of the positivist distinction between facts and values and the exorcism of values from the realm of knowledge. He asked whether the entire set of claims raised by positivism could be validated according to its own strictures about knowledge. Was the claim that only scientific knowledge counted as knowledge itself a scientifically (i.e., empirically) established thesis? Was the claim that values could not rationally be established scientifically established? Did our inability to resolve some very difficult questions of "value conflict" mean that no knowledge of "value" is possible, or that all conflicts are irresolvable ("WIPP," 22–23)?

Strauss denied, furthermore, that the alleged logical distinction between facts and values could be maintained. Positivistic social science cannot demonstrate that social science itself is good, Strauss observed, because that would be a value judgment. Positivist social science cannot even describe human social life accurately, since it is impossible to account for phenomena like corruption or crime without using evaluative terms.

Strauss argued that the positivist demand that a social scientist treat good and evil equally and indifferently necessarily fosters moral obtuseness and the related vices of "conformism and philistinism."[16] The "ethical neutrality" of the social scientist amounts to an "alibi for thoughtlessness and vulgarity: by saying that democracy and truth [for example] are values, he says in effect that one does not have to think about the reasons why these things are good, and that he may bow as well as anyone else to the values that are adopted by his society" ("WIPP," 20). Accordingly, Strauss observed, most social scientists take very definite moral and political positions. Apart from the perceived warrant for thoughtlessness and conformism contained in the doctrine of values to which they adhere, these social scientists do not perceive the nihilistic consequences of the fact-value distinction, because they think: if there is no reason to prefer one value to another, all values must be equal. And if all values are equal, they ought to be treated as equal. So if there is a conflict among values, the majority ought to decide, a conclusion reached only by ignoring the Is-Ought distinction. In other words, there is a close, if unacknowledged, connection between the widespread acceptance of the fact-value distinction and democratic political prejudices. The blatant inability of a "value-free" social science to provide politically relevant information and guidance has gone largely unperceived, because the outcome of World War II and its aftermath made scientific progress and the spread of egalitarian politics appear to be "the wave of the future." People need not investigate what is good or bad, if the future is already determined.[17]

To take a simple example of the core problem of distinguishing facts and values: how might one distinguish a representation of something from the thing it represents? This is apparently a question of fact. But how do we tell the difference between a clock and the model of a clock? A clock is a device that tells time; a model that has no "works" to allow it do so is not a clock. But if a clock is a time-telling device, then there is an inherent standard of good implicit in its very factuality—a clock that does not tell time is not a good clock, because what it is to be a clock already contains a reference to the standard of value, telling time. That is, the distinction between Is and Ought, or fact and value, is far less absolute than it is usually taken to be.[18]

In addition to the Husserlian and the ontological critique of social science positivism and its fact-value distinction, Strauss gives special weight to the internal dynamic according to which "positivism necessarily transforms itself into historicism" ("WIPP," 25). He gives this critique special emphasis for two reasons. First, the historicism into which positivism transforms itself is "the serious antagonist of political philosophy" (28). Second, the critique implicit in the transformation of one doctrine into another has the power that comes from its being an internal critique, not one coming from outside the position critiqued. The internally driven transformation testifies most effectively to the doctrine's incompleteness and deficiency.

Strauss gives an account of the transformation of positivism into historicism in his first lecture in the "What Is Political Philosophy?" series. He presents three arguments to support his contention. The ultimate conclusion of the chain of three arguments is the claim that in historicism "modern science comes to be viewed as one historically relative way of understanding things which is not in principle superior to alternative ways of understanding" ("WIPP," 26). Historicism so defined is a much more radical challenge to political philosophy or to traditional rationalism than is positivism in that positivism embraces relativism in a limited (but crucial) sphere, the sphere of value, and retains a commitment to the possibility of objective truth in the realm of science (fact), whereas historicism relativizes "all the way down."

The first part of the transformation critique is not theoretical but takes up the point of view of a sophisticated and self-aware practitioner of social science. The social scientist, following the model of the natural scientist, attempts to formulate general laws of social or political behavior based on data, i.e., empirical observations. As a scientist she is aware that one cannot formulate such general laws based on a narrow range of observations. One cannot provide a scientific account of the behavior of water under conditions of changing temperature if one restricts one's observations to a range of temperatures between 70 and 90 degrees. Likewise, one cannot formulate general laws of political behavior on the basis of observations limited to the United States or the Western democracies. Social science, if not each and every social scientist, must become comparative or "cross-cultural" and historical ("WIPP," 25).

Once the social scientist comes into a different cultural or historical setting she necessarily becomes aware that she must take account of the "cultural meanings" prevalent in the society under study in order to identify the phenomena she wishes to study comparatively. Let us say she is interested in legislative behavior. She may begin with ideas of legislatures based on the U.S. Congress and the British Parliament and other bodies of that sort, but she may soon discover that applying these ideas elsewhere is not always straightforward. Is the English Parliament of the sixteenth century a legislature? What of the Roman comitia? The Afghan loya jirga? In order to begin to identify the phenomena, in order to judge whether a certain institution or practice belongs to the universe of phenomena she is attempting to study, she will need what Strauss calls "historical understanding," by which he means she will have to "attempt to understand those cultures as they understand or understood themselves." "Historical understanding," Strauss concludes, "becomes the basis" or at least the prerequisite for "a truly empirical science of society." At this stage of the argument the transformation of positivism into historicism is practical, not theoretical. In order to identify the phenomena, one must become historical, but one does not need to give up the aspiration to science or even jettison the fact-value distinction. Yet, Strauss observes, "if one considers the infinity of the task of historical understanding, one begins to wonder whether historical understanding does not take the place of the scientific study of society" ("WIPP," 25). As a practical matter, the never-ending task of historical study supplants the ultimate aim of formulating scientific laws.

The second part of the demonstration of the transformation of positivism goes deeper. Although unnamed in the lecture "What Is Political Philosophy?," the thinker Strauss identifies, in his 1965 lecture course, with his second argument is R. G. Collingwood, who, in his *The Idea of History*, discussed the dialectic of question and answer. Strauss restates the Collingwood position or adapts it to his point about social science positivism as follows: "Social science is said to be a body of true propositions about social phenomena. The propositions are answers to questions. What valid answers, objectively valid answers, are, may be determined by the principles of logic. But the questions depend on one's direction of interest, and hence on one's values, i.e., on subjective principles" ("WIPP," 25). Strauss's first argument focused on the object of inquiry and the need to, in effect, historicize the object in order to proceed with one's empirical observations. The second argument shifts focus away from the object of inquiry to the inquirer or the subject. Since all inquiries are conducted by a subject, the objects inquired about are determined by the subject and his "direction of interest." That direction is therefore necessarily subjective in the sense science seeks to avoid, i.e., determined by the subject's interests or values, for the interests of the subject establish what is important and worthy of inquiry. The judgment of importance is necessarily an evaluative one. Similar to the first argument, this one leaves us with the possibility of a hybrid "science"—partly objective in that it relates data to conclusions via logic, and partly subjective and value laden. This hybrid does not and cannot segregate the fact and the value elements as neatly as the positivist model demands, because "the objective answers receive their meaning from the subjective questions" (26).

Strauss's third argument is to demonstrate that the transformation of positivism into historicism develops the question-answer position in a yet deeper-going way. Observing that the inquirer approaches his scientific inquiries with questions shaped by his subjective interests, Strauss moves to the conclusion that "not only is social science superseded by historical studies; social science itself proves to be 'historical'" ("WIPP," 26). Among the "interests" that the scientist brings to his inquiry is the interest in science itself, i.e., the commitment to knowledge of a certain sort or that meets certain criteria, the criteria of scientific method. This commitment to science is not more evident or necessary—no less a value—than a commitment to voodoo or theology. The historicization of inquiry in which the self-conscious and sophisticated scientist engages confirms this, for historicization reveals that "science" has not been a commitment, an interest, or a value of all societies, but only of a few fairly recent ones. If no values can be pronounced truer than any other, then the orientation toward science of our societies and our scientists has no more objective standing than any value judgment a positivist would be inclined to set aside. The upshot is that "modern science comes to be viewed as one historically relative way of understanding things which is not in principle superior to alternative ways of understanding" (26).

The critique of positivism from its self-transformation into historicism is a critique on which Strauss places much weight, for reasons we have stated above, but it is not the critique he finds most cogent, for it depends in crucial places on accepting the fact-value distinction, or rather the position the philosophers of social science call value noncognitivism. That is not a position Strauss accepts. Perhaps the best way to put Strauss's position is to say that he finds positivism to be an untenable halfway house. Either both facts and "values" can be objective and true, or neither can. That is the ultimate point of the proof from transformation. Although the political science of his time was largely committed to positivism, and remains so to this day, he did not consider it as serious a challenge to the possibility of political philosophy as historicism. For that reason he devoted much more of his philosophic energy to attempting to respond to historicism, as we will see in chapter 2. Nonetheless he was an unrelenting opponent of positivism, in part because he taught in a political science department where the fact-value distinction had come to be "the common sense of the subject" and in part because neither political philosophy nor the problem of political philosophy in its many forms was at all visible to the positivist eye.

In a rare response to his critics, in his 1965 lecture course Strauss defended his critique of positivism at some length. In *Political Theory: The Foundations of Twentieth-Century Political Thought* (1959), Arnold Brecht had accused Strauss of misrepresenting Max Weber's position in *Natural Right and History*.[19] According to Brecht, Weber did not argue that all values are equal; he maintained simply that their validity was "equally indemonstrable." That was true, moreover, only of "ultimate" values. In Brecht's account, Weber recognized of course that each value can be judged scientifically as to its accordance with known standards—"*as long as these standards are not themselves at issue.*"[20] Strauss responded, however, that "from the point of view of social science, the standards are necessarily at issue, since all value judgments are rationally questioned."[21] Thus positivist social scientists have to put words such as "crime" in quotation marks, because the words themselves convey disapproval and refer to a set of "standards" that posit values. Brecht also challenged Strauss's claim that positivist social scientists cannot recognize the superiority of civilization to cannibalism. In reply Strauss pointed to the work of anthropologists such as Ruth Benedict as instances of extreme relativism, and then stated more generally: if social scientists could demonstrate the superiority of civilization to cannibalism, they would have shown that value judgments can be validated scientifically and so disproved the fundamental positivist contention. And if one "value judgment" could be rationally validated, why not others?

Strauss believed that Ernest Nagel's response to his arguments in *Natural Right and History* went further than Brecht's.[22] In *The Structure of Science: Problems in the Logic of Scientific Explanation* (1961) Nagel conceded, contrary to Brecht, that "a large number of characterizations sometimes assumed to be purely factual descriptions of social phenomena do indeed formulate a type of value judgment."[23] He acknowledged, moreover, that it is often difficult to separate means entirely from ends, and that values can be attached to both. Nagel thought that he still could rescue the positivist position by distinguishing value judgments that express approval or disapproval from those that express an estimate of the degree to which some commonly recognized type of action, object, or institution is embodied in a given instance. Nagel had in mind something like this: one could speak of the citizens of a nation as "very law-abiding" without necessarily approving of the laws to which those citizens rendered obedience or of their law-abidingness. The key point, Strauss thought, was that Nagel admitted that such "characterizing" value judgments are inevitable.

Most significantly, Nagel was an unwitting witness for Strauss's claim that positivism collapses into historicism. By characterizing the principle of causality, upon which all modern science rests, as "only a contingent historical fact . . . for it is logically possible that in their efforts at mastering their environments men might have aimed at something quite different," Nagel admitted that the scientific orientation is just one possible, but historically contingent thinking orientation that human beings may take in the world, no more inherently true than others.[24]

Strauss thought that historicism constitutes a more serious challenge than positivism to the possibility of political philosophy, because historicism begins by recognizing that human existence is not like all other existence. Contrary to certain popular forms of "cultural relativism," historicism does not rest merely on the observation that human beings disagree about the answers to the most fundamental questions. Like positivism, historicism grows out of a certain understanding of the history of philosophy. As we show in chapter 2, Strauss thus devoted a great deal of thought to responding to the challenge posed by historicism and the understanding of the history of philosophy on which it was based.

CHAPTER TWO

The Problem of Historicism and the Fusion of Philosophy and History

Historicism was the threat to political philosophy that Strauss took most seriously; he wrote about it both more often and more extensively than he wrote about positivism. He defined historicism as the replacement of philosophic questions with historical questions; and he labored to rescue philosophy from what he called historicism, but what we, in the years after Strauss's death, might call postmodernism. Yet in doing so, Strauss paradoxically engaged in historical studies and defended his own work by arguing for the necessity of a "fusion" of philosophy and history in our time.

On the Necessity of Studying the History of Philosophy—in Our Time

Strauss clearly and emphatically distinguished philosophical from historical inquiry:

> Political philosophy is not a historical discipline. The philosophic questions of the nature of political things and of the best, or the just, political order are fundamentally different from historical questions, which always concern individuals: individual groups, individual human beings, individual achievements, individual "civilizations." ("PPH," 56)

It thus followed for Strauss that "political philosophy is fundamentally different from the history of political philosophy." The former seeks to answer "the question of the nature of political things," whereas the latter seeks to discover "how this or that philosopher or all philosophers have approached, discussed or answered the philosophic question." The one question, Strauss insisted, "cannot possibly be mistaken" for the other ("PPH," 56).

Strauss sought to revive political philosophy, yet the overwhelming bulk of his work is this other thing that he so clearly distinguished from political philosophy. As a result, Strauss has sometimes been dismissed as unphilosophic, as a "mere" historian of ideas. What can account for this apparent disparity between Strauss's aspiration and his efforts and achievements? Why, it is sometimes asked, did he engage in historical studies rather than constructive and original political philosophy, as did, for example, John Rawls?

Strauss touched on this momentous question many times in his writings, but he devoted one extended text exclusively to it. In 1949, well before *Natural Right and History*, the work for which he became best known in the American academy, Strauss published an essay, "Political Philosophy and History," in which he attempted to refute the historicist "assertion that the fundamental distinction between philosophic and historical questions cannot in the last analysis be maintained" ("PPH," 57), and yet argued for a certain kind of "fusion of philosophic and historical studies" (73). Such a fusion characterized his own work. This essay, much neglected in the now-voluminous literature on Strauss,[1] is thus crucial for understanding his historico-philosophic project. It presents not merely the rationale for but also an explanation of the distinctive way in which he approaches the history of political philosophy. It thus deserves careful examination.

THE "TRADITIONAL VIEW" AND THE "HISTORICIST" CHALLENGE (¶¶1–2)[2]

In "the traditional view," Strauss emphasizes, political philosophy and history constitute two essentially different kinds of inquiries about essentially different kinds of objects.[3] But, he immediately adds, that does not mean "that political philosophy is absolutely independent of history" ("PPH," 56). Even in the traditional view, historical knowledge plays two important, if preliminary and auxiliary, roles in the development of political philosophy: First, the question that animates political philosophy, the question of the nature of political things and the best order, would never arise "without the experience of the variety of political institutions and convictions in different countries and at different times." And second, "only historical knowledge can prevent one from mistaking the specific features of the political life of one's time and one's country for the nature of political things"

(56–57).[4] Contrary to the assertions of many of his critics, Strauss does not deny the importance of historical knowledge for the study of political philosophy. But he does insist that historical and philosophical knowledge are not the same.

Strauss recognizes, however, that the traditional view has been challenged by "historicism." Indeed, he concedes, the "historicist" challenge may appear "to go deeper to the roots, or to be more philosophic, than the political philosophy of the past." By raising doubts about whether "the very questions of the nature of political things and of the best, or the just, political order" as such can ever be answered for all times and places, historicism brings the very possibility of political philosophy into question; and it thus "creates an entirely new situation for political philosophy" ("PPH," 57).

ON THE RISE OF HISTORICISM (¶¶3–8)

Although Strauss doubts that the complete fusion of philosophy and history as advocated by "historicists" has been or ever can be achieved, he concedes that such a fusion appears to be the natural goal of the victorious trends of the political thought of the nineteenth and early twentieth centuries. He thus briefly describes that development. It begins in the sixteenth century when the opposition to previous political philosophy is marked by a novel emphasis on history.[5] That early turn to history was "absorbed by the 'unhistorical' teachings of the Age of Reason," so that even rationalist philosophy came to speak of "the spirit of a time" by the end of the seventeenth century. The term "philosophy of history" was coined in the mid-eighteenth century (by Voltaire); and "the teaching of the outstanding philosopher of the nineteenth century, Hegel, was meant to be a 'synthesis' of philosophy and history" ("PPH," 58).[6] The "historical school" of the nineteenth century brought about the historicization of previously unhistorical sciences like jurisprudence, politics, and economics. But these historicists were, in turn, criticized by their twentieth-century successors for losing themselves in a passive contemplation of the past. "The typical historicism of the twentieth century demands that each generation reinterpret the past on the basis of its own experience and with a view to its own future" (59). As a result, the questions of traditional political philosophy concerning the nature of political things, of the state, and of the nature of man have been replaced by questions about the modern state, the present political situation, and so on, as if we could know what the modern state is without knowing what a state is. More thoughtful historicists therefore admit that it is not possible to abandon the universal questions of traditional philosophy, but they insist that any answers to them are dependent on the specific situation in which they are suggested and cannot be universally valid.

Strauss suggests that the most fundamental historicist claims can be summarized in two widely shared assumptions: (1) that the object of historical knowledge, "History," is a "field" or "world" fundamentally different from "Nature"; and (2) that "restorations of earlier teachings are impossible, or that every intended restoration necessarily leads to an essential modification of the restored teaching" ("PPH," 60).[7]

THE CRITIQUE OF THE COMMON CASE
FOR HISTORICISM (¶¶ 9–15)

Admitting that these widespread historicist assumptions cannot be disproven without a full critical analysis of modern philosophy, Strauss turns to the more manageable task of giving reasons why his readers should not take either of the two claims for granted. He begins by attempting to dispel a popular misunderstanding and moves step by step toward addressing the deepest philosophical claims made on behalf of the historicist thesis. The first widespread misunderstanding can be traced back to the attacks of early historicism on the political philosophy that led to the French Revolution.[8] It is often claimed that earlier philosophers conceived and proposed a "right" or "rational" political order that could be implemented at any time and any place. But, Strauss counters, it is not the philosophers but their critics who fail to distinguish properly between the abstract character of a philosophical definition of the best regime and the limitations placed upon its practical implementation by concrete circumstances. Philosophers knew "that all political action, as distinguished from political philosophy, is concerned with individual situations" ("PPH," 61).[9] They never expected that their account of the best regime would be put into practice without regard for specific conditions and traditions.

Many others accept the historicist thesis, Strauss suggests, simply on the grounds that what comes later must be better. But there are many reasons why this simple thought is problematic. First, unless we worship mere success, we will not identify the victorious cause with the truth. Second, even if we do identify the truth with the victorious cause, we do not know how history will end. We do not and cannot know what is true, therefore, on the basis merely of what comes later; we would at least have to know what will come last.

Another argument allegedly supporting historicism takes the "scandalous disagreements" among political philosophers to show that there are no answers valid for all times and all places. Rather than teaching us that the political philosophies of the past refute each other, Strauss responds, history shows us merely that they contradict each other. Just as historical knowledge of the differences among regimes gave rise to the question that animates political philosophy—namely, what is the best regime—so historical knowledge about the variety of answers to that question offered by political philosophers over the ages ought to give rise to the question of which, if any, is true. "If the 'anarchy of systems' exhibited by the history of philosophy proves anything, it proves our ignorance concerning the most important subjects (of which ignorance we can be aware without historicism), and therewith it proves the necessity of philosophy" ("PPH," 62).

Strauss concedes, however, that historicists have a stronger case than the mere variety of conflicting past philosophical doctrines. They can also point to the close relation that can be found between each political philosophy and the situation in which it emerged. Strauss is not particularly impressed by this observation, however, because historical evidence of the connection between any given philosophical doctrine and its historical setting has a much more limited bearing on the question of whether there can be universally valid answers to enduring questions than historicists think. Strauss does not deny that there is some connection between doctrines and history. He contends rather that the meaning of the connection is not as unambiguous as the historicists assume. First, historicists do not pay sufficient attention to the possibility that political philosophers in the past deliberately adapted the outward expressions of their views to the prejudices of their contemporaries. Many political philosophers do not present their teachings in scientific treatises proper; they write what might be called "treatise-tracts," hybrids of philosophic discourses and "tracts for the times." These philosophers do not restrict themselves to expounding the truth and nothing but the truth; they combine their exposition of what is true with what they consider desirable or feasible in the circumstances in which they find themselves, or what they think will be intelligible on the basis of generally received opinion. Strauss does not exclusively relate the attempts of past philosophers to adapt the expression of their views to the circumstances and opinions of their contemporaries to a desire to avoid persecution. Some philosophers, he suggests, were attempting to affect the political opinions and thus the practices of their contemporaries. He recognizes the "performative" character of their writings that Quentin Skinner, explicitly incorporating J. L. Austin's notion of a "speech act," emphasizes.[10] By explicitly acknowledging that some political philosophers sought to make their arguments more intelligible to their readers by adapting the expression of those arguments to the opinions of their contemporaries, Strauss also recognizes their use of the linguistic conventions that J. G. A. Pocock, relying on present-day analytic philosophy, stresses.[11] Strauss differs from these historicists in pointing out that the relation between a philosophy and the historical situation in which it is articulated may not be the same under all historical circumstances. "The obvious possibility is overlooked that the situation to which one particular doctrine is related, is particularly favorable to the discovery of *the* truth, whereas all other situations may be more or less unfavorable" ("PPH," 64). One cannot stop at ascertaining, loosely, that there is "a relation" between a philosophical argument and its historical origins. One has to determine more specifically what that relation is; and to discover what the relation is, one must try to determine whether the doctrine in question is true or false. The fundamental problem with historicism and the reason that it does not, in fact, raise the most important questions about the possibility of political philosophy, Strauss concludes, is that it cuts off inquiry into the question of the truth or falsity of any philosophical argument from the very beginning. Without examining it, historicists deny from the outset that any argument or doctrine articulated by a philosopher in the past can be true now.

THE CRITIQUE OF HISTORICISM AS HISTORY (¶¶16–22)

Strauss indicates the difference between his own understanding and the current historicist view by observing that "the old-fashioned, not familiar with the ravages wrought by historicism, may ridicule us for drawing a conclusion which amounts to the truism that we cannot reasonably reject a serious doctrine before we have examined it adequately" ("PPH," 64). He thus leads his readers to ask why, more precisely, historicists claim that past doctrines cannot possibly be true now. The answer he gives "briefly, and in a most preliminary fashion," is that historicists observe that the particular political phenomena about which political philosophers in the past wrote, particularly classical political philosophers, no longer exist. How can what they claimed about the *polis*, for example, be true about the modern state?

Strauss responds to this "most important example" first by observing generally that "every political situation contains elements which are essential to all political situations."[12] If not, how could we "intelligibly call all these different political situations 'political situations'?" ("PPH," 64). Second, and in some ways more significantly, Strauss argues that classical political philosophers did not contend that the "city" was the most perfect form of political organization merely because they had inherited it from their ancestors and were ignorant of other possible forms of political organization. On the contrary, these philosophers argued that the "city" was superior to the two basic alternatives known to them, the tribe and the Eastern monarchy, on the basis of two standards or desiderata derived from those two alternatives—the freedom that "we can say tentatively" characterized the tribe but was destroyed by monarchy, and the "civilization (high development of the arts and sciences)" present in the monarchy but absent in the tribe. And, Strauss observes, "this preference was not a peculiarity bound up with their particular historical situation. Up to and including the eighteenth century, some of the most outstanding political philosophers quite justifiably preferred the city to the modern state which had emerged since the sixteenth century, precisely because they measured the modern state of their time by the standards of freedom and civilization."[13] Only in the nineteenth century did the modern state become able to claim that it was superior to the Greek city on these very grounds. Strauss does not deny "that the emergence of modern democracy in particular has elicited, if it has not been the outcome of, such a reinterpretation of both 'freedom' and 'civilization' as could not have been foreseen by classical political philosophy." In other words, he is not claiming that classical political philosophy is simply true or simply superior to modern political philosophy. Indeed, he acknowledges that "there are definite reasons for considering that reinterpretation intrinsically superior to the original version" (66). Those reasons do not, however, include the "fact" that "modern democracy has superseded earlier forms of political association" or that "it has been victorious." Some philosophers have questioned the validity of these standards, moreover. Even in antiquity, some of them preferred the Eastern monarchy to the city.[14] Strauss insists merely that we cannot know which, if any, of the philosophers has stated the truth about such political matters until we have subjected their doctrines to a philosophic critique.

In order to engage in philosophy proper, i.e., to subject past doctrines to a philosophic critique concerning their truth or falsity, it is necessary to understand the thought of a philosopher exactly as he understood it himself. "All historical evidence adduced in support of historicism presupposes as a matter of course that adequate understanding of the philosophy of the past is possible on the basis of historicism." However, "this presupposition is open to grave doubts" ("PPH," 66).

Ironically, contemporary historicists are guilty of exactly the same error they pointed out in earlier, explicitly "progressive" history. Because they assumed that current thought is superior to the thought of the past, progressive historians understood past thought only as a preparation for the present. In studying a doctrine of the past, they "did not ask primarily, what was the conscious and deliberate intention of its originator? They preferred to ask, what is the contribution of the doctrine to our beliefs?" By asking what a past doctrine meant "in the light of later discoveries or inventions," such historians "took it for granted that it is possible and even necessary to understand the thinkers of the past better than those thinkers understood themselves." Strauss agrees with the historians who "rightly protested [against their predecessors] in the interest of historical truth, of historical exactness. The task of the historian of thought is to understand the thinkers of the past exactly as they understood themselves, or to revitalize their thought according to their own interpretation. If we abandon this goal, we abandon the only practical criterion of 'objectivity' in the history of thought" ("PPH," 67).

Strauss acknowledges that "the same historical phenomenon appears in different lights in different historical situations; new experience seems to shed new light on old texts"; and that "observations of this kind seem to suggest that the claim of any one interpretation to be *the* true interpretation is untenable." But, he insists, such observations do not justify this conclusion. "For the seemingly infinite variety of ways in which a given teaching can be understood does not do away with the fact that the originator of the doctrine understood it in one way only, provided that he was not confused" ("PPH," 67). All other "interpretations" of his doctrine constitute attempts to understand the thought better than its originator.

"Historicism is constitutionally unable to live up to the standards of historical exactness which it might be said to have discovered," Strauss concluded. "For historicism is the belief that the historicist approach is superior to the non-historical approach, but practically the whole thought of the past was radically 'unhistorical'" ("PPH," 68). The historicist reader thus approaches the nonhistoricist text with a prejudgment on the possible truth and possible meaning of historical texts that cannot help but stand between the reader and the text and cannot but hinder the reader in understanding the text "historically," i.e., as its author understood it. A good example of Strauss's point is the early Skinner, who professed to know the a priori possibilities of the meaning of historical texts on the basis of his "knowledge" of the historical context.[15]

THE CRITIQUE OF HISTORICISM AS PHILOSOPHY (¶¶23–28)

Contrary to the assumptions of many historians, Strauss argued, the historicist thesis cannot be proved solely on the basis of historical evidence. The
most a historian qua historian can show is that all political philosophies are
related to specific historical settings, or that only people living in a specific
historical situation will be apt to accept a given political philosophy. He
cannot prove that the historical setting of one particular political philosophy is not the ideal condition for the discovery of *the* political truth without determining that no political philosophy articulated in the past is true.

On the basis of the historicist assumption that the validity of every political philosophy is limited to its particular time and place, a contemporary student of the history of political philosophy might be tempted to
inquire not about the best regime per se, but only about the "operative
ideals which maintain a particular type of state."[16] But, as A. D. Lindsay
points out, any thorough discussion of those ideals must eventually raise
the question of the absolute worth of those ideals. "Nor," Strauss adds, "can
the question of the best political order be replaced by the question of the
future order." Even if we knew with certainty that the future will bring a
communist world society, we would know only "that the communist world
society is the only alternative to the destruction of modern civilization, and
we should still have to wonder which alternative is preferable" ("PPH," 69).
It is not possible to replace the fundamental questions of traditional political philosophy about the best regime with questions about present and
future possibilities. What the historicist thesis can reasonably claim ("if the
philosophic analysis on which it is based is correct") is not that the questions change from time to time, but that no answer to the universal questions is going to be valid for all times and places, because all the answers are
"historically conditioned."

Were its philosophic analysis correct, the historicist thesis would mean
"that there is an inevitable contradiction between the intention of philosophy and its fate" ("PPH," 70). The contradiction is inevitable, because
thinkers will continue not only to raise the fundamental questions that
arise, naturally, as it were, out of human existence, but also to find seemingly universal answers to those questions. That attempt will necessarily
fail, however, if all human thought is in thrall to opinions and convictions
that differ from historical situation to historical situation. Philosophers
who come to this tragic conclusion would no longer be able to believe that
any answer they found or formulated could be simply true. Moreover, they

would not be able to know the precise reason why their answers were defective, because that reason would be found in the deepest prejudice of their time, which would be hidden from them. Such philosophers could not help but raise the fundamental questions that occur to all thoughtful people, but they would have to join their philosophic effort to coherent reflection on their historical situation in order to free themselves as much as possible from the prejudices of their age. "That historical reflection would be in the service of the philosophic effort proper, but would by no means be identical with it" (70).[17]

Historicist philosophy claims to be superior to nonhistorical philosophy for three reasons, all of which Strauss disputes. He initially concedes that the attempts of historicist philosophers to identify the connection between philosophies and their historical situations might appear to be at a higher level of reflection and thus more truly philosophic than the "naïve" nonhistorical philosophy of the past. By casting doubt on the adequacy of any answers, such reflections might appear to make historical political philosophy less apt to degenerate into mere dogma than its nonhistorical predecessor. But, Strauss retorts, "a moment's reflection suffices to dispel that delusion" ("PPH," 71). For nonhistorical philosophers, all the answers suggested in former ages are potentially true until proven otherwise; historicist philosophers dogmatically exclude all the answers suggested in former ages before examining them. Nor does reflection on their historical situation necessarily mean that historicist philosophers are thinking more deeply or at a higher level than their nonhistorical predecessors, who were not greatly concerned with their historical situation. "For it is quite possible that the modern philosopher is in much greater need of reflection on his situation because, having abandoned the resolve to look at things *sub specie aeternitatis*, he is much more exposed to, and enthralled by, the convictions and 'trends' dominating his age" (71).

Historicist philosophy also claims to be superior to past, nonhistorical philosophy because it proceeds explicitly in light of an unknown future and thus has an "open horizon," whereas past, nonhistorical philosophy occurred within a closed horizon, restricted to the possibilities known at the time. But, Strauss objects, "the possibilities of the future are not unlimited as long as the differences between men and angels and between men and brutes have not been abolished." Moreover, it may be impossible to foresee all possible developments, even within the boundaries imposed by human nature, but it is equally impossible to say anything about possibilities that are at present not even imagined. "We must leave it to the political philosophers of the future to discuss the possibilities which will be known only in the future" ("PPH," 72).

The third and most fundamental reason historicist philosophy claims to be superior to nonhistoricist philosophy is that historicist philosophers know that the fundamental questions cannot be answered, whereas previous philosophers thought that they could. Strauss responds to this claim by observing that every philosophic position implies that there are answers to fundamental questions that are final and true for all times. Historicism merely replaces one kind of finality by another kind of finality, "by the final conviction that all human answers are essentially and radically 'historical.'" Historicism could claim to have done away with all pretenses to finality only if it presented the historicist thesis not as simply true, but as true for the time being only. "In fact," Strauss concludes, "if the historicist thesis is correct, we cannot escape the consequence that that thesis itself is 'historical' or valid, because meaningful, for a specific historical situation only" ("PPH," 72). Historicism, to be self-consistent, must itself be historicized. When that is done, the historicist thesis itself no longer can support its universalist claims, but opens again the nonhistoricist possibility.

HISTORICISM AS THE TRUTH OF OUR TIME (¶¶ 28–36)

If the historicist thesis is applied to itself, Strauss concludes, it will "reveal itself as relative to modern man; and this will imply that it will be replaced in due time, by a position which is no longer historicist." Strauss admits that some historicists would see such a development as a manifest decline; but, he argues, in doing so they would be ascribing "to the historical situation favorable to historicism an absoluteness which, as a matter of principle, they refuse to ascribe to any historical situation" ("PPH," 73).[18]

Applying the historicist thesis to itself, Strauss asks what it is about the modern situation that leads modern thinkers, in contrast to premodern, to be so concerned about history. To answer that question he gives the argument in favor of the fusing of philosophic and historical studies that he finds most convincing. "Political philosophy is the attempt to replace our opinions about political fundamentals by knowledge about them. Its first task consists therefore in making fully explicit our political ideas, so that they can be subjected to critical analysis." The problem for modern political philosophers is that "our ideas" are partial abbreviations or residues of the thoughts of past thinkers. "These thoughts were once explicit and in the center of consideration and discussion. It may even be presumed that they were once perfectly lucid. By being transmitted to later generations they have possibly been transformed, and there is no certainty that the transformation was effected consciously and with full clarity." So, Strauss concludes, "if we want to clarify the political ideas we have inherited, we must actualize their implications, which were explicit in the past, and this can be done only by means of the history of political ideas." Thus "the clarification of our political ideas insensibly changes into and becomes indistinguishable from the history of political ideas. To this extent the philosophic effort and the historical effort have become completely fused" ("PPH," 73).

Once we recognize our need to engage in historical studies in order to clarify our own ideas, Strauss adds, we also become aware of the fact that premodern political philosophers perceived no such need. "The most natural, and the most cautious explanation of this paradoxical fact would be, that perhaps our political ideas have a character fundamentally different from that of the political ideas of former ages" ("PPH," 74). In earlier ages, Strauss observes, political ideas were based, like our ideas of things like dogs, on firsthand experience. The idea of the modern state is not like that, however. "It emerged partly owing to the transformation, or reinterpretation, of more elementary ideas, of the idea of the city in particular. Ideas which are derived directly from impressions can be clarified without any recourse to history; but ideas which have emerged owing to a specific transformation of more elementary ideas cannot be clarified but by means of the history of ideas" (74).[19]

Strauss supports this analysis by quoting the first and foremost "philosopher of history," G. W. F. Hegel:

> The manner of study in ancient times is distinct from that of modern times, in that the former consisted in the veritable training and perfecting of the natural consciousness. . . . Philosophizing about everything it came across, the natural consciousness transformed itself into a universality of abstract understanding which was active in every matter and in every respect. In modern times, however, the individual finds the abstract form ready made.[20]

Strauss glosses Hegel's statement by observing that classical philosophers articulated the fundamental concepts of political philosophy by starting from political phenomena as they present themselves to "the natural consciousness," which is a prephilosophic consciousness.[21] "These concepts can, therefore, be understood and their validity tested by direct reference to the phenomena as they are accessible to 'the natural consciousness.'" These concepts remained the basis of the philosophic efforts of the

Middle Ages and were "partly taken for granted and partly modified by the founders of modern political philosophy. In a still more modified form they underlie the ... political science of our time." Because "modern political philosophy emerges not simply from 'the natural consciousness,' but by way of a modification of ... a tradition of political philosophy, its fundamental concepts cannot be fully understood until we have understood the earlier political philosophy from which, and in opposition to which, they were acquired, and the specific modification by virtue of which they were acquired" ("PPH," 75).

It is not merely the fact that modern political philosophy is "dependent" on earlier philosophy that requires philosophers now to study the history of philosophy, Strauss emphasizes. Medieval philosophy was dependent upon ancient philosophy, but the relation between medieval and ancient philosophy was different from that between modern and premodern. For medieval philosophers, "Aristotle was *the* philosopher." However a medieval philosopher "might deviate from Aristotle in details, or as regards the application of the true teaching to circumstances which Aristotle could not possibly have foreseen [including, most importantly, the rise of universalist, monotheistic religions, as opposed to the particularistic gods of the ancient cities], the basis of the medieval philosopher's thought remained the Aristotelian teaching." Because most medieval philosophers thought that Aristotle's teaching was the true teaching, the basis of the medieval philosopher's thought was present to him; and because the basis of his thought was present to him, the medieval philosopher did not need to engage in a historical study, for example, of Aristotle. That is, he could treat Aristotle, in effect, as a contemporary.

The kind of dependency modern political philosophy has on ancient philosophy is different, precisely because the basis of modern political philosophy in ancient philosophy is no longer present to modern philosophers. Because "modern thought is in all its forms, directly or indirectly, determined by the idea of progress," modern thinkers assume that they can build on foundations that have already been laid without going back and reexamining the validity of those foundations. As a result, the foundations of modern political philosophy gradually become covered over.[22] If we are to understand the bases of the ideas we have inherited and to determine whether those ideas are well founded or not, we have to unearth these bases in earlier philosophy. "This philosophic inquiry is the history of philosophy or of science" ("PPH," 76).

Such a philosophic inquiry into the origins of modern philosophy and science is necessary in order to revive an appreciation of the distinction between "inherited knowledge . . . a man takes over from former generations" and "independently acquired knowledge . . . the philosophic or scientific knowledge a mature scholar acquires in his unbiased intercourse, as fully enlightened as possible as to its horizon and presuppositions" ("PPH," 76–77). That distinction has unfortunately been clouded if not covered over in our time by talk about a "body of knowledge" or "the results of research," in which people "tacitly assign the same cognitive status to inherited knowledge and independently acquired knowledge" (77). Strauss concludes that "modern political philosophy or science, as distinguished from pre-modern political philosophy or science, is in need of the history of political philosophy or science as an integral part of its own efforts, since . . . it consists to a considerable extent of inherited knowledge whose basis is no longer contemporaneous or immediately accessible." But, he insists, "the recognition of this necessity cannot be mistaken for historicism. For historicism asserts that the fusion of philosophic and historical questions marks in itself a progress beyond 'naïve' non-historical philosophy, whereas we limit ourselves to asserting that that fusion is . . . inevitable on the basis of modern philosophy, as distinguished from premodern philosophy or 'the philosophy of the future'" (77).

Strauss's somewhat ironical evocation of Nietzsche's call for a "philosophy of the future" at the conclusion of his essay on history highlights the fundamental issue. Will there be political philosophy in the future? Will philosophers continue to raise the fundamental questions? Or, if they continue to raise these questions, will they be discouraged from vigorously pursuing answers by a historicist conviction that they will never find an answer whose validity is not "historically conditioned" and thus limited in a way they themselves will never be able to perceive? By the mid-1930s Strauss had become convinced that Nietzsche, in his attempt to recapture ancient virtue, had not sufficiently freed himself from the idea of progress that is not only fundamental to all modern thought but was even implicit in Nietzsche's call for a "philosophy of the future."[23] What was needed, Strauss suggested in the title of a series of talks he gave a few years later, was not an attempt to make further "progress" on the basis of past achievements, but rather, first, an attempt to "return" to understanding past thinkers as they understood themselves.[24] In the many historical studies that comprise the bulk of his corpus Strauss sought to demonstrate that political philosophy in its original meaning is still possible, even though he argued that political philosophy now requires a preliminary historical critique of received opinions, a critique he pursued in his many studies of past political philosophy, studies with the aspiration to understand the thinkers as they understood themselves and with the goal of uncovering the permanent questions that persist and thus refute historicism.

Strauss's Philosophical Response to "Radical" Historicism

Strauss returned to the critique of historicism in his classic 1953 study *Natural Right and History*. He reiterated his fundamental objection to "historicism" early in that book: The "historicist" proposition that all thought is historically conditioned or limited is self-contradictory, because the truth of that proposition is not restricted to its own time and place. The proposition that all thought is historically limited, but that this insight is available only to people living at this time, evades the self-contradiction but requires a philosophical justification. The "radical historicist" Martin Heidegger had offered just such a justification.[25] To refute the historicist thesis, it was necessary to confront Heidegger's claims about the fundamentally historical character of human existence and the history of "Being."

Strauss summarized "the thesis of radical historicism" as follows:

All knowledge, however limited and "scientific," presupposes a frame of reference . . . [or] horizon . . . within which understanding and knowing take place. Only such a comprehensive vision makes possible any . . . observation . . . [or] orientation. The comprehensive view of the whole cannot be validated by reasoning, since it is the basis of all reasoning. Accordingly, there is a variety of such comprehensive views, each as legitimate as any other. . . . Strictly speaking, we cannot choose among different views. A single comprehensive view is imposed on us by fate.

No one controls the time or place at which he or she is born. According to Heidegger, we are, nevertheless, "free either to choose in anguish the world view and standards imposed on us by fate or else to lose ourselves in illusory security or in despair" (*NRH*, 26–27).

Strauss agreed that all understanding or knowledge presupposes a comprehensive view. It is not possible to understand any "object" or particular kind of being in isolation from all others. That is the reason earlier philosophers sought knowledge of the whole. Strauss also agreed that modern natural science makes it difficult, if not impossible, to achieve such a comprehensive view now. Strauss agreed with Heidegger that by analyzing and so reducing everything to miniscule particles of matter or energy in infinitely expanding space, modern natural science makes it impossible to recognize anything distinctively human ("WIPP," 39). There are really no stable, particular forms of existence or a limiting, defining "horizon" of the whole.

Strauss thus agreed with the radical historicist that we live in a time of crisis—philosophical as well as political. The historical explanation of the way in which human beings acquired their distinctive faculties was developed by philosophers attempting to make our understanding of human life consistent with a modern natural scientific view of the universe. But this historical understanding of human life culminated in showing that modern natural science is itself a human activity or product, shot through with the subjectivity of the subject scientist. Because it does not allow for a distinction between human and other forms of being, modern natural science cannot give an account of its own origin or foundation. Indeed, neither history nor science can show why human beings should persist in a search for knowledge that does not result in knowledge, strictly speaking, because knowledge can only be knowledge of the whole. In modern philosophy, the search for knowledge had been justified by promises of its beneficent effects on human life. But in the twentieth century the threat of nuclear war or various forms of environmental devastation and genetic engineering had made the beneficence of science increasingly questionable.[26] Like Heidegger, Strauss thus thought that the question why human beings should seek knowledge or philosophize had arisen in the twentieth century in a way it had not arisen before.

The "crisis of our times," according to both Heidegger and Strauss, was not simply philosophical or "scientific," however. It was also political. On the basis of the analysis of human existence he gave in *Being and Time*, Heidegger proclaimed the need for a new kind of practical stance in the face of fundamental uncertainty—resolution. In his notorious 1933 address as rector of the University of Freiburg, as well as in the lectures he gave in 1936 as an "introduction to metaphysics," Heidegger found that resolution embodied politically in German National Socialism. Confronted by the failure of the biologist Nazis to adopt his own historical understanding of the situation as well as by their failure to lead Germany to planetary rule, Heidegger later adopted a more passive, "poetic" stance. He argued that the dangerous truth revealed by the potential of modern technology to transform everything was a necessary result of Western rationalism, and that Western rationalism was, in turn, a necessary outgrowth of Greek philosophy and its fundamental, if usually unrecognized, conception of Being as presence. Heidegger thought he could perceive the limits of the understanding of Being as presence that had first been announced in ancient Greece because he lived at the time at which the possibilities of that understanding could be seen to have been fully worked out by previous thinkers.[27]

Strauss thought that Heidegger's analysis of the working out of the implications of the original experience of "Being" in ancient Greece, i.e., his "*destruktion* of the traditional understanding of the history of philosophy," had made it possible to reexamine the traditional understanding of that history in a way it had not been reexamined for centuries (*JPCM*, 450, 462). But, Strauss argued, a fresh examination of the origins of Western civilization in the works of Plato and Aristotle, on the one hand, and the Hebrew Bible, on the other, led to very different conclusions about the defining limitations or characteristics of human existence as well as about the origins and history of Western philosophy from those Heidegger had announced.

According to the phenomenological analysis Heidegger presented in *Being and Time*, human beings ask what an object is—in itself—only when it stops working, i.e., performing its function or being useful. In other words, Heidegger suggested, human beings initially and originally perceive "things" in the world in terms of their use; theory and thus the theoretical question concerning their essence or "being" is secondary and derivative. And since it is derivative from practical experience, which is itself limited by time and space, "theory" or philosophy is defined and limited by its temporal origins in a way that was not recognized earlier.

Human beings discover that their existence is limited by time and space, according to Heidegger, when, seeking the source of a general but undefined anxiety they feel, they realize that they can cease to exist at any moment. They do not necessarily continue to live as a result of their natural or animal instincts or mere chance; they can choose to die. But if and when they choose to live, they project what they have been in the past into an unknown future.

Strauss objected that the anxiety Heidegger thought revealed the fundamental character and limitations of human existence through a confrontation with the ever-present possibility of one's own death was, in fact, an experience peculiar to our time. As a result of the apparent success of modern natural science in providing human beings not merely with knowledge but with the ability to manipulate things, the view developed that anything that could not be studied with the techniques employed by modern natural scientists could not be known. Among the "things" that could not be shown to be true by the collection and analysis of data are human judgments about good and bad, right and wrong. Told that their judgments about such fundamental matters were merely irrational expressions of feeling or arbitrary "values," people became uncertain about the rightness or wrongness, truth or falsity, of their judgments and so, anxious. In previous times, human beings who believed in a divine or even merely a necessary natural order of things might have feared death, but they did not feel the same uncertainty or general "anxiety" about the goodness or badness of their existence that Heidegger took to be the key to its fundamentally temporal character and limitation. What one finds in human societies at all times and places are these judgments, varying to be sure, of good and bad.

In *Natural Right and History* Strauss sought to counter Heidegger's claims about the history of philosophy by giving a different account of the origin, first of philosophy itself, and then of political philosophy, that is, of the human attempt to obtain knowledge about what is just, noble, and good. In prephilosophical societies (like that described in the Hebrew Bible), human beings understand things in terms of their characteristic "ways." The most important of those "ways" are our own ways, the ways of our community. These ways, having been established, are said to be best because they are oldest. But to identify the good with the old, communities had to understand the originators of the old ways to be better than the current inhabitants, i.e., to be gods or pupils of gods. Questions about the goodness of their own ways arose when it was observed that there was a variety of ways or customs. To determine which ways were best, one had to distinguish between what was conventionally said in each community and what human beings could observe for themselves. At the same time inquirers became aware of the distinction between that which was man-made and that which was not. Questions about the status of the laws and the divine sources of the laws became joined with questions about the origins or causes: were they products of human action, i.e., established by convention, or did they exist independently of human beings, by nature? "Philosophy . . . came into being when nature was discovered . . . by some Greek twenty-six hundred years ago or before" (*NRH*, 82). "The philosophic quest for the first things presupposes not merely that there are first things but that the first things are always," because, according to a fundamental premise of reason, "no being emerges without a cause" (89). In other words, the traditional equation of being itself with eternal, unchanging being was a requirement of reason or intelligibility itself. It was not, as Heidegger had maintained, the product of a faulty, because limited, understanding of Being as presence.

The Greek discovery of "nature" as a term of distinction denoting those things which did not come into being as products of human art or convention pointed toward, but did not itself constitute, the insight fundamental to political philosophy. Political philosophy arose after and out of philosophy, when Socrates raised the question about the best form of life for human beings. Socrates's famous turn to "the human things" did not mean that he turned away from any or all inquiries into nature. "Socrates was forced to raise the question as to what the human things as such are" by his observation that to be means to be something, i.e., that "being" is essentially differentiated (see *CM*, 19–21; *RCPR*, 126, 132–33). And, Strauss pointed out, "it is impossible to grasp the distinctive character of human things as such without grasping the essential difference between human things and the things which are not human, i.e., the divine or natural things. This, in turn, presupposes some understanding of the divine or natural things as such" (*NRH*, 122).

In asking whether human beings should choose to live justly, and thus what justice is, Strauss observed, in the *Republic* Plato shows that Socrates was forced to rise from discussions concerning merely human matters to questions concerning the structure and intelligibility of the whole.[28] Indeed, the question raised in the *Republic* about the best way of life constitutes both the origin of the human search for knowledge and the framework in which the character and limitations of that search become evident. He concluded his own controversial reading of the *Republic* by stating:

> The teaching of the *Republic* regarding justice can be true although it is not complete, in so far as the nature of justice depends decisively on the nature of the city—for even the trans-political cannot be understood as such except if the city is understood—and the city is completely intelligible because its limits can be made perfectly manifest: to see these limits, one need not have answered the question regarding the whole; it is sufficient for the purpose to have raised the question regarding the whole. (*CM*, 138)

Like Heidegger, Strauss emphasized that human understanding requires a limited framework. We cannot come to know or define anything, much less orient or understand our relation to other things, if we are not able to determine the limits of the particular world in which we find ourselves.

Unlike Heidegger, however, Strauss was led by his rereading of Plato to conclude that this framework was provided not by "time," but by the "city."

> Socrates makes clear in the *Republic* of what character the city would have to be in order to satisfy the highest need of man. By letting us see that the city constructed in accordance with this requirement is not possible, he lets us see the essential limits, the nature, of the city. (*CM*, 138)

Human beings come to understand the "transpolitical" only by seeing the limits of the political. Whereas Heidegger argued that time constitutes the "horizon" of our vision and conceals what lies beyond it, Strauss argues that the limits of the city make us aware not merely of our desire to find and come into contact with something beyond them, but of our intimations that there is something "good in itself," even if we do not know and probably never will know exactly what that is (*NRH*, 31–32; "WIPP," 55).

"Far from legitimizing the historicist inference," Strauss concluded, "history seems rather to prove that all human thought, and certainly all philosophic thought, is concerned with the same fundamental themes or . . . problems." Is "being" or the universe eternal? Does it have an intelligible order? A beginning or an end? Philosophers ancient and modern have asked such questions. And "if the fundamental problems persist in all historical change, human thought is capable of transcending its historical limitation or of grasping something trans-historical" (*NRH*, 23–24). By showing that there are "fundamental problems" that "persist in all historical change, however much they may be obscured by the temporary denial of their relevance and however variable or provisional all human solutions to these problems may be," Strauss thought he had demonstrated how "the human mind liberates itself from its historical limitations." He did not think that anything more was "needed to legitimize philosophy in its original, Socratic sense" (32).

Strauss's Rediscovery of the Art of Writing

Strauss's refutation of the historicist contention had two parts: the philosophical response to "radical historicism" that he presents primarily in *Natural Right and History* (1953) and the literary and empirical or historical response to historicism that he presents thematically primarily in *Persecution and the Art of Writing* (1952) and in practice in many of his historical studies.[29] As should now be clear, Strauss turned to studies in the history of political philosophy with a dual purpose. On the one hand, he meant to show empirically that the historicist claim that all thought belongs to its time was false. He wished to demonstrate that philosophic thought could be and often was "untimely."[30] But he turned to the history of political philosophy also in pursuit of the peculiar fusion of philosophy and history that he saw to be necessary in our day. Contrary to the historicists, who insisted that we, looking at historical thinkers from the vantage of our different historical moment, could never understand them as they understood themselves, Strauss insisted that aiming to understand a thinker as he understood himself was the necessary methodological mandate for studies in the history of thought, for only that could count as genuine understanding.[31]

But how to understand a thinker as he understood himself? Strauss hesitated to lay down any strict hermeneutical rules for reading. All readings, he insisted in an exchange with Hans-Georg Gadamer, are irreducibly "occasional."[32] Yet Strauss did promulgate what became a famous and controversial claim about interpretation—the so-called esotericism thesis. Past thinkers, Strauss maintained, often employed an art of writing in which they overemphasized their agreements with the leading opinions of their times and downplayed their divergences from those opinions. That practice contributed to the later emergence of historicism, for it led to the impression of a relatively snug fit between a given mode of thought and the historical situation in which it found expression.

Strauss's discovery of esotericism occurred in the course of his studies of the Jewish philosopher Maimonides and his Islamic mentor, Alfarabi. Medieval Jewish and Islamic philosophy developed in a context quite different from that in which Christian philosophy arose. Where revelation was considered to be a matter not of doctrinal belief, as in Christianity, but of law, as in Judaism and Islam, the opposition between the unquestioning obedience demanded by the command of God and the questioning characteristic of philosophy was very clear. Both Maimonides and Alfarabi appeared to be followers of Aristotle who argued for the compatibility of reason and revelation. But further study showed Strauss that both took their understanding of philosophy and its relation to the "gods of the city" more from Plato than from Aristotle. Taking Socrates as the exemplar of the philosophic life, Maimonides and Alfarabi not only recognized the conflict between philosophy and the laws of the city that had led to Socrates's death but also came to understand philosophy to consist in a Socratic quest for wisdom rather than in the possession of knowledge. Philosophy is love of rather than attainment of wisdom.

These medieval Islamic and Jewish writers were Strauss's teachers with respect to the "art of writing" he became so well known for expounding.[33] Recognizing that they themselves were in danger of being persecuted for impiety, Strauss argued, these medieval philosophers practiced an "art of writing" that disguised the extent to which they were challenging accepted opinions. They endorsed orthodox doctrines about the creation and order of the world, the good, and the just, particularly at the beginnings and conclusions of their writings. They indicated their dissent, however, by carefully planted hints, or even by contradictions of their own pious statements, especially in the center of an argument, where the contradiction was least apt to be noticed. They also stated heterodox opinions through the mouths of other characters or authors, and raised doubts about the adequacy of the position or arguments they were purportedly defending by remaining silent about crucial topics. One of the most significant examples of such a silence was Alfarabi's failure to mention either the Platonic ideas or the immortality of the soul in his book *The Philosophy of Plato*, even though he claimed to be summarizing the content of all the dialogues including *Phaedo* and the *Republic*, where these two doctrines receive prominent treatment.[34]

Recent historians of political thought fail to recognize the "art of writing" that philosophers utilized in the past, Strauss argued, because these historians have shared the presuppositions of their liberal societies. Taking "for granted the essential harmony between thought and society or between intellectual progress and social progress," these historians do not understand the conflict that philosophers in the past recognized between philosophy and society, a conflict that led them to develop an indirect mode of communicating their most radical thoughts "between the lines." Insofar as contemporary "historical" accounts of the works of past authors proceed on the basis of modern liberal assumptions about the relation between thought and society, however, these accounts are fundamentally, if ironically "unhistorical." Liberal societies are relatively rare, recent developments. Most philosophers did not live or write in societies that gave them complete freedom to say or publish what they thought. On the contrary, many past authors who openly disagreed with prevailing, officially endorsed opinions suffered penalties ranging from social ostracism to torture and capital punishment.

The threat of persecution was only the first and most obvious reason, however, that past authors did not state their thoughts completely and explicitly. Because questioning accepted opinions creates doubt about the validity as well as the application of established moral norms, some premodern authors concluded, a completely public presentation of an unfettered philosophical search for truth is not compatible with the requirements of maintaining a stable political order. Attempting to act (or write) in a "socially responsible" manner, these authors sought to conceal their most radical questions and conclusions from all but their most careful readers.

There was a third reason, moreover, that some authors chose to communicate their thoughts incompletely and indirectly. Truly philosophical authors write not so much to propagate doctrines as to encourage younger readers to follow them in a life of inquiry. Such authors artfully attempt to provoke questions in the minds of their most attentive readers and then provide hints concerning the way those questions might be answered; but these authors leave their readers to think out the answers and the problems with these possible answers for themselves. Plato, who wrote only dialogues in which he presented conversations among others, was Strauss's model of such an author.

Strauss's ideas about concealed writing were controversial in his time, but they were historically rather commonplace. For instance, Strauss notes, Maimonides spoke openly of concealed meaning in texts, and until the end of the nineteenth century, many philosophers and theologians thought that Thomas Hobbes and Baruch Spinoza were really atheists, concealing their true views by referring repeatedly to God, divine law, and the truth of Scripture in order to avoid the censors. There was a very widespread consensus that some if not all ancient and medieval authors wrote esoterically. So widespread was knowledge of the practice that John Toland in the seventeenth century wrote a treatise on esoteric writing.[35]

Strauss's theory of esotericism was subtle and nuanced. He distinguished, for example, between heterodox modern philosophers who, looking forward to the abolition of persecution as such, "concealed their views only far enough to protect themselves as well as possible," and older authors who, "convinced that philosophy as such was suspect to, and hated by, the majority of men," concluded "that public communication of the philosophic or scientific truth was impossible or undesirable, not only for the time being but for all times" (*PAW*, 33–34).

Strauss never claimed that all authors write esoterically. Indeed, he set up criteria that must be met before one has a right to posit esotericism in a text, one of the chief ones being that one has to read the text "on the lines" before one tries to read "between the lines." Only when problems—contradictions, noticeable gaps, and other anomalies—appear in the "on the lines" reading ought one to think of a "between the lines" reading. Strauss's techniques of reading are not undisciplined as some critics assert. As a historian, Strauss observed, a scholar has to begin by trying to give an account of what an author literally wrote. If a coherent and accurate account of the content of any given text can be given on the basis of the author's explicit statements, the analysis ends there. But Strauss cautioned, "The context in which a statement occurs, and the literary character of the whole work as well as its plan, must be perfectly understood before an interpretation of the statement can reasonably claim to be adequate or even correct." If an obviously intelligent and knowledgeable author makes "such blunders as would shame an intelligent high school boy, it is reasonable to assume that they are intentional, especially if the author discusses, however incidentally, the possibility of intentional blunders in writing." Emphasizing the importance of the literary form, Strauss added, "the views of the author of a drama or dialogue must not, without previous proof, be identified with the views expressed by one or more of his characters." Most important (and in the context of modern historical scholarship, most controversial), he concluded, "the real opinion of an author is not necessarily identical with that which he expresses in the largest number of passages" (*PAW*, 30).

Given the differences and nuances that he recognized, Strauss did not lay out one hermeneutical "method" to be applied to all texts.[36] In *Persecution* he first pointed out some of the kinds of indications or hints on the part of an author that should lead a careful reader to look for that author's true thoughts beneath the surface of the text. In analyzing specific works by four different authors, Strauss suggested a few general strategies for reading such texts. According to the classical teachers of forensic rhetoric, he noted, things placed in the middle are least exposed to superficial readers.[37] In explicating Alfarabi's treatment of Plato in *On the Philosophy of Plato and Aristotle*, Strauss thus observed that "at the beginning of the treatise *On the Attainment of Happiness* with which he prefaces his summaries of the philosophies of Plato and Aristotle, Farabi employs the distinction between 'the happiness of this world in this life' and 'the ultimate happiness in the other life'; [but] in the *Plato*, which is the second and therefore the least exposed part of a tripartite work, the distinction of the two kinds of happiness is completely dropped" (*PAW*, 13). The observation that some topic or point comes in the middle of a list or text does not prove anything in itself, however. It merely gives the reader a hint of what to look for and think about. An independent account of the significance of the central points must be provided (13–14).

Likewise, Strauss suggested, we often learn how an author writes by observing how he reads another text. Explicating the literary character of the *Guide of the Perplexed*, Strauss pointed out "hints" provided by Maimonides's own reading of the Torah that help a careful reader decipher the "secrets" Maimonides stated he was communicating only in intentionally disordered "chapter headings."[38] Strauss began his essay "How to Study Spinoza's *Theologico-Political Treatise*," however, with a long and complex analysis of the reasons we cannot and should not try to read Spinoza the way he read the Bible or Euclid (*PAW*, 150).[39] Finally, although Halevi was the only author Strauss treated in *Persecution* who wrote a dialogue, Strauss did not conclude that Halevi used the form, as Plato did, to defend philosophy. Following his own "rule" about taking account of the literary form and not identifying the author with the views of any particular character, Strauss argued that Halevi did not necessarily or in all cases subscribe to the arguments the scholar gave in order to persuade the pagan king to convert to Judaism. Nevertheless, Strauss concluded: "In defending Judaism, which, according to him, is the only true revealed religion, against the philosophers, [Halevi] was conscious of defending morality itself and therewith the cause, not only of Judaism, but of mankind at large" (*PAW*, 141). In sum, Strauss did not read the works of all four philosophers in the same way. In each case, he paid particular attention to the literary form and identified places where they contradicted themselves or the orthodox principles of their communities.

The Strauss thesis about the "art of writing" has been met with skepticism based on three kinds of arguments or intuitions. First, as we have already noted, many denizens of modern liberal societies find it difficult to imagine or credit the difficulties of writing in a nonliberal society. But it surely is possible that a thinker may have something to say that will be highly offensive to powerful figures in his or her community or to public opinion at large. It is not implausible that a thinker may hesitate to put himself at risk by being completely open in his public expression. A thinker may come to conclusions that are at odds with claims important to the moral and political consensus of his society and even to the moral and political health of that society.[40] An example Strauss often used of such a conflict is the belief that just and unjust behavior are rewarded and punished in an afterlife. Surely it would be no surprise if many philosophers concluded that there is no reasonable evidence for such a belief and yet did not argue explicitly against it, thinking that such a belief supports moral order in society.

Second, some fall back on historicist views about the relation of thought to its times. The only basis for the a priori and out of hand rejection of such possibilities as outlined above is the dogmatic commitment to historicism, i.e., the commitment to the view that thinkers never think outside the box of their time and place. But that stance is simply question begging and too loaded with a priori elements to provide a reliable method for interpretation.

Of most merit is the objection that Strauss's methods can never produce readings that satisfy "scientific" criteria for interpretation, including such things as easy replicability, interpersonal stability of interpretation, and ability to account univocally for all the "data" in a text.[41] Indeed, this objection points to a tension between Strauss's aims and his methods. The aim of his studies is to understand the philosophers as they understood themselves. In place of the historicists' contention that historical distance prevents us from understanding a thinker as he understood himself, Strauss finds intentional concealment to be a potential barrier to understanding. If Strauss is correct about the way in which older writers wrote, then it becomes extremely difficult to nail down a reading as *the* reading intended by the author. In his main thematic work on this kind of writing, *Persecution and the Art of Writing*, Strauss in effect concedes that no incontestable reading of a philosopher allegedly engaging in esoteric writing can ever be established (*PAW*, 30). The point of such writing was to make it difficult to prove that the thinker held views such as emerge in an esoteric reading. If there were a clear-cut and incontestable reading of an author who wrote in this way, the author would then have to be judged a failure at achieving what that mode of writing aimed to achieve: to establish at the very least "plausible deniability" for the doctrines not allowed to be seen in public. Thus, to take one example where Strauss's way of reading has stirred the most controversy, Locke certainly provided much ammunition for those who would see him as an anti-Hobbesian writer or as a Christian thinker at bottom. Although Strauss argued that deeper analysis showed Locke to be neither anti-Hobbesian nor deeply Christian, his texts contain a great deal of evidence to support those theses. More broadly, there will *always* be contrary evidence to any esoteric reading of a text.

The burden that an esoteric reading has to bear is extremely heavy, Strauss admitted, and such readings never can be established to the satisfaction of all readers. However, given the possibility that some writers wrote that way, a reading that does not pursue the esoteric meaning even more definitely fails at the task of understanding the author as he understood himself. Many of Strauss's critics fail to see that underreading a text can be as much an error as overreading and often entail a much greater loss.

So while the esotericism methodology unquestionably poses difficult issues of verification and objectivity, the alternative falls even shorter. Strauss understood the difficulties and the risks, but he accepted them. He recognized that he would never persuade all the people all the time, yet he chose to strive toward understanding thinkers who wrote in ways that have become alien to contemporary taste and practice.

Part II

Strauss and the Philosophers

CHAPTER THREE

Strauss's Rereading of the History of Political Philosophy

An Overview

S trauss's concern with historicism and his conclusion that our time required an unprecedented fusion of history and philosophy, a fusion to be paradoxically conducted in full awareness of the radical difference between philosophy itself and history of philosophy, led him to a strenuous effort to reread the history of political philosophy. Strauss is well known for his many detailed studies of individual philosophers, but he also set that rereading into the context of, or rather extracted from that rereading, an overarching narrative of the history of political philosophy. Not only did he overturn standard and accepted readings of individual philosophers— as in his famous claims about philosopher-kings in Plato's *Republic* or about Maimonides's orthodoxy or about Locke's concealed and only mildly transformed Hobbesianism—but he also put forth a new narrative about the course of Western philosophy. In this chapter we consider that overall narrative. In later chapters we consider some of the high points of his studies of individual philosophers.

Heidegger opened the way for Strauss's radical rereading of the tradition.[1] First, by insisting on what we might call the unified character of Western philosophy, constituting one tradition, held together by a common if unrecognized conception of Being, Heidegger encouraged Strauss to think about the philosophic tradition holistically. Moreover, Heidegger reversed the polarities normally brought, consciously or not, to the study of philosophy in the modern era. He rejected the idea that philosophy was a progressive enterprise moving toward ever truer or more sophisticated or better formulations. Rather, he contended that the Western tradition was built on a "primordial" experience of Being, an experience or disclosure that opened up the possibility of philosophy or metaphysics as we have known it in the West. One implication Heidegger drew from this origin of philosophy was that we moderns were not more advanced, but had regressed, that we were further away from that "primordial" disclosure and thus saw less clearly than those nearer to it. Heidegger thus prepared the way for a kind of "return to the ancients." It was to be a provisional return only, for it was in the service of the "destruktion" of the tradition, not the reembrace of it. As became clear as Heidegger's work progressed in the 1930s, he had in mind not a return but a new beginning, the prerequisite for which was the critical return to the origins in Aristotle, Plato, and eventually in the pre-Socratics (see especially the *Beiträge*). But in making that return with a critical eye, Heidegger also approached the older thinkers with a fresh eye and gave philosophers like Aristotle a sharp new reading that astonished and magnetized young men like Strauss.[2] As Richard Velkley said of the effect that Heidegger's readings of past philosophers had on Strauss: "Modern philosophy came into being through a refutation of the Aristotelian philosophy, but Heidegger showed that the founders of modern philosophy had refuted only the Aristotelians of their time without understanding Aristotle himself." Velkley quotes Strauss's conclusion from his experience of Heidegger's new readings of the traditional thinkers: a thinker "cannot have been refuted if he has not been understood."[3] The entire history needed to be reconsidered in light of that single fact.

But Strauss's novel understanding of this history of philosophy proved to be quite different from Heidegger's. The latter concluded that the moderns had not "refuted" the earlier philosophers but only modified their thinking, remaining in thrall to the same disclosure of Being that produced metaphysics. The moderns broke far less with their predecessors than they believed. Strauss came to disagree profoundly with Heidegger about the course and meaning of Western philosophy. Heidegger had a narrative that could be interpreted as a narrative of decline, and that stood in strong contrast to the narrative of thinkers like Comte, Hegel, and Marx, who saw the story of philosophy as progressive, as the ascent of reason to its proper vocation, and even completion, in modern times. Heidegger did not share in this celebration of modernity and modern thought, but his is only in a certain sense a narrative of decline. It is rather a narrative of the working out and completing of the original disclosure of Being in the pre-Socratics. In Heidegger's fully developed history of Western philosophy Nietzsche stands as the completion in the sense of the bringing forth and making explicit of the nihilistic implications always already present in the Western experience of Being as presence;[4] with Nietzsche the need for a new beginning became visible, as it did to Nietzsche himself, who called for a "philosophy of the future."

Strauss shared with Heidegger and indeed depended to a degree on Heidegger for the insight that the nineteenth-century narratives of Western philosophy as a progress leading up to a culmination in the present were false. He shared with Heidegger the notion that in order to understand our present situation one must dig deep into the thought of the past.[5] But in his mature thought he rejected most emphatically Heidegger's version of that history as one history from the pre-Socratics to Nietzsche, one history working out what was implicit at the very beginning. Rather, according to Strauss, that history had two breaks, two turns that were neither predictable nor the working out of what was preexisting in the previous thinking. Strauss recognized both a "Socratic turn" and a "Machiavellian turn," or as he more usually put it, the birth of political philosophy in Socrates and the birth of modernity in Machiavelli. These "turns" were products of conscious choices or insights, not of necessity.

Strauss devoted perhaps his most strenuous thinking to attempting to understand these two "turns." The "Socratic turn" was the subject of his books *Natural Right and History* and *Socrates and Aristophanes*, as well as of much of *The City and Man*. The character of the Socratic turn was further developed in his two late books on Xenophon. The Machiavellian turn was also the subject of some of his most intense study and writing, being the dominant theme of his *Thoughts on Machiavelli*, as well as of many other writings.

From his theory of the two turns derived two of the important sets of distinctions that marked his thinking—the distinction between political philosophy and nonpolitical philosophy, and that between ancients and moderns. One way to describe Strauss's alternative to Heidegger's narrative, then, is to say that philosophy began in the pre-Socratics, and was succeeded and to some degree displaced by Socrates's "second sailing," which initiated political philosophy. The latter prevailed in some important alternative forms through the Middle Ages until challenged by Machiavelli and his modernist successors. The development of the modernity ushered in by Machiavelli led, finally, to the eclipse of political philosophy in the twentieth century, as captured by Strauss's observation that the leading thinkers of the first half of that century—Bergson, Whitehead, Husserl, and Heidegger—were no longer political philosophers of either the ancient Socratic or the modern Machiavellian type (*WIPP*, 17). Those twin demons, positivism and historicism, seemed to write the obituary for political philosophy. But here is another place where Strauss broke greatly with Heidegger. Instead of calling for a "destruktion" of the tradition and a new beginning, Strauss called for a rediscovery and reconstruction of the Socratic part of the tradition and a "return."[6] Strauss's theme of "return" will be the subject of the next chapter; the remainder of this chapter will be devoted to an overview of Strauss's rereading of the history of philosophy.

The "Homeric" Turn and Its Aftermath

Before political philosophy there was philosophy; before philosophy there was the "natural understanding."[7] According to Strauss, the emergence of philosophy is "coterminous" with the "discovery of nature." The "natural understanding" that precedes all philosophy or science is for Strauss both immensely significant and *relatively* little spoken of. One of the most important Husserlian vestiges remaining in Strauss's mature thought is the proposition that science or philosophy rests on a world that is "radically pre-scientific or pre-philosophic."[8] Science or philosophy is a modification of that "natural world or the world of common sense." Strauss sides with Heidegger rather than Husserl, however, in seeing that the commonsense world "is not the object or product of a theoretical attitude" as Husserl posited it in his transcendental phenomenology. Like Heidegger, Strauss thought the prescientific world a world of "things" or "affairs" (*pragmata*) with which we are concerned (*NRH*, 79; "Epilogue," *LAM*, 210–12; *CM*, 12–13).

On this central question of the prescientific stratum of human thinking Strauss differed from Heidegger's analysis in *Sein und Zeit* in two ways, however. First, the paradigmatic "pre-theoretical dealing with things" for Heidegger was the relation between man and tools. The "things" were grasped as instruments of use, the "ready at hand." Strauss differed in part because he did not rest his analysis of the prescientific in the kind of abstract reflection on original "being-in-the-world" in which Heidegger had indulged. Instead, he relied on the firmer and more empirical evidence supplied by classical philosophy in its reports of its origins, "supplemented by considerations of the most elementary premises of the Bible" (*NRH*, 80). The prephilosophic or commonsense view is, in a retrospective view from the perspective of philosophy, an absence, the absence of "nature": there is, Strauss emphasized many times, no word for nature in the Hebrew Bible. Instead of the idea of nature, for the Bible and other manifestations of the prephilosophic, "the characteristic behavior of anything or class of

things was conceived of as its custom or way" (82). "Way" equally characterized the behavior of what we would now recognize as natural entities—
animals, the sun, and so on—and human customs and other kinds of behavioral regularities. The way of particular concern to any group of humans
was their way—the way inherited from their ancestors. This is "the right
way." This way has normative force backed up by the universal understanding that gods were the source or the support for the right way. The "way"
or "the law"—divine and holy—characterizes the prephilosophic: again, in
our terms, the prephilosophic is eminently moral and religious, not a mere
matter of ready-at-handness. The prephilosophic world is a world full of
the divine and of norms; it is "prescriptive" (83). Nietzsche's "value-laden"
insight is a corrective to Heidegger's "pragmatism."[9] It is a sphere of practice not theory, but Strauss amends Heidegger's characterization by bringing out the place of the divine and the prescriptive as the decisive or most
characteristic features of the prephilosophic, i.e., of the natural consciousness, which must be always kept in mind as the substratum of philosophic
or theoretical thinking. Strauss understands the prescientific "world" differently from Heidegger in yet another way. For Heidegger the "theoretical
attitude," that is, the "looking at" that leads to the formulation of the object as an in-itself—what he calls "present-to-hand" as opposed to "ready-
at-hand"—occurs when the object somehow breaks down in its use. The
decisive break in consciousness for the Heidegger of *Being and Time* occurs
in this way. The object, no longer an object of use, becomes—an object. In
that moment was born the "theoretical attitude," the prerequisite for the
emergence of philosophy or science.

For Strauss, the decisive event leading to the emergence of philosophy
is not this kind of breakdown. As we have said, the decisive thing is the
"discovery of nature." Nature and philosophy are coterminous. Nature is,
Strauss insists, a "term of distinction." It refers not to "the totality of phenomena" but to a subclass of phenomena that previously were said to be
"ways"; way splits up into "nature" and "convention" or "laws"' (*NRH*, 82).

The term "nature" appears in Greek literature first in Homer, in whose
Odyssey the term appears once, referring to the "nature" of a plant called
"moly." Strauss makes no claim that Homer was the first human to discover
nature, but his text is the oldest in which the concept recognizably appears.
"'Nature' means here the character of a thing, or of a kind of thing, the way
in which a kind of thing looks and acts, and the thing, or the kind of thing,
is taken not to have been made by gods or men" (*HPP*, 2). In the *Odyssey*
moly has a significant power or nature: it can counter or neutralize Circe's

power to transform men into swine. Moly is a "drug" that can fix the beings, i.e., allow them to persist in their characters. Moly not merely has a nature, but vouches for nature altogether as fixed character, possessed inherently by the things or kinds of things. That there is nature in this sense demonstrates that the world is not universal flux. "The whole history of philosophy," Strauss affirms, "is nothing but the record of the repeated attempts to grasp fully what was implied in that crucial discovery" of nature, for the observation of relatively fixed entities does not yet vouch for the validity of the category "nature" (NRH, 82).[10]

Strauss offers only a tentative or even whimsical explanation for the discovery of nature. "If we were entitled to take a poetic utterance literally, we could say that the first man we know who spoke of nature was the Wily Odysseus who had seen the towns of many men and had thus come to know how much the thoughts of men differ from town to town or from tribe to tribe" (HPP, 2–3; see "PPH," 56–57, and chap. 2 above). The serious thought here is that the experience of different "ways" was the precondition for discriminating between those aspects or ways that change or vary and those that are constant. Thus fire burns everywhere the same, while the ways of men differ from town to town.

The most significant implication of the discovery of nature for political philosophy is the clear distinction between nature, fixed and independent of human making, and convention or law, seen to be manmade in light of the discovery of nature. Of the two, nature had the higher dignity (NRH, 1, 89). If the natural things are the unmade things, then it is perfectly intelligible that the initial inquiries by the first inquirers into nature, the first philosophers, should be into "the first things," i.e., "certain 'first things' which are not strictly speaking 'things' but which are responsible for the coming into being and perishing of everything that comes into being and perishes." These are the things that are truly "by themselves": they are or have natures in the most emphatic sense (CM, 14). Thus the so-called pre-Socratic philosophers sought knowledge of the archai, the first things or principles of all things.

The pre-Socratics sought, that is, to give a naturalistic account that no longer appealed to the gods to explain events (NRH, 82–89). Good examples were the seriocomical naturalistic accounts of heavenly phenomena in Aristophanes's Clouds, in which it is matter-of-factly announced to the bumpkin Strepsiades that "Zeus is not."[11]

As significant for political philosophy was the way these first philosophers construed the phenomena of law (nomos) and justice (dikê). One possible way to understand those parts of the "ways" that are not taken up into the category of "nature" is to see them as nothing but conventions, norms that have authority only from the conscious or unconscious decisions or agreements of human beings. Strauss notes as "the crucial pre-Socratic text" the following saying by Heraclitus: "In God's view, all things are fair [noble] and good and just, but men have made the supposition that some things are just and others unjust."[12] A version of this kind of conventionalism makes its way into Plato's *Republic* in the mouth of Glaucon and into Plato's *Gorgias* in the mouth of Callicles. If there is such a thing as natural justice or natural right, it is the "right of the stronger," but those who are weaker band together to establish "justice" in terms of the ostensible common good or the due or right of all. Such a view is in the interest of the many, though not in the interest of the naturally "stronger" or better. Justice as contained in the laws is entirely conventional, therefore; indeed it covers over the truth about nature, both in the substantive standards it endorses, and in the divine authorities to which it appeals. Not the gods but the agreements of the mediocre sorts of men are the source of justice as defined in the *nomoi* (*NRH*, 107). Philosophy, in its discovery of nature and its resulting turn away from the *nomoi* or laws that claimed authority over the nascent philosophers, as they did over everyone in the community, necessarily has the character of revolution: it rejects the authority to which it has been subject. From this situation Strauss infers one of his most common themes: the tension between philosophy and the city. Philosophy in its nature is opposed to the city and to the authorities to which the city looks as the origin and guarantors of its laws, the gods of the city.

The Socratic Turn and Its Aftermath

Strauss was fond of citing Cicero to the effect that "Socrates was the first to call philosophy down from heaven, to establish it in the cities, to introduce it also into the households, and to compel it to inquire about men's life and manners as well as about the good and bad things" (*CM*, 13, citing *Tusculan Disputations* 5.10 and *Brutus* 31). The Socratic turn away from nature as pursued by the pre-Socratics in favor of inquiry into the "human things" comprised the Socratic innovation that brought *political* philosophy into being. As we will see, Strauss did not understand this turn in the manner popularized by Aristotle,[13] who presented Socrates as a philosopher concerned exclusively with moral matters, beyond whom both Plato and Aristotle himself moved in broadening their purview to include all of nature and cosmology. Strauss rather saw Plato and Aristotle as firmly within the Socratic tradition of philosophizing, in part because he denied outright the Aristotelian claim: "Contrary to appearances, Socrates' turn to the study of human things was based, not on disregard of the divine or natural things, but upon a new approach to the understanding of all things" (*NRH*, 122; see *RCPR*, 132, 141).

With Socrates, philosophy becomes political philosophy. Strauss never gave a causal account of the emergence of Socratic philosophizing, but he frequently spoke of the philosophic deficiencies of pre-Socratic thinking that made the Socratic turn necessary. He appears to have thought that it was accidental or merely adventitious that the particular individual Socrates effected this shift in the nature of philosophy.

Strauss most often portrayed the Socratic turn in the context of the dual and somewhat parallel critiques of Socrates mounted by Aristophanes in the *Clouds* and Nietzsche in *The Birth of Tragedy* and other writings (*SA*, 3–8). Although some readers of Strauss attribute the turn to the Aristophanic critiques, Strauss himself never made that claim, and indeed the dating of the turn, at least as related in the account of Socrates given by Plato, cannot sustain the hypothesis that Aristophanes somehow prompted the change in the Socratic mode of philosophizing. The conversation recounted in Plato's *Protagoras*, it is generally believed, occurred in 433–432 BCE, just prior to the Peloponnesian War. In this dialogue the "Socratic" Socrates, as opposed to the pre-Socratic Socrates we hear of in *Phaedo*, is clearly on display. The *Clouds*, however, was performed only in 423, that is, a decade after the conversation in *Protagoras* is presented as having taken place. At least according to Plato, whom Strauss tacitly seems to follow, Aristophanes's critique cannot have provoked Socrates to change direction.[14]

Strauss saw the *Clouds*, however, as bringing to the fore many of the deficiencies of the older philosophic orientation that political philosophy remedied. He read the *Clouds* not as the hostile attack on the philosophers it is often taken to be, but rather as a friendly warning. Strauss emphasizes in his reading of the play that Aristophanes presents the clouds as the patron "divinities" of the philosophers, and presents himself as a cloud. That is to say, Aristophanes places both the philosophers and himself as a poet in the same genus, if not quite in the same species, as Socrates.[15] Indeed, Strauss saw Aristophanes's poetry as a whole to be informed by the philosophic conception of nature (*RCPR*, 133). In so judging he takes a cue from Plato's *Symposium*, where Aristophanes, overcome by the physiological phenomenon of a fit of hiccups, cannot take his allotted turn in the speechmaking and is replaced by the physician Eryximachus, an indication, Strauss believes, of the interchangeability of Aristophanes and the naturalists as represented by the physician.[16]

Although Aristophanes and Socrates belong to the same genus, Strauss believed, Aristophanes could warn Socrates, because he belongs to the species poet. That species differs from the species philosopher in that it pays primary attention to the human things: the poets are imitators of human speeches and actions. As a poet Aristophanes sees two major deficiencies in the nonpoetic, "pre-Socratic" Socrates. He is ignorant of the setting in which his philosophizing necessarily occurs and of the effects of his activity on that context; i.e., he is insufficiently attuned to the city (RCPR, 125). He also lacks self-knowledge; his eye is keen for what is in the heavens and beneath the earth, i.e., nature as manifest in the nonhuman world, but he knows little of himself as a human being. The Clouds is a warning, Strauss argued, because in it Aristophanes informs the philosophers about the dangers to themselves that their relatively unself-conscious activity threatens: at the end of the play the simpleton Strepsiades burns down Socrates's school, a comic foreshadowing of the fate of Socrates himself.[17]

The philosophers as shown by Aristophanes may be in the city but surely are not of it. The philosophers are barely aware of or provident for their own needs as embodied beings (SA, 49; RCPR, 166). They do not make sufficient provision for their food; they dismiss other humans as mere "ephemerals," of little value or concern compared with what is always, nature, and the things that truly are (SA, 49; RCPR, 120). Despite their efforts to look away from the city, they remain dependent on the provision for bodily needs that it makes possible and on the civic order that it provides. The distance between Athens and Sparta is for them a mere matter of geography; for Strepsiades, who has a citizen's perspective, it is a matter of how far off Athens's enemy is.[18] But, Aristophanes reminds them, philosophers too depend on the protection provided by the city.

Philosophers pay little attention to their need for protection, however, and have little sense of the nature of the city. They depreciate the gods who are understood to stand behind the nomoi and who demand worship; instead they explain the world in terms of impersonal natural forces, leaving no room and having no regard for the gods. They make light of the family, seeing it as only conventional. They find the relations between roosters and their offspring more revealing of nature than the human family.[19] Philosophers thus have no regard for the sacred and no piety toward gods or fathers. In the *Clouds* Socrates countenances father beating and incest, as well as more common forms of civic injustice. The difference between Aristophanes's philosopher and the poets is indicated clearly enough by the difference between Socrates in the *Clouds* and Oedipus in Sophocles's play with regard to family crimes of parricide and incest (*SA*, 52).

Not noticing, or rejecting as merely conventional, the sacred and just things as understood in the city, the philosophers are vulnerable to the citizens' righteous anger. In the *Clouds* Strepsiades attacks Socrates's school; and we know that the city of Athens not only later indicted and executed Socrates but also threatened many other philosophers. The philosophers, who so strongly break with the commonsense or everyday way in which most men view the world, need a warning that their cause is threatening to the community and reflexively dangerous to themselves. The "Aristophanean Socrates," says Strauss, "is wholly unaware of the devastating effect which his indifference to practical matters must have on the city, if non-theoretical men should become influenced by Socrates' sentiments" (*RCPR*, 123–25).

Not merely do the philosophers stand in danger if they fail to mend their ways, but Aristophanes argues that without the wisdom of the poets, i.e., without knowledge of human being, they fall greatly short of their own goal of knowledge of the whole. Aristophanes would teach them more than prudence, more than the need to be aware of the political setting of their activity. They need to understand the human character of their activity as well (*SA*, 312–14).

Aristophanes would have the philosophers "be integrated into a whole which is ruled by poetry" (*RCPR*, 134 also see *SA*, 313). Strauss thus sees Aristophanes as having a most elevated sense of his own calling: "Poetry is both the foundation and the capstone of wisdom within which philosophy finds its place, or through which philosophy is protected and at the same time perfected" (*RCPR*, 134). Socratic philosophers in part follow the line Aristophanes laid out, but they insist, contrary to the poet, that the two must be integrated into a whole in which philosophy remains the dominant element (*RCPR*, 134; *SA*, 314).

Socratic philosophy resists being integrated into poetry because the turn to the human things had for Socrates a dual character, an internal and an external. The external aspect is what we have thus far emphasized in the Aristophanic critique and proposed reformation of philosophy. The poet,

as Strauss saw him, built a body of thought based on a pre-Socratic understanding of nature supplemented by a poetic understanding of the human.

> The internal aspect of the turn goes deeper, however, and is more revolu-
> tionary: The recognition by philosophy of the fact that the human race is
> worthy of some seriousness is the origin of political philosophy or political
> science. If this recognition is to be philosophic, however, this must mean
> that the political things, the merely human things, are of decisive impor-
> tance for understanding nature as a whole. (*RCPR*, 126)

The turn to the human things is the Socratic turn proper and leads to political philosophy in the decisive sense, i.e., political philosophy as the character of philosophy as a whole and not merely one branch of philosophy, akin
to philosophy of art or philosophy of sports. Political philosophy brings
with it a reorientation of philosophy away from the reductionism of earlier
philosophy. As Strauss understands him, "Socrates did not limit himself to
the study of the human things but was concerned, as is every other philosopher, with the whole—only he thought that the human things are the clue
to the whole" (*RCPR*, 132).

Contrary to his predecessors, who sought the *archē* from which the
things of the world derive, Socrates concluded that "the whole is characterized by noetic heterogeneity" (*RCPR*, 132; see "WIPP," 39). The whole
consists of "classes or kinds, the character of which does not become clear
through sense perception," but is apparent only to the eye of the mind, or
reason. The world as composed of things or classes of things is the world
as it appears to us in our opinions, not in perception per se. Strauss could
thus describe the Socratic turn as a return—a "return to common sense."
Strauss has an almost Hegelian picture of the development of political philosophy. The initially given is the commonsense world of "things with properties," complete with the sacred and value dimensions they carry within
ordinary life. With the discovery of nature this world of common sense is
negated, transcended in favor of the search for "true being," the underlying
principles or substance truly present in our illusory, commonsense world.
The pre-Socratics fail to generate a stable doctrine of the *archai*: some say
Being is one and motion impossible, others that Being is nothing but flux;
some that the principle is water, others that there are four principles. The
instability or unsettled character of pre-Socratic thinking could well have
led Socrates to conclude that there was something wrong with the entire
enterprise of pre-Socratic philosophy (*RCPR*, 142). He thus effects his re-

turn to common sense, but not at the original level of common sense, for he restores common sense in light of the philosophic insight into and search for nature.

Opinion is the sphere in which the beings become visible, and thus Socrates reorients himself around opinion in order to discover being as a whole. The relation between opinion and knowledge necessarily becomes thematic for Socratic philosophy. Socrates thus takes seriously the matters around which opinion forms—the divine, the noble and the base, the just and the unjust—in a way his predecessors did not. As Strauss puts it, "the discovery of noetic heterogeneity means the vindication of . . . common sense." It is a return from madness to sobriety. "Socrates discovered the paradoxical fact that, in a way, the most important truth is the most obvious truth, or the truth of the surface" (*RCPR*, 142; see also *TM*, 13). Contrary, one suspects, to both Heidegger and all mystics, Strauss concludes that "the fact that there is a variety of beings, in the sense of kinds or classes, means that there cannot be a single total experience of being" (*RCPR*, 143).

The philosophic turn to opinion has two almost opposite-seeming consequences. On the one hand, it reminds the philosopher of the inescapable rootedness of philosophic knowledge in common sense or opinion. It reminds of "the mystery" of knowing ("Epilogue," *LAM*, 211). But, on the other hand, it also opens up the distance between opinion and knowledge and turns attention toward the resistance of opinion to being transformed into knowledge. Political philosophy becomes deeply aware of "the power of that in man which is recalcitrant to reason and which therefore cannot be persuaded into submission, but must be beaten into it" (*RCPR*, 131). Given that resistance, Strauss concluded that the Enlightenment hope of universal rationality and the modern philosophic project of overcoming the political were doomed to remain unfulfillable dreams. Human life is and will remain ineradicably political, i.e., a realm of opinion and ultimately coercion. Philosophy is unable to change fundamentally the character of society. The limits to the possibilities of rational transformation of society mean that the theoretical man must approach political life in a spirit of moderation, which requires among other things "the recognition of opinions which are not true, but which are salutary for political life" (*RCPR*, 133).

Political philosophy thus understood as grounded in opinion but attempting the ascent to knowledge implies or rests on the openness of the human soul, the opinion-forming faculty, to the whole. The human things can be "the clue to all things, to the whole of nature" only if "they are the link or bond between the highest and the lowest, or [if] man is a micro-cosm" (*RCPR*, 133). The core of philosophy for Socrates is not the kind of physiological natural science to which even the poet Aristophanes renders allegiance, "but a certain psychology . . . is both the foundation and cap-stone of wisdom" (*RCPR*, 134; *CM*, 314). The human soul is open to the whole—as the very possibility of any knowledge implies—and therefore the soul is that part of the whole most worthy of attention, in part because it is *the* access humans have to that whole. The highest theme of Socratic philosophy is thus the soul, but not as a mere supplement to physiology. As Strauss quite beautifully said, "By becoming aware of the dignity of the mind [as the opening to the whole], we realize the true ground of the dig-nity of man and therewith of the goodness of the world, whether we under-stand it as created or uncreated, which is the home of man because it is the home of the human mind" ("WILE," 8). Thus Strauss could conclude his masterwork on the turn away from Socratic philosophy: "It would seem that the notion of the beneficence of nature or of the primacy of the good must be restored by being rethought through a return to the fundamental experiences from which it is derived. For while 'philosophy must beware of wishing to be edifying,' it is of necessity edifying" (*TM*, 299, quoting Hegel, *Phenomenology*, preface).

Understanding the Socratic turn differently from the way it was under-stood in standard accounts of the history of philosophy (and differently from Heidegger's innovative reading as well), Strauss was prompted to at-tempt a comprehensive rereading and reinterpretation of classical politi-cal philosophy. Strauss regularly spoke of classical political philosophy as a more or less unified thing; in two very conspicuous places, "What Is Politi-cal Philosophy?" and *Natural Right and History*, he presented a composite account of classical political philosophy in contrast to very particularized accounts of modern political philosophies. But Strauss recognized three broad schools or approaches within the Socratic tradition, which, he main-tained, stretched well into the Christian era, for he included the Thomis-tic natural law as one of the three. The other two were the Platonic-Stoic and the Aristotelian. Strauss tended to present Aristotle's as the most ex-emplary version for displaying a Socratic or classical approach to political life. We will on that account present a sketch of Strauss's understanding of Aristotelian political science, a sketch to be supplemented and corrected in chapter 6 below.

The novelty of Strauss's rereading of classical philosophy is visible, per-haps first and foremost, in his presentation of it as a composite rather than as a series of individualized doctrines. Unlike most students of the subject, he does not see Plato and Aristotle, Xenophon and Cicero, as holding fundamentally different political philosophies. As we will see in chapter 5, he read Plato's *Republic* very differently from the way most or all twentieth-century scholars did. It is a text meant to show the nature or boundary of the city and the political, not to present a doctrine of the best regime. It is not that Strauss recognizes no differences among the classical Socratic philosophers, but he finds more significant their common character as Socratics.

Strauss also almost silently rejects the most common approach to the classical philosophers of the past century or so, the attempt to read them developmentally, as in the effort to identify early, middle, and late Platonic writings or Werner Jaeger's attempt to reconstruct an Aristotelian development. He rejects the basic premise from which most recent Platonic scholarship proceeded—that Plato began very near to the "mere moralist" Socrates, and from there modified his position by becoming in stages more metaphysical and cosmological. As we have seen, Strauss saw Socrates to be concerned with "the whole" from the start. Partly because any notion of the development of the ancient thinkers must remain purely conjectural, given the absence of solid historical evidence on dates of composition, to say nothing of traditions from antiquity that Plato kept his manuscripts and revised them periodically, Strauss treated the extant texts of each of these authors as though they had been written contemporaneously. Unlike most of his contemporaries, Strauss began with a hermeneutic principle that one ought to take as a working hypothesis that the texts are consistent with each other. Differences among them, such as, for instance, between Plato's *Republic* and *Laws*, ought to be understood in terms of different intentions for the works rather than as signs of Platonic development.

Strauss's interpretations of the ancients are distinguished from those of his contemporaries also by the particular combination of historical and nonhistorical reading that he gave them. Most of those who wrote on the classics in Strauss's time treated them as simply matters of historical interest, just like many other objects of inquiry for modern scholarship. Strauss recognizes, as we have pointed out above, the need for genuinely historical study of the texts of the past, but at the same time he treats these texts as speaking to us, or making claims of truth to us, claims that we need to take seriously as possibly true. Thus for Strauss classical political philosophy is not merely a matter of curiosity but, he argues, a guide to the better understanding of political life. He presents Aristotle to today's political scientists as a better basis for practicing their science than the newer behavioral science ("Epilogue," *LAM*, 205–7). More than that, he did not present classical philosophy as a model merely for political scientists, but he thought that individuals within political life could benefit from it just as Aristotle did when he addressed his *Politics* to political men. Since Strauss wrote, others, like Hannah Arendt and Alasdair Macintyre, have come forward to propose the classics as writers whom we can or need to learn from, not just to learn about. Neither Arendt nor Macintyre sees the same lessons in the classics that Strauss did, but he clearly pioneered the effort to take them as living voices addressed to us, making claims of relevance to us.

Strauss's rereading of the Socratics differs from that of others in that he takes his bearings toward these texts from his insight into the nature of the Socratic turn as a turn toward opinion, the prephilosophic or natural understanding as *the* necessary beginning point for philosophy. He published his first systematic statement on the ancients in 1945 in an essay[20] in which he attempts to bring out "those characteristic features of classical political philosophy which are in particular danger of being overlooked or insufficiently stressed by the schools that are most influential in our time" (*WIPP*, 78). Nathan Tarcov has well summarized the main points of this essay: "The two features of classical political philosophy that Strauss stresses both concern its relation to political life but are quite different: that it was related to political life directly and that it transcended political life."[21]

What Strauss calls "the direct relation of classical political philosophy to pre-philosophic political life" is a direct result and embodiment of the Socratic turn itself. As Strauss says, this direct relation "was due not to the undeveloped character of classical philosophy or science, but to mature reflection" (*WIPP*, 92). It was due to the reflection that led Socrates and the Socratics back to a beginning point in opinion. "Philosophy, being an attempt to rise from opinion to science, is necessarily related to the sphere of opinion as its essential starting point, and hence to the political sphere. Therefore the political sphere is bound to advance into the focus of philosophic interest as soon as philosophy starts to reflect on its own doings" (92).

Political philosophy thus has a dual starting point, philosophy and political life itself. "There is a straight and almost continuous way leading from the pre-philosophic to the philosophic approach." Political life itself points toward the inquiries of political philosophy. "The question guiding classical political philosophy, the typical answer that it gave, and the insight into the bearing of the formidable objections to it, belong to pre-philosophic political life, or precede political philosophy" (*WIPP*, 81, 86). The dual beginning point—in political life and in philosophy as Socratically conceived—constitutes "the problem of political philosophy" that Strauss referred to in the first lecture of his series "What Is Political Philosophy?" (see chapter 1 above).

Understanding the genesis and nature of political philosophy as he does, Strauss rejected both the standard ways of interpreting classical political philosophy and Heidegger's innovative way of reading the philosophic tradition, even though the latter had prodded him to reconceive the tradition. In contrast to Heidegger, Strauss emphasizes the thoroughly practical character of classical political philosophy. "The attitude of classical political philosophy toward political things was always akin to that of the enlightened statesman; it was not the attitude of the detached observer who looks at political things in the way in which a zoologist looks at the big fishes swallowing the small ones" (*WIPP*, 90, 27). Heidegger's account of the origin and character of the "theoretical attitude" does not capture the character of classical philosophy. Philosophy is not the result of the breakdown of the natural or commonsense perspective or of the *Lebenswelt*; it stands in greater if not perfect continuity with the original "natural orientation" in the world.

Strauss is even further from the standard and accepted interpretations of the classic texts. The difference between his and the standard readings lies in a feature of the standard readings that his novel and unorthodox readings make more apparent than it normally is. The standard, "textbook" reading of the classical philosophers is thoroughly governed by the alleged theoretical commitments of the philosophers. Thus Plato's political philosophy is most often read in terms of his "doctrine of ideas." Accordingly, the proposal in *The Republic* for the rule of philosopher kings, knowers of the ideas, is taken as a straightforward proposal for a best or ideal kind of rule.[22] Likewise, Aristotle's political philosophy is read as one manifestation among many others of his teleological doctrine of nature. Accordingly, most readers of Aristotle emphasize the discussion in book 1 of the *Politics* of the naturalness of the city, the organic character of the political community, and its metaphysical priority over the individual.

Strauss's rereading of this part of the tradition is so novel because he almost entirely eschews or ignores these theoretical constructs in terms of which the writers are so often read and instead emphasizes "the direct relation to political life" of classical political philosophy (*WIPP*, 79; see 78, 84,

88, 27–28).[23] What determines "the orientation and scope," "the basic distinctions," "the primary questions," even "the method" of classical political philosophy were not the large theoretical concepts associated with these philosophers but the language, concepts, distinctions, goals, and concerns of political life itself (79–80). The philosopher looking at politics allows his inquiry to be shaped by the phenomena, not by a conceptual framework he brings with him. "The primary questions of classical political philosophy and the terms in which it stated them, were not specifically philosophic or scientific; they were questions that are raised in assemblies, councils, clubs and cabinets, and they were stated in terms intelligible and familiar ... from everyday experience and everyday usage" (80). Classical political philosophy then has an ineradicably practical character, for it seeks political knowledge in the first instance of the same sort as was sought within political life itself—for the sake of improving practice. Classical political philosophy is infinitely less "theoretical" than the kind of scientific political science that threatens political philosophy today.

His emphasis on its "direct relation to political life" led Strauss to discover at the center of classical political philosophy a different set of concerns and guiding questions from those the more standard interpreters found. Taking a cue from political life itself, which "is characterized by conflicts between men asserting opposed claims ... in the name of justice," classical political philosophy sets out to serve as an umpire, adjudicating the various claims. At bottom, the conflicts visible in political life are conflicts over what the philosophers called *politeia*, translated by Strauss as "regime" (*WIPP*, 80), which he defines as "the order, the form, which gives society its character. ... Regime is the form of life as living together, the manner of living of society and in society, since this manner depends decisively on the predominance of human beings of a certain type" (34). By "predominance" the classics mean "rule." Regime is identical to government. Book 3 of the *Politics* is much more central to Strauss's reading than book 1.

As the classical writers emphasized, "there is a variety of regimes"—best known through Aristotle's sixfold classification of regimes. Because of this variety and because of the conflicting claims raised on their behalves, the question naturally arises, which of them is better, or even best. Again taking issue with Heidegger, Strauss comments, "thus the regimes themselves, and not any preoccupation of mere bystanders, force us to wonder which of the given conflicting regimes is ... the best regime." The dominant concept in classical political philosophy is regime, and thus the inquiry is "guided by the question of the best regime" (*WIPP*, 34).

The classics press the question of the best regime and come to realize that "the actualization of the best regime depends on the coming together, on the coincidence of things which have a natural tendency to move away from each other (e.g., on the coincidence of philosophy and political power); its actualization depends therefore on chance" (*WIPP*, 34). The best regime is not strictly speaking impossible of realization, but it is highly unlikely in the normal course of human affairs. Thus classical political philosophy culminates in the depiction of "utopias" (*NRH*, 139). Strauss famously argues that Plato's proposal for the rule of philosophers in the best regime of the *Republic* is not entirely serious, at least as a practical proposal. The crux of the problem is that although the rule of philosophy answers to the needs and aspirations of the political community, neither the philosophers nor the nonphilosophers will take any of the steps necessary to bring such a regime into being. Given the great unlikelihood of the rule of the wise, "the practically best regime is the rule, under law, of gentlemen, or the mixed regime" (*NRH*, 142–43).

Strauss's rereading of the Socratic philosophers is rooted in his understanding of the Socratic turn as a "new approach to the understanding of all things." That new approach has at its core the insight that "the being of things, their what, comes first to sight, not in what we see of them, but in what is said about them or in opinions about them" (*NRH*, 124). The philosopher is driven to consider the opinions of men and thus leave his ivory tower at least long enough to investigate and converse "dialectically" about those opinions.

Let us here repeat a passage quoted earlier: "Philosophy, being an attempt to rise from opinion to science, is necessarily related to the sphere of opinion as its essential starting point, and hence to the political sphere. Therefore the political sphere is bound to advance into the focus of philosophic interest as soon as philosophy starts to reflect on its own doings" (*WIPP*, 92). This passage, juxtaposed with Strauss's depiction of the character of classical political philosophy as directly related to political life, brings us once more up against the "problem of political philosophy." In his presentation of classical political philosophy, Strauss presents it *as if* it grows directly out of political life. But it does not in fact do so. At best Strauss has shown that it *could* grow out of political life. But in fact it grows out of philosophy and its peculiar turn to the sphere of opinion—the cave or the political community. From that perspective "the political sphere" does indeed "advance into the focus of philosophic interest" when "philosophy starts to reflect on its own doings." But does philosophy in so reflecting need to engage in political philosophy as described by Strauss? Does it need to serve as umpire among the competing claims? Does it need to give detailed advice, as Aristotle does, on how to make a tyranny better, or a democracy of a certain sort more moderate?

In attempting to answer questions of this sort, Strauss presents an account of political philosophy that is different from what we have so far described. Socratic philosophy is more visible in the community than pre-Socratic philosophy needed to be, and thus it is much more likely that "other men . . . become aware of the possibility of philosophy." The philosophers, partly prompted by the others who see philosophy as a strange and perhaps hostile presence, are driven to ask, "why philosophy?" They ask not merely for themselves but for the sake of the community: what can they say to the public that can allow the public to see philosophy as good or at least as tolerable? As Strauss says, "the question 'Why philosophy?' means 'Why does political life need philosophy?'" (*WIPP*, 92–93). The philosophers are led "to supply a political justification for philosophy by showing that the well-being of the political community depends decisively on the study of philosophy." The philosophers are led to "justify philosophy before the tribunal of the political community," which "means to justify philosophy in terms of the political community, that is to say, by means of a kind of argument which appeals not to philosophers as such, but to citizens as such" (93). But if the city and its citizens reside in the realm of opinion, then political philosophy too must, in order to appeal to "citizens as such," remain in the realm of opinion, and not serve as the vehicle of ascending from opinion to what transcends opinion. Therein lies the problem of political philosophy—how it can both serve as justification of philosophy to the citizens as such, and serve as philosophic ascent from opinion. In any case, in light of this newly revealed character of political philosophy Strauss provides a new definition of his subject:

> From this point of view, the adjective 'political' in the expression 'political philosophy' designates not so much a subject matter as a manner of treatment; from this point of view, I say, 'political philosophy' means primarily not the philosophic treatment of politics, but the political, or popular treatment of philosophy, in the political introduction to philosophy—the attempt to lead the qualified citizens, or rather their qualified sons, from the political life to the philosophic life. (*WIPP*, 93–94)[24]

Political philosophy, as the practice of Socratic philosophizing, both goes beyond the political community in its questions and answers, and also remains in direct contact with and takes the perspective of the community. Given Strauss's understanding of classical political philosophy, it is thus easy to see how its practice is inseparable from the practice of esoteric expression.

The Machiavellian Turn and Its Aftermath

Here we may build on what has come before and be substantially briefer. Strauss made much of the fact that classical political philosophy emerged before there was a tradition of political philosophy. It had an unmediated relation to political life relative to later political philosophy and a keen awareness of the ways in which it was a response to the question "why philosophy?" Classical political philosophy survived within the three monotheistic religions of the Middle Ages. But its situation within the three differed. Within Islam and Judaism political philosophy faced an environment where the law of the community was a holy law, with its source in God. In this regard political philosophy faced a situation parallel to that in which political philosophy first emerged. Within Islam and Judaism the philosophers necessarily remained very attuned to the signature Strauss theme of the tension between philosophy and the city—and of the original meaning of political philosophy as the justification and presentation of philosophy to the city.

Classical political philosophy also survived or was revived within Christendom, but there the situation was somewhat different. Christianity was not a religion of law and left what was Caesar's to Caesar. Christianity remained open to more or less autonomous philosophic thought about politics. Christianity, moreover, was a doctrinal religion, ripe with claims puzzling to the human mind, preeminently claims about the Trinity. Christianity lent itself to the rise of a philosophy-like discipline, theology, rather than to the legal science of the other two religions. Philosophy eventually proved to be immensely helpful to theology and was welcomed within Christianity with a heartiness that was lacking within Islam and Judaism. But it was welcomed not in its original form but as "handmaiden" to theology. As Strauss saw it, but seldom said, it was no accident that modernity arose within Christendom and not elsewhere (*WIPP*, 43–44).

Strauss suggested that the study of the history of political philosophy ought to be divided according to a break or division announced by the philosophers themselves. At a certain point political philosophers like Machiavelli and Hobbes explicitly announced their rejection of previous philosophy as "unrealistic," and ushered in a new kind of philosophy, not aiming at virtue and "imaginary republics" as did the old philosophy. Machiavelli objected that these old writers had erred in taking their bearings by what human beings ought to do rather than by what they actually do, and thus he developed a new kind of "realism." That realism, according to Strauss, is the hallmark of modern philosophy (*WIPP*, 40).

Strauss devoted much of his attention, from his early books on Spinoza and Hobbes to the end of his career, to the question of the cause, meaning, and validity of this break with classical political philosophy. Strauss's conclusion regarding the cause and nature of the Machiavellian turn has its paradoxes. On the one hand, he identifies "anti-theological ire" as cause or facilitator of the Machiavellian reorientation of political philosophy. On the other hand, he insists that the Machiavellian critique of religion (one of the two chief bases of his turn against the tradition) "is not original." It is a restatement of the critique of religion mounted by "pagan philosophers" as refurbished by the "medieval school which goes by the name of Averroism" (*WIPP*, 41, 42). What is new and from Strauss's view most significant about Machiavelli, however, is his critique of morality.

The critique of morality culminated in Machiavelli's well-known realism. Machiavelli claimed not merely to give a truer view of human beings by emphasizing the passions that move most people most of the time, but also to provide a more "effectual" political science. To understand the near sovereignty of the passions that move human beings would facilitate the channeling or direction of those passions to achieve the ends most people desire—peace and prosperity. Machiavelli and his successors thus invited later readers to evaluate his proposals not only in terms of their truth, but also, if not preeminently, in terms of their results. But how can Strauss identify Machiavelli's great innovation as a result of his "anti-theological ire," i.e., his opposition to religion or at least to Christianity, and yet insist that Machiavelli's critique of religion contained nothing new, but merely related what was common coin among the ancient philosophers? How does the old and common produce the radically new and different?

These are not strictly contradictory positions; we can reconcile the various things Strauss says if we consider that although there was nothing novel in Machiavelli's philosophic critique of religion, his passions were so aroused that they carried him beyond critique of religion to critique of morality (and therewith of ancient political philosophy) (*WIPP*, 40). That is to say, Machiavelli's "anti-theological ire" might derive not from the old philosophic critique of religion, which he shared with pagans and Averroists, but from somewhere else, and that in turn resulted not in a critique of religion so much as in a critique or rejection of classical political philosophy.

As Strauss developed the thought, Machiavelli's break with past philosophy had something to do with the "profound changes the classical tradition . . . had undergone" by his time. The twin peaks of classical thought had both been transformed. The "contemplative life" (or intellectual virtue) "had found its home in monasteries." Likewise, "moral virtue had been transfigured into Christian charity," which had the effect of "infinitely increasing" the responsibility of human beings to and for one another. One result was the unattainability of moral virtue; another was the unleashing of "pious cruelty." Machiavelli "tended to believe that a considerable increase in man's inhumanity was the unintended but not surprising consequence of man's aiming too high." The element common to both transformations was the assimilation of classical philosophy and the classical moral orientation within Christianity. Machiavelli, apparently, was driven to reject classical philosophy out of antitheological ire because it had become more or less inseparable from Christianity and in the combined form had become particularly pernicious. Machiavelli's response to the synthesis of the Christian and the classical outlooks was to propose that we "lower our goals so that we shall not be forced to commit any bestialities which are not evidently required for the preservation of society and of freedom" (*WIPP*, 43).

In lowering the goals of political life, Machiavelli sought what he called "the effectual truth."[25] Strauss related that Machiavellian concern to his own construal of classical political philosophy in terms of the modern impatience with the utopian or chance-beholden character of classical thought. Machiavelli sought a truth that was reasonably realizable, i.e., not dependent on chance or on high moral efforts and achievements such as the virtues called for by the tradition. Although Machiavellian politics is surely strenuous, there was solid evidence in the history of Rome that it was realizable in this world.

Strauss links the Machiavellian concern with actualizability and thus with lowering the sights with the theological issue through his reflections on the synthesis of the biblical and the classical. That synthesis is particularly problematical because the combination of the two makes for an immoderation that either alone does not. Although the classical conception aims high, at an unrealizable utopia, its point is to establish a case for the highest political virtue, moderation, and an appreciation for the fact that what is higher than the political is not politically realizable. The paradox of classical political philosophy is that what validates and justifies political life is well beyond political life. In any case, in Strauss's famous interpretation Plato's *Republic* offers a lesson in moderation by providing a cure for the immoderate yearning for justice, for political reform, in the souls of the young. The heights of aspiration and the ultimate transcendence of the political realm in the classical philosophic notion of the true human good reconcile us to the imperfections of political life.

The biblical God, however, produces a "longing for justice and the just city" that "fills the purest hearts and the loftiest souls with [unmatched] zeal" (*WIPP*, 9). That longing, when combined with Greek ethical and philosophical aspiration, produces the "pious cruelty" and other perversions of moral and political life in the late medieval era. Religion per se, even the biblical religions, is not the source of the problem. Thus the old and tried critique of religion may have detached philosophers from an inner attachment to the gods of their cities, but it did not lead them to "anti-theological ire" or to attempt to overturn the moral and political understanding contained in classical political philosophy. As both Plato and Aristotle repeatedly observed, the city requires institutions and practices of piety (see especially Plato's *Laws*).

It is the combination of philosophical and biblical elements that overcomes the inherent moderation of classical political philosophy. The "holy God" infuses man with a zeal for justice and holiness that threatens to break out of the chains of moderation: "Extremism in pursuit of justice and goodness is no vice." It is the biblical God, particularly perhaps the incarnated God of Christianity, who introduces the demand for actualization. "Be perfect as thy father in heaven is perfect." The high or utopian aspirations of classical philosophy in their Christianized form demand to be actualized— with the result Machiavelli decried.

Given the demand for actualization, the ill results can be blunted only by lowering the sights, i.e., by aiming at what can be more readily achieved; that means in practice, by making peace with those subrational things in human beings, the passions, that both biblical religion and classical moral philosophy try to repress. The lower goal, the goal friendly to the passions, can be achieved with much greater likelihood. An extremely clever person like Machiavelli even thought (according to Strauss) that he could nearly guarantee the actualization of the best (understood in his new way), i.e., he thought chance could be largely conquered.

Strauss's Machiavelli thus presented himself as a benefactor of mankind. He would benefit his fellows by showing them how to achieve the goals they actually sought—"freedom from foreign domination, stability or rule of law, prosperity, glory or empire"—by building on forces within them that most human beings experienced most of the time (*WIPP*, 42). Machiavelli would thus endow the passions and bless their objects. He would speak to the problem of political philosophy, i.e., of the relation between philosophy and the city, by making political philosophy the willing ally of most men; i.e., he would answer the question "why philosophy?" by promising to satisfy the basic human desires. "Modern philosophy comes into being when the end of philosophy is identified with the end which is capable of being actually pursued by all men" (*LAM*, 19).

Although Machiavelli may have experienced his antitheological ire on behalf of the independence of thinking, his strategy of aligning with the desires of most men required a more open turn against the theological forces that blocked the satisfaction of worldly desire—especially the grand desires for fame and glory—and against the theologically supported moral doctrine that preached against pride in human achievement and gave men a bad conscience over it. Machiavelli may have thus broken no new ground in his critique of religion, but he was novel in attempting to rally opinion in the general direction pointed to by that critique. "He attempted to destroy Christianity by the same means by which Christianity was originally established." Or, as Strauss put it more broadly, Machiavelli "desired to bring about a change of opinion which in due time would precipitate a change in political power" (*WIPP*, 45).

Strauss questioned the value of Machiavelli's intended benefaction; he wondered whether the continent this "new Columbus" had discovered was "habitable"—because in breaking with classical political philosophy Machiavelli had in effect decapitated political philosophy by excising its most important themes—the philosophic life and political philosophy itself as a certain way of living with the limits of the political.

Machiavelli initiated the turn that brought modern political philosophy and eventually modern politics, but Strauss did not see the modern tradition to be quite so unified as the classical (*WIPP*, 40). He argued that modern political philosophy had developed, dialectically and logically, in three basic stages or "waves." By urging political leaders or "princes" to act not on the basis of what human beings should do, but on what people commonly fear and desire, Machiavelli had been the first political philosopher explicitly to break with the view of human nature according to which human beings should seek to achieve their full potential. The break he announced was both generalized and strengthened by modern natural scientists, who sought not to discover and contemplate the intelligible order of nature but to analyze and reduce natural materials to their smallest component parts so that they could be reorganized to serve human ends better. Hobbes improved upon Machiavelli not only by using modern natural science to support the new view of human nature they both promoted. He also proposed a new understanding of natural right that made the new institutional arrangements based on the new understanding of human nature not merely effective but just. John Locke made the new understanding of human beings and the purpose of political organizations even more palatable by observing that men did not fear violent death so much as they desired to acquire the means of living a safe, comfortable life—in a word, property. In sum, Strauss concluded, the first "wave" of modern political philosophers argued that human beings could achieve the ends most people seek most of the time, if they "lowered their sights."

That "lowering of the sights" provoked a reaction, however, first and most vehemently from Jean-Jacques Rousseau. Whereas "ancient politicians spoke unceasingly of manners and virtue," he protested, "ours speak of nothing but trade and money." Strauss observes that Rousseau opposed "both the stifling spirit of the absolute monarchy and the more or less cynical commercialism of the modern republics" ("TWM," 89); but he could not simply reaffirm the classical understanding of human virtue or excellence, because he accepted the truth of modern natural science. Rousseau thus sought to discover what human beings were like by nature before they entered civil society. He objected to Hobbes's description of man's "natural condition," by observing that Hobbes had not reached nature, and in mistaking social man for natural man, Hobbes had thus fallen short of his own theoretical aim. In nature human beings were characterized simply by the immediate pleasure they took in feeling that they were alive (the "sentiment of their own existence"), by a certain compassion for the suffering of other sentient beings, so long as it did not come into conflict with their own self-preservation, and by an ability to adapt to changing circumstances, called by Rousseau "perfectibility." Contingent events like population growth forced natural men into society; they began to form families and then tribes. They developed their linguistic and rational capacities, and began to compare themselves with others. Wishing to be esteemed, they began to fight—first, for the sake of honor, but later, after some had successfully laid claim to certain pieces of land, for wealth and political power. As a result, they lost the freedom and equality they had enjoyed by nature. Rousseau concluded that the only way that human beings could recapture their original natural freedom and equality in civil society would be for each to legislate simultaneously for himself and all others as part of the "general will." Only people who gave themselves laws would be free, but these laws would be just and the people living under them free and equal only if the laws applied and were endorsed by everyone subject to them. Rousseau's thought was developed by later thinkers like Kant, Hegel, and Marx into a philosophy of history, formalizing Rousseau's insight that humans become what they are through history and that morality is to be understood in terms of freedom and rationality, rather than nature. In what Strauss termed the second "wave of modernity," nature was thus replaced by history as the source both of what distinguishes human beings from all others and of the definition of what is just or right.

Hegel's successors were not persuaded by his account of the end of history. Thinkers like Nietzsche protested that the life of a nineteenth-century middle-class German burgher could not represent the acme of human excellence. Nor, it was pointed out, had Hegel provided the rational account of the whole he had promised. But if history had not come to an end, Nietzsche saw, history could not be said to be rational. And if human life and knowledge were historically limited and defined, the pressing question became what if anything could give human life meaning, since history had undermined all claims on the part of human beings to have access to an eternal truth. By denying that human beings could know anything to be eternally true, Strauss thought, Nietzsche initiated the third "wave" of modernity. As he and then Heidegger saw clearly, the contention that all human knowledge is historically limited meant that philosophy as it had traditionally been understood was no longer possible. The end result of modern political philosophy was thus the historicism Strauss criticized.

Strauss observed that the three "waves" of modern political philosophy he had described corresponded to the three major kinds of regimes or political "ideologies" in the mid-twentieth century. But, he warned, the fact that the "second" and "third" waves of modern political philosophy had been used to justify oppressive forms of communist and fascist politics did not mean that it was possible to return to early modern political philosophy. The criticism later modern political philosophers had made of their predecessors was valid. Political life, however, does not simply follow nor is it determined by the logic of political philosophy. And there were powerful sources of support for modern liberal democracies in premodern political thought. The extreme political consequences of the modern rejection of classical political philosophy meant that the grounds of that initial rejection ought to be reexamined. Strauss thus came full circle in calling for a return to premodern thought.

CHAPTER FOUR

Reviving Western Civilization from Its Roots

Strauss's Return to Premodern Thought

erhaps the most widely known of Strauss's ideas were his claims about esoteric writing and his call for a return to premodern thought. That call for return was understood by him to stand in contrast to the normal intellectual orientation of our day toward progress—going forward not back. He made the contrast between these two orientations of thinking thematic in a remarkable series of lectures he delivered in 1952, very near in time to the publication of *Natural Right and History*. The lecture series was called, appropriately, "Progress or Return? The Contemporary Crisis in Western Civilization."[1] As the title indicates, in these lectures Strauss made two main points—about "progress" and "return." First, Strauss argued that the modern idea of progress is fundamentally incoherent, because it is based on an untenable combination of concepts drawn from the two fundamentally incompatible "roots" of the Western tradition: ancient philosophy and biblical revelation. Second, in light of the failure of the modern project to conquer nature, Strauss urged his contemporaries to return to the two "roots" of the Western tradition, each of which is more coherent and provides the basis of a more stringent form of morality than later attempts to synthesize them.[2]

The discovery that the two roots of Western civilization are fundamentally incompatible might initially be disconcerting. But "if the very life of Western civilization" arises from this "fundamental tension," "there is therefore no reason inherent in the Western civilization itself . . . why it should give up life" ("PR," 289–90). If that civilization is to persist, however, advocates of the two incompatible roots will have to recognize the irresoluble tension between them. Theologians will have to credit the philosophers' testimony that they are able to live happily without revelation, and philosophers will have to recognize their own inability to disprove the possibility of revelation. Neither will be able to refute the other; but by continually confronting the challenge posed by the other, each will be forced to recognize its own character and limits. The lecture series thus culminates in Strauss's paradoxical call for the West to "live the tension" instead of trying to overcome it with faulty and impossible syntheses.

Progress

In order to make progress, Strauss explained, it is necessary to begin in a defective condition from which one can move to a better. That improved condition or goal must, moreover, be attainable, lest all "progress" toward it appear, in the end, to be vain.

Although modern thought is characteristically committed to the idea of progress, ancient Greek philosophy was also progressive insofar as it contained the promise of some gain in wisdom.[3] But the improvement promised by ancient Greek philosophy was extremely limited. Under conditions of scarcity, only a few individuals would have both the natural capacity and the economic resources needed to devote their lives to study. These individuals might try to transmit their learning to later generations in writing, but the Greek philosophers recognized that knowledge, strictly speaking, could not simply be inherited or received. Each individual would have to expend the effort necessary to acquire understanding for himself. There were also improvements in the arts that could be learned and passed on by practice or apprenticeship, but the Greek philosophers observed that improvements in technical knowledge were not necessarily accompanied by moral and political gains. They thought that even the limited progress in knowledge individuals and their societies could make would eventually come to an end. Observing that the visible universe has come into being, some argued that it would necessarily perish again. (If the world comes to an end, so obviously does "progress.") Others, like Aristotle, who held that the visible universe is eternal, asserted that there are periodic destructions of the gains human beings have made in floods or other natural disasters, so that periods of progress are followed by decay and destruction.

The ancient conception of progress thus differs from the modern idea in two decisive respects. First, the ancients did not think that intellectual progress would necessarily be accompanied by social progress. And, second, modern progress is not thought to end in telluric or cosmic catastrophes.

The modern idea of progress developed in two steps or stages. The first was the introduction of the idea of method in the seventeenth century. "Method brings about the leveling of the natural differences of the mind," because "methods can be learned in principle by everyone. Only discovery remains the preserve of the few" ("PR," 261). Gains in wisdom would no longer be restricted to a few as they had been in ancient philosophy. Thanks to the discovery of the "scientific" method, the fruits of knowledge accumulated over generations could be enjoyed by many. Intellectual progress would thus be accompanied by moral and social progress. The second distinctive characteristic of the modern idea of progress, the prospect "of an infinite future on earth not interrupted by telluric catastrophes" was developed in the eighteenth century. Believing that modern scientific research had shown that the human race began only seven thousand or so years ago, eighteenth-century rationalists concluded that humanity was in its infancy. The future was open, but the immense progress human beings had made in this relatively short period of time made it likely that they could and would make infinitely more progress in an infinite future. "The decisive point," Strauss emphasized, was that "there is a beginning and no end" ("PR," 262).

It is, however, precisely this notion of a beginning without an end that makes the modern idea of progress incoherent. Although the origin of this idea may be found in Plato's *Timaeus*, where the title character presents a "myth" in which a "demiurge" creates a world that becomes eternal, that "myth" is presented in the context of a "history" of regular telluric disasters. The source of the notion of a beginning without an end thus "has to be found in a certain interpretation of the Bible, which we find, for example, in Maimonides, where you have the beginning—the creation—and no end, and cataclysms are excluded, not by natural necessity, but by the covenant of God with Noah." Therein lies the fundamental difficulty. "On the basis of the Bible, the beginning cannot be imperfect." Instead of striving to move away from a defective beginning, the Bible teaches human beings to repent of their sins and strive to return.[4] "The availability of infinite time for infinite progress appears, then, to be guaranteed by a document of revelation which denies the other crucial elements of the idea of progress. Progress in the full and emphatic sense of the term is a hybrid notion" ("PR," 262). The modern idea of progress thus "underwent a radical modification in the nineteenth century," because modern natural science suggested that the ascent would eventually be followed by a decline. Strauss quotes a statement by Friedrich Engels as an example of this rather weak-kneed modification: "Truth can no longer be found in a collection of fixed dogmatic propositions but only in the process of knowing, which process ascends from the lower to ever higher stages. All those stages are only perishable phases in the endless development from the lower to the higher. There is no final absolute truth and no final absolute stage of the development. Nothing is imperishable except the uninterrupted process of the coming and perishing of the endless ascent from the lower to the higher." But, Strauss notes, Engels concludes by conceding that "at present natural science predicts a possible end to the existence of the earth and a certain end to the inhabitability of the earth." He takes comfort merely in the fact that "we are certainly still rather remote from the point where decline begins to set in" (263).[5]

Strauss acknowledges that this notion of an infinite increase in human knowledge through a never-ending accumulation of further information is compatible with the modern understanding of natural science as essentially hypothetical. But he does not base his argument concerning the fundamental incoherence of the modern idea of progress on the explicitly hypothetical findings of modern natural science. He argues more radically that without a source or basis in an omnipotent God there is no reason to hope for never-ending improvement or "progress." Such "progress" would be possible only if nature, especially human nature, could be entirely transformed. In "Jerusalem and Athens," he points out: "According to Socrates, the coming-into-being of the best political order is not due to divine intervention; human nature will remain as it always has been; the decisive difference between the best political order and all other societies is that in the former the philosophers will be kings or that the natural potentiality of the philosophers will reach its utmost perfection. In the most perfect social order as Socrates sees it, knowledge of the most important things will remain, as it always was, the preserve of the philosophers, i.e., of a very small part of the population. According to the prophets, however, in the Messianic age 'the earth shall be full of knowledge of the Lord, as the waters cover the earth' (Isaiah 11:9), and this will be brought about by God Himself. As a consequence, the Messianic age will be the age of universal peace. . . . The cessation of evils that Socrates expects from the establishment of the best regime [does] not include the cessation of war" (SPPP, 171–72). And in "Progress or Return?" he concludes: "The idea of progress was bound up with the notion of the conquest of nature, of man making himself the master and owner of nature for the purpose of relieving man's estate. . . . We all know of the enormous successes of the new science and of the technology which is based on it. . . . But we have also to note that there is no corresponding increase in wisdom and goodness." Indeed, "this development of modern science culminated in the view that man is not able to distinguish in a responsible manner between good and evil." We no longer believe that we have or can have firm knowledge or standards of what is right or wrong, because we think that we can have scientific knowledge only of facts, not "values." As a result, "nothing can be said responsibly about the right use" of the immense power modern natural science has conferred on human beings ("PR," 264).

The Failure of "Modernity"

To understand the crisis of Western civilization, Strauss concludes, "one cannot leave it at understanding the problematic character of the idea of progress, for the idea of progress is only a part, or an aspect, of a larger whole, of what we shall not hesitate to call modernity" ("PR," 265). The distinction he often draws between the "ancients" and the "moderns" is a distinction not between two time periods so much as between two different understandings of the human condition. Indeed, he observes, "because premodern traditions of course survived and survive throughout the modern period, there has been a constant movement against this modern trend" (269).[6] Although Strauss acknowledges the difficulty of defining "this modern trend" completely in a brief statement, in the second "Progress or Return?" lecture he identifies the three most salient and defining features of what he calls "modernity" and at the same time indicates the reasons for its failure, laying the groundwork for his call for return.

ANTITHEOLOGICAL IRE

Since human beings would not seek knowledge to transform the world so long as they regarded that world as the creation of a good and omnipotent God, Strauss finds "anti-theological ire" at the bottom of the modern philosophical enterprise. Modern philosophers saw widespread belief in a Creator God as *the* obstacle to the human attainment of knowledge that would massively improve our condition. Resting on indemonstrable claims to divine revelation or miracles, these philosophers maintained, biblical religion was fundamentally irrational.[7]

As Strauss often points out, however, neither revelation nor miracles claim to be based on reason. The truth of revelation cannot be "disproved," therefore, simply by showing that revelation is not reasonable; it can be disproved only by showing that everything in the world can be rationally explained. Hegel claimed to give such a proof, but his "proof" proved inadequate. Insofar as modern natural scientists posit the availability of ever more information or data, and thus the possibility of an infinite increase in our knowledge, they suggest that human beings will never possess a complete rational account of the whole.

RETENTION OF BIBLICAL MORALITY
WITHOUT THE BIBLICAL GOD

"Modern rationalism rejected biblical theology and replaced it by such things as deism, pantheism, atheism. But in this process, biblical morality was in a way preserved. Goodness was still believed to consist in something like justice, benevolence, love, or charity" ("PR," 265).

Other commentators on the works of modern political philosophers like Spinoza, Hobbes, and Locke have objected to Strauss's readings of them as atheists who sought to cover up their atheism with obfuscating references to traditional Jewish or Christian beliefs.[8] Strauss responded to the critics who maintained that these modern philosophers were "believers" by pointing out that, as the lives of Spinoza and Hobbes demonstrate, it was dangerous to appear not to accept the tenets of the established religion. Their professions of belief were thus prudent, and the texts of the philosophers, when thought through, pointed elsewhere. Strauss was not their only reader to suspect heterodoxy: many critics contemporary with these philosophers objected to their "unconventional" views despite their many gestures toward orthodoxy. It was only in the nineteenth century that commentators began to insist that repeated references to the Bible meant that authors were believers (*PAW*, 26–28).

Strauss thought that these philosophers had nonetheless retained ideas with a biblical foundation ("PR," 265; *LAM*, 233–57). He also agreed with Nietzsche that biblical morality had no basis without biblical faith. And it was impossible for modern philosophers to be true believers for two reasons. As philosophers, they insisted that nothing should be held to be true that could not be shown to be in accord with reason. Moreover, insofar as they thought that human life and the world needed to be fundamentally transformed, they did not accept the biblical idea that life is inherently good or that God's providence could be relied upon.

THE ELEVATION OF FREEDOM AND HISTORY
AS THE ESSENTIAL HUMAN TRAITS

Although modern political philosophers retained a biblically based notion of morality, Strauss thought, their works nevertheless expressed a fundamental shift in moral orientation. Rather than emphasize human subordination to God or to an impersonal fate, modern philosophers increasingly emphasized human freedom.

First, modern philosophers maintained, human beings are the source of all knowledge. "We know only what we make," according to Thomas Hobbes. Likewise Immanuel Kant declared, "Understanding prescribes nature its laws."

Second, since human beings did not have any reliable knowledge of a divine or natural order, modern philosophers concluded, a good or virtuous form of human existence could no longer be understood in terms of duty defined by the precepts of a natural or divine order. Morality was, consequently, increasingly defined in terms of "rights" rather than right: claims individuals raise rather than duties prescribed (*PPH*, 156). These rights, preeminently of self-preservation, were associated with instinctive passions. Beginning with Hobbes, these "rights" were also seen to consist in liberties. As a result, human beings were increasingly seen to be distinguished from other living things not by their reason, but by their freedom. In modern political philosophy, Strauss concluded, "freedom gradually takes the place of virtue" as the definition of the good life. "The good life does not consist, as it did according to the earlier notion, in compliance with a pattern antedating the human will, but consists primarily in originating the pattern itself. . . . Man has no nature to speak of. He makes himself what he is; man's very humanity is acquired" ("PR," 271).

But the philosophical development that seemed initially to celebrate human knowledge and power culminated, ironically, in demonstrating their limits. Having accepted the natural scientific view of the world as composed merely of matter in motion, modern philosophers gradually came to see that they could not consistently posit the existence of a distinctively human nature. How, then, could they explain the origin of humanity's distinctive abilities? The answer that emerged to that question, beginning with Rousseau but coming to its full fruition in the works of a series of German philosophers—Hegel, Marx, Nietzsche, and Heidegger— was "history."[9] Human beings had acquired their distinctive traits and abilities as the unintended results or effects of their own actions; the arts and institutions they developed gradually changed the human beings who were their origin.

This modern philosophical understanding of history has to be distinguished from the simple recording of what had happened, characteristic of ancient "historians" like Herodotus and Thucydides, or the record of

God's works to be found in the Bible. Unlike ancient records, the modern conception of history entails a fundamental progress in human events. And the most extreme claims about the character and results of that progress— Hegel's claim that history culminated in the replacement of philosophy or the search for knowledge with science, followed by Marx's claim that the practical application of science or technology would relieve human beings of need and enable them to live as they wished—provoked equally extreme responses from Nietzsche and Heidegger. Nietzsche

> rejected the view that the historical process is rational. . . . He taught . . . that all human life and human thought ultimately rests on horizon-forming creations which are not susceptible of rational legitimization. The creators are great individuals. . . . His creative call to creativity was addressed to individuals who should revolutionize their own lives, not to society or to his nation. But he . . . hoped that his call . . . would tempt the best men of the generations after him to become true selves and thus to form a new nobility which would be able to rule the planet.

Because he was convinced that modern Western men had become completely tame, Nietzsche "preached the sacred right of 'merciless extinction' of large masses of men with as little restraint as his great antagonist [Marx] had done. . . . He thus prepared a regime which, as long as it lasted, made discredited democracy look again like the golden age" ("WIPP," 54–55).

Finally, the difficulties Nietzsche encountered when he "tried to articulate his understanding both of the modern situation and of human life as such by his doctrine of the will to power" led Heidegger to deny that human beings have access to anything eternal.[10] Strauss concludes:

> Modern thought reaches its culmination, its highest self-consciousness, in the most radical historicism. . . . For oblivion of eternity, or, in other words, estrangement from man's deepest desire and therewith from the primary issues, is the price which modern man had to pay, from the very beginning, for attempting to be absolutely sovereign, to become the master and owner of nature, to conquer chance. ("WIPP," 55)[11]

Return

Strauss's analysis of "the crisis of modernity" led him to call for a return to premodern thought. But that call for a return necessarily led him to a second question: "Return to what?" Strauss traced the incoherence of the modern idea of progress to the attempt to combine the two fundamentally incompatible "roots" of the Western tradition in Greek philosophy and the Bible in an understanding of the world as infinitely expanding and malleable and as having its source in the biblical God. But Strauss knew very well that modern philosophers were not the first to try to synthesize the two "roots" of Western civilization.[12] The failure of the explicit attempts on the part of medieval thinkers to show that ancient philosophy and scriptural revelation were compatible was not as obvious, perhaps, as the antagonism between modern science and the Bible. But in his third lecture Strauss argued that neither Christian theologians like Thomas Aquinas nor medieval Islamic and Jewish philosophers like Alfarabi and Maimonides had, in fact, achieved a genuine synthesis.

CHRISTIANITY AND PHILOSOPHY

At first glance, Strauss conceded, Christian thinkers like Aquinas seemed to have succeeded in achieving a state of peaceful coexistence, if not synthesis or harmony, between revelation and reason by making philosophy explicitly subservient to theology. Philosophy could and should provide arguments in support of faith. But, Strauss observed, as a result of its subordination to revealed truths, philosophy lost its defining characteristic as a life of questioning and became, rather, a source of arguments, a discipline or university department. As exemplified by Socrates, Strauss objected, "philosophy is . . . not a set of propositions, a teaching, or even a system, but . . . a way of life, a life animated by a peculiar passion, the philosophic desire or *eros*, not . . . an instrument or a department of human self-realization. Philosophy understood as an instrument or as a department is, of course, compatible with every thought [or understanding] of life, and therefore also with the biblical way of life. But this is no longer philosophy in the original sense of the term." The original meaning of philosophy had been lost in "the Western development, because philosophy was certainly in the Christian Middle Ages deprived of its character as a way of life" ("PR," 297).

PHILOSOPHY AND THE MEDIEVAL JEWISH AND ISLAMIC PHILOSOPHERS

In contrast to Christian theologians, Strauss discovered, medieval Jewish and Muslim philosophers had retained the original understanding of philosophy as a way of life. The conflict between scriptural revelation understood in terms of law, which requires unquestioning obedience on the part of human beings, and philosophy, which just as unambiguously and absolutely requires questioning, was obvious. Although Christian theologians could demonstrate the compatibility of philosophy with faith by making arguments to support propositions based, ultimately, on faith, Jewish and Muslim philosophers could not raise questions about the basis or meaning of the law without seeming to challenge the law itself.[13]

Strauss emphasized two results of the Islamic and Jewish understanding of revelation in terms of law rather than faith. First, when Islamic and Jewish philosophers reflected on the law, what came to sight "was not a creed or a set of dogmas, but a social order, if not an all-comprehensive order, which regulates not merely actions but thoughts or opinions as well" (*PAW*, 9–10). Understanding revelation as law, the *falasifa* (the Arabic translation of the Greek word for philosophers) thus took revelation to specify the most perfect political order. Arguing that revelation is intelligible to human beings "only to the extent to which it takes place through the intermediacy of secondary causes, or to the extent to which it is a natural phenomenon," the *falasifa* then attempted to justify their own study of philosophy by arguing that "the founder of the perfect order, the prophetic lawgiver, was not merely a statesman of the highest order but at the same time a philosopher of the highest order" (*PAW*, 10). In other words, in attempting to justify the study of philosophy before the law, the *falasifa* employed the Platonic conception of a "philosopher-king" rather than the Aristotelian conceptions of causation and being that became so prominent in Christian theology.

On first reading, Strauss acknowledged, both the Jewish philosopher Moses Maimonides and his Islamic teacher Alfarabi appeared to be arguing that an essentially Aristotelian understanding of the cosmos is compatible with the law. But this first impression is mistaken. The second feature of the writings of medieval Jewish and Islamic thinkers he emphasized in his new and controversial readings of their works was their esoteric character. Rather than demonstrating the way in which their philosophical investigations supported the law, the works of these philosophers revealed sotto voce the fundamental conflict between reason and revelation.

In his studies of Maimonides's *Guide of the Perplexed*, Strauss emphasized its "literary" character. Addressed to a young man named Joseph, a student of theoretical philosophy who wanted to learn the secrets of the Torah from Maimonides, Maimonides's "speeches" shared the ad hominem character of Socratic arguments.[14] In deciding whether and what to teach Joseph, Maimonides faced two difficulties. First, according to the ordinance of the Talmudic sages, teaching the secrets of the Torah was expressly forbidden by the law, except if it were to one man who was wise and able to understand by himself. But Maimonides could not know whether any or which of the readers of the *Guide* would be a wise man, able to understand things by himself. As a result of the Diaspora, which prevented the close connection between student and teacher the Talmudic rule required, but which also threatened the future existence of the law, Maimonides was forced to disobey the letter of the law by writing this book. He nevertheless preserved the spirit of the law by making his explication of the "secrets" far from clear.[15] He tested his readers' acumen by presenting both an exoteric teaching supporting the law and an esoteric questioning of the truth of its foundations or "roots."

In his introduction to the *Guide* Maimonides said that he had given only the "chapter headings" of his teaching and that these were "not presented in an orderly fashion, but are scattered throughout the book." Strauss thus began his explanation of "how to begin to study the Guide" with an outline of its contents. In the order indicated by Maimonides's own chapter and section headings, we see that "the account of the Chariot (III 1–7)" (*LAM*, 141–42) is central. *Ma'aseh merkabah* (or the account of the chariot in Ezekiel 1 and 10) is *the* secret the Talmudic sages declared should not be revealed, unless to one wise man. On the basis of the outline of the content of the sections Strauss juxtaposed with the order of Maimonides's chapter and section headings, however, readers see that the account of the creation (*ma'aseh bereshit*) is central. According to Strauss, the only respect in which Maimonides thinks the philosophers and the adherents of the law disagree is whether the world is created or eternal.[16] But, Strauss also observed, that disagreement is decisive.

Having detailed the twists and turns of Maimonides's initial showing that God does not have the corporeal features suggested by the text of the Bible (which is thus shown to contain traces of Sabianism [idol worship]) that would make it impossible for him to be One, Strauss brings out the problematic character of Maimonides's central discussion. "The Kalam [a kind of Islamic theology that used philosophical arguments to prove the truth of its theological first principles] proves that God as the Creator is, is one, and is incorporeal by proving first that the world has been created; but it proves that premise only by dialectical or sophistical arguments. The philosophers prove that God is, is one, and is incorporeal by assuming that the world is eternal, but they cannot demonstrate that assumption. Hence both ways are defective." Maimonides suggests, however, that the two defective arguments can be combined to prove that God is one, incorporeal, and eternal. "For, he argues, 'the world is eternal—the world is created' is

a complete disjunction; since God's being, unity, and incorporeality necessarily follow from either of the only two possible assumptions, the basic
verities have been demonstrated by this very fact (I 71, II 2)." But, Strauss
points out, "the results from opposed premises cannot be simply identical.
... The God whose being is proved on the assumption of eternity is the un-
moved mover, thought that thinks only itself and that as such is the form
or the life of the world. The God whose being is proved on the assumption of creation is the biblical God who is characterized by Will and whose
knowledge has only the name ['knowledge'] in common with our knowledge" (*LAM*, 180). A world ordered by pure thought is in principle accessible to the human mind and thus knowable by human beings at all times
and places. The intentions and works of a God "who will be what he will
be" are entirely unpredictable and unknowable, unless he chooses to reveal
them (and, according to the Bible, he reveals himself and his works only to
some chosen individuals or peoples at specific times and places). The two
"proofs" of the existence of God do not produce different results merely
with regard to human knowledge, moreover; they also have markedly different results with regard to human morality and social practice. "For while
the belief in God's unity, being, and incorporeality is required by the Law,
that belief, being compatible with the belief in the eternity of the world,
is compatible with the unqualified rejection of the Law: the Law stands or
falls by the belief in the creation of the world" (*LAM*, 182).[17]

Rather than showing that the arguments of the philosophers concerning the eternity of the world are compatible with the biblical assertion of
its Creation, Strauss concluded, it became "incumbent on Maimonides to
show that Aristotle or Aristotelianism is wrong in holding that the eternity
of the world has been demonstrated." Maimonides was thus led to assert
that "Aristotle had indeed perfect knowledge of the sublunar things, but
... that man as man ... has knowledge only of the earth and the earthly
things." This conclusion is supported by Psalm 115:16: "The heavens, even
the heavens, are the Lord's; but the earth hath he given to the children of
Man." But, Strauss reminded his readers, "it was knowledge of heaven that
was said to supply the best proof, not to say the only proof, of the being of
God" (*LAM*, 180–83).[18]

According to Maimonides, the God of the Bible is fundamentally mysterious, which is to say that he is fundamentally different from Aristotle's
purely intelligible first mover. Writing the *Guide* "as a book written by a Jew
for Jews," Maimonides seemed to adhere to the "old Jewish premise that
being a Jew and being a philosopher are two incompatible things" (*LAM*,

142).[19] But, Strauss noted, Maimonides also wrote at least one philosophical book.[20] And in that "philosophical book" Maimonides indicated that the function of the law (or religion) was fundamentally political.

Unlike the *Guide*, Strauss observed, the *Treatise on the Art of Logic* was written by Maimonides "in his capacity as a student of logic" to "a man of high education in the Arabic tongue who wished to have explained to him as briefly as possible the meaning of the terms frequently occurring in the art of logic." In other words, Maimonides wrote his *Treatise on Logic* not as a Jew to a Jew but as a philosopher to a student of logic. In this *Treatise* Maimonides first distinguished theoretical philosophy (mathematics, physics, and theology) from practical philosophy—man's governance of himself, the household, city, and great nation or nations. Observing that many of the books of the philosophers on these subjects have already been translated into Arabic, Maimonides noted that "the books of the philosophers on politics proper" are "useless for 'us' 'in these times.'" Strauss pointed out that the meaning of this statement is unclear. "We are naturally inclined to believe that 'we' means 'we Jews': we Jews do not need the political teaching . . . of the philosophers, since we have the Torah which guides us perfectly in every respect." But, he noted, "this is not precise enough. In the first place, whereas Maimonides says in regard to politics proper, or a part of it, that we do not need the books of the philosophers on this subject, he says in regard to ethics merely that the philosophers have many books on ethics: he does not say that we do not need the books of the philosophers on ethics." And, Strauss added, "he says nothing whatever in this context about the books of the philosophers on theoretical subjects." What Maimonides suggests then "is that of all genuinely philosophic books, only the books on politics proper . . . have been rendered superfluous by the Torah. This implies that the function of the Torah is emphatically political." But Maimonides adds an important qualification to his statement; he says that we do not need these books "in these times." If the Torah made the books of Greek philosophers on politics superfluous, it would have done so for all times. Maimonides must be referring to not "the Jews as such, but the Jews in exile, the Jews who lack a political existence." If so, he was suggesting that "the Torah is not sufficient for the guidance of a political community." That implication led Strauss to reconsider his understanding of whom Maimonides means by "us." In this book, he observed, Maimonides "describes himself as a student of logic, and he describes the immediate addressee as an authority on the sciences based upon divinely revealed law, as well as on Arabic eloquence." Because Maimonides does not describe himself or his addressee as a Jew, Strauss was "tempted to say that the *Logic* is the only philosophic book which Maimonides ever wrote" and that by "we" he means "we men of theory." If so, Maimonides must then "be understood to say that the men who speculate about principles or roots do not 'in these times' need the books of the philosophers which are devoted to politics proper because of the dominance of divinely revealed laws." In suggesting "that the need for the books of the philosophers on ethics and, especially, on theoretical philosophy has not been affected by the rise to dominance of revealed religions," he is also suggesting "that the function of revealed religion is emphatically political." He "regards as useless 'in these times' only the books of the philosophers on 'the laws, the *nomoi*, the governance by human beings in divine things.' He does not deny the validity of the basic part of the political teaching of the philosophers." He thinks that they "distinguish adequately between true and imaginary happiness and the means appropriate to both, and that they have an adequate knowledge of the rules of justice." Moreover, if Maimonides thinks that only the most practical part of the political teaching of the philosophers "is superfluous 'in these times' because its function is at present fulfilled by revealed religions; if, therefore, the function of revealed religion is emphatically political," Maimonides then thinks that "political philosophy is as necessary 'in these times' as in all other times for the theoretical understanding of revealed religion" (*WIPP*, 157–59).[21]

Strauss thought that Maimonides himself took such a "theoretical" view of the Law.[22] In the *Guide* Maimonides showed how the traditional understanding of the Law needed to be purified and improved with knowledge that could be obtained only through the study of philosophy. He did not show that Aristotelian philosophy was compatible with the teaching of the Bible; and in his only truly "philosophical" work, Maimonides suggested that the Law itself should be understood primarily in terms of its political function. In his "Note on Maimonides' *Letter on Astrology*," Strauss concluded, moreover, that Maimonides did not think that the Law, as traditionally understood and practiced, had performed its political function well, because it did not promote the art of war.[23]

Strauss found the same political view of religion in the works of "Farabi, whom Maimonides, the greatest Jewish thinker of the Middle Ages, regarded as the greatest among the Islamic philosophers, and indeed as the greatest philosophic authority after Aristotle" (*PAW*, 9). Wishing to restore philosophy "after it ha[d] been blurred or destroyed" (*PAW*, 12), Alfarabi followed Plato's example in the *Republic* by presenting his own philosophy in an emphatically political context.[24]

Like Plato, Alfarabi wanted to show the utility of philosophy to non-philosophers. In the first part of his treatise *On the Attainment of Happiness*, Alfarabi thus "discusses the human things which are required for bringing about the complete happiness of nations and of cities. The chief requirement proves to be philosophy, or rather the rule of philosophers" (*PAW*, 12).[25] At first glance, "philosophy and rule appears to require two different kinds of 'arts.'" Upon further reading, however, "the philosopher and the king prove to be identical ...; philosophy by itself is not only necessary but sufficient for producing happiness.... Farabi's Plato eventually replaces the philosopher-king who rules openly in the virtuous city, by the secret kingship of the philosopher who, being 'a perfect man' precisely because he is an 'investigator,' lives privately as a member of an imperfect society which he tries to humanize within the limits of the possible" (*PAW*, 12–13, 17). Contrary to the first impression Alfarabi gives his reader, a philosopher does not need to know how to rule in order to be a philosopher—nor does he need to rule in order to attain happiness. He can live quite happily as an "investigator" in an imperfect city, which he seeks to improve to the limited extent possible. Not merely does he not need to rule; he does not need to possess knowledge of any kind (which to be knowledge, strictly speaking, would have to be knowledge of the whole). Like Socrates he can attain happiness merely by seeking knowledge.

Strauss suggests that Alfarabi's "praise of philosophy is meant to rule out any claims of cognitive value which may be raised on behalf of religion in general and revealed religion in particular. For the philosophy on which Farabi bestowed his unqualified praise, is the philosophy of the pagans Plato and Aristotle" (*PAW*, 13). Taking advantage of "the specific immunity of the commentator or historian," Alfarabi declared through the mouth of Plato "that religious speculation, and religious investigation of the beings ... do not supply the science of the beings, in which man's highest perfection consists, whereas philosophy does" (*PAW*, 13, 14). As we have seen, Alfarabi cautiously but surely dismissed religious claims on behalf of happiness in another life and affirmed this life as the only life. In his commentary on the *Nicomachean Ethics* he declares that there is only the happiness of this life, and that "all divergent statements are based on 'ravings and old woman's tales'" (*PAW*, 14). A skeptic might object that in his commentaries Alfarabi was merely presenting the views of the pagan philosophers, not his own. But, Strauss emphasized, Alfarabi very obviously did not simply report Plato's views. "Precisely as a mere commentator of Plato, Farabi was compelled to embrace the doctrine of a life after death. His flagrant deviation from the letter of Plato's teaching . . . proves sufficiently that he rejected the belief in a happiness different from this life, or the belief in another life" (*PAW*, 14–15).[26]

In sum, Strauss's study of Maimonides and Alfarabi convinced him that these thinkers had not tried to reconcile or combine ancient philosophy with revealed truth, because they recognized that philosophy and law were fundamentally opposed. Their arguments in support of the law were designed to preserve the political communities that made the pursuit of wisdom by a few rare and fortunate individuals possible. And if the subordination of ancient philosophy to theology by the Christian scholastics was not a necessary result of the conjunction of philosophy with scriptural religion, Strauss concluded, the attack on scholastic definitions of incorporeal substances waged by early modern philosophers like Hobbes and Locke did not show that ancient philosophy was untrue any more than Spinoza's showing that miracles were irrational disproved the truth of revelation, because these attacks did not reach ancient philosophy as it was originally conceived and practiced by Socrates. If reason and revelation were as fundamentally opposed as the medieval Jewish and Islamic philosophers suggested, moreover, later modern philosophical attempts to synthesize rational natural science with biblical morality or ancient virtue were also fundamentally misguided. Each of the parts was more tenable than the attempted combinations.[27]

Strauss learned about the fundamental tension between reason and revelation from his study of Maimonides and Alfarabi, but, we should note, his way of treating that tension was completely different from that of these medieval philosophers. They sought to conceal the conflict between philosophy and the law in order to preserve both philosophy and the law (or a decent political community). Strauss seeks to bring out the fundamental tension between reason and revelation, because he sees that the modern attempt to synthesize them threatens to culminate in the destruction of both. An unprecedented situation calls for an unprecedented response.[28]

Living the Tension

Strauss thought that "what has taken place in the modern period has been a gradual corrosion and destruction of the heritage of Western civilization." Modern political philosophy culminated in Nietzsche's declaration that "God is dead" and Heidegger's conclusion that philosophy had come to an end. The "historical" turn in philosophy ended up destroying the grounds of earlier assertions of human freedom and progress by showing that human beings had been unalterably shaped, in unintended ways, by the deeds of their predecessors. And, as we noted earlier, the development of modern natural science and the historical understanding of human life it fostered had erased the foundations of all moral standards.

> The soul of the modern development . . . is a peculiar "realism," the notion that moral principles and appeal to moral principles . . . is ineffectual, and therefore that one has to seek a substitute . . . [first] in institutions and economics, . . . [but ultimately in] what was called "the historical process." . . . Once it became clear, however, that historical trends are absolutely ambiguous and, therefore, cannot serve as a standard . . . no standard was left. ("PR," 268)

Strauss's studies of medieval Jewish and Islamic philosophy had persuaded him, however, that neither the end of rational inquiry nor the undermining of morality was an inevitable consequence of the history of philosophy. There was a "solution" to the "crisis of Western civilization." That was to "return" to its opposed "roots" and to "live that conflict," because "this unresolved conflict" between the biblical and the philosophic notions of the good life "is the secret of the vitality of Western civilization." Western civilization would persist "only if we live that life, if we live that conflict" ("PR," 289–90). But what does it mean to "live" this conflict?

MORALITY

One reason the opposition between the two roots had not been perceived or fully appreciated, Strauss suggested, was that the Bible and Greek philosophy agreed on many of the core propositions of traditional morality, e.g., that murder, theft, and adultery are unqualifiedly bad. Both agreed, further, "that the proper framework of morality is the patriarchal family, which . . . forms the cell of a society in which the free adult males, and especially the old ones, predominate." Both also denied the legitimacy of worshiping any human being. Finally and most importantly, both "agree in assigning the highest praise among the virtues, not to courage or manliness, but to justice." Both agreed, moreover, "regarding the problem of justice, the difficulty created by the misery of the just and the prospering of the wicked" ("PR," 275–76).

Because the unjust appear to succeed better than the just, both the Bible and Greek philosophy agree, justice requires suprarational or supra-societal support. But, Strauss emphasized, the Bible and Greek philosophy disagree fundamentally about the character of the necessary support. "According to Greek philosophy, that [support] is *theoria*, contemplation"; according to the Bible, it is "piety, the need for divine mercy or redemption, obedient love" ("PR," 291). As a result, the corresponding understandings of "morality" also differ. In the *Nicomachean Ethics* Aristotle describes "magnanimity" or "great-souledness" as the comprehensive virtue of an individual in addition and contrast to "justice," which concerns an individual's relations with others. But "biblical humility excludes magnanimity in the Greek sense. . . . Magnanimity presupposes a man's conviction of his own worth. It presupposes that man is capable of being virtuous" ("PR," 277). In order to become virtuous, the Greeks also thought, a man needs a certain amount of wealth.[29] "The Bible, on the other hand, uses poor and pious or just as synonymous terms. Compared with the Bible, Greek philosophy is heartless in this as well as in other respects" ("PR," 277). A virtuous human being will not feel guilty or repent.

> Greek philosophy has frequently been blamed for the absence from it of that ruthless examination of one's intentions which is the consequence of the biblical demand for purity of the heart. "Know thyself" means for the Greeks, know what it means to be a human being, know what is the place of man in the universe, examine your opinions and prejudices, rather than "Search your heart." ("PR," 279)

As Maimonides shows, "the root of the matter is that only the Bible teaches divine omnipotence, and the thought of divine omnipotence is absolutely incompatible with Greek philosophy. . . . In Greek thought, we find in one form or the other an impersonal necessity higher than any personal being; whereas in the Bible the first cause is, as people say now, a person. This is connected with the fact that the concern of God with man is absolutely, if we may say so, essential to the biblical God; whereas that concern is, to put it very mildly, a problem for every Greek philosopher" ("PR," 281–82).[30]

THE TENSION BETWEEN THE ROOTS

If everything that happens occurs because God wills it, the composers of the Bible saw, the one true god has to be omnipotent. Otherwise, this god will not be simply responsible or the cause of what happens. If there is more than one god, the others will check and confound his will. But an omnipotent god is not intelligible or predictable (and thus potentially controllable by those who come to understand him). Especially if the law he gives to one particular people is to be understood to be *the* divine law, God must be understood to be essentially free, to be as he shall be and do as he shall will. As Maimonides recognized, God and his will thus remain essentially mysterious. Right will prevail, if God wills it, but human beings will never be able to see how or to fathom the reasons why.

According to the Greek philosophers, the source of justice and injustice, order and disorder, right and wrong has to be sought in the impersonal forces that determine the character of the cosmos. As presented in Maimonides's *Guide* (and as more generally traditionally understood), *the* difference between the Bible and philosophy concerns the creation or eternity of the world. If the world is created, everything depends ultimately on God's will. If the world is created, it is possible that someday swords may be made into plowshares, i.e., that human nature will change, so that wars will no longer occur. Everything is contingent (on the will of God); nothing exists necessarily or in itself. According to Greek philosophy, however, the gods, like everything else, are subject to higher, more impersonal forces.[31] Although they disagreed about the specific character of these forces— be they the fates, properties of matter, or purely intelligible ideas—in no case did Greek philosophers think that anything could be *fundamentally* changed or altered. "What distinguishes the Bible from Greek philosophy is the fact that Greek philosophy is based on this premise: that there is such a thing as nature, or natures—a notion which has no equivalent in biblical thought" ("PR," 282).

The difference between "revelation" and "reason" cannot be settled at this "metaphysical" level, Strauss insisted, because revelation does not rest on reason. The One Omnipotent God of the Bible is beyond human ken. Human reason is not capable of showing that it is impossible for such a God to exist. Nor can the difference be decided on the basis of an argument about "human nature," because "the nature of man cannot be fully clarified except by an understanding of the nature of the whole" ("PR," 297), and such an understanding is not—and probably never will be—available.

THE TWO PEAKS OF HUMAN EXISTENCE

How then are human beings supposed to live? Are our only alternatives to live in pious obedience from fear and love of the Lord or to rely on autonomous human reason, however faulty? Human beings appear to be confronted with an "abysmal," ungrounded choice.

In *Natural Right and History* Strauss explained that Max Weber had such an ungrounded choice in mind when he concluded that the conflict between values could not be resolved by human reason:

> Man cannot live without light, guidance, knowledge; only through knowledge of the good can he find the good that he needs. The fundamental question, therefore, is whether men can acquire that knowledge ... by the unaided efforts of their natural powers, or whether they are dependent for that knowledge on Divine Revelation. ... The dilemma cannot be evaded by any harmonization or synthesis, for ... the one thing needful proclaimed by the Bible is the opposite of that proclaimed by philosophy.

Strauss commented,

> If we take a bird's-eye view of the *secular* struggle between philosophy and theology, we can hardly avoid the impression that neither of the two antagonists has ever succeeded in really refuting the other. ... Revelation is always so uncertain to unassisted reason that it can never compel the assent of unassisted reason ... but ... [man] yearns so much for a solution ... and human knowledge is always so limited that the need for divine illumination cannot be denied and the possibility of revelation cannot be refuted.

And, he concluded, it was this state of affairs that *seemed* to decide irrevocably against philosophy and in favor of revelation.

> Philosophy has to grant that revelation is possible. But to grant that revelation is possible means to grant that philosophy is ... not necessarily, not evidently, *the* right life. Philosophy, the life devoted to the quest for evident knowledge available to man as man, would itself rest on an unevident, arbitrary, or blind decision. This would merely confirm the thesis of faith, that there is no possibility of consistency ... without belief in revelation. The mere fact that philosophy and revelation cannot refute each other would constitute the refutation of philosophy by revelation. (*NRH*, 74–75)

Scholars such as Steven Smith have concluded that Strauss himself saw "the alternatives of reason and revelation as resting on an act of choice or faith," i.e., the position we later call "decisionism."[32] But at the conclusion of "Progress or Return?" Strauss explicitly states that "this difficulty underlies *all present-day philosophizing*" and "is at the bottom of what in the social sciences is called the value problem" ("PR," 310, emphasis added). It does not apply to Socratic or classical political philosophy, because Socratic philosophy begins differently by raising the primary question of the right life.

In fact, Strauss argues, the "choice" between "faith" and "reason" cannot be made as such. It is not clear that one can "choose" to believe or to love God; one can at most act as if one does. Mere adherence to the law does not give one a righteous heart. Nor can one ground a life of pure reason on a choice without reason; such a "choice" would constitute "an act of will, of belief, and that being based on belief is fatal to any philosophy" (*LAM*, 256).[33]

The tension Strauss sees at the heart of "Western civilization" is not between two "beliefs," between which one must choose arbitrarily; it is between two incompatible understandings of the right way of life for a human being. By raising the question concerning the right way of life Strauss himself takes a philosophical stand. Showing none of the "anti-theological ire" that animated modern political philosophy, however, he states his belief "that the Bible sets forth the demands of morality and religion in their purest and most intransigent form" (*TM*, 133). He thus treats the teaching of the Bible very respectfully. In concluding his "Progress or Return?" lectures, he writes: "If one can say colloquially, the philosophers have never refuted revelation and the theologians have never refuted philosophy, that would sound plausible, considering the enormous difficulty of the problem from any point of view. And to that extent we may be said to have said something very trivial" ("PR," 309). What is not trivial, he emphasizes, is the necessity that philosophers see as a result of their inability to refute revelation that philosophy is possibly not the right way of life and that they must begin, therefore, by showing that it is. As a Socratic, Strauss thus investigates the chief alternative opinions proposed in our own Western tradition in answer to the question concerning the right way of life for a human being.

Strauss finds the first of the conflicting understandings of the right way of life in the Hebrew Bible or Torah. Rather than approach the Bible literally as the word of God, or accept the dismissive results of the historical-critical study of the Bible by philosophers like Spinoza, in his essay "Jerusalem and Athens" Strauss suggests that we read the Bible as the compilation of many generations of "memories of ancient histories." Such "memories of memories are not necessarily distorting or pale reflections of the original; they may be re-collections of re-collections, deepenings through meditation of the primary experiences." By proceeding in this way, he thinks "we shall start . . . where both the traditional and the historical study of the Bible necessarily start." And "we avoid the compulsion to make an advance decision in favor of Athens against Jerusalem. For the Bible does not require us to believe in the miraculous character of events that the Bible does not present as miraculous. God's speaking to men may be described as miraculous, but the Bible does not claim that the putting together of those speeches was done miraculously" (*SPPP*, 151–52).

Strauss then begins reading the Bible at the beginning and observes that it begins reasonably with *the* beginning. One sees, moreover, that there is an intelligible order to the events recounted. A modern natural scientist may think it strange, if not "irrational," that "light" is created before the sun. Believing in the goodness of the One God and his Creation, however, the compilers of the Bible recognized that creation proceeded in stages, marked by distinctions (like Platonic *diaireseis*) or separations of different kinds of beings. The most important such distinction is between those things which do not move themselves (created in the first three days) and those which do (created in the last three days). All stages of creation are said by God to be good—except for the heavens and man. The creation of the heavens was not unambiguously good, because the compilers of the Bible knew that many peoples worshiped the heavenly bodies rather than the one true God. And, as the second creation story shows, human beings were not simply good because not simply obedient. Our nature is such that we had to learn about good and evil. Indeed, it took many generations and much suffering to teach human beings that they should obey, of their own free will, the covenant or law freely offered to them by a mysterious and free God.[34] Human beings are images of the ruling principle of the world insofar as we are free, free to choose to do good or evil. In contrast to the Greek philosophers, the Bible thus suggests that human beings are distinguished not so much by our rational faculty as by our freedom and, consequently, our morality.

Precisely because human beings are free, it is not clear how we must or should live our lives. The ancient Greek philosophers Plato and Aristotle thus suggested that we need to use our reason, our most distinctive faculty, in order to find out. What is most important, according to these philosophers is not that human beings are free to choose to do what is right or wrong. So long as human beings lack knowledge, this freedom can and probably will be used badly. What is most urgent and necessary for human beings is, therefore, to seek knowledge of the right way to live. The philosophic life as the proffered answer to the question of the right life is based on the perception that the right way of life is and remains a question that "makes quest for knowledge the most important thing, and therefore a life devoted to it the right way of life" ("PR," 298).

Strauss identifies this original understanding of philosophy with Socrates. Since Socrates was aware of his own imperfect "human wisdom," Strauss notes, it may be difficult to understand why he did not seek divine wisdom. The reason implied in the *Apology of Socrates* is that "as a philosopher, he refuses assent to anything which is not evident to him, and revelation is for him not more than an unevident, unproven possibility. Confronted with an unproven possibility, he does not reject, he merely suspends judgment." But, Strauss objects, a human being cannot merely "suspend judgment regarding matters of utmost urgency," i.e., matters of life and death. And if revelation is true, the philosopher's disbelief will be fatal. His rejection of revelation would appear to be warranted only if revelation were disproved. Strauss suggests, however, that the philosopher would reply that the question of utmost urgency that cannot be suspended is how one should live. "This question is settled for Socrates by the fact that he is a philosopher. As a philosopher, he knows that we are ignorant of the most important things. The ignorance, the evident fact of this ignorance, evidently proves that quest for knowledge of the most important things is the most important thing for us." Socrates might thus appear to have begun with a choice or decision for philosophy. But, Strauss adds, not only does Socrates see the necessity, first and most urgently, to ask about the right way of life before asking whether we should fear the apparently inevitable end of our lives. Socrates also sees his decision "confirmed by the fact that he finds his happiness in acquiring the highest possible degree of clarity which he can acquire. He sees no necessity whatever to assent to something which is not evident to him" ("PR," 296–97). And if he were threatened with eternal damnation, Strauss suggests, like the philosophers of the past he would have been "absolutely certain that an all-wise God would not punish with eternal damnation or with anything else such human beings as are seeking the truth or clarity." Strauss postpones consideration of "whether this reply is quite sufficient." What he emphasizes is that "philosophy is meant, and that is the decisive point, not as a set of propositions, a teaching, or even a system, but as a way of life, a life animated by a peculiar passion, the philosophic desire or *eros*, not as an instrument or a department of human self-realization." This is the understanding of philosophy that "has been greatly obscured . . . by the Western development, because philosophy was certainly in the Christian Middle Ages deprived of its character as a way of life and became just a very important compartment" ("PR," 297).

Strauss then restates "why philosophy cannot possibly lead up to the insight that another way of life . . . is the right one. Philosophy is quest for knowledge regarding the whole. Being essentially quest and being not able ever to become wisdom, as distinguished from philosophy, the problems are always more evident than the solutions." One of those problems is that "the right way of life cannot be fully established except by an understanding of the nature of man, and the nature of man cannot be fully clarified except by an understanding of the nature of the whole. Therefore, the right way of life cannot be established metaphysically except by a completed metaphysics, and therefore the right way of life remains questionable. But the very uncertainty of all solutions, the very ignorance regarding the most important things, makes quest for knowledge the most important thing, and therefore a life devoted to it, the right way of life" ("PR," 297–98).

Strauss thus concludes, "philosophy in its original and full sense is then certainly incompatible with the biblical way of life. Philosophy and Bible are the alternatives or the antagonists in the drama of the human soul. Each . . . claims to know or to hold the truth . . . regarding the right way of life. But there can be only one truth: hence, conflict between these claims . . . ; and that means inevitably argument" ("PR," 298). Each of the two opponents has tried for millennia to refute the other. Neither, Strauss argues, has succeeded or can succeed.

Greek philosophers did not know the Bible, nor did the compilers of the Bible know Greek philosophy. But, Strauss observed, each nevertheless indicates awareness of the alternative. Anticipating the Greek view, the Bible suggests that *the* sin to be avoided is worship of the heavenly bodies. The authors of the Bible did not think that human beings should be encouraged to contemplate the motions of the heavenly bodies with wonder or to seek the intelligible source of life on earth in them. Anticipating the biblical view, Greek philosophers suggest that tragedy presents a popular, but ultimately false view of human existence as fundamentally "guilty," arousing pity (or piety) and fear ("PR," 287–88).

Just as Maimonides took a "theoretical" view of the Law, so it seems that Strauss took a philosophical view of the tension between reason and revelation. Because he understood philosophy to consist in a quest for knowledge rather than the possession of it, he emphasized the perennial problems that made philosophy always a search.[35] He acknowledged that "philosophy is victorious as long as it limits itself to repelling the attack which theologians make on philosophy with the weapons of philosophy. But," he insisted, "philosophy in its turn suffers a defeat as soon as it starts an offensive of its own, as soon as it tries to refute, not the necessarily inadequate proofs of revelation, but revelation itself" ("PR," 305).

Strauss argued that modern philosophy was animated by "anti-theological ire." But classical political philosophy, as he understood it, was not. In arguing that Strauss thought that philosophy could and did refute revelation by giving an account of its origin and historical development, Heinrich Meier does not appear to be persuaded by the distinction Meier himself quotes from Strauss, between "a philosophy which believes that it can refute the possibility of revelation—and a philosophy which does not believe that: *this* is the real meaning of la querelle des anciens et des modernes."[36] According to Strauss, ancient philosophers like Socrates recognized the limits of their knowledge, whereas modern philosophers like Spinoza and Hegel did not. These modern philosophers thought that they could refute revelation by giving a rational account of the whole. Strauss explained: "The historical refutation of revelation . . . presupposes natural theology because the historical refutation always presupposes the impossibility of miracles, and the impossibility of miracles is ultimately guaranteed only by knowledge of God." A refutation of revelation on the basis of natural theology thus presupposed "a proof that God's nature is comprehensible, and this in its turn requires completion of the true system of the true or adequate account of the whole." But, Strauss concluded, "since such a true or adequate, as distinguished from a merely clear and distinct, account of the whole, is certainly not available, philosophy has never refuted revelation ("PR," 309).[37]

Strauss also insisted that "revelation, or rather theology," has never refuted philosophy. "For from the point of view of philosophy, first, revelation is only a possibility; and secondly, man, in spite of what the theologians say, can live as a philosopher, that is to say, untragically." Attempts by Pascal and others "to prove that the life of philosophy is fundamentally miserable presuppose faith" ("PR," 309).

"By showing as no one has done in four hundred years that the claims of Reason and Revelation are inherently untouched by modernity," Ernest Fortin suggests, "Strauss may have performed as great a service for theology as he has for philosophy."[38] Strauss was, however, clearly more concerned about philosophy than about theology. He wanted philosophers to "admit the possibility of revelation," because such an admission would amount to an acknowledgment that philosophy might not be the right way of life.

And if philosophy were not evidently the right way of life, philosophers would again have to ask what the right way of life is. That is the question, Strauss argued, that gave rise to political philosophy in the first place. And in attempting to answer that question, Strauss also saw, philosophers would have to justify their questioning, not only to themselves but also to the city. It was the perceived need to justify philosophy, Strauss argued (*NRH*, 121–53; *WIPP*, 10–12, 90–94; *CM*, 19–20), that gave rise to Socratic political philosophy; and it is to Socratic political philosophy that Strauss sought to return.

A Revival Is Not Simply a Return

Strauss did not seek to revive or literally return to medieval Jewish or Islamic, or even to ancient, political philosophy. On the contrary, he explicitly recognized that such a return was neither possible nor desirable. In his introduction to *The City and Man* he cautioned:

> We cannot reasonably expect that a fresh understanding of classical political philosophy will supply us with recipes for today's use. For the relative success of modern political philosophy has brought into being a kind of society wholly unknown to the classics, a kind of society to which the classical principles as stated and elaborated by the classics are not immediately applicable. Only we living today can possibly find a solution to the problems of today. (*CM*, 11)

Strauss sought to reopen the questions that had given rise to ancient political philosophy by showing that neither the "progressive" accounts of the history of philosophy, which claimed that later philosophers had solved the problems posed by their predecessors, nor the more "pessimistic" late modern accounts of the end of philosophy were well-founded. By reraising the questions or irreconcilable tensions, Strauss explicitly admitted that none of the previously given answers or solutions was adequate.[39]

Like Alfarabi, Strauss understood himself to be attempting to revive philosophy "after it has been blurred or destroyed." Like Alfarabi, Strauss thus presented his philosophy in an explicitly political or "Platonic" framework.[40] Strauss saw that the future of philosophy as a way of life was threatened in an unprecedented way in modern times by the logic of the development of modern philosophy as well as by the possibility of the establishment of a totalitarian world-state whose ideology and technology would make all questioning or dissent impossible (*OT*, 211). New circumstances called for new responses, including new readings or critiques of the "Western tradition" and the history of philosophy. However, because Strauss was reconceiving the Western tradition from its very inception or "roots" in order to revive old questions and therewith the original understanding of philosophy as a way of life, he could and did describe his own work as a "return."

CHAPTER FIVE

Strauss's New Reading of Plato

S trauss's study of medieval Jewish and Islamic political philosophy not merely led him to see that the source of the vitality of Western civilization was to be found in the tension between its two roots. His studies of the writings, particularly of Alfarabi, also led him to give new readings of the classical political philosophy of Plato and Aristotle.[1] In this chapter we look at the studies of Platonic dialogues Strauss published in order to obtain a more comprehensive view of his understanding of "Platonic political philosophy." In the next chapter we then examine the one and only essay on Aristotle's *Politics* he published in some detail to show how he thought the original, Socratic understanding of philosophy as a way of life was already becoming lost.

The dominant understanding of the Platonic dialogues in the Western philosophical tradition emphasized the centrality of Plato's theories of the "ideas" and the immortality of the soul.[2] Strauss discovered that both doctrines were strangely lacking in Alfarabi's summary of "the philosophy of Plato."[3] Instead Alfarabi suggested that the conflict between philosophy and the "law" (which included both religion and politics for Jews, Muslims, and ancient Greeks) was at the core of Plato's thought. Looking back at Plato with fresh eyes after reading Alfarabi, Strauss developed a new way of reading the dialogues in terms of this conflict, a way of reading that gave Plato's thought renewed vitality and relevance.[4]

Strauss's new reading of Plato is to be found in an exemplary way in his commentary on Plato's *Republic*. He published the first version of this commentary in the essay "Plato" he wrote for *The History of Political Philosophy*, which he edited with Joseph Cropsey. In a short concluding section on the *Statesman* and *Laws* he argued that all three of Plato's major dialogues on politics point to the conclusion that the rule of law is the best practical outcome. The slightly longer version of his essay, "On Plato's *Republic*," in *The City and Man* was prefaced by reflections on how the dialogues should be read. He later wrote a series of essays on the dialogues connected to Socrates's trial. "On Plato's *Apology of Socrates* and *Crito*" and "On the *Euthydemus*" were reprinted in his posthumously published *Studies in Platonic Political Philosophy* to which, Joseph Cropsey tells us in the foreword, Strauss planned to add an essay on *Gorgias*.[5] Strauss's last works on Plato were concerned primarily with the *Laws*. Having published "How Fārābī Read Plato's *Laws*" in 1957, Strauss included an essay on the *Minos*, the dialogue traditionally considered to be an introduction to Plato's *Laws*, in *Liberalism Ancient and Modern* in 1968.[6] He had just finished his own commentary, *The Argument and the Action of Plato's "Laws,"* when he died in 1973. Both Strauss's selection of dialogues and the analyses he gave of them reflect the influence of Alfarabi, visible in the emphasis placed on the conflict between philosophy and politics.[7]

Strauss's Way of Reading Plato

Strauss did not simply follow Alfarabi's hints about the true character and content of Plato's teaching, however.[8] On the contrary, at the beginning of his essay "Plato's *Republic*" in *The City and Man*, he explained his own way of reading Plato.

In his dialogues, Strauss emphasized, Plato presents exclusively the speeches and deeds of others.[9] The dialogues must, therefore, be read like dramas in which one can never identify the views of the author with any particular character. Although it is tempting to take Socrates as Plato's spokesman, Socrates is not the only philosopher who appears in the dialogues, and if we take him as Plato's spokesman, we are confronted by the fact that he is explicitly said to be ironic. There is a notable difference between Socrates and his student, moreover: Socrates did not write. Plato has his character Socrates identify the fundamental defect of writing at the end of *Phaedrus*: writings say the same thing to all people. The Platonic dialogues must be understood as attempts to remedy this defect. For Plato "the proper work of a writing is . . . to reveal the truth to some while leading others to salutary opinions; . . . to arouse to thinking those who are by nature fit for it" (*CM*, 53). Plato thus shows Socrates saying different things to different people, because in each case he says what is suited to the person to whom he is speaking. Recognizing such differences is a requisite characteristic of both responsible and effective teaching. But, Strauss argued, the different teachings presented in the different dialogues do not merely reflect the different characters of the participants in the conversation, nor are they simply matters of rhetoric or persuasion.[10] "Plato's work consists of many dialogues because it imitates the manyness, the variety, the heterogeneity of being. . . . There are many dialogues because the whole consists of many parts" (*CM*, 61–62). Unlike numerical units, however, the parts cannot simply be added up to constitute the whole.

> The individual dialogue is not a chapter from an encyclopedia of the philosophic sciences. . . , still less a relic of a stage of Plato's development. Each dialogue . . . reveals the truth about that part. But the truth about a part is a partial truth, a half truth. Each dialogue, we venture to say, abstracts from something that is most important to the subject matter of the dialogue. (*CM*, 62)

In order to see the way in which the truth presented in each dialogue is only partial, readers have to pay particular attention to the dramatic elements. "The principle guiding the specific abstraction which characterizes [a] dialogue . . . is revealed primarily by the setting. . . : its time, place, characters, and action" (*RCPR*, 155). Plato presents the conversation as an actual historical event, that is, as an event that occurred at least partially by chance.[11] The task confronting the reader of a Platonic dialogue is thus to see the way in which the drama, i.e., the setting, characters, and action, shape the argument. Plato does not tell us what he thinks; he indirectly shows us by presenting the speeches and deeds of others.

Strauss's Reading of Plato's *Republic*

Strauss showed that his way of reading the dialogues produced a dramatically different understanding of Plato in his essay on the *Republic*, the dialogue that many commentators think contains Plato's most comprehensive statements about both politics and philosophy. He argued that attention to the setting of the dialogue alerts readers from the very beginning that the *Republic* may not contain a serious proposal for political reform, as many readers have thought, so much as a warning about the difficulties inherent in all such attempts. Although Plato does not identify the precise time of the conversation portrayed, "we are not left entirely in the dark" about "the political circumstances in which the conversation about the political principle took place." By setting the dialogue in the Piraeus, the Athenian seaport, where Socrates is compelled to speak to a group of ten men, Plato reminded his readers that

> some years after the conversation, men linked to Socrates and Plato by kinship or friendship attempted . . . putting down the democracy and restoring an aristocratic regime dedicated to virtue and justice. Among other things they established an authority called the Ten in the Piraeus. (*CM*, 63)

The composition of the two groups, the Ten who ruled and the ten who talked to Socrates about rule, was different, however. "Polemarchus, Lysias, and Niceratus [characters mentioned in the *Republic* as having been present at the conversation] were mere victims of the so-called Thirty Tyrants."[12] By discussing "justice in the presence of victims of an abortive attempt made by most unjust men to restore justice," Plato prepared his readers "for the possibility that the restoration attempted in the *Republic* will not take place on the political plane" (*CM*, 63). In the *Republic* Socrates's major interlocutor is Plato's brother Glaucon; and "Xenophon tells us that Socrates . . . cured him of his extreme political ambition. . . . Certain it is that the *Republic* supplies the most magnificent cure ever devised for every form of political ambition" (*CM*, 65).[13] In a century that had witnessed the attempts of two different totalitarian regimes to establish world domination, Strauss thought there was again a need for such a "magnificent cure."

The explicit question raised in the *Republic* is "what is justice?" Unlike many Plato scholars, Strauss took what appeared to be merely preliminary matters in the dialogues with the utmost seriousness. Thus, although Socrates's refutations of the three definitions of justice offered by Cephalus, Polemarchus, and Thrasymachus in book 1 appear abortive, Strauss found that they point both to a definition of justice and to the difficulty it entails, matters of real significance for the question of justice as it unfolds later. If, as Socrates's refutation of Cephalus's more traditional definition of justice as giving to each his or her due suggests, justice consists in giving each what is good for one, and if injustice consists, as Socrates's refutation of Thrasymachus is supposed to show, in one part of a community taking advantage of the other, justice becomes a problem if what is good for the community as a whole is not good for all of its members as individuals. Plato's *Republic* shows that this is indeed the case in the most important instance: it would be good for the community if a philosopher ruled, but not for the philosopher himself.

Socrates appears to push against that conclusion by suggesting that justice in the polity and in the individual must be essentially the same. When

Glaucon challenges Socrates to show that justice is choiceworthy for its own sake, Socrates responds that they first have to determine what justice is; in order to do so they should look for justice "writ large" in a city. From the perspective of the traditional reading of Plato primarily in terms of his theory of the ideas, Strauss pointed out, Socrates's mode of proceeding in the *Republic* appears anomalous. Rather than seek the answer to the question "what is justice?" in an eternal idea of justice in itself (which should be the same not merely in individual and city, but everywhere and at all times), he follows Glaucon's example by looking for it in the coming-into-being of a city, a new city that—unlike all others—has ostensibly been established entirely according to nature.[14] There is a significant difference, in other words, between the kind of education Socrates offers Plato's brothers in the dialogue and the education that he proposes for the "guardians" of his "city in speech."[15] In the conversation with Plato's brothers Socrates shows what justice is by tracing it to its origins in the need human beings have to live peacefully and cooperate with others in order to survive. But in the education Socrates argues is necessary for the philosophers who are to become the rulers of this city, he suggests that they will need to study five different kinds of mathematics in order to prepare them to acquire knowledge of the "ideas" of justice and the other kinds of virtues.

That there is no unqualifiedly natural basis for the city is shown by the fact that it has to be founded; cities are products of human making or art. The first "true" city Socrates describes is not humanly satisfying, moreover. Glaucon indicates as much when he passionately protests that Socrates has described a "city of pigs." He misses and desires the "relishes" or luxuries people conventionally seek. By having each person do what he does best by nature and exchange the results, the "true" city provides for the necessities of physical preservation. To develop any form of human excellence human beings have to possess more goods or leisure than is necessary simply for their preservation; and in striving to obtain those goods, Socrates suggests, they necessarily come into conflict with other cities. Armed guards thus become necessary to defend the city from invasion.[16]

Once a part of the city is armed, however, it becomes potentially dangerous to the other, unarmed part. The guardians must be carefully educated not to misuse their power. But, Strauss observed, "the whole discussion partakes of the character of myth" (*CM*, 98). The explicitly unrealizable character of the educational prescriptions, especially the "noble lie" in which they culminate, shows that Socrates is not putting forth a practical program. The content of the prescribed education is nevertheless instructive.

The difficulties point to the reasons why the institution of a perfectly just regime is impossible.

These difficulties arise right at the beginning of the guardians' education. According to the traditional stories, the gods, who were supposed to defend justice, were themselves pleasure seeking and unjust, and thus questionable guardians of justice. Socrates thus begins his account of the education of the warriors with two laws concerning what Adeimantus calls "theology": (1) gods shall be said to cause only good; and (2) as an apparent corollary of the first, gods shall not be said to change their shape (*eidos* or *idea*, Strauss noted) or to lie.[17] Such gods are more akin to justice, but Adeimantus is troubled by the second law, because it suggests the gods cannot rule (which Socrates later shows requires deceit) or therefore be just.[18]

Strauss shows that the purportedly "natural" foundation of the city is just as problematic as its "divine" support in his analysis of the "noble lie" with which Socrates's account of the warriors' education ends. Part of the lie attempts to convince citizens that they were born from the piece of land upon which they live, a response to the fact that no particular people has an unqualified or natural or simply just claim to possess any particular part of the earth (*CM*, 102). (Indeed, it is not evident that any political association that does not include the whole human race has a simply natural basis.) By stating that the founders will also have to convince the citizens, again contrary to easily observable fact, that the different classes have different types of blood, Socrates also indirectly admits that the conventional order in the city does not perfectly reflect a natural order of talent and, therefore, cannot be simply just.

Justice proves to be difficult to find in the city they have established, moreover. "Justice is said to consist in each part of the city or of the soul 'doing the work for which it is best fitted by nature.' . . . If each part of the city does its work well, the city is wise, courageous, and moderate and therewith perfectly good; it does not need justice in addition." But "the case of the individual is different. If he is wise, courageous, and moderate, he is not yet perfectly good; for his goodness toward his fellows, his willingness to help them. . . , as distinguished from unwillingness to harm them, does not follow from his possessing the three first virtues" (*CM*, 110). Looking for a definition of justice solely in the internal relations citizens have to one another, Strauss notes, Socrates does not raise a question about the city's relations to others. Although he admitted that even his "true" or "simple" city would need to import goods from others and that the need for guardians arose from the need to defend the city against others who would seek to seize its territory unjustly, in drawing the parallel between the city and the soul of an individual Socrates treats the city as if it were self-sufficient.[19]

To maintain the parallel between the city and the individual Socrates has to find the same parts or "natures" in the individual as in the city. But, Strauss pointed out, that parallel depends upon an abstraction from the body, because the parts of the individual that parallel the classes of the city are parts of the soul.[20] The body, for the sake of which the city was originally established, is altogether ignored. It is ignored, we discover later in the discussion, because the attachment each individual has to his or her own *bodily* existence is *the* source of injustice.

If justice consists in the good order or health of the soul, it is clear that justice is choiceworthy for its own sake, whether the individual enjoys a reputation for virtue or not. By the end of book 4 Socrates has thus satisfied Glaucon's demand in book 2 that he show that justice is good in itself, without regard to its extrinsic benefits or effects.[21] The difficulty is that, according to this definition of justice, "only the man in whom reason properly cultivated rules the other two parts . . . i.e. only the wise man . . . can be just . . . and the philosopher can be just without being a member of the just city" (*CM*, 109).[22]

Socrates and his companions first sought to find justice "writ large" in a city; they found that justice is good and possible for an individual, but not clearly for a city. The conversation thus begins anew, as it were, to discover whether it is possible to found a perfectly just city. As at the very beginning of the dialogue, Socrates's companions take a vote and, like a democratic assembly, compel him to serve them through a combination of persuasion and force. But this time, Strauss emphasized, Thrasymachus joins them. His joining their "city" is essential, because it turns out that the possibility of establishing a just city depends, to a great extent, on the power of his rhetorical art.

Strauss observed in an earlier essay that Alfarabi was the only commentator on Plato who had noted the central importance of Thrasymachus and his art for both the argument and the action of the dialogue.[23] But he did not refer to the Muslim philosopher in his published interpretation of the *Republic*, because he did not understand the role of rhetoric in the same way that Alfarabi did. According to the latter, Plato had combined the way of Socrates with the way of Thrasymachus in order to improve the opinions and thus the politics of his readers gradually over time. According to Strauss, in the *Republic* Plato showed that the propagation of salutary teachings would never suffice to produce a just polity; rational rule and popular enlightenment would always be limited by the needs of the body (which, Strauss reminded his readers, Aristotle said had to be ruled by the soul "despotically," that is, not by persuasion but by force).[24]

The explicit reason that Socrates's companions would not allow him to end the conversation by showing that justice is choiceworthy for the individual was that they wanted him to explain the "communistic" institutions he had said would be necessary in addition to the noble lie to prevent the guardians from pursuing their own self-interest at the expense of the common good. As in Aristophanes's play *The Assembly of Women*, from which Plato literally took his proposals, the abolition of private property and the community of women and children establish justice by removing the fundamental cause of injustice, the primary attachment rooted in the body that each of us has to his or her own existence. Just as Aristophanes showed that in order to maintain the equality of condition necessary to end oligarchic oppression and democratic envy, Praxagora had to impose severe constraints on the natural preference or *eros* people have for the young and the beautiful, so in the *Republic* Socrates subordinated *eros* entirely to the needs of the city. The guardians were to be bred like animals.[25]

But, Strauss observed, there was another way a just city might come into being—by making a just individual, that is, a philosopher, its absolute ruler. Socrates points to "the coincidence of philosophy and political power [as] not only the necessary but the sufficient condition of universal happiness" (*CM*, 122). The communistic institutions that appear to be so contrary to human nature may not be required. Because they desire only truth and have no interest in wealth or fame, philosophers will not seek to rule, however; they will have to be forced to do so. The many will not compel philosophers to take the reins of government unless or until they are persuaded it is desirable for them to do so. That is the function or role of Thrasymachus's art. The difficulty, according to Socrates, stems from the fact that once philosophers have seen "the light," they do not want to return to the "cave." The nonphilosophers will thus have to prevail on the philosophers, who will not put themselves forward. But, Strauss concluded, as the danger Socrates admits philosophers encounter if and when they return to the cave indicates, the nonphilosophers' passionate attachment to the opinions they have grown up believing and their hatred of those who question and thus appear to discredit these opinions make it highly unlikely, if not simply impossible, for philosophers to rule. The abstraction from the body that characterizes the *Republic* leads not only to a denigration of *eros*, but also to an overestimation of the power of rhetoric. Not even a master rhetorician like

Thrasymachus would be able to effect the convergence of philosophy with political power.

Although Socrates finally admits that the just city exists only "in speech," Strauss observed, the fiction of its possibility is maintained throughout the *Republic*. That fiction is necessary to arouse the spiritedness of lovers of justice like Glaucon against the injustice they find not only in existing regimes, but also in themselves.[26] The need to counter their own inner temptation is the reason Socrates goes on, after the depiction of the just regime, not only to sketch the inferior regimes into which it decays, culminating with the portrait of the tyrant, but also to reintroduce the question of the utility and status of poetry.

Socrates does not actually provide a better answer in the *Republic* to the question "what is justice?" than he does in *Euthyphro* to the question "what is piety?" But, Strauss concluded, Socrates does show us what the source or origin of injustice is—and how it is overcome in or by a few individuals. There will be no just city until a philosopher becomes king, not because philosophers know what is good, but because philosophers do not desire the wealth and esteem that lead other men, as Thrasymachus insisted, to seek to rule for their own advantage and thus unjustly.[27] *The* reason no political association will ever be just is, therefore, that no philosopher will ever want to rule. Anyone who seeks to exercise political power shows by virtue of that fact that he or she is not truly a lover of wisdom. Because their mortal nature makes it impossible for any human being entirely to obtain or retain knowledge, philosophers have to spend all their time and effort seeking it. They will feel obliged to help their fellows upon whom they depend for their own existence by giving them political advice, but they will not seek to rule full-time or at the expense of their search for wisdom (cf. *CM*, 124–38; *OT*, 193–202). As Plato shows in book 8 of the *Republic*, philosophers will not praise democracies or seek to see them established merely because democracies are the regimes in which it is easiest to practice philosophy. But, Strauss also points out, if we look at "the descending order of regimes . . . modeled on Hesiod's descending order of the five races of men . . . , we see at once that the Platonic equivalent of Hesiod's divine race of heroes is democracy" (*CM*, 130).

Strauss emphasized that Plato understood philosophy to be a way of life, not a set of doctrines. As embodied by Socrates, indeed, philosophy constitutes the only truly worthwhile and satisfying way of living for a human being.[28] That was the reason Plato did not write treatises containing his own arguments, but presented conversations, mostly between Socrates and others, to show what a philosopher would do and say. Although Socrates severely criticized other forms of poetry in the *Republic*, Strauss noted, poetry that presented philosophy as the best way of life would be allowed in the just city. Strauss concluded, as had Friedrich Nietzsche and Hans-Georg Gadamer, that Plato's dialogues constituted the example par excellence of such ministerial poetry. Rather than being attempts to convey truths or put forward arguments, the dialogues were intended above all to encourage their readers to engage in a search for wisdom and, if not to become philosophers themselves, to love philosophy (*LAM*, 6–8).

Reading Plato's *Republic* in his dramatic manner thus led Strauss to find in it a "lesson" quite different from and even opposed to the standard interpretations scholars had previously supplied. Rather than advocating a "totalitarian regime" ruled by philosophers or propounding a "theory of ideas," Strauss concluded, Plato's *Republic* shows that "even the transpolitical cannot be understood as such except if the city is understood—and the city is completely intelligible because its limits can be made perfectly manifest: to see these limits, one need not have answered the question regarding the whole; it is sufficient for the purpose to have raised the question regarding the whole" (*CM*, 138). Political philosophy constitutes first philosophy, because raising the question of the best way of life not only reveals the nature and limits of "the city" (or, in contemporary terms, "the political"). It also reveals the true nature of philosophy.

It is thus not surprising that Strauss's interpretation has been extraordinarily controversial. The controversy overspilled the confines of the scholarly world when Myles Burnyeat, a prominent classicist and student of ancient philosophy, dismissed Strauss's reading as entirely without foundation in the pages of the *New York Review of Books*.[29]

Plato's Defense of Philosophy

Strauss found the chief theme of the *Republic* to be not the convergence of politics and philosophy, but rather their divergence or opposition. The *Republic* shows philosophy to be a problem, an irritant within the political community. The city, once it becomes aware of philosophy, asks, "why philosophy?" It demands that philosophy give an account or defense of itself.

The picture most students have of the ancient conflict between the philosopher and the city is based on Plato's *Apology of Socrates*. But, Strauss argued, in his *Apology* and *Crito* Plato gives an explicitly popular and hence somewhat one-sided picture of the character and effects of Socratic phi-

losophy. In these dialogues Socrates presents himself as an innocent victim of political persecution who tries not merely to converse with but to
improve anyone he meets. However, a careful reading of these dialogues
(along with *Euthydemus*) shows that Socrates was not merely an innocent
victim but that he provoked the Athenians to kill him. Such a reading also
shows that Socrates was not the universal moral benefactor he claimed to
be. He was, in fact, not interested in conversing with everyone he came
across or who came to him, and his interest in the individuals he did wish
to converse with was not so much in their moral improvement as in their
potential for the philosophic life.

In his first speech in the *Apology*, Socrates shows that the official charges
were trumped up by angry fathers. Unable to answer questions raised by
youths imitating Socrates and in search of someone to blame for their own
incapacity, his accusers reiterated the old charges against philosophers.
This old prejudice might be traced partly to a certain comic poet; but, Socrates claims, he does not do or study any of the things Aristophanes ridi-
culed. Nor is it credible, as his new accuser, the poet Meletos, charges, that,
acting in opposition to the efforts of all other citizens, Socrates alone could
corrupt the youth of Athens.

Rather than impiously questioning the existence of the Olympian gods
like the philosopher in Aristophanes's *Clouds*, Plato's Socrates says he has
devoted his entire life to proving the wisdom of Apollo's oracle. By interrogating the men who claimed to have wisdom, he has shown why the oracle
declared him to be the wisest; unlike them, he knows that he does not
know. Responding to an anonymous interlocutor who asks what Socrates
has been doing, if he has not done what his accusers charge, Socrates compares himself to Achilles. Like the epic hero, the philosopher has chosen to
risk death rather than abandon the post at which the god stationed him.
Neglecting his own affairs, Socrates has devoted himself to exhorting his
fellow citizens to virtue. He has acted only as a private citizen and has not
gone into politics, because he was forbidden to do so by a certain divine
voice. In his defense, Socrates thus presents himself as a "god-fearing" man
who has always sought to be just.[30] The conflict between the philosopher
and his fellow citizens is, Socrates suggests in his second speech, a product
of a misunderstanding he could remedy, if only he had more time. If Athens
had a law forbidding one-day trials for capital crimes, he would have been
able to persuade the jury to acquit him.

Strauss saw reasons in Plato's text to question Socrates's claims, however. First, that Chairophon asked the oracle whether there were anyone

wiser than Socrates indicated that he had a certain renown for philosophy and engaged in it before undertaking his supposedly oracle-inspired mission. As Aristophanes showed in his *Clouds*, there was a pre-Delphic Socrates with whom Chairophon had investigated the things in the heavens and under the earth (the places in which the gods were traditionally said to dwell). Socrates's claim that he would be able to persuade his fellow citizens of his innocence if he had more time seemed, moreover, to contradict his earlier claim that he had been conversing with his fellow citizens all day long for many years. In fact, Strauss pointed out, we never see Socrates engaged in a conversation with an ordinary artisan or great politician in any of the other Platonic dialogues.[31] Nor does Plato report any conversation occurring in the agora. Socrates's speeches were more private and less public than he suggests in his *Apology*. That was one reason, perhaps, that the ancient prejudice against philosophers had persisted virtually unchallenged.

After the jury voted to convict him, moreover, Socrates admitted that his initial account of his piety was ironic. The philosopher had presented himself as serving the god, because if he had said "that it is the greatest good for a human being to engage every day in speeches about virtue and the other things about which they heard him converse and thereby examine himself and others . . . and that the unexamined life is not worth living for any human being" (*Apology* 38a), he would have convinced the jury even less than he did with his story about serving the god.

As Xenophon explicitly stated in his *Apology*, but Plato only showed dramatically in his, Socrates provoked the Athenians into killing him. The "penalty" he initially proposed as an alternative to death was "shocking." His claim that he deserved to be fed and housed at public expense like a victor in the Olympic games assumed that he had succeeded in improving the character of his fellow citizens. But the fact that they had unjustly accused and condemned him showed that he had not improved their characters any more than the Athenian statesmen — Perikles, Kimon, Miltiades, and Themistokles — whom he had criticized on precisely these grounds in the *Gorgias* (515b8–516e8). Socrates's claim that he needed public support was equally faulty; it ignored the fact, stressed in Xenophon's *Oeconomicus*, that the philosopher could count on his friends — as Socrates himself reminded his audience, when he subsequently proposed paying a significant fine with their help. By explaining why he did not propose exile, Strauss pointed out, Socrates indicated that "there always was an alternative to the death penalty." Socrates chose to die, because he thought it was better than the alternatives. But "the Platonic Socrates, as distinguished from the Xeno-phontic Socrates, d[id] not explain his conduct at the trial by his view that in his advanced years it was good for him to die" (*SPPP*, 50–51).[32]

In his *Apology of Socrates* Plato reported what the philosopher said and did, but he did not provide readers with any information concerning the philosopher's own deliberations or the reasons that persuaded him that he ought to remain and die. We are left to infer the reasons from his speeches and deeds.[33] Comparing himself to a tragic hero, Socrates presented him-self in his only public speech as willing to die rather than admit that he or his philosophy was wrong.[34] In his *Apology* Socrates suggested that, like a biblical prophet, he put himself in great danger by directly confronting rulers with their own injustice. Yet, Socrates admitted, he stayed out of politics until the very end of his life to secure his own preservation. Know-ing he was close to death in any case, Socrates took the opportunity offered by his trial to make a "statement," in deed as much as if not more than in speech, that would convince not only his compatriots but also their descen-dants that philosophy does not constitute a threat to political order.[35] That is, the death of Socrates on behalf of philosophy, more than his defense speech, is the true "apology of Socrates."

Why Socrates provoked the Athenians to condemn him to death is not the only question left explicitly unanswered in Plato's *Apology*, Strauss ob-served. There is also the question of the significance of the difference Soc-rates emphasized between the jurors who voted to acquit and those who voted to condemn. In *Gorgias* Socrates predicted that if he were ever forced to defend himself and his philosophizing in court, his position would be like that of a physician brought before a jury of children by a pastry cook who accused him of not giving them sweets. That is, he treated the demos as uniformly hostile to philosophy. But in the *Apology* Plato shows that this is not simply the case. If Meletos had not been joined by the politician Any-tus and the rhetor Lykon, Socrates predicted, he would have been acquit-ted. Neither the poets nor the people as a whole are the most serious critics of the philosopher; ambitious democratic politicians, concerned particu-larly about their sons' future, come to light as Socrates's most dangerous accusers.[36] Like Anytus, democratic politicians do not want to be refuted by Socrates or have their sons influenced by him, because a demonstration that they do not actually know what is noble and good would not merely raise questions about their claims to be qualified to rule the city, but dimin-ish the affection and respect of their children.

Many commentators have understood Plato to oppose philosophy particularly to sophistry.[37] The sophists were understood to have corrupted the young, whereas Socrates tried to benefit them. Early in his defense speech in the *Apology* Plato thus shows that Socrates takes care to distinguish himself from the sophists by reminding the jury that he did not claim to teach virtue or charge a fee for doing so. Yet in *Euthydemus*, Strauss argues, Plato shows that Socrates was partly responsible for people's mistaking his philosophy for sophistry. Socrates intentionally perpetuated the impression that philosophy was a useless endeavor to dissuade fathers of inept sons from pressing him to take them as students.

Rather than constituting a sign of his piety or divine inspiration, as many commentators have taken it to be, Strauss argues, in *Euthydemus* Plato shows that Socrates used his *daimonion* (his divine voice) as an excuse to do (or not to do) what he wanted.[38] At the beginning of *Euthydemus*, for example, Socrates tells Kriton that his *daimonion* warned him against leaving the dressing room of the gymnasium where he had been exercising. So he stayed and met, first, the sophists Euthydemus and his brother Dionysodoros, with their students, and then Alkibiades's grandson Kleinias with his train of lovers. By forbidding Socrates to leave, his *daimonion* seems to have imposed the subsequent conversation on Socrates; but, we see, the conversation is far from compulsory. The "divine" sign that gives no reasons for its directives appears to mark Socrates's own inclinations; he did not leave, because he wanted to stay and talk to the young men who tend to gather in such places.[39]

Plato indicates the similarity between Socrates's and the sophists' teachings at the very beginning of their exchange. Seeking students, the brothers gladly agree to demonstrate their ability to refute whatever is said and to enable anyone else to do the same in a short time. "This power is necessarily identical with virtue," Strauss observed, "if virtue is wisdom and if wisdom in the proper sense—knowledge of the most important things—is impossible" (*SPPP*, 70). Like Socrates, the brothers show that they are wiser and hence more virtuous than others by showing that those who think they know do not.

The difference between the sophists and Socrates becomes clear, however, in the subsequent action. The sophists discourage Kleinias from engaging in any further conversation by first refuting his contention that the ignorant learn, by pointing out that the stupid have proved themselves incapable of learning, and then refuting his second contention that it must be the wise who learn, by pointing out that the wise already know. Socrates, on the other hand, encourages the young man to seek wisdom in the protreptic speech with which he responds to the sophists' "playfulness."

But, Strauss pointed out, the positive effect of Socrates's speech on Kleinias obscures some of its more unsettling implications. When Socrates suggests that a person might need good fortune as well as wisdom, Kleinias is so elated by his newly regained self-confidence that he fails to notice the philosopher's vacillation as to whether wisdom can altogether overcome the power of chance. If it does not, the acquisition of wisdom alone would not be sufficient to guarantee that a man would live a good, virtuous, or happy life. Nor does Kleinias observe how Socrates's claims about virtue and wisdom involve a radical debunking of what Aristotle called moral virtue. According to Socrates's argument, it does not do an ignorant man any good to try to be just or courageous or moderate, because he does not know what is truly good. Indeed, few if any human beings do!

The drama also covers over Socrates's refutation of the sophists. Having convinced Kleinias that he must seek to be wise, Socrates turns back to the brothers with the question whether it is possible to teach anyone to be virtuous—or wise. The brothers comically argue that it is not possible for anyone to learn anything. Because the sophists seem to defeat Socrates's contention that everyone should try to learn to become wise by showing that it is impossible for anyone to learn anything, the ironical implication of Socrates's observation that if no one can learn, no one needs or can learn the sophists' "art," gets lost. Through the drama Plato nevertheless shows his readers that the arguments with which the brothers intend to show the young men who gathered around them at the gymnasium that they ought to come and study with the sophists defeat the sophists' primary purpose.

In the first half of the dialogue Socrates thus demonstrates his superiority to the sophists both in speech and in deed; but in the second half he lets himself appear to be bested. Why? Strauss characteristically argued that the reasons for Socrates's apparent aporia are to be found in the dramatic setting. Socrates is relating this conversation to his friend Kriton, who is looking for a teacher for his son Kritoboulos. By showing that his questioning of Kleinias in the end proved to be fruitless, Socrates discourages Kriton from asking him to become his son's educator.[40]

In a radically different interpretation from that given in conventional Platonic scholarship, Strauss suggested that because Socrates emphasized the elenctic, aporetic character of his philosophy in order to discourage the fathers of inept sons from pressing him to take their sons as students, many people were understandably unable to distinguish Socrates's philosophical investigations from the eristic refutations in which the sophists engaged. Plato dramatized the difference, however, in the argument and the action of the first part of *Euthydemus* as well as in the sophists' comic critiques of typical Socratic doctrines like recollection and the theory of ideas. Whereas Socrates claimed to know simply that he did not know, he held out the possibility of attaining knowledge. The sophists claimed to be able to refute any proposition, and thus to show that it is impossible to know anything, on the basis of a Zeno-like application of Parmenides's argument that one can neither say nor think what is not. By having Socrates praise their refutations of his characteristic teachings, Plato showed that both he and his teacher recognized the problematic character of Socrates's arguments.[41] According to Socrates, the partial intelligibility of the whole gives us grounds both to try to improve our understanding and not to overestimate the power of our intellect. Lacking full knowledge, we are never free, as he initially suggests to Kleinias, from the control of fortune or chance. Nor is it possible, as the sophists suggest, to establish one's preeminence over others simply by besting them in speech. In a world lacking a completely intelligible order, hierarchy cannot be established simply on the basis of *logos*; it requires force. As Aristotle concludes in the *Nicomachean Ethics*, so Plato shows in *Euthydemus*, the sophists were wrong to identify politics entirely with rhetoric.

Contrary to most other commentators, Strauss concluded, "Socrates was not the mortal enemy of the sophists nor were the sophists the mortal enemies of Socrates" (*SPPP*, 88). According to Socrates, the greatest enemy of philosophy, the greatest sophist, is the political multitude (*Republic* 492a5–e6). In the *Republic* he first suggested that the people might be persuaded to accept the rule of a philosopher by a rhetorician like Thrasymachus, but in describing the philosopher's return to the cave Socrates later admitted that the anger of the nonphilosophers would be aroused by anyone who questioned their long-held opinions. In the *Apology of Socrates*, however, Plato showed that when the philosopher was indicted for the capital crime of not believing in the gods of the city and corrupting the young, he used the opportunity to try to convince his fellow citizens (and Plato's readers) that the questions he posed did not undermine the laws of the city. Recognizing that people generally are persuaded more by facts or deeds than by speeches and that at seventy years of age he would die soon in any case, Socrates chose to stand trial and accept the death penalty. He acted more in order to protect philosophy from political persecution in the future than, as he claimed in his speech, to benefit his fellow citizens. But he also demonstrated the way in which philosophy can positively help the city by providing arguments that persuade citizens like Socrates's friend Kriton to obey the laws.

Plato's "Practical" Political Philosophy

In his commentaries on *Minos*, the *Statesman*, and the *Laws*, Strauss argued, as he had in his commentary on the *Republic*, that philosophy not only cannot but also will not rule. Philosophy can and should, however, benefit the city by providing reasons why the next-best and only practical alternative to the rule of the wise is rule of law. In the *Statesman*, Strauss notes, the Eleatic Stranger points out:

> Rule of law is inferior to the rule of living intelligence because laws, owing to their generality, cannot determine wisely what is right and proper in all circumstances . . . : only the wise man on the spot could correctly decide. . . . Nevertheless laws are necessary. The few wise men cannot sit beside each of the many unwise men and tell him exactly what it is becoming for him to do. (*HPP*, 74–75)

As Strauss emphasized:

> All laws . . . are crude rules of thumb which are sufficient for the large majority of cases. . . . The freezing of crude rules of thumb into sacred, inviolable, unchangeable prescriptions which would be rejected by everyone as ridiculous if done in the sciences and the arts is a necessity in the ordering of human affairs; this necessity is the proximate cause of the ineradicable difference between the political and the suprapolitical spheres. (*HPP*, 75)

The main problem with the rule of law is not its generality, however; it is the assumption that these crude rules should bind the wise man as well. As the Stranger explains:

> The wise man is subjected to the laws, whose justice and wisdom is inferior to his, because the unwise men cannot help distrusting the wise man, and this distrust is not entirely indefensible given the fact that they cannot understand him. They cannot believe that a wise man who would deserve to rule as a true king without laws would be willing and able to rule over them. The ultimate reason for their unbelief is the fact that no human

being has that manifest superiority . . . which would induce everybody to submit to his rule without any hesitation and without any reserve. The unwise men cannot help making themselves the judges of the wise man. No wonder then that the wise men are unwilling to rule over them. (*HPP*, 75)

Demanding that the wise man regard the law as simply authoritative, the unwise will bring charges of corrupting the young (a capital crime) against the man who, like Socrates, raises questions about the justice and wisdom of the established order.

The best practical solution to the division between the wise and the unwise presented in the *Statesman* seems to be for the philosopher to convince a legislator to enact a code of law, including provisions for the education of other wise men to administer the laws once enacted. That is precisely what the Athenian Stranger appears to do in the *Laws*. But, Strauss argued, by the end of the *Laws* we see that a philosopher is no more able or willing to act as a founder than he was to become a ruler in the *Republic*.

Since the *Laws* is the only Platonic dialogue in which Socrates does not appear, Strauss began his account of *The Argument and the Action of Plato's "Laws"* by asking about the relation between the Athenian Stranger and Socrates.[42] The difference seems to be a matter primarily of the setting— the interlocutors and the place.[43] Because the conversation takes place on Crete where the Athenian is a stranger and the old Dorians with whom he talks have no knowledge of philosophy, he does not confront the same prejudice against philosophers that Socrates did in Athens. Whereas Socrates always spoke to or in front of youths, the Athenian talks to two old men. When they begin to react angrily, like the Athenian elders, to his criticisms of their revered institutions, the Athenian reminds them of the

> Dorian law of laws . . . which forbids the young to criticize any of their institutions but stipulates that all should say with one voice that all their laws are fine since they were given by gods . . . ; yet one of their old men may make speeches of this sort when speaking to a ruler and men of his own age, provided no one young is present. (*AAPL*, 10–11)

If Socrates had not been so old at the time of his trial, he might have gone into exile in Crete. In *Crito*, Strauss reminds his readers, "the Laws" tell Socrates that

> if he left Athens he would go either to one of the well-governed cities nearby, where he would be utterly discredited by his unlawful escape, or

to Thessaly, which is utterly lawless. [They do] not discuss what would happen to him if he went to a well-governed city far away like ... Crete [which] he had mentioned ... shortly before. .... If Socrates had escaped from prison, he would have gone to Crete, where he was wholly unknown and would have come to sight only as an Athenian Stranger.

However, Strauss also observed, Plato's art was not constrained by the facts of Socrates's life. For example, in *Menexenus* he has Socrates repeat a speech that mentions events that occurred after his death.[44] There had to be another reason for Plato's replacing Socrates with an Athenian Stranger in his most practical political dialogue, the only dialogue in which the protagonist proposes an actual code of law.

In his commentary Strauss pointed out that the anonymity of the Athenian extends beyond his name to what he is—namely, a philosopher. The word *philosophy* does not appear in the dialogue until book 9, and then it is in the context of the discussion of how to punish possible infractions of the laws. Philosophy is presented as a possible source of infraction, because it brings into question the most fundamental laws concerning the gods. The Athenian's failure to mention philosophy in specifying what the laws ought to be also means he has not made the source and basis of his recommendations clear. He could not do so—and still persuade the old Dorians to accept them. Their conversations are a model, we learn in book 7, of the *poetry* the Athenian suggests the legislator ought to use to *persuade* rather than force people to obey. Only at the very end of the dialogue does the Athenian admit, in effect, that it will be necessary to abolish the "Dorian law of laws" in order to establish and maintain the new regime. In the Nocturnal Council the elders will discuss the foundations of the regime—the nature and unity of the virtues and the arguments for the existence of god—*with young people*. (Strauss pointed out they may be female as well as male.) The law based on intelligence cannot be maintained solely on the basis of tradition. Rulers of the new regime will have to be philosophically educated, and philosophy necessarily raises questions about "received wisdom" or tradition. By depicting an anonymous Athenian Stranger discussing a possible reform of Dorian law with two old statesmen in a private conversation that lasts but a day, Plato had suggested that cooperation between traditional and rational forms of authority might be possible. But he indicated at the end of the dialogue that such cooperation would never really exist. The Athenian is not willing to stay to help see his laws enacted; like Socrates's philosopher-king, he would have to be forced to rule. And, Strauss suggested, if the Dorians kept him and got to know him better, they would see more clearly just how critical he is of their ancestral laws. Their agreement is more apparent than real.

The reason Socrates does not appear in the *Laws*, Strauss concluded, is that he was prevented by his *daimonion* from engaging in politics. In other words, he could not engage in legislative activity without endangering his life. There was an unbridgeable opposition between philosophy, openly represented as such by Socrates, and legislation.[45]

That opposition seems, moreover, to parallel the most obvious difference between Socrates and Plato. "The laws proposed in the *Laws* are written." The only other Platonic dialogue that is set outside of Athens is *Phaedrus*, "which may be said to concern writing." The singular absence of Socrates from the *Laws* leads us to ask whether Plato indicated the way in which he thought the opposition between philosophy and politics could be overcome, by seeking gradually to alter the opinions of one's readers through writing rather than by directly challenging the opinions of the political elite as Socrates had done.[46]

That was the conclusion to which Alfarabi came, Strauss argued in his essay "How Farabi Read Plato's *Laws*."[47] And that essay provides the key to Strauss's own account. Strauss does not mention or cite Alfarabi in *The Argument and the Action*. He reminds his readers of the "Averroist" understanding, however, by prefacing his study with a quotation from the medieval Islamic philosopher Avicenna stating that "the treatment of prophecy and the Divine law is contained in ... the Laws" (*AAPL*, 1). One of the techniques of esoteric teaching Strauss claimed to have learned from Alfarabi was leaving out something of central importance to a discussion. By failing to cite Alfarabi in his own study of Plato's *Laws*, Strauss indicated his disagreement with Alfarabi's major conclusion.

Like Alfarabi, Strauss seems to present a mere summary of the dialogue, organized simply book by book, with a brief preface about the indirect character of Plato's writing. But, as Joseph Cropsey indicates in his foreword, repeated rereadings show Strauss's account to be much more than a summary.

According to Alfarabi, Strauss noted, Plato did not think it wise to declare the truth openly to all readers. To illustrate the way in which Plato could nevertheless communicate the truth to discerning readers by stating it baldly in a context that prevented most from understanding, Alfarabi related a story about a pious ascetic. Threatened with persecution by the rulers of the city, the ascetic dressed up as a drunk beggar and with clanging cymbals approached the gates of the city. Accosted by the guard, he declared that he was the pious ascetic they were seeking. Thinking the beggar was mocking him, the guard ordered him to pass through. If the ruse were later discovered, Strauss commented, the many would excuse the ascetic, believing he remained true to his character by telling the truth. But, in fact, the ascetic lied in deed. That lie was, however, the necessary condition for his ability to declare the truth safely.[48]

Strauss indicated the importance of the distinction between speech and deed for his own analysis in the title, *The Argument and the Action of Plato's Laws*. As in Alfarabi's story, so in the dialogue itself, the action is deceptive. Although the Athenian Stranger appears to be willing to give the Dorian founders of a new colony a code of laws and so to engage directly in political action, Strauss pointed out, he proves in fact willing merely to engage them in a conversation lasting one day (*AAPL*, 42, 64). The dialogue concludes with Megillos's announcement that the city they have projected in speech will not work unless they compel the Athenian Stranger to become a participant, a duty from which the Athenian had excused himself along with Megillos in book 6.[49] The conclusion of the *Laws* is the same as that of the *Republic*: the establishment of a just city is impossible unless and until a philosopher is compelled to become king.

Like Socrates in the *Republic*, the Athenian in the *Laws* describes a "city in speech." But unlike Glaucon and Adeimantus, Strauss pointed out, the interlocutors in the *Laws* know nothing of philosophy. The treatment of the city in the *Laws* thus initially appears to be quite different (*AAPL*, 6). "In the *Republic*, reason or intellect guides the foundation of the city from the beginning, and eventually rules the city in broad daylight without any dilution or disguise" (*AAPL*, 38). In the *Laws* the Stranger also suggests that the best condition for the founding of a city would be a combination of wisdom with tyrannical power.[50] But since the wise are few and the many strong, he concludes, the just claims of the wise to rule will have to be diluted by the necessity of recognizing the strength or power of the many, that is, by seeking their consent. "Rule of law is a kind of rule of the stronger while the rule of wisdom is not" (*AAPL*, 47).[51] The rule of law may be necessary and even, in light of the probable alternatives, desirable, but it is never entirely right or just. Political moderation consists in the "adaptation of wisdom to the opinions of the citizen body or to consent," but moderation is not, according to the Athenian, a virtue in and of itself. The combination of election and lot he proposes for the selection of magistrates does not constitute a just mixture of two kinds of justice or equality.

> According to an old saying, which is true, equality produces friendship, but there is a great difference, not to say opposition, between two kinds of equality. One kind demands that equal honor be given to everyone; this is achieved by lot . . . ; the second kind of equality gives more to the greater and less to the smaller by giving to everyone what is appropriate to his nature, . . . virtue and education. It is the second kind of inequality which . . . is . . . the political right, because it produces for the cities all good things. This implies that the first kind . . . is conventional.

Strauss concluded:

> There are, then, not two different and conflicting roots or principles of justice, say, freedom and good government; but the single principle of justice must be diluted on account of necessity—the compelling power of the many; . . . a rational society is not possible, unless it be the society ruled by a philosopher exercising tyrannical power. . . . We have here the core of the Athenian's political suggestions. (*AAPL*, 86–87)[52]

The way the Athenian presents his political suggestions disguises the difference between the many unwise, who need to be persuaded to consent to the law, and the intellect of the man who alone has a right to declare what the law should be. Beginning the conversation by inquiring about the origin of their laws, the Athenian initially presents himself as a student rather than as a teacher of the old Dorians. Even after the Stranger's questions about their institutions convince Kleinias and Megillos that he may have something to teach them, he continues to present the conclusions and effects of philosophical conversations without mentioning philosophy by name. Just as the Stranger's description of Athenian drinking parties (or possibly philosophical symposia like that described in Plato's *Symposium*) in book 1 has something of the effect of wine, if vicariously, on his elderly interlocutors, making them a bit more flexible and open to new ideas, so the Stranger's description of the highest Muse without mentioning its name in book 2 indicates the way the clarity of the mind of the philosopher must be reduced, as if he too were metaphorically feeling the dulling effects of wine on the sharpness of the intellect, so that his unphilosophic interlocutors can understand him. The harmony thus achieved "between

the few wise and the many unwise, the rulers and the ruled ... is moderation in the highest sense of the word" (*AAPL*, 20–21, 33).[53]

Strauss pointed out several examples of lack of clarity about the most
fundamental issues in the Athenian's speech that serve to obscure the difference between the Stranger and his Dorian interlocutors. Although he
first distinguishes the logos that should rule the individual from the law,
which is the reason accepted by the city, the Athenian later blurs that distinction without his interlocutors' noticing it, as he blurs the distinction
between the old and the wise (*AAPL*, 20–21, 33). He is unclear about the
question of the origins, the relation between the reverence due parents
(our natural origins) and that due the gods (*AAPL*, 63, 66, 165–66).[54] He
blurs the differences among intellect (*nous*), good sense (*phronēsis*), and
opinion (*doxa*).

The problems that arise from the Athenian's obscuring the character and
source of his own wisdom—that is, the "manifest absence of philosophy"—
come out at the end of the dialogue. To institute and preserve the laws he
has proposed, the Athenian has to educate successors who share his understanding. The Nocturnal Council is supposed to provide such an education,
but the composition of the Council is not made clear.

> Are all its members men each of whom can acquire within his soul science
> of the subjects in question [the unity and differences among the virtues,
> the ideas of the noble and the good, and the being and power of the gods]?
> Are its members potential or actual philosophers? A glance at Kleinias [the
> Athenian's unphilosophic Cretan interlocutor who will presumably found
> the colony under his guidance] is sufficient to make one see the pertinence
> of the question. The heterogeneous composition of the Council makes it
> impossible to give a simple answer. Hence the Athenian cannot, as Socra-
> tes in the *Republic* can, determine the subjects of study and the time to be
> allotted to each. (*AAPL*, 85)

When the Athenian suggests that he and Kleinias investigate the question
of the unity of the virtues by question and answer, the old Cretan does not
see the point. He does not understand the use or danger of engaging in
Socratic dialectics, which, Strauss pointed out, are as absent from the *Laws*
as their originator (*AAPL*, 114, 180).

Because the Athenian obscures the philosophical foundation of the
legislation he proposes, the word *philosophy* does not appear in the dialogue
until book 9. "Philosophy" is explicitly introduced only in the context of

the discussion of penal legislation because, its positive role in the formulation of the law not having been made manifest, it appears only in the form of a questioning of accepted opinions and thus as the potential source of the most heinous capital crime of impiety.[55]

In the *Laws* the tension between philosophy and politics at first appears to be overcome. As Strauss observed in his preface:

> The *Laws* opens with the word "god"; there is no other Platonic dialogue that opens in this manner. The *Laws* is Plato's most pious work. In the *Apology of Socrates* Socrates defends himself against the charge of impiety, of not believing in the gods in whom the city believes. In the *Laws* the Athenian stranger devises a law against impiety which would have been more favorable to Socrates than the corresponding Athenian law. (*AAPL*, 2)

The Athenian proposes that no capital crime be tried in one day. In the *Apology* (73a–b), we recall, Socrates claims that under such conditions, he could have convinced his judges to acquit him (but cf. *SPPP*, 49–50). But Strauss observed toward the center of his study of the *Laws*, "Whether Socrates would have fared better in Kleinias' or the Athenian's city than he fared in Athens cannot be guessed until one knows the Athenian's law regarding impiety and the prosecution of that crime" (*AAPL*, 91).

In fact, both the law and the terms of its prosecution turn out to be unclear. "It is not clear whether a man who believes in the kosmic gods, . . . without believing in the Olympian gods, is guilty of impiety" (*AAPL*, 156). (Socrates might have passed the first test, but could not pass the second.) The law recognizes that there are different kinds of atheists:

> Some have a character by nature good, hate the bad men, and through loathing injustice do not do wrong . . . , while others are incontinent, possess powerful memories, and are quick at learning; the man of the first kind is likely to be of utter frankness of speech regarding the gods . . . and by ridiculing others would perhaps make them, too, impious, if he were not punished; the other, . . . full of craft and guile . . . belongs to the class of men from which come . . . tyrants, public speakers, and . . . sophists. Of these two types the dissembling one (the ironic one) deserves not one death or two, but the other needs admonition together with imprisonment.

But, Strauss pointed out,

> The disjunction made by the law is not complete: what happens to the atheist who [like Socrates] is a just man and does not ridicule others be-

cause they sacrifice and pray and who to this extent is a dissembler? is it literally true of him that he deserves not one death or two, i.e., no death at all, nor imprisonment? . . . One could say that he will become guilty if he frankly expresses his unbelief—but what if he expresses his unbelief only to sensible friends? Can one imagine Socrates denouncing him to the authorities? (*AAPL*, 155–56)

According to the law, such just men are to be imprisoned in the *sōphronistērion*—the name of which reminds one of the *phrontistērion* in *The Clouds*—for "no less than five years, during which time no citizen may visit them except the members of the Nocturnal Council, who are to take care of their improvement; if after the lapse of the five years a man of this kind is thought to have come to his senses, he will be released; if he relapses, however, he will be punished with death (*AAPL*, 155).

The members of the Nocturnal Council are not to be allowed merely to profess belief "in the gods as the laws declare them to be and because the laws declare them to be"; they are supposed to prove to themselves and others that the gods exist. They will presumably have to raise the question "what is god?" and discuss it among themselves. A philosopher like Socrates might not be apt to denounce a counselor who expressed his doubts about the existence or beneficence of the gods. But, Strauss asked, what about a nonphilosophic counselor like Kleinias? Kleinias appears to believe "in the gods as the laws declare them to be and because the laws declare them to be" (*AAPL*, 3, 7, 11). How would he like his inability to defend his own opinions to be exposed before the youthful members of the Council? What would become of the fame the Athenian Stranger promises he will gain as founder? It seems likely that the elder members of the Council would finally react to the disruptive effects of the activities of a philosopher among them very much the way the Athenian fathers eventually did to Socrates.[56]

The tension between philosophy and the city does not become fully visible in the *Laws*, Strauss suggested, because "Socrates" is absent. As a result of the dramatic setting, there is no philosopher who arouses the anger of the fathers by explicitly bringing the authority of their opinions into question in front of their sons.[57] As the conclusion of the *Laws* indicates, however, the tension between the philosopher and the fathers can never be entirely eradicated; it is impossible for a philosopher to be a philosopher without raising questions about the validity of inherited views. The tension between philosophy and politics can at most be meliorated, as it was in both Xenophon's and Plato's writings, by the presentation of the philosopher primarily as a *phronimos*, a man of practical wisdom willing to teach potential princes. But, as Plato indicates in his depiction of both Socrates and the Athenian, there are limits on the extent to which the philosopher is willing to dedicate himself to playing such a role.

In contrast to Alfarabi, who thought the manifest absence of philosophy in the *Laws* suggested that the confrontational tactics of the moralist Socrates needed to be supplemented with the gradual reform of public opinion by the more theoretical Plato, Strauss concluded:

> We are no longer . . . sure . . . we can draw a clear line between Socrates and Plato. There is traditional support for drawing such a clear line, above all in Aristotle; but Aristotle's statements on this kind of subject no longer possess for us the authority that they formerly possessed. . . . The decisive fact for us is that Plato as it were points away from himself to Socrates. Plato points not only to Socrates' speeches but to his whole life, to his fate as well. (*SPPP*, 168)

As the highlighting of Socrates indicates, Plato's primary purpose in writing the dialogues was not effecting political reform through the gradual alteration of public opinion. Socrates was, after all, the philosopher who did not engage in political action. As Aristotle points out in his *Politics*, the best possible regime proposed in the *Laws* is ultimately as impossible to put into practice as the "city in speech" of the *Republic*. Plato's primary purpose in writing the dialogues appears, rather, to have been the protection and perpetuation of philosophy by convincing his readers that philosophy was not necessarily inimical to public order and morality.

Plato recognized that philosophy could undermine both public order and morality. As the Athenian explains in the *Laws* (10.886c–890a), the materialistic arguments of the "pre-Socratic" philosophers led to the conclusion that there were no gods and that justice was merely conventional. To show that philosophy was not inimical to morality, Plato had to persuade philosophers to moderate their speech. By dramatizing not only the speeches but also the life and death of Socrates, Plato reminded would-be philosophers of the reasons they should not pose certain questions— questions regarding the gods and the soul, that is, questions regarding not only the basis and intelligibility of the cosmos but also the sources of support for justice, both natural and supernatural—too publicly or directly. By keeping himself and his own opinions always hidden, like his teacher Socrates, Plato taught his readers, first and foremost, the need for self-

restraint. (Strauss contrasts Plato in this respect particularly with Nietzsche, who openly declared, among other things, that God is dead [*SPPP*,
174].) Plato thus taught his readers to be political philosophers in the sense
in which Strauss understands that term. As Strauss came to understand it,
largely through his study of Plato, political philosophy arises from the debates about good and bad orders in political life itself, but its philosophical
concerns ultimately transcend politics. Philosophy per se seeks knowledge
of the whole, of which political things form only a small part, but *political*
philosophers conduct their search for knowledge of the whole in a way designed to minimize its potentially destructive effects (*WIPP*, 94; see chapter 1 above).

As shown by his posthumously published *Studies in Platonic Political Philosophy*, Strauss did not understand "Platonic political philosophy" to refer
simply to Plato's own writings and thought. He used the phrase to describe
a distinctive understanding and style of philosophizing that he was seeking to revive. As Strauss observed in one of those "studies," Plato pointed
away from himself to Socrates. In other words, Plato made Socrates a kind
of model that he followed, although in a clearly modified form, in writing. Even more than Socrates, Plato examined the opinions of others rather
than putting forth his own. As Victor Gourevitch has observed, Strauss
seems to have adopted (and adapted) Plato's model in his own writing:

> Strauss rarely speaks in his own name. Except for Prefaces and Introduc-
> tions, that is to say except for what might be called public occasions when
> he is, as it were, compelled to speak in a popular manner, he prefers to ap-
> pear in the guise of the historian and the exegete. . . . By casting his thought
> primarily in the form of historical studies that take the entire history of
> political philosophy for their province, he implies that the relationship be-
> tween his views and the doctrines he studies is comparable to that between
> the views of a dramatist and those of his characters.[58]

As we argued in chapter 2, Strauss thought people today had to engage
in historical studies in order to engage in political philosophy, but he did
not think that political philosophy consisted merely in a history of past
thought. For him Plato and his exemplar Socrates represented examples of
the only truly satisfying form of human existence that could be lived now—
adapted, to be sure, to contemporary circumstances.

CHAPTER SIX

Why Strauss Is Not an Aristotelian

The call for a return to the ancients was a very broad theme in Strauss's work and was perhaps his signature idea. He was indeed one of the first non-Thomists to call for such a return. When he began his career the twin forces of progressivism and historicism had made the idea of return seem retrograde if not simply absurd (*CM*, 10–11). Since Strauss wrote, the idea of return has become more widespread, especially in the form of an Aristotle revival. Thinkers like Elizabeth Anscombe and Alasdair MacIntyre rediscovered what has now come to be called "virtue ethics," a form of Aristotelian ethical theory.[1] Thinkers like John Finnis and Joseph Raz rediscovered "practical reason," an idea borrowed from Aristotle and the basis for a "perfectionist" ethic with "flourishing" as its core.[2] It is thus no longer as unfashionable as it was when Strauss was writing to look to classical philosophers for guidance. Yet he still differs in one very important way from most if not all of the others who wish to so return: for Strauss Aristotle is not the central name in his concern with ancient philosophy. Instead, the central figure in his notion of return is Socrates. Thus those Strauss considers closer to Socrates, Plato and Xenophon especially, have been more important for him than Aristotle. As opposed to the many works Strauss devoted to Plato and Xenophon, he has remarkably few writings devoted to Aristotle, and only one on a particular Aristotelian text.

The Originator of Political Science

If, as has often been suggested, Leo Strauss's signature idea is "the return to the ancients," then his book *The City and Man* would seem to have a special place in his large corpus. Although most of the writings of his later

[144]

years did indeed focus on the ancients, only *The City and Man* focuses on ancient political philosophy at its peak. His book *Socrates and Aristophanes*, published two years after *The City and Man*, presents an interpretation and analysis of a Greek thinker, Aristophanes, who was a poet not a philosopher, and accordingly the book brings to light one of Strauss's most significant antinomies—philosophy and poetry. His book *Liberalism Ancient and Modern*, published another two years later, contains a series of essays written over the preceding decade or so. Strauss indicates the less fundamental character of that book when he describes his "earlier publications" as containing his attempt "to lay bare the fundamental difference between classical and modern political philosophy." This book, however, is devoted to "adumbrating that difference" (*LAM*, viii). *Liberalism Ancient and Modern* is thus part of the same project but deals at a less fundamental level with it. Strauss continued in his later years to produce books on ancient philosophy, including two books on Xenophon (1970, 1972)[3] and two posthumously published books, *The Argument and the Action of Plato's "Laws"* (1978) and *Studies in Platonic Political Philosophy* (1983). Strauss is well known for valuing Xenophon much more highly than most of his contemporaries, and for considering Xenophon a genuine philosopher. Nonetheless, he did not consider Xenophon to stand at the level of the philosophers he treated in *The City and Man*, where Strauss identifies the "men of the highest excellence" as Plato and Aristotle (*CM*, 49). As to the *Laws* of Plato, Strauss also considers this to be a most important dialogue—"the only political work proper of Plato" (*CM*, 29)—but he emphasizes its "sub-Socratic" level. That is to say, it is below the Socratic *Republic*, which, according to Strauss "brings to light . . . the nature of political things" and is the subject of the central essay in *The City and Man* (*CM*, 138).

The City and Man, let us tentatively say, is an especially significant work within Strauss's oeuvre because it presents his most sustained reflections on the "political thought of classical antiquity," and especially on the political thought of the two greatest thinkers who have left us any writings, Plato and Aristotle. The preface to *The City and Man* presents the task of the book in more modest terms, as a place where he "develops his views on a rather neglected aspect of classical political thought more fully than [he] otherwise might have done" (*CM*, v), and perforce than he did previously. He did, of course, develop his "views" on classical political thought on numerous earlier occasions, sometimes quite fully, including an "earlier and shorter version" of the chapter on Plato's *Republic* that appears in *The City and Man* (*HPP*, 33–89).

Strauss identifies the topic of this fuller development as "a rather neglected aspect of classical political thought," "rather neglected," it would seem, not only by him but by others who have written on the classics. But he does not tell us in so many words what that "rather neglected aspect" is. Perhaps it is the theme announced by his title: the city and man, i.e., the relation between the political community and the human beings who are its "matter" (*CM*, 46). But it seems strange to call that topic "rather neglected," for the relation between the individual and the political community is a frequently explored topic in studies in the history of political thought.

The City and Man is certainly not Strauss's first effort at explicating the political thought of classical antiquity. Prior to *The City and Man* he had written on Xenophon, including a comprehensive study of one Xenophontic dialogue in *On Tyranny* (1948). Mostly, however, his writings on classical political philosophy had the character of compendia, quite striking really in the contexts in which they were published. Thus in his very influential *Natural Right and History* Strauss paired a long chapter on "classic natural right" with an even longer chapter on "modern natural right." The chapter on the classics presented a composite doctrine—a construct of a doctrine attributed to the classic Socratics without distinguishing very much among them. In nearly every footnote of the first twenty-five paragraphs of the first chapter, Strauss cites a number of classical thinkers, including Plato, Xenophon, Aristotle, Cicero, and Thomas Aquinas. Only in the last seventeen paragraphs of the chapter, i.e., well beyond the halfway mark, does he "distinguish three types of classic natural right teachings, or three different manners in which the classics understood natural right" (*NRH*, 146). The common elements of the classic position are more prominent, or at least earn more sustained attention, than the areas of difference.

Strauss's treatment of the moderns in *Natural Right and History* is altogether different—he gives us not a composite view of "modern natural right" but a discussion individualized almost from the outset: there is only one paragraph before Strauss turns to a separate discussion of Hobbes and then Locke. The succeeding chapter on "the crisis of modern natural right" follows almost the same pattern; it consists of two long "subchapters," one on Rousseau, one on Burke.

The pattern present in *Natural Right and History* is even more emphatically visible in one of Strauss's other main statements on the classic as opposed to the modern position: in the famous essay based on the lecture series "What Is Political Philosophy?," Strauss devotes one lecture to "the classical solution" (in the singular) to "the problem of political philosophy," and another lecture to "the modern solutions" (in the plural). As in *Natural Right and History*, Strauss presents a more or less composite account of the classics, but a highly individualized account of the moderns.[4]

Since *The City and Man* has individual chapters devoted to Aristotle, Plato, and Thucydides, one might conclude that it develops more fully than Strauss has yet done the differences among the political thinkers of classical antiquity, or, perhaps better put, the individual voices or viewpoints of the different thinkers. Yet that too does not seem an "aspect" of classical thought "rather neglected," since many scholars have attended with great assiduity to this topic. Perhaps it is not so much the differences among the thinkers per se but some aspect of the differences that Strauss meant to address. That suggestion seems to get us farther because Strauss asserts in the introduction to *The City and Man* that "Aristotle's *Politics* contains the original form of political science," or that Aristotle is, in some significant sense, the first political scientist (*CM*, 12). That claim, he admits at the outset of the chapter on Aristotle, is open to the objection that not Aristotle but Socrates is the "originator of political philosophy or political science" (*CM*, 13). That objection leads Strauss to make a distinction, which comes to view at first as a distinction between political science and political philosophy. Socrates founds political philosophy, but Aristotle founds political science (*CM*, 19–21). Strauss means to say not that Aristotle's political science is nonphilosophic but that it is philosophic in such a way that it at the same time gives birth to political science. Strauss is tolerably clear on what he understands by this claim: "not Socrates or Plato, but Aristotle is truly the founder of political science as one discipline, and by no means the most fundamental or the highest discipline, among a number of disciplines" (*CM*, 21). Aristotle's political science is philosophic, then, but in a different way from Plato's political philosophy. Plato does not see political inquiry as one discipline among others, and he sees political philosophy as far more central or fundamental than Aristotle does: "in its original [Socratic or Platonic] form political philosophy broadly understood is the core of philosophy or rather the 'first philosophy,'" rather than metaphysics, which is "first philosophy" for Aristotle (*CM*, 20).

The emphasis in the Aristotle chapter on that thinker as the "originator" of political science, in contradistinction to Socrates or Plato as "originator" or promulgator of political philosophy, suggests that *this* is the particular difference between the two that Strauss means to develop more fully than hitherto has been done. That is indeed a "rather neglected aspect" of classical philosophy.

The conclusion that Strauss is probing the differences between two different kinds or understandings of political enquiry receives confirmation when we notice the third chapter of the book, on Thucydides's account of the Peloponnesian War. So as not to make it difficult for us, Strauss labels the first section of this chapter "Political Philosophy and Political History," and he labels the tenth and last section "Political History and Political Philosophy." Plato and Aristotle are identified in this context with political philosophy and Thucydides with political history (*CM*, 139, 236). Thucydides is thus interpreted in the light of his "discipline," political history. The conclusion is inescapable: the organizing principle of *The City and Man* is the investigation of the three disciplines or types of political enquiry practiced by the three thinkers engaged in the book. Chapter 1 is thus silently subtitled "Political Science," chapter 2 "Political Philosophy," and chapter 3 "Political History." It is the distinction among these three that has been "rather neglected" and that Strauss will develop more fully.

Although *The City and Man* is a book about three kinds of political enquiry, Strauss indicates that two of them are closer to each other than to the third: Plato and Aristotle are practitioners of political philosophy, and as such engage in "the quest for the best regime which is possible, although it never was or will be actual" (*CM*, 139). Thucydides's political history "seems to be an entirely different world," by implication not a quest for the best regime, and most definitely not indifferent to the actuality of its subject matter.

Aristotelian Political Science

It may seem odd that Strauss's chief extended discussion of the differences between Plato and Aristotle should occur in relation to the disciplinary topic propounded in *The City and Man*. It may not seem less odd, but it appears more premeditated, if we recall that in the same year that Strauss delivered the lectures that served as the basis for *The City and Man*, he published his "Epilogue" to *Essays on the Scientific Study of Politics*. A prominent part of his concluding essay was the call for a return to the "old political science" from the new "scientific" political science: "it is best" he said, "to contrast the new political science directly with the 'original' of the old, that is, with Aristotelian political science" (*LAM*, 205). In this context Strauss outlined five elements of Aristotelian political science. That is, he turned to Aristotle in the "Epilogue" in the context of discussing the disciplinary character of political science, and he took for granted what is *the* thematic claim of the Aristotle chapter in *The City and Man*, that his is the "original" political science.

Strauss's "Epilogue" is an attempt to encourage his fellow political scientists to withdraw their obeisance or deference to the new science, which takes its bearings from the philosophic doctrines of logical positivism and empiricism. He attempts to wean them away from the new science by both laying out an explicit alternative to it—the aforementioned Aristotelian political science—and mounting a critique of the presuppositions of the new science (see chapter 1 above). Strauss on many previous occasions criticized the distinction between facts and values, which is such a large part of the foundation of the new political science. In this context, he passes over this theme quickly by collapsing it into the critique of the empiricist commitments of the new political science. This latter theme comes to sight as more fundamental, both because it provides the deeper ground behind the fact-value distinction, and because it brings to light the chief ground of attraction, "the sympathetic chord," that accounts for the strength of the new political science. That attraction proceeds from the ordinary political scientist's intuition that political science must be an empirical discipline. Although as a student (mainly) of old texts, it might seem that Strauss would wish to resist this empirical orientation, in fact he embraces it wholeheartedly. "This is a demand of common sense" and one that the old political science he commends did in fact meet (*LAM*, 210). Strauss parts ways with the new political science and its philosophic projectors not over the need for an empirical science, but over how that need is understood: the new scientists are empiricists, not merely empirical.

The core difference between empirical inquiry and empiricism, as Strauss presents it, is that empirical inquiry as such, that is, the reliance on experience for knowledge of the political world, retains (willy-nilly) a commitment to the same common sense that underlies the demand for empirical inquiry in the first place. Although more than a few critics have challenged Strauss's notion of "common sense" as hopelessly obscure, he quite precisely tells us that "common-sense understanding is understanding in terms of 'things possessing qualities'" (*LAM*, 212). He means by common sense what he sometimes describes as "prescientific" or "primary awareness," a notion he appears to have taken over in the first instance from Husserl.[5]

Empiricism is a theory based on recognition of the "naiveté" or inadequacy of common sense or prescientific awareness. Empiricism is the effort to look more carefully at what is actually given in experience than "our primary awareness of things as things and people as people" does (*LAM*,

213). "What is perceived or 'given' is only sense data; the 'thing' emerges by virtue of unconscious or conscious construction: the 'things' which to common sense present themselves as 'given' are in truth constructs." "Scientific understanding" comes into being when the naiveté of the prescientific is fully recognized, and understanding by means of "unconscious construction" is replaced by "understanding by means of conscious construction" (*LAM*, 212).

While modern science, the new political science included, intends to reject the prescientific understanding, Strauss, following Husserl, maintains that this effort necessarily fails. One cannot, Strauss emphasizes, "establish empiricism empirically: it is not known through sense data that the only possible objects of perception are sense data" rather than "things" or "patterns" (*LAM*, 212). One can establish or attempt to establish empiricism only "through the same kind of perception through which we perceive things as things rather than sense data or constructs" (*LAM*, 213). Empiricism, then, must begin with the naïve prescientific awareness, and by a process of abstraction "sense data become known as sense data." This act of abstraction both depends upon and denies the legitimacy of such dependence on common sense. Strauss's Husserlian conclusion is that "there is no possible human thought which is not in the last analysis dependent on the legitimacy of that naiveté [of natural understanding] and the awareness or the knowledge going with it" (*LAM*, 213).

Strauss does not, however, mean to accept root and branch the deliverances of common sense. "The old political science was not unaware of the imperfections of political opinion, but it did not believe that the remedy lies in the total rejection of common sense understanding as such" (*LAM*, 213). Strauss's position is thus complex and elusive. It is clearly anti-Cartesian: beginning with universal doubt leads to the problematic stance of empiricism or other epistemologies that fail to take prescientific awareness seriously. Yet the prescientific or common sense is not itself sufficient either. One must move from it ("ascend," Strauss usually says), but one must do so in a way that remains consciously grounded on the prescientific. Adequate science or philosophy requires a clear grasp of the prescientific. But, as Strauss saw it, the long history of Western philosophy and science has obscured, although not destroyed, the prescientific awareness. "To grasp the natural world as a world that is radically prescientific or prephilosophic, one has to go back behind the first emergence of science or philosophy," for "the world in which we live," our "common sense" or "natural world," is already transformed by centuries of theoretical apprehension of it. "The world in which we live is already a product of science" (*NRH*, 79).

Although they may at first seem to belong to different universes of discourse, the links between Strauss's "Epilogue" and *The City and Man* are many and deep. It would not be much of an exaggeration to say that the latter is the sequel or completion of the former, the fleshing out of the nature of the Aristotelian political science for which the "Epilogue" calls. Perhaps even more importantly, *The City and Man* adumbrates the notion of common sense to which the "Epilogue" appeals, as well as an account of how science or philosophy relates to the prescientific.

The Philosophical Foundation
of Aristotle's Political Science

Strauss recommends Aristotle's political science to American political scientists, precisely because it stands in a more adequate relation to common sense than the newer scientific political science. More than that, Aristotle's *Politics* is "nothing other than the fully conscious form of the 'common sense' understanding of political things." Aristotle gives us both the "fully conscious form of the 'common sense' understanding" and at the same time "the original form of political science." It is the conjunction of these two claims that most characterizes Strauss's presentation of Aristotle. Strauss explains that conjunction straightforwardly: "classical political philosophy is the primary form of political science because the common sense understanding of political things is primary" (*CM*, 12).

Yet Strauss also stresses that his characterization of Aristotle's political science as containing that particular conjunction is "manifestly provisional" (*CM*, 12). Its provisionality is quite "manifest" by the time we come to the end of the book, for on almost its last page we learn that "the quest for the 'common sense' understanding of political things which led us first to Aristotle's *Politics*, leads us eventually to Thucydides's *War of the Peloponnesians and the Athenians*." That is, Thucydides articulates the "beginning of political understanding . . . in an unsurpassable, nay, unrivalled manner" (*CM*, 240). Thucydides presents us the "common sense" view in a way that even Aristotle does not. But that is not Strauss's first ground for calling his characterization of Aristotle "provisional": the provisional explanation for calling his own characterization "provisional" is that that characterization contains the term "common sense," a term meant to be understood in contradistinction to modern science, "whereas the *Politics* itself does not presuppose 'science'" (*CM*, 12; but cf. 19). But that too is an ambiguous explanation, for it seems to mean something obvious and historical—that Aristotle did not, indeed, could not have presupposed modern natural science. Yet Strauss perhaps has in mind something more general. Aristotle's *Politics* is independent not only of modern natural science but of science however understood, or at least of "theoretical science" as understood by Aristotle (*CM*, 25).

We cannot see why Strauss is not an Aristotelian until we see why Strauss both praises and recommends Aristotle in ways that might lead one to think that he is an Aristotelian. The central questions to be addressed seem to be two: (1) How does Strauss explain or defend his characterization of Aristotle as the "originator" of political science and at the same time as the "fully conscious form of the 'common sense' understanding of political things?" (2) What is it about the Aristotelian political science that is deficient? The only way to grapple with these issues is to begin with the surface of Strauss's chapter. That surface is its structure: it is divided into five untitled sections, subtly marked by dashes at the ends of sections.

Strauss prefaces his turn to the Aristotle chapter by announcing that he will "first attempt to reach a more adequate understanding of the *Politics* by considering the objections to which [his] contention is exposed." Given the opening of the chapter proper, it is clear that the "contention" or aspect of the contention to which he refers is the claim that Aristotle is the originator of political science, for he tells us that "according to the traditional view, it was not Aristotle but Socrates who originated political philosophy or political science" (*CM*, 13). The second section of the chapter is also addressed to an "objection" to his contention, but this time Strauss identifies the contention and objection as follows: "our provisional contention according to which Aristotle's political science is the fully conscious form of the common sense understanding of political things is open to the objection that the matrix of that science is not common sense simply but the common sense of the Greeks, not to say the common sense of the Greek upper class" (*CM*, 30). What might appear to be two contentions are in fact one; Aristotle originates political science *because* he presents the fully conscious form of the commonsense understanding of political things.

The third section of the chapter is devoted to "a few words about Aristotle's alleged anti-democratic prejudice" (*CM*, 35, 21). This appears to be an adumbration of the same objection or the extension of the objection addressed in the second section, i.e., the assertion that Aristotle's political science is an expression of "the common sense of the Greek upper class," with their opposition to democracy and their valorization of inequality.

The first three sections then treat the "objections" that will help us to a "more adequate understanding of the *Politics*." The last two sections of the chapter deal with the Aristotelian political science itself, explaining in turn two—perhaps the two most characteristic—claims Aristotle raises. In the fourth section Strauss explains the famous Aristotelian affirmation that "the city is the natural association *par excellence*" (*CM*, 41; cf. 16–17). In the fifth section Strauss brings out the fact that the central theme of the *Politics* is not in fact the city but the *politeia*, the regime. That, in turn, is the basis for the centrality of the question of the best regime for the old political science.

Certainly Strauss's most striking claim is the assertion that Aristotle is the originator of political science because he gives the fully conscious form of "common sense," the latter part of this contention understood to be provisional. That claim is strikingly developed in the first section of the chapter, the section devoted in effect to the objection that not Aristotle but someone else is the originator of political science. There are two candidates or sets of candidates for the "someone else": as we have seen, the "traditional view" names Socrates; the nontraditional view, presumably the modern scholarly view (see *LAM*, 26–64), identifies the pre-Socratic sophists as the first to turn "to the study of the human things" (*CM*, 14). Strauss devotes a part of his first section to responding to this modern scholarly claim (paras. 2–7), and the remainder of the section to replying to the "traditional view" (paras. 8–15).

Strauss emphatically rejects the modern scholarly view that the pre-Socratic sophists originated political science. They proceeded on the basis of the distinction between nature and convention and relegated the human things proper, the just and the noble things, to the realm of convention (*CM*, 14). Accordingly they thought the only significant politically relevant knowledge was knowledge of rhetoric, for convention, being merely an agreement, is subject to the art of persuasion (*CM*, 17). Strauss insists that even the pre-Socratic Hippodamus, whom Aristotle seems to identify as the first political scientist, failed to find that science, because he merely attempted to impose some broader theory of nature onto the human world. In other words, "he did not pay attention to the peculiar character of political things: he did not see that the political things are in a class by themselves" (*CM*, 19).

The man who apparently first saw the uniqueness of the political was

Socrates, ironically because he applied to the political a general theory about nature as a whole: he asked "what is the political?" just as he asked of everything the "what is . . . ?" question. Socrates's discovery of "noetic heterogeneity" in the whole made possible his turn to the human things as human things. Strauss significantly attributes to Socrates the view that raising the "what is . . . ?" question represented a "return . . . to sanity, to 'common sense'" (CM, 19). Strauss says this because it represented "a turn away from the question" that had obsessed Socrates's predecessors, the attempt to discover the "first things," or roots "which are responsible for the coming into being and perishing of everything that comes into being and perishes" (CM, 14). The Socratic turn is a turn to "common sense," i.e., to the way the world is experienced, because "the roots of the whole are hidden, [but] the whole manifestly consists of heterogeneous parts" (CM, 19). Strauss and Socrates (and Aristotle) would no doubt point to the phenomenon of speech, in which the different beings or parts are named with different yet stable names (cf. CM, 17).

The Socratic turn is the necessary but apparently not the sufficient cause for the emergence of political science; despite the fact that Socrates effected a return to common sense, he did not originate political science. The question of why Aristotle not Socrates founds political science amounts to the question, then, of how Socrates returns to common sense yet apparently does not give us "the fully conscious form of the common sense understanding of political things." In the eighth paragraph of the chapter Strauss affirms on the basis of his account of the Socratic turn that "not Socrates or Plato but Aristotle is truly the founder of political science: as one discipline . . . among a number of disciplines" (CM, 21). His point here is to show why Socrates and Plato could not found political science. Socrates and Plato endorsed the Socratic thesis that "human wisdom is knowledge of ignorance." Knowledge of ignorance is not the same as pure ignorance; it is the recognition that "there is no knowledge of the whole but only knowledge of parts, hence only partial knowledge of parts, hence no unqualified transcending . . . of this sphere of opinion" (CM, 20; see also WIPP, 38–39). "Partial knowledge of parts" means not only that knowledge of the whole escapes us but also that the knowledge of the parts is also somehow "elusive." Each part is "open to the whole" in the sense that knowledge of it is subject to the uncertainty imposed by the elusiveness of the whole. This odd kind of "openness" of each part, including the political part, "obstructs the establishment of political philosophy or political science as an independent discipline" (CM, 21). Political science, like every sort of knowledge, is not self-contained but implicates sooner or later this whole, which itself cannot be nailed down. The implication of this discussion would seem to be that Aristotle achieves, or believes he achieves, that knowledge of the whole that precluded Plato and Socrates from founding political science as a separate discipline.

At the end of his eleventh paragraph, Strauss indeed concludes that Aristotle "could found political science as an independent discipline among a number of disciplines in such a way that political science . . . is the fully conscious form of the 'common sense' understanding of political things" (*CM*, 25). Presumably what should occur between the end of the eighth paragraph and the end of the eleventh paragraph is a discussion of how Aristotle surpasses the Socratic understanding of philosophy as knowledge of ignorance. Indeed that *seems* to be what happens, for in drawing his conclusion that Aristotle does "found political science as an independent discipline," Strauss cites as one of the bases for the Aristotelian achievement the view "that theoretical wisdom (knowledge of the whole, i.e., of that by virtue of which 'all things' are a whole) is available" (*CM*, 25).

Aristotle completes philosophy in a way that Plato does not, and therefore can articulate the place of the human things in a fixed and determinate way that Socrates and Plato could not. Although we are in a sense prepared for this assertion by Strauss because of what he said about Socrates in paragraph 8, it is striking how little prepared we are for it by the intervening discussion, for, contrary to our expectation, Strauss does not develop in any way whatsoever the Aristotelian claim to complete philosophy. It is, quite literally, a parenthetical comment. Strauss radically underattends to this central claim. Among other things, he gives us no idea of whether he considers Aristotle's claim to go beyond Socrates and Plato sound or not, and therefore whether he considers Aristotle's political science to be sound or not. Judging from other works by Strauss, in which he endorses the Socratic/Platonic position on philosophy, it would seem that Strauss does not endorse the Aristotelian claim and hence does not endorse Aristotelian political science (cf., e.g., *WIPP*, 5).

Instead of attending to this all-important issue of the status or possibility of knowledge of the whole, Strauss takes up another topic, the status of prudence, in the text intervening between paragraphs 8 and 11. Prudence, the virtue of the legislator or statesman, is knowledge of the ends of human life and of the means to achieve them, and is available to human beings, "independently of theoretical science" (*CM*, 25).

It would seem that knowledge of the whole is not necessary for the establishment of political science, for its self-contained character, its independence from theoretical science, would imply that whatever might turn out to be the truth with respect to cosmology or the whole, the human sphere is secure and sui generis. This is indeed what Strauss assumes in his "Epilogue," where he denies, in effect, that the differences between modern natural science and Aristotelian philosophy of nature render Aristotelian political science outdated (see esp. *LAM*, 205–7).

It would seem that the crucial premise for the emergence of political science is not the Aristotelian knowledge of the whole but the intelligibility and "closedness" of the sphere of prudence, that is, "the ends in the light of which prudence guides man" (*CM*, 25). This seems to be both the necessary and the sufficient condition for the emergence and existence of Aristotelian political science. Accordingly, Strauss says no more about Aristotle's alleged knowledge of the whole in the sequel, but concentrates instead on further elucidation of the claim about prudence.

The further exploration of prudence is introduced by a brief paragraph that, among other things, contrasts Aristotle's position on the relations among nature, art, and law with the views of the pre-Socratics and with "another extreme view." The latter is particularly of interest because it is introduced without any preparation and apparently without any follow-up. And, it almost goes without saying, Strauss does not identify the holders of the "extreme view" of which he speaks. The extremists believe that "nature and law became fused and oppose themselves to the arts which thus appear to defile a sacred order" (*CM*, 25). Judging from comments Strauss makes elsewhere it appears that the source of this view is the Bible, according to which "the *polis* and the arts and knowledge" are "a kind of rebellion against God" ("PR," 288). But why is Strauss injecting from left field, so to speak, this biblical sentiment in the midst of his very unbiblical account of Aristotle? Whatever the answer to that question, we must note that it stands, somehow, as a preface to the further explanation of prudence.

That further explanation leads to a reformulation of the original Straussian contention: "Aristotle is the founder of political science because he is the discoverer of moral virtue," rather than because he is the philosopher who achieves knowledge of the whole (*CM*, 27). There is a profound connection between the previous representation of Aristotle as promulgator of the thesis of the closed sphere of prudence, and Aristotle as "discoverer of moral virtue." "Prudence is that kind of knowledge which is inseparable from 'moral virtue,'" because "according to Aristotle it is moral virtue that supplies the sound principles of action, the just and noble ends, as actually

desired" (*CM*, 24, 25). What distinguishes moral virtue from virtue simply
or from desirable qualities of character in general is that the deeds to which
it points—the "just and noble deeds"—are conceived of "as choiceworthy
for their own sake." That is to say, they are experienced as "absolutes" or as
good in themselves, and not as means to some other end, be it some trans-
moral end of the individual or a purpose that is "essentially in the service
of the city," that is, a necessary means to social goods (*CM*, 27). Because
prudence requires the acceptance of the moral virtues as themselves the
proper ends of action, prudence is possible only for the moral individual,
the kind of person Strauss, following Aristotle, calls the gentleman (*CM*,
24–25). Thus Aristotelian political science takes the internal perspective of
the political actor, of the citizen or statesman who faces the political world
as a field of action, not a field merely to observe in theoretical detachment.
In this sense, Strauss's Aristotelian political science reveals its "existential"
dimension. "Aristotelian political science . . . has the character of categorical advice or exhortation" (*LAM*, 207).

Moral virtue thus stands as the ground of political science as the highest
prudence, and of political science as "the fully conscious form of the common sense understanding of political things." For the commonsense understanding is nothing other than "the perspective of the citizen or statesman,"
which by implication is the perspective of moral virtue, or of "the just and
noble things" as goods or ends in themselves.

Yet Strauss insists that for Aristotle "the highest end of man by nature
is theoretical understanding or philosophy and this perfection does not
require moral virtue as moral virtue" (*CM*, 14). That is to say, either moral
virtue is not *the* end or good in itself of human life, or it is not even a good
in itself. According to Strauss, to show that moral virtue is the end or good
in itself would require showing that "the practice of moral virtues is the end
of man by nature." This, in turn, would require knowledge of the human
soul, which is theoretical knowledge, not knowledge of the human things
(*CM*, 1, 13–14), but "Aristotle . . . does not even attempt to give such an account." Instead "he remains within the limits of an unwritten *nomos* which
is recognized by well-bred people everywhere" (*CM*, 26). There seems to be
a serious gap in the Aristotelian account.

It might appear from the discussion thus far that Leo Strauss is not
an Aristotelian because he sees Aristotle to be building his political science on an account of moral virtue that is merely a matter of generaliz-
ing from the moral beliefs, grounded in the moral education or prejudices,
of Greek "gentlemen." This is not his point, however, as is evident from

the next of the two objections that he takes up in this chapter: the objection that Aristotle's political science embodies not the "common sense of the subject" but "the common sense of the Greeks or of the Greek upper class." The decisive answer to the contention that moral virtue is merely a prejudice of the Greeks is Strauss's very important explanation of the relation between the "philosophic way of life" and the gentlemanly life and its virtues. Aristotle "shows them [the gentleman readers] as far as possible that the way of life of the perfect gentleman [i.e., the life to which they aspire] points toward the philosophic way of life" (CM, 28). Aristotle thus ultimately transcends the point of view of the moral life but retains from it the central idea of morality: that there is a way of life "choiceworthy for its own sake," to which is linked the moral life as usually understood, not so much as means to an end but as echo or reflection. The moral life, or the norms and virtues that compose it, derive much of their content indeed from the requisites of the city—the virtues are in large part the habitual practices needed for the survival and thriving of the political community. But, Strauss insists, Aristotle also shows us that "moral virtue is not . . . intelligible as [simply] a means for the only two natural ends which could be thought to be its end" (CM, 27). Not merely is it a means to the philosophic or the social and political life, but it is the embodiment of the truth of the human situation that there is a human good in itself beyond the self and the goods of the body, which exerts its call in one form or another on human beings. While Strauss's Aristotle (and it would seem, Strauss himself) is not a Kantian, neither is he an Aristotelian in the normal meaning of that term, i.e., an ethicist who grounds moral virtues in a consequentialist, teleological theory of the human person or soul.

Defense of Aristotle's Political Science

Strauss connects the value of the moral life to the value of the "philosophic way of life" (CM, 28). The latter is in itself an ambiguous phrase in the Straussian lexicon, for it may mean that contemplative life that Aristotle is taken to describe as the attainment of wisdom in the knowledge of God, or it may mean the Socratic life of the *quest* for wisdom. Usually Strauss speaks of the philosophic life in the Aristotelian context as "contemplation," but in this context toward the end of his reply to the first objection he uses the Socratic formulation instead, and thus draws Aristotle much closer to Socrates and Plato than he has hitherto done. Thus Strauss can conclude this section by speculating that perhaps Socrates was not essentially foreclosed from founding political science, but failed to do so only because he lacked the leisure for any political activity whatever, including founding political science (*CM*, 29). This is a significant proposition. Not only does it redraw the line of distinction between Socrates and Aristotle in a decisive way, eradicating the theme of the differences between their understandings of the philosophic life, but it also affirms that the founding of political science is itself a political, not a theoretical act. That follows because it is in various ways an intervention into politics—what Strauss calls the "umpiring" role of the philosopher. The philosopher who founds or promulgates political science intervenes in political life to improve or aid political life so far as he is able.[6] But most importantly in this context, the philosopher engages in a political action by clarifying the meaning of political life for political life, most especially by revealing the ground and rationale (if that is the correct term) for moral virtue, the matrix of political life itself.

Strauss's attempt to clarify the nature of Aristotelian political science at the same time represents an attempt to clarify the nature of common sense, or of the "pre-scientific awareness." Strauss, of course, is not the first thinker in modern times to set himself that task: he was preceded by two of the philosophers he identified as among the four greatest of the twentieth century, Husserl and Heidegger. Both saw the need to get behind the "tradition." Neither, Strauss believed, succeeded in getting to the "natural awareness," as indicated by the fact that he once cited them as examples of twentieth-century philosophers who reveal in their own work "how ... thoroughly political philosophy has become discredited," i.e., how non-political they are (*WIPP*, 12). But what Strauss brings out in his presentation of the commonsense or prescientific understanding is how implicitly political, because explicitly moral, it is. (See, in general, *SPPP*, 29–37.)

Strauss does not rest content with having uncovered the original form of political science. As he did in the "Epilogue," but in a philosophically deeper way, he attempts to defend the Aristotelian political science against modern objections and alternatives. Thus all but one paragraph of the second section (paras. 16–20) is devoted to arguing for the superiority of the *polis* (the city) to the modern equivalences, society or culture, as the focus around which to orient the science of the human things (*CM*, 31–35). Likewise, the third section (paras. 21–24), devoted to replying to the objection that Aristotelian political science reflects the prejudices of the Greek upper classes, leads Strauss to contrast the Aristotelian view of democracy with the modern view. In part, Strauss means to vindicate Aristotle by arguing that Aristotle's negative judgment about democracy concerns a different kind of democracy from ours, and that modern democracy in many ways transcends the democracy Aristotle rejected (*CM*, 35–37). Yet there is a deeper set of issues involved in the Aristotelian critique of democracy, a set of issues that is relevant to a critique of modern democracy as well. That set of issues concerns the question of human equality: Strauss defends the Aristotelian affirmation of inequality over and against the affirmation of equality by the moderns. That is, the third section contains Strauss's vindication of classical political philosophy over modern political philosophy.

Strauss's consideration of the objection to his claim about Aristotle as founder of political science thus contains his response to Husserl and Heidegger on the nature of the natural or prescientific awareness, as well as an explanation of his judgment in favor of the ancients over the moderns. No small things. But more than that, it contains his account of how Aristotelian political science coheres with and supplements the prescientific awareness. It also coheres with, more fully explains, and justifies his commendation of Aristotelian political science in the "Epilogue." Once we note that his Aristotle is very different from the standard Aristotles one sees in the literature, it seems eminently plausible to see Strauss as an Aristotelian, for his Aristotle is plausibly a Socratic, a Socrates with greater leisure or public spirit than Socrates himself.

Aristotle and the Origin of Modern Political Philosophy

Yet Strauss does not present Aristotle's teaching as the peak, or as *the* comprehensive philosophy, as the preceding account would suggest. In *The City and Man* Aristotle is a prologue, an introduction to his study of Plato's *Republic*, the book that "brings to light . . . the nature of political things . . . the essential limits, the nature, of the city" (*CM*, 138). The *Republic* thus provides the answer par excellence to the "what is . . . ?" question about the political. Strauss does not claim that much for the *Politics*. It cannot be an accident that, despite his praise for and recommendations of Aristotelian political science, Strauss is generally understood to be some sort of Platonist and not an Aristotelian.

The fourth section of the chapter on Aristotle, the first section not addressed to answering an objection to his contention about Aristotle, takes up Aristotle's famous claim that "the city is by nature" (*CM*, 41). If Strauss has hesitations about Aristotle such that it is Plato and not he who brings out the "nature of the city," it is here in the discussion of the naturalness of the city that we might expect these to appear.

Strauss's treatment of this Aristotelian thesis is itself remarkably brief— one paragraph—and is followed by an examination of the poets' objections to, and then "the modern criticism" of, Aristotle's "principle." No longer is it Strauss's contention about Aristotle as the founder of political science that is under examination, but Aristotle's own. The argument has taken a turn, it seems. The greatest part of this section is devoted to a consideration of the "modern criticism." This comparison of Aristotle and the moderns differs from the previous ones, however. Here the point is not to defend the classical conception from modern criticism but to show how the modern position can be seen as the development of a central thesis or claim of Aristotle's. That is, Strauss brings out a kind of continuity, or perhaps better, a way in which Aristotle, though distant from the moderns, prepares the way for them.

Strauss's account of Aristotle on the naturalness of the city takes its point of departure in the thought that the city is natural because men are inclined by nature to it. Strauss does not seem to mean a natural inclination in the direct and obvious sense, such as in the claim that men are inclined by nature toward food. Not all human beings live in cities—some live in tribes, for example—whereas all human beings who survive take nourishment. As Strauss presents it, there is an intermediate variable: "Men are by nature inclined to the city because they are by nature inclined to happiness, to living together in a manner that satisfies the needs of their nature." The inclination to happiness is primary over the inclination to the city. Human beings are not only inclined toward but capable of happiness. Nature or the whole is "friendly to man" in this way, as witnessed by the claim that Strauss cites from Aristotle, that the animals are made for men. Nature provides— that is the premise underlying Aristotle's affirmation of the naturalness of the city, according to Strauss, who calls this view "'optimism' in the original sense of the term" (CM, 41).

Yet if human beings are both inclined toward and endowed by nature with the capacity for happiness, why do so few achieve it? If the city is part of this endowment, then why do so many cities fall manifestly short of being the good city to which nature aspires? Aristotle's answer is that the "nature [of man] is enslaved in many ways" (CM, 41, 42). But if man's nature is so enslaved, can it really be said that nature provides, or that the "optimistic" view is justified?

Strauss subtly suggests that it is *this* conundrum that ultimately leads the moderns in their distinctive direction, and not the more frequently posited modern rejection of Aristotelian cosmology and teleology. Other classical philosophers had rejected teleology and not gone where Bacon, Descartes, and the others went. Strauss puts the decisive transition as follows: "If one ponders over the facts which Aristotle summarizes by saying that our nature is enslaved in many ways, one easily arrives at the conclusion that nature is not a kind mother but a harsh stepmother to man, i.e., that the true mother of man is not nature." That thought lies near the center of the modern enterprise: "The consequent resolve to liberate man from that enslavement by his own sustained effort" (*CM*, 42). This is a more fundamental expression by Strauss of the core of modernity than his usual claims about actualizability, or "the rejection of the classical scheme as unrealistic" (*WIPP*, 39). Strauss spends most of his remaining space in his fourth section tracing the various manifestations of this effort at liberation within modern thought and practice (paras. 26–29). But he passes over remarkably hastily the pregnant suggestion he has let drop—that the moderns take their point of departure from an Aristotelian thought.

It is neither the rejection of teleology nor the conclusion that nature is a "harsh stepmother to man" that propels modernity. The latter conclusion is not even "peculiar to modern thought" (*CM*, 42). Strauss would appear to have in mind the non-Socratic (e.g., Epicurean) classical thinkers who rejected a teleological cosmos and who saw nature as a "harsh stepmother," and yet who did not set out on the path of modernity (*LAM*, 96, 100, 105, 122, 124). There are, it appears, two ways to be anti-Aristotelian, the Epicurean and the modern. One difference between these two sorts of anti-Aristotelians is that Lucretius, our main source of knowledge of Epicurus, shows "amazing silence about Plato and Aristotle" (*LAM*, 91), and this cannot be said of the pioneers of modern philosophy. According to Strauss, Machiavelli in effect rewrites Aristotle's *Ethics*. The role of Aristotle as an authority to be wrestled with in Hobbes's philosophic writings is so evident as not to require documentation. The moderns, those who drew the anti-Aristotelian conclusions and then embarked on the "conquest of nature," differ from those who drew the un-Aristotelian conclusions without embarking on the modern venture in that Aristotle was a large a presence for the former but not the latter.

Is there something about Aristotle, the man who founded political science, the man who discovered moral virtue, that leads to modernity in a way that, say, Plato, on the one side, and Epicureanism, on the other, do not?

The answer, Strauss is subtly suggesting, is yes, but to tease out that answer seems very difficult. Let us attempt a rough stab at it. Aristotle differs from both Plato and the non-Socratics in being "optimistic" in the sense Strauss indicated, but at the same time falling short, as in the Aristotelian conundrum identified above. Aristotle promises happiness as underwritten by nature in a way that the others do not, a promise captured, Strauss suggests, in his claim that the city is natural. Plato clearly is not such an "optimist." Among other things, according to Strauss, he denies that the city is natural (see *CM*, 43, 48, 60, 96, 102, 117). Aristotle makes certain promises, holds out "human excellence" as a "universal end," yet he—or nature—cannot deliver on this promise: it is "very rarely achieved" (*CM*, 44). Beginning from Aristotle (rather than from, say, Plato), modern thinkers are particularly driven to the conclusion about the stepmotherliness of nature, but this conclusion coexists with the promise of universally available happiness, i.e., the natural character of moral virtue or human excellence. The moderns appear to be those who hold on to the Aristotelian promise but see that Aristotelian reliance on nature, which amounts to a reliance on chance, is insufficient (*CM*, 42). Human beings must instead liberate themselves by their own effort, or must conquer chance. In the context, this means a liberation from nature, not a liberation to nature, as even the Epicureans had it.

Strauss's suggestion of a link between Aristotle and the emergence of modernity in *The City and Man* is a novel theme in his writing. It must be a partial theme as well, for it does not take account of competing explanations he supplied for the coming of modernity, for example, the emphasis elsewhere on Machiavelli's "anti-theological ire" (*WIPP*, 44). Jerusalem, as well as Aristotle's Athens, had something to do with the coming of modernity, a reminder of which fact Strauss gave in his injection of the biblical alternative into his discussion of Aristotle on prudence and art. Aristotle shares something extremely significant with Jerusalem. Insofar as he discovers or affirms moral virtue, i.e., "just and noble deeds as choiceworthy for their own sake," he takes a stance on human life very close to the biblical position. In some respects, Strauss indicates, the biblical doctrine is more consistent with Aristotle's presentation of moral virtue than is Aristotle's own doctrine. "Moral judgment seems then to lead up to the postulate that a God concerned with justice has created all men equal as regards their possibility of becoming good or bad. Yet 'matter' might confound this intention of the just God. One must therefore postulate creation *ex nihilo* by an omnipotent God who as such must be omniscient, by the absolute sovereign God of the Bible who will be what he will be, i.e., who will be gracious to whom He will be gracious" (*CM*, 39). It would seem no accident, then, that after a bit of struggle Aristotle was so readily taken up into Christianity.

A certain line of thought in Aristotle, that line of thought that led him to his discovery of moral virtue, that led him to affirm the naturalness of the political, and that allowed him to become the originator of political science, merges easily if not perfectly with biblical views and provides the setting for the harsh reaction that was modernity. Strauss's point seems to be this: biblical religion alone would not and did not produce modernity; non-Aristotelian Socratism, as in Plato or Xenophon, would not and did not produce modernity. The combination of biblical religion and Aristotle achieved what the classical Socratics and revelation could not produce. We might tentatively conclude, then, that Strauss was no Aristotelian because, insofar as Strauss considered modernity to be problematic, he saw Aristotle, especially that Aristotle who is the founder of political science, to be implicated in its emergence.

The Political in Aristotle's Political Science

But the role of Aristotle in the coming of modernity is not Strauss's last word on Aristotle. The concluding section of the chapter turns to the consideration not of the city (*polis*) but of the regime (*politeia*) as the center of Aristotle's political science. The centrality of the *politeia* is a frequent topic in Strauss's discussions of classical political philosophy. What he does not always do is bring out the deeper significance of the fact that not the city but the regime is the "theme of the *Politics*." The fifth section of the Aristotle chapter is brief—four paragraphs spread out over less than five pages. And it would be overstating to say that Strauss explicitly addresses the question we have just raised. Yet that does indeed seem to be the very question he is implicitly addressing.

To think the political in terms of *politeia* or regime turns out to be very different from thinking politics in terms of *polis*, city, or political community. *Politeia* is "divisive." It raises a "political issue," in the sense of an issue that is contested. There are different political regimes, i.e., different forms of rule, which engage in a contest within and among political communities (*CM*, 45). Each regime has its own form of virtue: indeed much of what is contested in political life concerns the question of which moral way will dominate. A good citizen is an individual who possesses the virtues suitable to or relative to the regime. A good democrat does not possess the same moral qualities as a good aristocrat or a good courtier in a monarchy. The different kinds of citizens differ according to the different regimes. The different kinds of citizens are dedicated to radically different ends (*CM*, 47).

The regime or "political" understanding of politics differs fundamentally from the understanding of politics in terms of the city per se. In Aristotle's rendition, the city is "natural"; its naturalness is an indication or a reflex of the natural directedness of all human beings to happiness or human excellence, or virtue, understood as one table of virtues as in the *Ethics*. To speak of politics in terms of the city is to speak of *the* universal directedness to *the* one end of moral virtue. But to speak of politics in terms of the regime is to recognize that "through a change of regime the political community becomes dedicated to an end radically different from its earlier end" (*CM*, 47). The understanding of the political in terms of the city, of naturalness, and therefore in terms of moral virtue per se is illusory: "what Aristotle said" about regimes may "run counter to our notions," but "it does not run counter to our experience" (*CM*, 46). It runs counter to our notions because "our notions" are like those of the "patriot," who takes the political community to be the reality and the "regime" to be a merely superficial phenomenon. More to the point, our notions, the common sense of the matter, conceive the political community to be a substance with qualities. But the Aristotelian doctrine of regime is truer to experience, i.e., to the reality of political life, than the patriot's view. The patriot's view corresponds to Aristotle's presentation in book 1, in terms of the naturalness of the city. The truer view corresponds to Aristotle's presentation in book 3 in terms of regime. Strauss's Aristotle is not an Aristotelian in the ordinary sense, and he appears not to be an Aristotelian even in Strauss's sense.

Aristotle's own view, Strauss implies, is the view of book 3. Book 1 presents a preliminary or tentative, or even exoteric, view of the political. But so far as that is true, so is the Aristotelian account of the moral virtues preliminary or tentative or exoteric. Within a political horizon virtue is in fact more variable, more relative than the explicit Aristotelian ethical teaching seems to allow.[7] This is not, of course, to say that Aristotle or Strauss is a relativist. True human excellence consists in contemplation or philosophy, a pursuit not relative to regime, indeed, an activity that is "trans-political," or "supra-political" (*CM*, 49). Aristotle's political science, which is "a political inquiry strictly and narrowly conceived," abstracts from this fact about true human excellence and the inability of the city to embody it (*CM*, 49). Unlike the moderns, who presuppose "a fundamental harmony between philosophy and the people" (*CM*, 37), Aristotle presupposes a disharmony, but in his political works, he suppresses the fact that he subtly asserts: "man transcends the city." But for Aristotle man transcends the city only by what is "highest in man" (*CM*, 49).

It would seem then that the character of the political regime, or rather contest over regime, is a result of the incomplete truth of the claims about moral virtue on which Aristotle rests his political science. If Aristotle's discovery of moral virtue were simply true, the truth of politics would be revealed in book 1 and not in book 3. Or in modern terms, the theme of political science would be the state and not the regime. Aristotle's political science, by virtue of being the "fully conscious form of the common sense understanding of political things" falls short of achieving or presenting the full truth about those political things, or perhaps better put, it is the kind of political science that emerges out of political life rather than from philosophy. Aristotle's political science is the developed form of political inquiry that emerges from and stays in immediate contact with political life itself. The contrast between Aristotelian political science and Platonic political philosophy is thus an instance of the "problem of political philosophy" as Strauss developed it in the first part of "What Is Political Philosophy?"

The task of adumbrating the alternative approach to politics, approaching it from the transpolitical perspective of philosophy, was performed in advance, so to speak, by Plato, but it lies ahead for Strauss in the second chapter of *The City and Man*. In that place Strauss clarifies the nature of moral virtue in a way he has done only by implication in his chapter on Aristotle. Thus he shows that, according to Socrates in the *Republic*, the "political" virtues of citizens are actually only opinions or habits. True virtue or excellence belongs only to the philosopher. So far as Aristotle leaves the relation between moral or political virtue and the true virtue of the philosopher in a kind of haze of practice, Strauss finds Plato philosophically more satisfactory, but he finds Aristotle to be sufficient and sound enough for most practical purposes. Aristotle gives us politics as it is experienced from the inside, in particular how moral virtue and thus politics seem to the nonphilosopher, and thus he captures the truth also. Strauss shows himself here as elsewhere to be the Anti-Kant, for it was Kant who rejected the saying that something may be true in theory but untrue in practice. Strauss finds Aristotelian political science to be less than the whole truth in theory but true (enough) in practice. It is the truth of practice.

CHAPTER SEVEN

At the Crossroads

Strauss on the Coming of Modernity

As is well known, Strauss at first identified Thomas Hobbes as the originator of modern political philosophy but later changed his mind and accorded the honor or blame to Niccolò Machiavelli instead. Strauss gave more or less extended accounts of Machiavelli's achievements several times, the most extensive of which was, of course, his 1958 book *Thoughts on Machiavelli*. But even after that magisterial volume he returned to Machiavelli several times, raising the question for us of what more did he have to say after *Thoughts*? The return to Machiavelli of greatest interest is probably his last effort on the Florentine, an essay added to the second edition of the *History of Political Philosophy* that he and Joseph Cropsey edited. That essay was published in 1972, just one year before Strauss's death.

Among many features that make this essay of such interest is the way it is paired with the essay that precedes it in *History*, the essay on Marsilius of Padua, which appeared in the original 1963 edition of *History*. Despite the nearly ten years that separated the appearance of the two essays, Strauss signals in multiple ways that they belong together. The last word of the Marsilius essay in fact is "Machiavelli," identified as the one who "broke with the classical tradition" and in whom "political philosophy . . . took on an entirely new character" (*HPP*, 294).

The essays on Marsilius and Machiavelli were also republished in separate collections of Strauss's writings, the former in *Liberalism Ancient and Modern*, and the latter in the posthumous *Studies in Platonic Political Philosophy*. But even in their severed publication form Strauss indicated their linked character. Not only does the Marsilius essay end with the reference forward to Machiavelli, but the Machiavelli essay in *Studies* is immediately preceded by an essay on Maimonides's *Treatise on the Art of Logic*, whose last words are "Marsilius of Padua's *Defensor Pacis*" (*SPPP*, 209). Strauss's persistent linking of the two philosophers and thus of the two essays makes immediate sense when we consider more fully the way Strauss concludes the essay on Marsilius:

> Marsilius was driven to take this view to some extent by his anticlericalism. When antitheological passion induced a thinker to take the extreme step of questioning the supremacy of contemplation, political philosophy broke with the classical tradition, and especially with Aristotle, and took an entirely new character. The thinker in question was Machiavelli. (*HPP*, 294)

Marsilius and Machiavelli faced similar situations—the theological-political order of late medieval times in Italy. Both reacted in an anticlerical if not an antitheological manner, but one reacted in a way that remained within the classical tradition of political philosophy, while the other went beyond and ushered in that new "kind of thought which is philosophic indeed but no longer Greek: modern philosophy" (*HPP*, 297). It is as though Marsilius and Machiavelli, traveling on the same road away from the Rome of their day, came to the same crossroads, Marsilius veering back toward Athens, i.e., proceeding on the basis and within the capacious confines of classical political philosophy, and Machiavelli heading off toward what appears at first to be ancient Rome but actually turns out to be a "new moral continent"—New York, let us say (*HPP*, 277, 306; *TM*, 85).

Another way to see almost the same point is to note that when Strauss published the Marsilius essay in his *Liberalism* collection he placed it in a unit of chapters devoted to illustrating "the liberalism of premodern thinkers." Marsilius is thus emphatically identified as a premodern thinker in a volume devoted to "adumbrat[ing] ... the fundamental difference between classical and modern philosophy" (*LAM*, viii).

Strauss further indicates the character of the relation between Marsilius and Machiavelli in a subtle number game that he plays. In the twenty-seventh paragraph of the essay on Machiavelli Strauss puts forth a claim he previously voiced in *Thoughts*: the number 26 (or twice 13) is particularly significant for Machiavelli. Strauss organizes his discussion of the *Discourses* in the Machiavelli essay in part around chapters whose numbers are multiples of 13 and suggests further that "we might profitably consider the other chapters of the *Discourses* whose numbers are multiples of 13" (*HPP*, 313). Looking back to the Marsilius essay, we notice that it contains, in its *History* version, two sections of twelve paragraphs each. Marsilius moves in the same direction as Machiavelli (12), but does not go so far (13) as his Florentine successor does. (Strauss changed the paragraphing of the Marsilius essay in reprinting it in *Liberalism*: in that version it has two sections of twelve and thirteen paragraphs respectively, or a total of twenty-five paragraphs, signaling perhaps Strauss's second thought that Marsilius was even closer to Machiavelli than he had originally believed. We will later suggest other reasons that may have led Strauss to modify the paragraphing of this essay.)

To say that Marsilius approached Machiavelli but did not reach him is to suggest that they shared something but that that something was not what it takes to define modern political philosophy. The pair of essays before us thus provides a particularly open window onto the question of just what Strauss took to be the defining characteristics of modern political philosophy, and conversely, of just what gives classical political philosophy its character. The pair of essays might thus be taken to give Strauss's answer to the Socratic question "what is modern political philosophy?"

Marsilius and Machiavelli

Let us begin by identifying some of the ways Marsilius approaches Machiavelli, i.e., some of the features his thought shares with that of the Florentine. The opening and closing paragraphs of Strauss's Marsilius essay announce some of the chief features of Marsilius's thought that resemble, or even match, that of Machiavelli. The opening paragraph contrasts Marsilius with the "most celebrated Christian Aristotelian Thomas Aquinas," who is the subject of the immediately preceding essay in *History*. Marsilius stands between Thomas Aquinas and Machiavelli, and Strauss is attempting to clarify the differences between Marsilius and his Aristotelian predecessor, as well as between Marsilius and his modernist successor. "Marsilius," says Strauss, "lives as it were in another world than Thomas" (*HPP*, 270). That other world does not appear to be *the* "other world," for philosophers, "as philosophers, did not believe in another life," and Marsilius is identified elsewhere by Strauss as an Averroist (*NRH*, 158), a breed of philosophers "who as philosophers refused to make any concessions to revealed religion" (*HPP*, 314).[1] Although Strauss does not explicitly identify Marsilius as an Averroist in the essay devoted to him, he does so in several places elsewhere, and in the Marsilius essay itself he makes a point of the fact that Marsilius accepts "the philosophic concept . . . of the 'sect' as a society constituted by belief in a peculiar divine law or by a peculiar religion" (*HPP*, 278). To accept the philosophic concept of the sect is, Strauss affirms in the Machiavelli essay, to "go in the way of Averroism," the very way in which Machiavelli himself goes (*HPP*, 314; cf. *TM*, 225).

So far as Marsilius lives in another world, or stands toward the other world differently from Thomas Aquinas, he appears to stand or live with Machiavelli: both are Averroists or, rather, adherents of "the view characteristic of the *falāsifa* (i.e., of the Islamic Aristotelians) as well as of the Jewish Aristotelians" (*NRH*, 158). As Strauss says on several occasions, and as we have noted earlier, "the substance of Machiavelli's religious teaching is not original" (*HPP*, 314). It is not original because "it amounts to a restatement of the teaching of pagan philosophers, as well as of that medieval school which goes by the name of Averroism" (*WIPP*, 41; cf. *TM*, 202, 225, 232). Marsilius the Averroist thus approaches Machiavelli the Averroist in his understanding and critique of religion: modernity does not consist essentially in critique of biblical religion.

In the final paragraph of the Marsilius essay, Strauss makes a claim about Marsilius that may be even more surprising to those who have followed Strauss on the meaning of modernity: "Marsilius says much less than Aristotle even in his *Politics* about the highest end which is natural to man. For the reasons indicated above *he lowered his sights*" (*HPP*, 293, emphasis added; cf. *TM*, 207–8).

As we have seen, if there is one theme running through Strauss's various discussions of modernity, it is the theme of "lowering the sights." For example, according to his synoptic statement of the modern position in "What Is Political Philosophy?," "Machiavelli consciously lowers the standards of social action. His lowering of the standards is meant to lead to a higher probability of actualization of that scheme which is constructed in accordance with the lowered standards. Thus the dependence on chance [so integral to classical conceptions] is reduced: chance will be conquered" ("WIPP," 41; cf. *NRH*, 178). In his synoptic restatement a decade later in his essay "The Three Waves of Modernity," Strauss repeats nearly the same points in nearly the same language. According to Machiavelli, "one must start from how men do live; one must lower one's sights" ("TWM," 86).

But Marsilius has already "lowered his sights"—not thereby ushering in modernity. Strauss's statements are not necessarily contradictory; "lowering the sights" could be a necessary but not sufficient marker of modern political philosophy, or one could lower one's sights in various degrees. Or one might say that it is not the lowering of sights per se that characterizes modern political philosophy, but the motive for the lowering. Machiavelli and his successors lower their sights for the sake of actualization of the best or the good order. Perhaps Marsilius failed to found modern political philosophy because he lowered his sights for a different reason.

Seeing what Marsilius and Machiavelli share—features that seem so relevant to Strauss's typical accounts of modern political philosophy—leads us to pay closer attention to the differences that Strauss explicitly identifies between them. Let us consider the concluding paragraph of the Marsilius essay—that which stands at the place of convergence of the two thinkers, and which is thus figuratively the locus of the crossroads itself. Strauss identifies two differences. First, they differ in motive. "Marsilius was driven to some extent to take this position by his anticlericalism." Machiavelli, however, was "induced" by "antitheological passion" to his position. Both react negatively to the theological-political ordering of their day, but the nature of the reaction differs, with Machiavelli opposing theology per se and Marsilius only clericalism. One can surely be anticlerical without being antitheological. Furthermore, Machiavelli is said to be moved by "passion" or "ire." Strauss does not characterize Marsilius's state of mind but suggests not only that his anticlericalism is "cooler" than Machiavelli's parallel passion, but that it is more rational as well—it is an "ism," i.e., a doctrine of some sort.

As to substance, Strauss identifies the crucial step Machiavelli took that ushered in a new kind of political philosophy as "questioning the supremacy of contemplation," implying that Marsilius did not take this further step. This is merely another way of getting to the same conclusion we have already reached—neither the critique of religion nor the "lowering of the sights" per se characterizes modern political philosophy. Strauss's explicit identification of these differences—a difference of motive and a difference of substance—poses the main challenge in understanding Strauss's two essays: what does he take to be the relation between the motives and the substantive change? A second challenge follows from this one: why is questioning contemplation as the end the decisive move that ushers in modern philosophy?

Motives

Marsilius is "driven" by anticlericalism, Machiavelli "induced" by "antitheological passion." Both are moved by their stance toward the theological-political order of Christendom. That observation helps make sense of the opening of the Machiavelli essay with Strauss's evocation of the fundamental differences that amount to a "conflict" between Athens and Jerusalem (*HPP*, 296–97). This conflict is "unresolved," as Strauss affirmed many times, but especially in his lecture series "Progress or Return?" (See chapter 4 above.) To say that it is unresolved is to say that the apparent resolution represented by Christian Aristotelianism, the school of thought with which Strauss identifies both Thomas Aquinas and Marsilius, is only an apparent resolution. As we have seen, Strauss identifies Marsilius with the Averroists, a set of philosophers who opt philosophically for reason and opt humanly for philosophy. That is, the Marsilian type of Christian Aristotelianism is not meant to be a resolution of the "unresolved conflict that has prevented Western thought from ever coming to rest." If Aquinas lives in "another world" from Marsilius, then we might conclude that Strauss finds Aquinas to have failed to achieve alleged resolution in the opposite way, a conclusion that is affirmed in Strauss's systematic statement on the law of nature as explained in chapter 8 below. This "conflict" is "perhaps . . . at the bottom" of the Machiavellian founding of modern political philosophy (*HPP*, 297). That is to say, the chief difference between classical and modern political philosophy consists in the different character of their attempts to negotiate the conflict between Athens and Jerusalem.

Strauss's presentation of Marsilius's anticlericalism and its consequences for the Paduan's political philosophy as a whole is complex, befitting the complex manner of Marsilius's own presentation. The key to Strauss's exegesis of Marsilius's thought appears in the thirteenth paragraph of his essay: "both reason and revelation speak against the rule of priests" (*HPP*, 285). That is to say, Marsilius finds grounds in both Aristotelian philosophy and biblical teachings to reject the role that priests took in medieval Christendom. In the opening paragraph of the Marsilius essay Strauss distinguishes two threads of Marsilius's argument, identifying one as political philosophy and the other as political theology. He appears to restrict himself to an explication of the former. He disclaims any intention to "go into Marsilius' doctrine of the Church, although it was of the greatest importance, especially during the Reformation, for that doctrine belongs to political theology rather than political philosophy" (*HPP*, 276). Since "his doctrine regarding the Christian priesthood," an extremely important part of his doctrine of the church, "supplies the key to almost all the difficulties in which his work abounds," it is difficult to see how Strauss can avoid "going into" Marsilius's political theology. Indeed, he does not avoid treating the political theology, for that "principle [i.e., the doctrine on the priesthood] explains his only explicit deviation from the teaching of Aristotle," and Strauss devotes much of his essay to explaining that deviation and its root in Marsilius's opposition to the structure and claims of the church of his day.

Strauss does not necessarily contradict himself in so proceeding. Although he discusses various aspects of Marsilius's ecclesiology extensively, he is careful to signal when he is speaking of political philosophy as opposed to political theology, or as he sometimes puts it, the "Christian law." Thus at least five times within the essay, Strauss uses the phrase "the confines of political philosophy" or something very similar to signal the character of the Marsilian teaching under examination. In one of these places, Strauss puts it in terms of "returning" to the "confines of political philosophy" (*HPP*, 282), while in others he speaks in a way that indicates a difference between what can be said "within the confines of political philosophy" and Christian political theology (*HPP*, 279, 287–89, 290). Similarly, Strauss speaks on many occasions of Marsilian points that derive from the "'law of Christians,' and only [from] that law," as opposed to claims that Marsilius derives from both reason and revelation (*HPP*, 279, 287–89, 290).

It is not the case, then, that Strauss completely sets to the side Marsilius's political theology in favor of his political philosophy. Indeed, Strauss has made clear why that is impossible to do. But it remains true that Strauss does not "go into" Marsilius's political theology, if by "go into" we take him to mean to examine the validity of the claims made within the political theology. That is, Strauss does not do what a theologian might do; he refrains from comparing Marsilius's arguments from the New Testament on the nature of the church with the New Testament sources on which they are allegedly based. This failure to probe Marsilius's biblically based arguments stands in strong contrast with Strauss's treatment of Marsilian claims allegedly resting on Aristotle. Strauss does not hesitate to make pronouncements like the following: "his teaching ascribed to Aristotle is much more democratic than Aristotle's authentic teaching" (*HPP*, 281). He never makes any such judgment on the "authentic" biblical teaching compared with Marsilius's presentation of it.

Marsilius's strategy of, in effect, distinguishing political philosophy, or doctrines based on reason and demonstration, from political theology, or doctrines based on the Christian faith, apparently rests on an understanding that is quite similar to that of Thomas Aquinas concerning philosophy and faith. For Marsilius "revelation is indeed above reason, but not against reason" (*HPP*, 276, 279). Because revelation is above reason, Aristotle could not know the true doctrine of the Christian priesthood, which is revealed in the New Testament, especially in the examples of Jesus and the apostles. But there is an important parallelism between the conclusion to the rational or Aristotelian doctrine of the priesthood and biblical doctrine according to Marsilius (*HPP*, 275–78). Although Aristotle did not know the true Christian doctrine, "this does not mean that his teaching regarding the priesthood is entirely wrong. On the contrary, within political philosophy that teaching is in the main correct" (*HPP*, 277). Aristotle and the New Testament agree that "the priesthood forms a necessary part of the commonwealth . . . but cannot be the ruling part: priests cannot have the power to rule or to judge" (*HPP*, 277–78). But in the Europe of Marsilius's day the clerics claimed just this power; indeed Marsilius set himself most decisively against the claim of "papal plenitude of power" (*HPP*, 277).

That claim to plenitude of power passes beyond what both reason and revelation teach regarding clerical power. The New Testament does not agree completely with Aristotle about the priesthood (*HPP*, 278), but in its authentic teaching, as opposed to the bogus claims of the clergy, it separates the priests even more decisively from politics than Aristotle did:

> For according to [Marsilius] the New Testament not only does not authorize government by priests, especially in secular matters, but positively forbids it. In the Christian law, and only in the Christian law, the action of the priest as priest is most perfect of all. But this action requires a spirit and way of life which are incompatible with rulership, for it requires contempt for the world and the utmost humility. (*HPP*, 287–88)

The extreme claims raised by the church to share in or to exercise supreme secular power not only are contrary to the church's own scriptural grounds of authority but wreak havoc with ordinary civil life. These claims violate the rational teaching regarding the priests, but also the rational (and scriptural) teaching regarding political authority. The ecclesiastical claim to supreme power "renders any government impossible, for it destroys the unity of the government and of the legal order" (*HPP*, 279). The divided claims to authority "endanger not only the good life or the fruits of peace, for the sake of which the commonwealth exists, but mere life or mere peace which is merely the condition . . . for the realization of the true end of the commonwealth" (*HPP*, 278; cf. 277).

Thus Strauss identifies Marsilius's "venture" as "the eradication of papal plenitude of power and everything reminding of it" (*HPP*, 285). It is tempting on the basis of what we have seen thus far in the Marsilius essay to conclude that Strauss intends the distinction between anticlerical, as in Marsilius, and antitheological, as in Machiavelli, to be meaningful and definitive. Marsilius opposes the political pretensions of the priests on political philosophic and theological grounds. He is not opposed to Christian theology, but he builds on it. Strauss cites unnamed scholars who assert that "the *Defender* is inspired by nothing but anticlericalism," i.e., not by antitheological urges as well (*HPP*, 284–85). Those scholars would appear to support our conjecture.

It would be a mistake to succumb to that conjecture, however, for, apart from Strauss's general inclusion of Marsilius among the Averroists, immediately after citing those scholars Strauss suggests otherwise. He turns to "a Marsilian doctrine which is not affected by either political theology or antitheological preoccupations" (*HPP*, 285). This is the one and only time Strauss applies the term "antitheological" to Marsilius, but the point is clear: Marsilius's anticlericalism is accompanied by or part of "antitheological preoccupations." The point is reinforced when a few paragraphs later Strauss modifies his earlier statement about the relation between reason and revelation in Marsilius: "revelation is not simply above reason but against reason" (*HPP*, 289). In this respect too Marsilius differs greatly from Thomas Aquinas, and from the impression they (Strauss and Marsilius) leave on the surface regarding how Marsilius stands toward Athens and Jerusalem. In other words, like the other Averroists, Marsilius makes no concessions at the level of philosophy to the claims and deliverances of revelation. If Marsilius is antitheological as well as anticlerical, then the difference in motive between him and Machiavelli must lie in the passion Machiavelli adds to what he, Marsilius, and the other Averroists share.

Although Strauss denied in "What Is Political Philosophy?" any originality to Machiavelli's critique of religion, he did find Machiavelli to be "a great master of blasphemy." In the context of a series of lectures delivered in Jerusalem Strauss chooses to keep Machiavelli's blasphemies "under the veil" beneath which he hid them ("WIPP," 41). But Strauss returns to the blasphemies in his later writings on Machiavelli; in both *Thoughts on Machiavelli* and the 1972 essay, Strauss is more than willing to "lift the veil" (cf. *TM*, 49, 188, 51). In both places he adverts to the same example of a blasphemy marked by "charm and gracefulness" ("WIPP," 41). It might seem strange that in an essay placed in an undergraduate textbook Strauss is more forthcoming than in the lecture in Jerusalem. The reason, we believe, has to do with the pairing with the Marsilius essay, for the question guiding that pairing concerns the difference between Marsilius's anticlerical or his antitheological preoccupations and Machiavelli's antitheological passion. That Machiavelli blasphemes as he does is a sign of that passion.

The blasphemy in question occurs in the twenty-sixth chapter of the *Discourses*, the significance of which Strauss explains in his own twenty-seventh paragraph: his point of view is not identical to Machiavelli's despite his willingness to expose Machiavelli's blasphemy. As Strauss summarizes the point of *Discourses* 1.26: "a new prince who wishes to establish absolute power in his state must make everything new; he must establish new magistracies with new names, new authorities, and new men; he must make the rich poor and the poor rich, as David did when he became king. . . . In sum he must not leave anything in his country untouched, and there must not be any rank or wealth that its possessors do not recognize as owing to the prince" (*HPP*, 312). In the context of depicting the tasks facing the new prince, Strauss notes that Machiavelli quotes a passage from the New Testament, the lone New Testament quotation appearing in either the *Discourses* or the *Prince*.

As Strauss says, "the quotation forms part of the Magnificat, the Virgin Mary's prayer of thanks after she heard from the angel Gabriel that she would bring forth a son. . . . He that 'hath filled the hungry with good things, and sent the rich empty away' is none other than God himself" (*HPP*, 312, quoting Luke 1:53). The conclusion Strauss draws is the "most horrible blasphemy." "In the context of this chapter this means that god [*sic*] is a tyrant, and that King David, who made the rich poor and the poor rich, was a Godly [*sic*] king, a king who walked in the ways of the Lord because he proceeded in the tyrannical way" (*HPP*, 312). In *Thoughts* Strauss has a long discussion of what Machiavelli "meant by indicating that the Biblical God is a tyrant" (*TM*, 187–88). In the Machiavelli essay Strauss does not move in that direction—his gaze in this shorter statement is much more focused than in *Thoughts*. He is focused on the essential question raised by the pairing of Marsilius and Machiavelli. In that context he instead goes on to discuss at greater length the character of Machiavelli's blaspheming, rather than the content of his blasphemy. He considers an objection "someone" might raise to his explication of the blasphemy: "the blasphemy is not expressly uttered but only implied." Although this may be meant to be an extenuating claim, "far from helping Machiavelli, [it] makes his case worse." Strauss appears here as a prosecutor, speaking on behalf of those offended by the "most horrible blasphemy," but from a philosophic point of view his more serious point is the following: "A concealed blasphemy," Strauss says, "is so insidious . . . because it practically compels the hearer or reader to think the blasphemy by himself and thus to became an accomplice of the blasphemer" (*HPP*, 312). In adding his particularly insidious kind of blasphemy to the understanding of religion that he shares with Averroists like Marsilius, Machiavelli turns in this quasi-open (but legally innocent) way against the biblical religion and attempts to bring his readers along with him. As opposed to the Averroists, who maintained an inner freedom from revealed religion but supported it outwardly, Machiavelli makes a kind of warfare against Christianity.

This more or less open but subtle warfare expresses an antitheological passion that Strauss does not find in Marsilius or the other Averroists. The differences are strikingly evident in the most surface features as well as in the subtleties of Strauss's two essays. So, as we have seen, in the Marsilius essay, Strauss goes out of his way to emphasize the way Marsilius makes arguments deriving from both reason and revelation; there is nothing of that sort in the Machiavelli essay. Strauss shows Marsilius deferring to innumerable scriptural passages; Machiavelli uses only one. Machiavelli makes no concessions to political theology. More subtly, Strauss calls attention (in passing only) to the place in Marsilius's book where he takes up "the question concerning the ground of the belief in the truth of the Bible" (*HPP*, 292). Until that point, Strauss emphasizes, "the reader can only guess whether Marsilius was a believer or unbeliever" (*HPP*, 292). However, the Marsilian chapter to which Strauss calls our attention, *Defensor Pacis* 2.19, might still leave readers guessing. It is much more subtle and ambiguous than the Machiavellian blasphemy. Strauss does not explicitly commit himself in this essay on whether he takes Marsilius to be a believer or not, but given his general identification of Marsilius as an Averroist and his general view of the Averroists, it is difficult to believe that he thought Marsilius was a believer.

It would be beside our present purpose to attempt an extensive independent interpretation of the chapter in question, but we will note a few things that seem to us to support what we take Strauss's position to be. First, in his summary of the main conclusion of the entire book in 3.2, Marsilius lists first and foremost the conclusions of 2.19. That we must believe in the truth only of divine or canonic Scriptures in order "to gain eternal beatitude" is the first premise of the political-theological part of Marsilius's argument. These arguments take the Bible as the authoritative statement of truth and reason from it, as reason does from self-evident truth. It is most important here to distinguish between writings that "arise from human invention" and those that "are handed down by the direct inspiration of

God, who cannot be deceived nor wishes to deceive" (2.19.4). One must, therefore, have a way of distinguishing between these two different kinds of writings. No men but those to whom the revelation is directly vouchsafed have direct experience of God's inspiration. All others must somehow depend on their word. The Scriptures that deserve belief and obedience are those that have been held to be canonic, perhaps by church councils (2.19.5–6), but what is the basis on which the church or church councils have assembled the canon? Marsilius is both complex and vague on that all-important topic. His most precise conclusion appears to be that "we must in piety hold that what the catholic or universal church says in matters concerning the faith has been directly revealed by the Holy Spirit" (2.19.10). That in turn must be believed because according to Matthew 28, Jesus said, "and lo, I am with you always, even unto the end of the world." Jerome takes that passage to mean that Jesus "promises he will be with his disciples even unto the end of the world . . . and he will never leave those who believe in him" (2.19.2). Marsilius applies this thought more directly to the topic at hand by concluding that "therefore, the gathering of the faithful in a general council truly represents, through succession, the gathering of the apostles and other elders of the faithful at that time." He directly applies this conclusion to the claim that general councils have the right to "resolve doubtful senses of Scripture," but it would seem to apply with equal or greater force to the claims of the church, as a gathering of the faithful, to identity the canonic, i.e., truly divinely originated writings (2.19.2). As he says, "one must in piety hold that the holy spirit always accompanies such people [i.e., gatherings of the faithful] for the preservation of faith" (2.19.2).

It is noteworthy that in all the places where Marsilius draws conclusions about the authoritative text, he employs the phrase "in piety." Piety requires that one believe the canonic texts to be authentic revelations from God. What criteria are there to determine what piety requires us to accept? That Marsilius has begged the question is evident when we notice that the main reason in favor of taking the church's traditional determination of the holy books is that the passage from the book of Matthew can be or has been interpreted to vouch for the determinations by the church of the canon. But this means that the book of Matthew is being used to establish its own authority, and we have no way to know whether it is actually from God or is the product of mere human invention. Marsilius's argument in 2.19, then, has implications that speak against his being "a believer," but he surely does not parade this conclusion, nor does he bring his readers to think unorthodox thoughts. Indeed, the surface thrust of the chapter tends to validate the authority of the canonic books. There is nothing comparable in Machiavelli's books.

Strauss thus subtly displays Machiavelli's antitheological passion and its absence in Marsilius, but does he help us understand the source of this passion and thus the ultimate motive, as he understand it, for Machiavelli's departure from the tradition of Western political philosophy? Here we meet with real difficulties in reading Strauss, for he writes with an amazing reserve. He reminds much of Montesquieu, who said of a particularly important topic: "But we must not always so exhaust a subject that one leaves nothing for the reader to do. It is not a question of making him read but of making him think" (*Spirit of the Laws* 11.20). Strauss makes us both read and think.

Strauss's first formulation of the antitheological motivation for Machiavelli's thinking appeared in his essay "What Is Political Philosophy?," written several years before *Thoughts on Machiavelli* and about a decade before the Marsilius essay where he repeats the point. In the earlier statement Strauss puts it like this: "I would then suggest that the narrowing of the horizon which Machiavelli was the first to effect, was caused, or at least facilitated, by anti-theological ire—a passion which we can understand but of which we cannot approve" ("WIPP," 44). Let us note in passing two differences between his earlier and later formulations of the thesis. First, Strauss first spoke of antitheological ire but later of antitheological passion. That difference appears to be blunted by his identification of that ire as a passion. The second difference may be related. In the "What Is Political Philosophy?" version of the thesis, Strauss backs away from the claim that antitheological ire motivated Machiavelli's philosophic turn. The *History* version lacks that hesitation: "anti-theological passion induced" Machiavelli to take "[his] extreme step." If we may take the later statement to be the more mature or considered formulation, we can conclude that Strauss came to a more nuanced appreciation for Machiavelli's undertaking. "Induced" is more precise than the ambiguity contained in "caused, or at least facilitated." "Induced" is weaker than "caused" but more focused than "facilitated." "Induced" can mean "led toward," but it is much less determinative than "caused." And it specifies the relation much more precisely than "facilitated."

Strauss is also much more forthcoming in supplying an explanation for Machiavelli's antitheological ire in the earlier statement. Christian charity, the transfigured form of moral virtue, raised the level of man's responsibility to his fellows, for one arguably had some sort of responsibility for the salvation of their souls. This "concern for the souls of others seemed to permit, nay to require courses of action which would have appeared to the classics, and which did appear to Machiavelli to be inhuman and cruel: Machiavelli speaks of the pious cruelty of Ferdinand of Aragon, and by implication of the Inquisition, in expelling the Marranos from Spain." It is perhaps not an accident that Strauss selects this particular example in this essay, originally delivered as a lecture in Jerusalem. In any case, as we noted in chapter 3, Strauss affirms that Machiavelli "seems to have diagnosed the great evils of religious persecution as a necessary consequence of the Christian principle, and ultimately of the Biblical principle. He tended to believe that a considerable increase in man's inhumanity was the unintended but not surprising consequence of man's aiming too high." The conclusion Strauss attributes to Machiavelli, then, is that it is better to aim lower "so that we shall not be forced to commit any bestialities not evidently required for the preservation of society and freedom" ("WIPP," 44).

Even though the 1972 Machiavelli essay is introduced by a statement very similar to what Strauss wrote earlier of Machiavelli's motives, there is no direct connection made in the later essay between Machiavelli's antitheological animus and pious cruelty. Strauss does not, for example, repeat the point about Ferdinand and the Marranos, or, more significantly, about the Inquisition as a response to the heightened moral demands within Christianity. He does repeat the conclusion he drew in the earlier presentation: Machiavelli "loathed oppression which is not in the service of the well-being of the people and of effective government" (*HPP*, 314–315). Duly expanded, this could be construed to endorse the earlier point about "pious cruelty," which is cruelty not in the service of the well-being of the people. Nonetheless, it is striking that Strauss does not in this case connect the point explicitly to Christian practices like the Inquisition or to Machiavelli's antitheological passion.

Strauss is more explicit—or closer to explicitness—about matters such as Christian pious cruelty in the first of our two paired essays. In his essay on Marsilius he emphasizes that Marsilius denies that under the divine law "it is permitted to coerce heretics or infidels." "No divine law as such has any coercive power in this world unless by virtue of a human law" (*HPP*, 289). Marsilius concedes that "the Christian human legislator, not as Christian but as human legislator, may use coercion against heretics and infidels in this world" (*HPP*, 289). Whether the legislator does so or not "will depend on his judgment" on what is needed to promote "virtuous conduct in this world," but not on what is needed to effectuate the divine law (*HPP*,

290). If Marsilius's legislator engages in such practices it would thus arguably meet Machiavelli's criterion of eschewing "oppression which is not
in the service of the well-being of the people." That is, it would not be the
gratuitous or unnecessary (so far as mortal rulers can judge such things)
cruelty that Strauss said aroused Machiavelli's antitheological ire.

Marsilius too opposed such gratuitous religion-inspired oppression and
went to lengths to promulgate a doctrine of ecclesial power designed to
prevent it. From the example of Marsilius, Strauss thus shows that one
can oppose and even perhaps hate such policies allegedly in service to the
divine laws and yet not be moved by antitheological passion or ire. Accordingly in the 1972 restatement on Machiavelli Strauss retreats from the
earlier account of what moves Machiavelli.

But does he have something to put in its place? We believe he does, but
in order to see it we must carefully follow out some of his hints. At one
point in his Machiavelli essay, Strauss engages in one of those practices that
earned him the bemused or irritated attention of his fellow scholars—the
numerology that led him to count chapters and look for centers of lists. In
this case he is looking for an explanation of the significance of the number
26 in Machiavelli's writings. He concludes that 26 ("twice thirteen") "might
mean both good luck and bad luck, hence altogether: luck, *fortuna*" (*HPP*,
311). In this context he asserts that 26 is thus linked to Machiavelli's "theology." Since Machiavelli's theology is intimately tied to his antitheology,
the same number 26 can stand for or point toward that kind of theology
Machiavelli opposes. If we follow out Strauss's suggestion we might turn
first to the various chapters that are multiples of 13 or 26 in Machiavelli's
writings, which Strauss does, with striking results for understanding
Machiavelli on theology, as we saw in Strauss's discussion of Machiavelli's
lone New Testament quotation. But we are particularly interested in trying
to understand Strauss's attribution of antitheological passion to Machiavelli, which is not a claim that Machiavelli himself makes. Turning to paragraph 26 of Strauss's essay, we indeed find the answer we are seeking.

In order to understand that paragraph we must find the proper context
for it as set in the Marsilius essay. Marsilius promulgated what he considered a "cure" for the "disease" he found in Christian Europe, the corruption
of political life by the church. The cure was to be the demonstration within
the confines of the Christian law that "the action of the priest is the most
perfect of all" the elements in the city, including the rulers. This was one of
the places where, on the basis of Christian doctrine, Marsilius found Aristotle wanting, for Aristotle held that "the action of the priest is less noble

or perfect than the action of the rulers" (*HPP*, 279). Marsilius modifies Aristotle by elevating the status of the priesthood far higher than Aristotle left it. But the true basis for this greater dignity of the priests means that the priests cannot rule or share in secular government or possess any coercive powers whatever. To repeat a passage from Strauss that we have already cited, but that is crucial in our present context: "In the Christian law ... the action of the priest ... is the most perfect of all. But this action requires a spirit and a way of life which are incompatible with rulership for it requires contempt for the world and the utmost humility" (*HPP*, 287–88). Marsilius hoped to reform Christendom by removing the priests from the political equation by teaching the forgotten truth about the priesthood and the relation of the ecclesial to the secular authorities. If the priests would follow the path of humility, poverty, and obedience, then, Marsilius suggests, the grave disease of the age could be cured.

Strauss's twenty-sixth paragraph takes up book 3, chapter 1, of the *Discourses*, the chapter or quasi-chapter Strauss listed as the central one of the five he would cover in the second half of his essay. That chapter presents the well-known thesis that "if one wishes a sect or a republic to live long, it is necessary to draw it back often toward its beginning" (*Discourses* 3.1, title). Machiavelli discusses three types of mixed bodies—republics, sects, and kingdoms. Strauss pays the most attention to the sects. Treating "our religion" as one among all the other "worldly things" he discusses in his chapter, Machiavelli claims that if Christianity "had not been drawn back toward its beginning by Saint Francis and Saint Dominick," it would by Machiavelli's time have been "altogether eliminated." Those two saints "with poverty and the example of the life of Christ ... brought back into the minds of men what had already been eliminated there" (3.1.1–4). They had renewed and thus preserved Christianity.

The character of this renewal bears a marked resemblance to Marsilius's agenda of reform. He too would call the priests back to the original poverty and humility of Christ, the apostles, and the early church. Without his noticing it, Marsilius's solutions had already been put into effect by Francis and Dominic, but the results that Machiavelli saw were completely different from, indeed the opposite of, what Marsilius sought. Rather than taming the church hierarchy and peeling it away from politics, Machiavelli thought the monastic reforms "were so powerful that they are the cause that the dishonesty of the prelates and of the heads of the religion do not ruin it" (3.1.4). Reforms of the type sought by Marsilius led only to the further entrenchment and solidification of the clergy's political position. The reform did not merely leave the status quo intact but made things worse: "the Franciscans and the Dominicans live still in poverty and have so great credit with the people through confession and preaching that they convince the people that it is evil to speak evil of evil and that it is good to live in obedience to the prelates, and if the prelates sin, to leave them for punishment to God" (3.1.4; Strauss's translation, *HPP*, 310). The piety inspired in the people by the reforms allowed the church leaders to get away with being scoundrels. Indeed, it encouraged them: "Thus the prelates do the worst they can, for they do not fear the punishment they do not see and in which they do not believe" (3.1.4).

One can feel Machiavelli's passion in these passages. It is passion compounded of anger at the successful hypocrisy of the prelates and the utter failure of the classically inspired solution promoted by Marsilius. As Strauss implicitly suggests, the reform instigated by Francis and Dominic did not go the full length of the reforms sought by Marsilius, for it "left intact the Christian hierarchy" (*HPP*, 310). Marsilius would have changed the hierarchy by making the prelacy subordinate to the church as the body of the faithful, and by cutting back on the pretensions to power of the prelacy, especially the papacy. But Machiavelli points to the utopian or unrealistic character of Marsilius's proposed solution: he would have restored the priesthood to its original piety, humility, and poverty, and, as the great embodiments of the way of Christ, affirm it to consist of the highest or most perfect kinds of men. And yet at the same time he would have elevated the great body of the people over it in the form of the church laity or general councils, which were supposed to prevent the emergence of the hybrid church of which Machiavelli speaks, a church composed of pious and admired monks and priests topped off by a rich, proud, and corrupt hierarchy.

Machiavelli's passion is antitheological because the arrangement he despises is made possible by the Christian promise. Recall Machiavelli's quotation of the Magnificat. The Christian God favors and affirms the poor and the lowly. He offers consolation here and promises of rewards in the life to come. The poor and lowly by necessity are greatly moved by those who are poor and lowly by choice, i.e., the Franciscans and Dominicans. The poor and lowly will not readily accept themselves as superior to those who validate their hopes and both allay and arouse their fears. The Marsilian agenda, Machiavelli believes, is self-contradictory and unachievable, as history has shown.

Machiavelli's passion, as Strauss understands it, is not aroused merely by the church hierarchy's taking advantage of the gullibility, the decency, and the piety of the people. He frequently praises the Roman nobility for similar deceptions. He does not oppose the "very natural" desire to acquire—it would do no good to do so. But, as Strauss points out, "what prompted [Machiavelli in his seeking of new modes and orders] was the natural desire that he always had, to do those things that in his opinion bring about the common benefit of each" (HPP 306, quoting chap. 1, proem; also see TM, 282–83). Machiavelli desires "the common benefit," but the Christian order he describes in 3.1 spectacularly fails to achieve that. The people receive no real return for their willingness to indulge and support the manner of life of the higher clergy. Machiavelli's "natural desire" is thwarted by the present theological-political order, and the best the classical tradition can do, in the person of Marsilius, is to propose solutions that make matters worse. Machiavelli's "anti-theological passion" is thus constituted by his natural desire to benefit his fellows, compounded with his insight into the way the Christian order frustrates that desire and is immune or apparently immune from genuine reform (though see TM, 286–87). Every reform that remains within the orbit of Christianity and classical political philosophy necessarily fails and even makes matters worse.

Substance

Recall that in his thematic statement for the paired Marsilius and Machiavelli essays Strauss put the issue into this nutshell: "When antitheological passion induced a thinker to take the extreme step of questioning the supremacy of contemplation, political philosophy broke with the classical tradition, and took on an entirely new character. The thinker in question was Machiavelli" (HPP, 294). Despite its "entirely new character," however, modern philosophy as initiated by Machiavelli "is philosophic indeed but no longer Greek." Although he suggested in some of his earlier writings that modern thought is not truly philosophic, by the time of his Machiavelli essay Strauss is certain that it is. But it is different. In this place he describes that difference differently from any other time in his career: it is "no longer Greek," as if Greekness defined the tradition of political philosophy prior to Machiavelli. Here Strauss sounds more like Heidegger, or like a garden-variety historicist who derives the character of a given body of thought from the cultural-historical nexus from which it emerges. Strauss's assertion is especially striking, for as we have emphasized, he makes so much of the Socratic turn. The Socratic tradition surely shares much with prior or non-

Socratic Greek thinkers, but Strauss was more impressed with what it did not share, with its return to common sense or sobriety.

However, all Greek philosophic thought, as philosophic, shared a recognition of nature and therewith of the distinction between nature and convention and an affirmation of nature as normative. If this is an adequate formulation of what Strauss means in pointing to the Greekness of pre-Machiavellian philosophy, then we have an important pointer toward what he sees as central to modern philosophy as a whole: a shift in the understanding of nature and its relation to convention such that nature is no longer the norm. At the end of the Marsilius essay, Strauss promised to explain the "extreme step" by which Machiavelli broke with the classical tradition. That step consisted in "questioning the supremacy of contemplation." At the beginning of the Machiavelli essay, in its first paragraph to be precise, Strauss indicates a somewhat broader intention in his treatment of the thought of the Florentine: "It is in trying to understand modern philosophy that we come across Machiavelli" (HPP, 297). These two ways of stating his intention are not at all contradictory, but they are somewhat different. In the one case the focus is on Machiavelli and the step he was induced to take by his antitheological passion. In the second formulation the concern with Machiavelli is not the chief focus but is instrumental to this larger enterprise—"to understand modern philosophy." We cannot help but notice also that Strauss speaks here of "modern philosophy" altogether, not modern *political* philosophy. That coheres with our earlier suggestion that Strauss is speaking of something more comprehensive than the political philosophy of the Socratics.

We cannot allow Strauss's broadening of this issue to distract us from our primary task. Now that we understand the nature of Machiavelli's antitheological passion, we need to understand how that leads him to question "the supremacy of contemplation" and how that, rather than "lowering the sights" or seeking "actualization" per se, defines Machiavellian modernity. But we now have a further task: to understand how the modern philosophy Machiavelli originates breaks with Greek philosophy, as understood above (and as developed in chapter 3) and yet remains "philosophic indeed."

MARSILIUS

Strauss's formulation of the Machiavellian achievement clearly implies that Marsilius did not challenge "the supremacy of contemplation," but developed the novel features of his political philosophy (relative to Aristotle's) while maintaining the supremacy of contemplation or the philosophic life. That inference is indeed explicitly confirmed by Strauss:

> As regards the principles of political philosophy, Marsilius presents himself as a strict follower of Aristotle. . . . He explicitly agrees with Aristotle regarding the purpose of the commonwealth: the commonwealth exists for the sake of the good life, and the good life consists in being engaged in the activity becoming a free man, i.e., in the exercise of the virtues of the practical as well as of the speculative soul. While practical or civic felicity "seems to be" the end of human acts, in fact the activity of the metaphysician is more perfect than the activity of the prince who is the active or political man *par excellence*. (*HPP*, 277)

On the basis of reason, Marsilius affirms contemplation as the *highest* or "most perfect"; on the basis of revelation or alleged revelation, he affirms that "the action of the priest is the most perfect of all," in particular more perfect than "the action of the ruler" (*HPP*, 279). But that conclusion holds, we have seen, "in the 'law of the Christians,' and only in that law" (*HPP*, 279).

In order to pursue his anticlerical agenda, Strauss maintains, Marsilius modifies Aristotle in several more or less significant ways. Most importantly, he develops a far more democratic or more popular-sovereignty-oriented theory than Aristotle did, and he asks less of the political regime with regard to pursuing virtue. In these ways he "lowers his sights" and appears to approach Machiavelli. Marsilius makes these modifications in service to the chief requirements of his project. That project set him the following problem: "how to reconcile the Aristotelian principle (the men dedicated to the most noble practical activity ought to rule in their own right) with the Christian principle (the activity of the priest is more noble than that of the gentleman)" (*HPP*, 280).

The Marsilian solution can be understood in these terms: "he needed for his anticlerical agenda a populist basis because he had to appeal from the accepted opinions regarding the Church to the New Testament. . . . The New Testament apparently gives some support to the view that decisions in such matters rest with the whole body of the faithful as distinguished from the priests alone. Marsilius' 'whole body of the citizens' is merely the philosophic or rational counterpart of the 'the whole body of the faithful'" (*HPP*, 284–85). Strauss attributes that explanation to "some scholars" and he finds it "defensible," but he also thinks it does not go far enough. One needs, for example, to notice the way in which "Marsilius' populist teaching" is only "provisional or . . . tentative" (*HPP*, 284). That is to say, Marsilius moves back toward the more aristocratic Aristotelian doctrine in almost every part of his theory. The core of Strauss's reading of Marsilius as a Socratic, however, lies in his understanding of the Paduan's treatment of the relation between moral and intellectual virtue. Marsilius responds to an obscurity in Aristotle's treatment of moral virtue in a way similar to what Maimonides did. Marsilius thus "deviates" from the way Aristotle rhetorically or "for practical reasons" presented the virtues in his *Ethics*, but he agrees in principle with Aristotle in his *Politics*, which Strauss considers the more revealing statement of Aristotle's position on virtue (*HPP*, 295; cf. chapter 6 above). The central point Strauss insists on is that Marsilius "deduces the necessity of those [moral] virtues from the purposes of civil society, and the necessity of that purpose from the end or ends of man [i.e., intellectual virtue]." Despite his gestures in the direction Machiavelli is to take, Marsilius remains firmly in the camp of classical political philosophy by retaining the notion that the perfection of man is philosophy or contemplation, even while affirming with Maimonides that "the only law properly so-called is the human law which is directed toward the well-being of the body" (*HPP*, 294).

ANTITHEOLOGICAL PASSION AND THE
SUPREMACY OF CONTEMPLATION

Strauss presents at least sketches of accounts of Machiavelli's "questioning of the supremacy of contemplation" on three different occasions. In the lecture "The Modern Solutions" in "What Is Political Philosophy?," Strauss points out that "by Machiavelli's time the classical tradition had undergone profound changes. The contemplative life had found its home in monasteries" ("WIPP," 43). Although Strauss does not explicitly draw the connection, his idea seems to be this: moved by "anti-theological ire," Machiavelli rejected all things Christian; contemplation, now attached to the Christian monastic life, was a victim of his wholesale angry opposition to Christianity ("WIPP," 44).

In *Thoughts on Machiavelli* Strauss develops a much richer account of Machiavelli's turn against contemplation or philosophy as the highest human end. In this version Strauss is less concerned to explore the origin of Machiavelli's questioning the supremacy of contemplation and instead aims to explore the paradox of Machiavelli's notion of the ultimate human good. As Strauss presents it in *Thoughts*, according to Machiavelli "the most excellent man, as distinguished from the most excellent captain, or soldier of war or love, acquires full satisfaction and immunity to the power of chance through knowledge of 'the world'" (*TM*, 290). This knowledge revealed to Machiavelli "the delusions of glory and the limitations of the political." There is a diremption between Machiavelli's understanding of the highest excellence of human being as human being and his understanding of the highest goods available to the political community. Machiavelli's grasp of that diremption is not like the understanding of an apparently similar diremption Strauss attributes to the "Greeks." The city, Strauss regularly emphasizes, cannot philosophize, but the classical philosophers thought of the political good in relation to their understanding of philosophy as the highest human good. They conceived the political as a dimmed reflection of, or a preparation for, or means to the highest good of philosophy. "The classics understood the moral-political phenomena in the light of man's highest virtue or perfection, the life of the philosopher or the contemplative life. The superiority of peace to war or of leisure to business is a reflection of the superiority of thinking to doing or making. . . . Philosophy transcends the city, and the worth of the city depends ultimately on its openness, or deference, to philosophy" (*TM*, 295–96).

Machiavelli's "new moral continent" consists in severing that link between the good of philosophy that he himself, according to Strauss, continued to recognize, and the political. "Machiavelli's philosophizing . . . remains on the whole within the limits set by the city qua closed to philosophy. Accepting the ends of the *demos* as beyond appeal, he seeks for the best means conducive to those ends." Philosophy no longer exists within his political philosophy as an end or measure for political life, but rather is presented as a powerful means or ally to the *demos* in their search after their ends. "He achieves the decisive turn toward the notion of philosophy according to which its purpose is to relieve man's estate or to increase man's power or to guide man toward the rational society, the bond of which is enlightened self-interest or the comfortable self-preservation of each of its members" (*TM*, 296). In these passages we come to understand Strauss's terminology in his programmatic formulation in the Marsilius essay of Machiavelli's achievement: he questioned the primacy of contemplation. Sometimes Strauss uses that term in contrast to the questing or zetetic character of Socratic philosophizing. But here he is using it to stand for the philosophical goal of understanding for its own sake rather than as an instrument for increasing human power. Machiavelli breaks with what we might crudely call both the Aristotelian and the Socratic versions of the philosophic life.

Despite his perhaps surprising effort to affirm the high place of philosophy in the classical sense in Machiavelli's thinking, Strauss maintains that "one is entitled to say that philosophy and its status is obfuscated not only in Machiavelli's teaching but in his thought as well. . . . As a consequence he is unable to give a clear account of his own doing. What is greatest in him cannot be properly appreciated on the basis of his own narrow view of the nature of men" (*TM*, 294). Strauss is aware—and makes his readers aware—of the obfuscation of the role philosophy plays in Machiavelli's thought that results from his refusal to construe the political in light of the transpolitical. But in *Thoughts on Machiavelli* Strauss does not explain *why* Machiavelli did not take account of his own experience of the satisfactions of philosophy.

It is our contention that the 1972 Machiavelli essay, when paired with the 1963 Marsilius essay, means to solve that puzzle, for it is here that Strauss makes clear the ground of Machiavelli's decision. Strauss wants his readers to view Machiavelli's project in light of Machiavelli's perceptions of the failure of Marsilius's somewhat similar effort according to which recalling the priests to the "true Christian way" would resolve the theological-political crisis. The examples of Francis and Dominic persuaded Machiavelli that such reforms would not solve the problem. Their example of the "true way" only attached the people more firmly to the church and reconciled them to the abuses and hypocrisy of the church hierarchy. More would be needed to wean the people away from their obeisance to the higher clergy and their willingness to leave them to the judgment of God (*Discourses* 3.1).

Machiavelli's political philosophy represents the effort to give the people more. His philosophy would look not to what men ought to do, but to what they do, what most men do (*HPP*, 299). Those men previously seen as extraordinary would be interpreted along the same lines as the ordinary run of men. The desires to acquire and maintain, the desire for security and comfortable preservation would be taken as the horizon for construing the human world. Whatever might seem higher would be analyzed into a modification or concealed version of the "natural desires." Machiavelli preconceives the political and moral spheres so that "the ends of the *demos*" are "beyond reproach." All ends that appear higher than those ends are in fact illusions, "grounds for imagined kingdoms and republics." Out of his "antitheological passion" and in order to defeat the hold of Christianity on the world, Machiavelli not only endorses the Averroist understanding and critique of religion but goes well beyond the Averroists and rejects the moral orientation of the Averroists and other Socratic philosophers, who looked at the moral and political in light of the transpolitical good of philosophy as the highest human life.

The Marsilius and the Machiavelli essays together thus clarify one theme left obscure in *Thoughts on Machiavelli*. But there is another, related issue that is not yet clear. What does Strauss believe led Machiavelli to set to the side what he knew to be true—that the philosophic life or the life of understanding is in fact the highest life? Strauss at least suggests that Machiavelli was moved by benevolence or a kind of humanity toward his fellow human beings. Machiavelli suggests as much in the proem to book 1 of the *Discourses*: as Strauss restates it, "what prompted" Machiavelli in his Columbus-like quest for "unknown waters and lands" was the "natural desire that he always had to do those things that in his opinion bring about the common benefit of each" (*HPP*, 306).

Machiavelli, Strauss suggests, "was a generous man," who at the same time knew "very well that what passes for generosity in political life is most of the time nothing but shrewd calculation" (*HPP*, 315). But what about the case of Machiavelli himself? Is his generosity too a matter of shrewd calculation? In the Machiavelli essay Strauss does not directly address that question, but in *Thoughts* he does. "If the desire to work for the common good is natural in Machiavelli, one should expect that it is by nature effective, if in different degrees, in all men. This expectation is not borne out by his teaching. What then is 'the factual truth' of Machiavelli's natural desire?" (*TM*, 286). Strauss's first surmise is that Machiavelli "hopes to be rewarded for his achievement. The reward would consist of nothing but praise," ultimately "the highest glory [that] goes to the discoverer of the all-important truth, of the truth regarding man and society, of the new modes and orders which are in accordance with nature" (*TM*, 288). But, as we have seen, Strauss attributes to Machiavelli a "clear awareness" of the delusions of glory and of the limitations of political honor. "Immortal glory is impossible, and what is called immortal glory depends on chance. Hence to see the highest good in glory means to deny the possibility of happiness" (289). Machiavelli thus does not place the highest good for himself in glory; "knowledge of the world" rather gives Machiavelli his satisfaction and is responsible for a kind of "humanity" in him (*TM*, 290). His good—what's in it for him—is thus not his natural benevolence or his desire for glory. But if it is the desire for knowledge, he is like the Socratics. Why then should he choose to set this aside in his political philosophy and take the way of the *demos* entirely? The answer we have reached thus far is—his antitheological passion. Machiavelli's reason was swept aside by his passion.

But this does not appear to be Strauss's last word either. In the Machia-velli essay he subtly incorporates his interpretation of Machiavelli's analysis according to which philosophy is the highest human good. He calls atten-tion to Machiavelli's extravagant praise for the Roman captain Camillus; going well beyond Livy's already strong praise, "Machiavelli . . . calls Camil-lus 'the most prudent of all Roman captains'" (*HPP*, 315). Referring to *Dis-courses* 3.31, Strauss points out that "Machiavelli traces Camillus' superiority to the whims of fortune to his superior knowledge of the world." That is, "knowledge of the world" is the basis for genuine freedom and satisfaction, just what Strauss argued about Machiavelli in *Thoughts*. Strauss is treat-ing Camillus as a kind of stand-in for Machiavelli. But not as a complete stand-in. As much as Machiavelli praises Camillus, he also identifies a grave error Camillus committed, an error that caused the populace to exile him. Strauss identifies Camillus's error in chief as staging a triumph in which his chariot was drawn by four white horses. This gave the people the impres-sion that he was claiming to be equal to a god. According to Machiavelli this action produced hatred in the people. "Appearing proud and swollen . . . cannot be more hateful to peoples, and especially to free ones. Although no disadvantage arises for them from that pride and that pomp, nonethe-less they hold whoever uses them in hatred. A prince ought to guard him-self from that as from a reef, because to draw on hatred without profit for oneself is a policy altogether rash and hardly prudent" (*Discourses* 3.23).

Strauss believes that Camillus's "rather shocking act of *superbia* was in Machiavelli's eyes a sign of Camillus' magnanimity," i.e., "of claiming high honors for oneself with understanding that one is worthy of them" (*HPP*, 315, 296). Recall that Strauss presents Camillus as a stand-in for Machiavelli or, probably better put, as a stand-in for the "supremacy of contemplation" or the philosophic life as the only life capable of conquering *fortuna*. As such a stand-in, Camillus symbolically raises the same claim that the clas-sical philosophers claimed for themselves, the claim that their life, the life of philosophy, is the peak of human existence and is indeed divine or god-like. Such claims, Machiavelli tells us, needlessly arouse the peoples' hatred. That is to say, philosophers who raise claims on behalf of philosophy do not cure but play into what Strauss called the tension between philosophy and the city. The exile of Camillus is the equivalent of the death of Socrates.

Machiavelli greatly admires Camillus, but he eschews the way of Camil-lus. He does not raise a claim to the divinity of the way of contemplation; he suppresses all public claims on behalf of philosophy and instead gives him-self without reserve to the claims of the *demos*. But at the same time he has a silent reservation on behalf of philosophy. He forgets philosophy for the sake of better securing philosophy from the hatred of the people. The problem of philosophy and the city had indeed been transformed by Machiavelli's time. Philosophy had won a more or less secure place by becoming "handmaid to theology," i.e., putting itself in the service of Christianity and thus ostensibly in the service of the people as affirmed and secured within Christianity, though actually at the service of the church hierarchy, who were the real beneficiaries of the Christian order.

Machiavelli, like Marsilius, wished to free philosophy from its subservience to the church and to enable it to regain its stance of true freedom from the shadows of the cave. Marsilius's example was instructive for Machiavelli. He did not succeed in his attempt to tame the church—quite the contrary—or to secure the independence of philosophy. Disrupting the existing accommodation between philosophy and the reigning theological-political order, he suffered the punishment of excommunication and required the protection of strong political allies to preserve himself. Marsilius followed the way of Camillus. In order to secure philosophy as an independent enterprise and to better secure the "common benefit of each," Machiavelli found a "new path" toward resolving the tension between philosophy and the city. Thus Strauss could treat modern philosophy as initiated by Machiavelli as a "solution to the problem of political philosophy." It is the solution that forgets or ignores the true point of philosophy in order to put philosophy at the service of the *demos* and thus to erase the people's fears, suspicions, and potential hatred of it. Ironically, it is Strauss's view that Machiavelli decided as he did against philosophy for the sake of philosophy itself.

Philosophic but Not Greek

Unlike philosophy departments today, but like real and recognized philosophers of the past such as Spinoza, Bacon, and Hobbes (*HPP*, 298–99, 367; cf. *LAM*, 246–47), Strauss pronounces Machiavelli's thoughts to be "philosophic indeed." The reason for that should now be evident. Given the way that Strauss understands and describes philosophy in such places as "What Is Political Philosophy?," Machiavelli, as read by Strauss, surely qualifies. The philosopher is marked not by adherence to this or that doctrine or by promulgating doctrines on this or that topic but rather by the quest for knowledge of the whole, by the attempt to replace opinion by knowledge.

Moreover, according to Strauss, Machiavelli, not unequivocally to be sure, shares the philosophic commitment to philosophy as the highest or best life for a human being. It is the only life that gains one genuine freedom from the rule of *fortuna*. Machiavelli emphatically also qualifies as a *political* philosopher for Strauss: he appreciates the disparity between the philosopher and the city (as Strauss formulated it), and his philosophic activity was meant to respond to that disparity on behalf of both philosophy and public benefit. That is, he was not only a philosopher but a public-spirited one. That public-spiritedness distinguishes him from certain classes of thinkers to whom he is sometimes compared, such as the Sophists or the non-Socratic ancients like Epicurus and Lucretius (*HPP*, 316–17; *TM*, 292).

Strauss's concluding observation in the Machiavelli essay is thus that "Machiavelli and Socrates make a common front against the Sophists" (*HPP*, 317). But that should not blind us to the further claim that he also raises: although Machiavelli's thought is philosophic, it is "no longer Greek" (*HPP*, 297). If our previous conjecture is correct as to the distinguishing marks of "Greek" philosophy, Socratic and non-Socratic alike, then this claim would amount to the view that Machiavelli either no longer distinguishes between nature and convention, or that he no longer treats nature as the standard or norm. For the Florentine, "justice is precisely not, as Augustine had said, the *fundamentum regnorum*; the foundation of justice is injustice; the foundation of morality is immorality; the foundation of legitimacy is illegitimacy or revolution; the foundation of freedom is tyranny. At the beginning there is Terror, not Harmony or Love" (*HPP*, 302). Nature, or what is originally given, is not a standard to follow but a deplorable situation to escape. Strauss expands the point, significantly in his twenty-sixth paragraph: "at the beginning there is not Love but Terror; Machiavelli's wholly new teaching is based on this alleged insight (which anticipates Hobbes' doctrine of the state of nature)" (*HPP*, 310). This insight, in turn, is prompted by Machiavelli's location within a Christian society. The reform effected by Francis and Dominic, it will be recalled, only entrenched the hypocritical rule of the clergy by convincing the people that "it is evil to speak evil of evil and that it is good to live in obedience to the prelates, and if the prelates sin, to leave them for punishment to God" (*HPP*, 310; quoting *Discourses* 3.1). Strauss comments: "The Christian command or counsel not to resist evil is based on the premise that the beginning or principle is love. That command or counsel can only lead to the utmost disorder or else to evasion" (*HPP*, 311). Machiavelli sees two things about this premise. It validates a particularly shabby moral and political order and it readily turns into its apparent opposite—pious cruelty. Although he does not say so explicitly, Strauss suggests that Machiavelli's endorsement of the opposite, characteristically modern principle derives from a perhaps over-hasty negation of the principle of love affirmed in the Christian order.

According to Machiavelli, human beings construct justice, morality, legitimacy via their political orders for the sake of escaping nature. The manmade or the conventional is simply superior to the natural. Of course, Machiavelli endorses the Baconian principle that nature can be conquered only if one obeys her ("WIPP," 47). But even so, it is nature in the form of undeniable force and not nature as a source of norms that retains power in Machiavelli's thinking. So far as he sets in motion the line of thinking that orders nature and the whole in this manner, Machiavelli is the key to "trying to understand modern philosophy" (*HPP*, 297; also see 311). The moderns thus differ, according to Strauss, not only from the Socratics but from the premodern non-Socratics as well. To bring out that point is one of Strauss's main intentions in his essay on Lucretius, the chief source that we have for ancient Epicureanism. Lucretius, like Machiavelli, recognizes "the defective character of the world." But "the realization of the badness of the world does not induce Lucretius for a moment to think of rebellion or conquest" (*LAM*, 96).

Strauss recognized a kind of inconsistency in Machiavelli's thinking on this very topic, however (see *TM*, 289–99). So far as the Florentine reaffirms the philosophic life and the philosophic quest, he would seem not to wholeheartedly commit himself to his own chief insight. That is just Strauss's point. Machiavelli's thought is marked by willful blindness to himself. "He is unable to give a clear account of his own doing" (*TM*, 294). In the Machiavelli essay Strauss expresses this thought via his observation that Machiavelli looks to Xenophon more than to any other Greek philosopher, but in looking to Xenophon, "he takes no notice of Xenophon's Socratic writings. . . . Half of Xenophon, in Xenophon's view the better half, is suppressed by Machiavelli" (*HPP*, 316; see also *TM*, 291). It is the "suppression" of Socrates, and by extension of the Socratic in himself, that leads Machiavelli to believe in his new moral universe. "It is true that in Machiavelli everything appears in a new light, but that is due, not to an enlargement of the horizon, but to a narrowing of it" (*HPP*, 316). In light of that insight into the character of Machiavelli's thinking, Strauss concludes that "many modern discoveries regarding man have this character" (*HPP*, 316). Machiavelli does indeed help us in the effort of "trying to understand modern philosophy."

Strauss's alternative to what we might call the Machiavellian turn is visible in one of his most terse and yet revealing expressions at the very end of *Thoughts on Machiavelli*. "It would seem that the notion of the beneficence of nature or the primacy of the good must be restored by being rethought through a return to the fundamental experiences from which it is derived. For while 'philosophy must beware of wishing to be edifying,' it is of necessity edifying" (*TM*, 299, quoting Hegel, *Phenomenology of Spirit*, preface).

CHAPTER EIGHT

Strauss on Locke and the Law of Nature

Machiavelli, according to Strauss, introduced modernity, but he needed many lieutenants and eventually even foot soldiers for modernity to triumph. And he got them. Bacon, Spinoza, Hobbes, Bayle, and many others carried on the Machiavellian project, though often in much modified form. Strauss also identified John Locke as a lieutenant or even a general in Machiavelli's army and a particularly successful one. His success, Strauss thought, derived from two features of his thought. In place of Machiavelli's muscular and martial form of modern philosophy, Locke substituted an economic solution. As Strauss once said, economism is Machiavellianism come of age ("WIPP," 49). The Lockean form of modernity was much more attractive to the many than the Machiavellian form and far less provocative. Locke's other major innovation was to clothe his doctrine in much more traditional garb. He regularly appealed to what seemed a version of traditional natural law, and he cast his argument in many places in theistic terms. Locke could be and indeed often was taken for some sort of Christian Aristotelian. In *Natural Right and History* Strauss argued that this appearance was mostly a clever subterfuge. Locke was, if not quite an orthodox follower of Hobbes, far closer to him and thus to Machiavelli than he was normally taken to be.

In a letter to Willmoore Kendall, Strauss commented that of all the unorthodox readings of canonical political philosophers he had produced, none had caused as much controversy and raised as much ire as his interpretation of Locke in *Natural Right and History*. Strauss's later essay on Locke in *What Is Political Philosophy?* needs to be seen in the context of that controversy, for the original *Natural Right and History* chapter had been written prior to the 1954 public appearance of the text on the law of nature that was found in Locke's papers. The new text, published a year after *Natural Right*, was relevant because, as the editor of the Norton Critical Edition of Locke's political writings put it, it "described a theologically based natural law theory that rejected Hobbesean self-interest as the basis of moral obligation."[1] That is to say, Locke's *Essays on the Law of Nature* was seen as a definitive rebuttal to Strauss's version of Locke.[2]

Vindication

Strauss published his Locke essay in the *American Political Science Review* in June of 1958.[3] It was the most recent of all the essays reprinted in *What Is Political Philosophy?* In connection with writing that essay Strauss had offered a seminar on Locke in the winter quarter of 1958. It is clear from the transcript of that course that Strauss was just then working through *Essays* and no doubt wrote his essay then or soon thereafter.

In neither his seminar nor his essay does Strauss show any signs of realizing that Locke's *Essays* would be taken by many to be the definitive refutation of his very unorthodox Locke, but whether aware of that or not, Strauss nonetheless oriented his treatment of the newly published text around the issue as it would emerge in the literature. His main theses were in effect a response in advance to the critics who would rely on *Essays*. That text, Strauss maintained, appeared to present a version of traditional natural law doctrine reminiscent in many places of Thomas Aquinas and Richard Hooker (*WIPP*, 198). Locke's text also, however, "deviates from the tradition" in a number of ways (198). Strauss was also impressed with the number of outright and elementary contradictions that were to be found in it (204). In line with his general approach to reading, he concluded that such contradictions were "deliberate" and intended "to indicate [Locke's] thought rather than to reveal it" (206). Strauss concluded that Locke "indicated" not an endorsement of traditional natural law but a subtle critique, or at least a raising of serious questions and reservations about it (206–14). In place of the traditional doctrine, Locke pointed toward an alternative — much more Hobbesian — natural law doctrine (214–20). Thus, completely contrary to the critics who saw *Essays* as the refutation of Strauss's chapter on Locke, Strauss viewed it as the decisive confirmation. Indeed, Strauss thought his reading so compelling that he offered an explanation of why Locke failed to publish these essays: "he rightly did not publish [them], because here the self-contradictions, and the other shocking things are so obvious" that they would be readily spotted and would prevent the work from having "the tremendous success which the *Treatises* [on government] had."[4] Strauss believed, in other words, that *Essays* was too crude, too obvious to serve Locke's purpose of moving his readers subtly away from traditional and toward modern natural law.

If Strauss's main concern was to vindicate his *Natural Right and History* reading of Locke, then his treatment of the last of Locke's *Essays* should have sufficed, for this essay was taken, as Strauss seems to have anticipated it would be, as the decisive proof that Locke was not the kind of thinker Strauss had claimed him to be. Paul Sigmund, for example, refers to the last essay as the place where Locke "rejected Hobbesean self-interest as the basis of moral obligation."[5] That essay would seem to do what Sigmund says; it is addressed to the question "Is the private interest of each the basis of the law of nature?" to which Locke answers no. Since Hobbesian natural law is a series of moral rules derived by reason conducive to the preservation (or more broadly the interest) of each, it certainly appears that Locke's essay repudiates Hobbesian natural law.

But Strauss shows that such a conclusion would be based on a careless reading of Locke's text. Strauss traces Locke's step-by-step definition and redefinition of the question he is addressing in this text until, it turns out, Locke is refuting a claim that is not at all the Hobbesian position. Locke begins with the Carneadean challenge to natural law (or right): "there is no natural law [or right—*jus naturale*], for all, both men and animals, are driven to their own interest [*utilitas*] by nature's guidance" (*ELN*, 204). Nature prompts men not to right but to their own interest. Locke is very admiring of Carneades, so much so that he does not dwell on Carneades himself but focuses on some very zealous followers of his. The followers lack Carneades's "virtues" and "gifts of mind," and thus are easier targets. For reasons related to their inferiority and resentment, they reformulate Carneades's maxim about natural law: "every right and equity [should be] determined not by an extraneous law but by each person's own self-interest" (*ELN*, 205). As Strauss points out, "Locke does not even attempt to refute Carneades' assertion that each man is by nature driven to seek his own interest and not to act justly" (*WIPP*, 216); what he does attempt to refute is a particular interpretation of the position of Carneades's inferior followers. That interpretation proves to be both easy to refute and largely irrelevant to the Hobbesian law of nature.

In a remarkable sleight of hand, Strauss points out, Locke identifies "the *basis* of natural law with the *basic* natural law" (*WIPP*, 216, emphasis added). Locke's translation of the Hobbesian thesis is almost comical. He transforms what in Hobbes is a right (a liberty) into a duty (an obligation); that is, Hobbes says: in a state of nature it is morally permissible to do whatever, in your judgment, it takes to secure your preservation (your interest). This right, however, is shown by Hobbes to lead to the famous state of war, which men find to be an unacceptable state. Thus in two stages he derives an escape from the state of war. The first stage is the generation of so-called laws of nature from the Hobbesian right of nature. These are rules that, if followed, lead to peaceful relations among men. Without government to enforce the rules, however, they cannot be maintained; therefore the laws of nature themselves point toward the second stage, the social contract creating the sovereign. Both the "laws of nature" and the contract depend on men's renouncing the original right of nature that grants them the liberty that produces the state of war. They must instead agree to obey a sovereign and his laws. The "basis" of the Hobbesian laws of nature is indeed the "private interest of each," for the laws are the rules that specify how to achieve what each most seeks—peace and the preservation to which peace conduces (cf. 200).

According to Locke's transformation, the Hobbesian escape from the state of nature would be impossible, indeed prohibited. To turn private interest from the *basis* of the law of nature into the *basic* law of nature commanding or requiring that each pursue what Hobbes said men have only a right or liberty to do means it is unlawful for men to renounce their rights to everything (their "private interest") and adhere to the rational rules that make for peace by obeying the sovereign. The numerous scholars who believe that *Essays on the Law of Nature*, especially the last essay, somehow refutes the Straussian Locke are thus quite mistaken.

It might appear that Strauss's aim in his essay is to reaffirm his Hobbesian reading of Locke, but that turns out to be only partly the case. He reaffirms his earlier view that Locke does not accept "the traditional natural law teaching" (*WIPP*, 214), but he also attempts to show that Locke does not precisely accept the thesis that "private interest is the basis of the law of nature." In the last of the *Essays* Strauss's Locke modifies the Hobbesian formulation because the "fundamental harmony between private interest and the law of nature . . . does not mean that that harmony is complete" (218). Strauss cites, as an instance, the Lockean doctrine of revolution. It protects against governmental misdeeds that arouse "the great body of the people," but it does not protect each and every individual, for some tyrannical acts affect only a few and do not arouse the opposition of the "great body of the people." Thus Strauss reformulates the Lockean position: "For all practical purposes it may therefore be better to say that the basis or end of society is not the private interest of each but the public interest, i.e., the interest of the large majority" (218). That reformulation allows Strauss to account for the maxim Locke endorsed in the *Two Treatises*—*Salus Populi suprema lex esto*—but the limits of his reformulation are indicated by his reaffirmation that the "root of the public interest is the private interest of each" (218).

Strauss identifies another significant shift away from Hobbes in Locke's presentation of the natural law. Hobbes, Strauss pointed out in an earlier essay, refused "to speak of laws ordering non-human beings" (*WIPP*, 175). Locke, however, "speaks of a natural law which cannot be transgressed" (203, 204) and which applies to nonhuman as well as human beings. Indeed, the law that cannot be transgressed and that governs much beside man is one of Strauss's great concerns in the Locke essay in *What Is Political Philosophy?*

Strauss thus uses the occasion of his essay to modify somewhat his position on Locke. Just as his essay on Hobbes in *What Is Political Philosophy?* is the locus for adjustment to his earlier reading of Hobbes, so he has revised his position on Locke. Perhaps the key to *What Is Political Philosophy?* as a book is not so much the title essay as the "Restatement on Xenophon's *Hiero*"—the collection is held together by its revisionist character. That in turn coheres with the title essay, for in that essay Strauss emphasizes the Socratic, i.e., necessarily incomplete, character of philosophy: it is not the possession of the whole truth and nothing but the truth but a quest, necessarily incomplete and hence always open to revision (*WIPP*, 11).

The original *APSR* version of the essay is quite helpful in capturing Strauss's chief strategy in dealing with Locke's *Essays*. The *APSR* version is nearly identical to the reprinted version, but with differences of three sorts. First, Strauss modified the paragraphing of the essay from 28 in the original to 17 in the reprinted text. Second, Strauss has edited the text slightly, so far as we can tell for style and readability. We have not found any of these slight modifications to affect the meaning of the text in any significant way. Third, and most important, the *APSR* version had section titles. The essay was divided into five parts, titled respectively: I. Description of Locke's early essays on Natural Law (paras. 1–4 of *WIPP* version); II. A Natural Law which cannot be transgressed (paras. 5–8); III. Is the Natural Law based on speculative principles? (paras. 9–11); IV. Is Natural Law duly promulgated? (paras. 12–13); V. An alternative to the traditional Natural Law teaching (paras. 14–17).

The section headings identify three different forms of what might be called natural law in Locke's text: the natural law that cannot be transgressed, i.e., laws like the law of gravity; the traditional "natural law proper, i.e., . . . a natural law which man can transgress"; and finally the quasi-Hobbesian sort of "law" we have already had occasion to discuss. Strauss makes sense of the "confusions" in Locke's text by claiming that he is speaking of these three different kinds of natural law without being explicit that that is what he is doing and without sorting out for the reader which claims belong to which law. The nontransgressible natural law allows Locke to speak of natural law in a much more extended—and confusing—sense than Hobbes did.

History of Political Philosophy

Strauss believes that the editor of *Essays*, Wolfgang von Leyden, falls short as an editor, translator, and interpreter of Locke's text because von Leyden is convinced before confronting the text that it deals with "a topic now regarded by many"—which seems to include himself—"as obsolete" (*ELN*, v). "As a consequence of his dogmatism," Strauss observes, "the editor's interest in Locke's teaching cannot but be purely antiquarian or must lack that philosophic concern without which the adequate understanding of philosophic teachings is impossible" (*WIPP*, 201). Strauss's complaints against von Leyden are instances of his more general concerns about historicism as developed in the essay "Political Philosophy and History," also reprinted in *What Is Political Philosophy?* As he says in that essay, "our understanding of the thought of the past is liable to be the more adequate, the less the historian is convinced of the superiority of his own point of view, or the more he is prepared to admit the possibility that he may have to learn something, not merely about the thinkers of the past, but from them" (68).

Historical studies inspired by historicist assumptions cannot produce good historical, much less philosophical, understanding. Historicists assume that the thinker reflects his age, an assumption that can lead to one of two related defects (cf. *WIPP*, 63). On the one side, readers like the editor of *Essays* think that philosophical questions are settled by history and can thus become obsolete, like last year's model iPhone. On the other side, readers like the editor of the Norton edition of Locke's writings believe that thinkers fit so snugly into their times that they are unlikely—or even unable—to disagree with the dominant opinions of their day. Historicists do not take seriously enough the possibility that a given thinker may indeed differ from the reigning consensus in his society, but may think himself able to convey that disagreement only subtly, between the lines.

Such is Strauss's view of Locke's position regarding the law of nature. Locke appears to endorse the "traditional view" that is politically and intellectually dominant in his time, but by his "contradictions" and other quiet indications tells readers that he is greatly "doubtful of the traditional natural law teaching" (*WIPP*, 218). Although Locke pays more than obeisance to those traditional views, Strauss insists that a proper historical grasp of a past thinker requires that one not merely take at face value his professions of faith, especially when these fit so comfortably into reigning views, the denial of which would be problematical in one way or another for the thinker. One must not merely pay attention to what a writer like Locke says he is saying, but take seriously what he actually says or clearly implies. This means that the historian must engage in philosophic activity. That is, as Strauss puts it, "the philosophic effort and the historical effort have become completely fused" (23). To be a political philosopher one must for now be a historian, but the reverse holds true as well.

Paradoxically, Strauss holds that "the philosophic questions of the nature of political things and of the best, or the just, political order are fundamentally different from historical questions. . . . The question of the nature of political things," i.e., the philosophic question, "and the answer to it cannot possibly be mistaken for the question of how this or that philosopher or all philosophers have approached, discussed, or answered the philosophic question mentioned" (*WIPP*, 56). One may not require the answer to the philosophic question in order to write the history of philosophy, but one must engage in the philosophic activity of subjecting "the doctrines concerned to a philosophic critique concerned exclusively with their truth or falsehood" (66).

At times Strauss speaks as if history of political philosophy can precede political philosophy proper, as if one first ascertains the historical doctrines and then subjects them to "critique concerned exclusively with their truth or falsehood." However, that is mistaken, for the relation between historical and philosophic inquiry is much more intimate and dialectical than that description suggests, even if at the end of the day the two activities remain in principle somewhat separable. To be more specific in the case of Locke, many scholars have noticed Locke's affirmations of the traditional doctrine, but they have failed to note or to take seriously the many ways in which

Locke differs from and even rejects the traditional view. The traditional view as Strauss identifies its elements

> derives man's duties from man's natural constitution or his natural inclinations; it assumes that each man is by nature ordered toward virtue; it also presupposes that each man and each nation is ruled by divine providence, that men's souls are immortal, and that the natural law is sufficiently promulgated in and to the conscience of all men. (*WIPP*, 218)

The bulk of Strauss's essay is devoted to showing that Locke questions or rejects each and every one of these elements of the traditional natural law. A particularly important element of traditional natural law that Locke rejects is the role of the natural inclinations. According to Thomas Aquinas, "reason naturally grasps as goods all those things to which man has a natural inclination, and consequently to be pursued in action, and the contrary of these are grasped as evils to be avoided. Therefore, there is an order of the precepts of the law of nature that follows the order of the natural inclinations" (*Summa Theologica* 1–2, Q94, A2). Locke, however, denies that "the law of nature can be known from man's natural inclination" (*WIPP*, 198, cf. 215; *ELN*, 158). The significance of Locke's denial is often overlooked for two reasons. First, the scholars, like von Leyden, are often unaware of how important the claim about the natural inclinations is to the traditional natural law doctrine and therefore are unprepared to appreciate the reach of Locke's denial. Second, Locke's denial occurs in one of the three "essays" for which Locke supplied a title in the form of a question, and a one-word answer to the question, but no elaboration of the answer. Von Leyden seems to believe that these three are not properly part of the work, but, apparently not sharing the editor's view, Locke included them in the consecutive numbering he gave to the entire series of "essays." Not believing that this "essay" is truly part of the work, von Leyden consigns it to a footnote in very fine print, placed so that the English-language reader is not likely even to see it.

The second aspect of traditional law is the assumption "that each man is by nature ordered toward virtue." But, Strauss points out, Locke rejects this also, for he affirms that "those who have no other guide than nature itself, those in whom the dictates of nature are in no way corrupted by positive customs, live in such ignorance of every law as if no attention had to be paid to the right and honorable" (*WIPP*, 221; *ELN*, 141). Nature, Locke avers, guides not to virtue but to the opposite.

Strauss also brings out Locke's reservations about providence by calling attention to one very subtle theme in *Essays* regarding divine power, and a less subtle point regarding divine care for man. Divine providence can rule only if God is all-powerful, i.e., capable of overriding any and all potentially resisting forces in the world. Otherwise, we cannot be certain that it is providence rather than chance or nature or some other power that rules. But Locke is very careful, Strauss points out, not to affirm divine omnipotence in his proofs for the existence of God (and thus in the place where he speaks most precisely of God's nature). He speaks rather of "an artificer" who is "powerful" and "wise" but is not affirmed to be omnipotent or omniscient in this important context (*WIPP*, 207; *ELN*, 182).

Moreover, even if God were omnipotent and therefore capable of provident care for mankind, Locke sets a landmine under the notion of divine providential care. As Strauss restates Locke's point: "After having proved the existence of God from the perfect order of the world . . . Locke shows parenthetically that man could not have been made . . . by man himself: if man were his own maker, he would give himself, i.e., every human individual, everlasting existence, for man cannot be conceived to be so full of hate and enmity against himself as to deprive himself of all the charms of life" (*WIPP*, 213; *ELN*, 152). Strauss concludes, therefore, that according to Locke, "it would appear to follow that the creation of man as a mortal being which knows of its mortality cannot be due to a being which loves man" (214).

Strauss brings home the thought that God does not show loving care toward man in his discussion of the problem of the promulgation of the law of nature. "Nature—and, it would seem necessary to add, the author of nature—has not been so kind to man as to provide him with innate knowledge of natural law . . . but rather withholds knowledge of the natural law like a secret. . . . Therefore if nature is supposed to demand obedience to the natural law from man as man, nature would be a most cruel tyrant and not at all the kind mother of all" (*WIPP*, 214; citing *ELN*, 124, 126, 114, 228, 190, 192).

Of the five aspects of traditional natural law, Strauss pays most attention to the fourth, the requirement that rational proof of immortality of souls be given. It is Locke not Strauss who calls attention to the key place of immortality of souls in Locke's list of rationally accessible knowledge necessary to establish natural law (*WIPP*, 210; *ELN*, 172, 174). Since Locke mentions immortality only a few times, von Leyden and other orthodox scholars tend to pass it over and take little notice of the fact on which Strauss dwells: "in the essays Locke does not even attempt to demonstrate the immortality of the souls although that immortality is a necessary presupposition of the natural law" (*WIPP*, 210). No immortality, no natural law. Strauss teases out of some Lockean hints an answer to the question of why Locke does not offer a proof of immortality; the soul, Locke believes, is not a separate immaterial substance but itself matter (211–12).

The traditional view held that natural law was sufficiently promulgated through the conscience, or in Aquinas's technical language, synderesis. If the law is not directly implanted or innate, then promulgation in this way seems necessary, for the law is obligatory for all and must be known (somehow) by all in order for all to be capable of acting on it and for all to be justly held to account for not obeying it. But Locke denies that the law is known through conscience (*WIPP*, 204, 205). Instead he says that the law is secret and hidden, but knowable by those who put in the necessary effort to discover it. Those who do not are guilty for not doing so. Ignorance is no excuse—ignorance is itself guilty. This proves not to be a satisfactory substitute, however, for, to say nothing of all the nations that Locke identifies as entirely ignorant of the law of nature, there is the further problem that men need some direct knowledge of their obligation to hunt for the hidden and difficult knowledge of the natural law, if they are to be held guilty for not doing so and for not obeying the law of nature. In order to escape an infinite regress, that knowledge must be available either innately or via conscience. But Locke affirms no such thing. The inescapable conclusion, therefore, is that the law of nature is insufficiently promulgated and thus cannot be known to or binding on men, and thus cannot exist as law (212–13).

In measuring Locke's discussion of the law of nature against the "traditional" notion, Strauss at the same time displays Locke's doubts about his own particular or idiosyncratic version of natural law, for Locke picked out three of the traditional features as necessary presuppositions for his theory: the lawgiver, his will, and immortality. Since the historicist-inspired scholars are not interested in pressing the philosophic question of the adequacy of what Locke says, they are not driven to press the question of whether Locke's version of the "traditional" doctrine can hold up without the elements of the traditional doctrine that he jettisons.

Locke says that he has rationally established the existence and content of the law of nature; in fact he has failed to do so according to his own standards, and he has failed in a way that must be evident to him and indeed part of his intent. Watch what he says, not what he says he says. Strauss's insights into Locke on the law of nature illustrate well the result of his fusion of history and philosophy that we discussed in chapter 2 above. He takes seriously the historian's task of probing the philosophic claims of the subject thinker as part of the effort to understand the thinker historically. The historicist-inspired historians fail to do that and are indifferent to whether Locke's argument succeeds or fails, even according to Locke's own stated criteria for success or failure. The historians thus not only fail to achieve a philosophical understanding of the topic at hand but fail at their self-appointed task of historical understanding.

Political Philosophy

If Strauss's aim was to validate his general understanding of Locke as an adherent of modern natural right and not of traditional natural right or law, then his essay must be judged a success. Contrary to what many of the critics have said, Strauss more than adequately shows that *Essays* does not make a case for Locke as a traditionalist. This is a good historical conclusion. But is it enough? The essay on Locke appears in a collection entitled *What Is Political Philosophy? and Other Studies*, in the title essay of which political philosophy is said to be "the attempt to replace opinion about the nature of political things by knowledge of the nature of political things" (11–12, 73). Political philosophy thus understood is "fundamentally different from the history of political philosophy itself" (56, 76–77). "The question of the nature of political things and the answer to it cannot possibly be mistaken for the question of how this or that philosopher . . . approached, discussed, or answered the philosophic question mentioned" (56). The transformation of the one (history of political philosophy) into the other (political philosophy) is achieved via subjecting "the doctrines concerned to a philosophic critique concerned exclusively with their truth or falsehood" (66, 286). To make this inquiry, political philosophy would require a "critique concerned exclusively with . . . [the] truth or falsehood" of the traditional natural law or of the Lockean critique of the traditional law. Does Strauss's essay achieve that critique?

What exactly does Strauss believe he has achieved in this essay? He has a final paragraph beginning "In conclusion." But that paragraph is devoted to "some peculiarities of the edition and translation for which we have not found a convenient place" (*WIPP*, 219). These are almost entirely issues of translation. The final item in the final paragraph does not appear to fit the description given, however, for it does not concern a "peculiarity of the edition and translation." Rather it concerns a "slip" Locke "apparently made" in quoting from Aristotle on natural right. Locke *apparently* made a slip, but, Strauss concludes, "he *certainly* understood the passage in exactly the same way in which it had been understood by Averroes"—the last words of the essay (220).

Without further adumbration one would have to say that the conclusion of Strauss's conclusion is opaque. The Aristotelian passage that Locke "certainly" understands in the Averroistic manner is the very passage to which Strauss devoted the concluding pages of his chapter "Classic Natural Right" in *Natural Right and History*. Among other things, Strauss there explains what the Averroistic way of understanding that passage is. The Averroistic way is there contrasted with the Thomistic way and Strauss's own conjecture of the authentic Aristotelian way of understanding the doctrine of the changeability of all natural right.

The reference to the Averroistic understanding of natural right leads us to revisit *Natural Right and History*. Strauss's characterization of his intentions in that book helps make the significance of this return to it in *What Is Political Philosophy?* clearer. Strauss presents *Natural Right and History* as a response to the present "need of historical studies in order to familiarize ourselves with the whole complexity of the issue" of natural right. We must, Strauss continues, "for some time ... become students of what is called the 'history of ideas'" (*NRH*, 7). That is to say, according to the distinctions drawn in *What Is Political Philosophy?*, *Natural Right and History* is history of political philosophy, not political philosophy itself.

Strauss nowhere else so clearly demarcates the difference between these two pursuits as he does in *What Is Political Philosophy?* with its title containing *the* Socratic "what is ...?" question. The conclusion to which these various observations are tending is that, contrary to their general reputations, *What Is Political Philosophy?* is the more fundamental and far-reaching book, the book in which Strauss transcends history of political philosophy and engages in political philosophy itself. However, the essay on Locke, to say nothing of many other parts of *What Is Political Philosophy?*, still looks much like history of political philosophy; it explicates Locke's thought with subtlety and care, but the "critique concerned exclusively with ... truth or falsehood" is nowhere evident. Perhaps we must look harder for it.

The Aristotelian passage misquoted by Locke in *Essays* is the subject of Strauss's comments at the end of his chapter on "classic natural right" in *Natural Right and History*. Strauss has presented to that point a composite account of the classic position, as though the premodern philosophers all understood natural right in the same way. The last forty percent (or so) of the chapter is devoted to disaggregating the classic position by distinguishing "three types of classic natural rights teachings"—the Socratic-Platonic-Stoic, the Aristotelian, and the Thomistic. The Socratic-Platonic-Stoic view affirms that "civil life requires the dilution of natural right by merely conventional right" (*NRH*, 152–53). The Aristotelian view denies that natural right must be diluted, for "man is by nature a political animal" and therefore what is required by civil life must be in accordance with nature. However, Aristotle also affirms that "all natural right is changeable" (156–57). Finally, the Thomistic view, the perspective of the traditional natural law that Locke appears to endorse but in fact criticizes, is, as Strauss puts it, "free from the hesitations and ambiguities" of the other two versions of classic natural right. Thomistic natural law rejects the Platonic-Stoic claim that natural right must be diluted to find a place in civil society: the dictates of natural law are binding in society without need for "diluting" or admixture. Moreover, Aquinas interprets Aristotle's dictum on the changeability of natural right in a way that blunts the force of Aristotle's puzzling claim. Aquinas makes a distinction between the principles and the specific precepts or rules of natural law. The latter are derived from the former and change somewhat according to circumstance, but the principles remain always the same. Thus Thomistic natural right to a great extent rejects those aspects of the Platonic and Aristotelian doctrines that contain "hesitation" or "ambiguity" in identifying right as it exists at any time in even the best regime with natural right per se.

The specific part of the discussion of the "types of classic natural right" to which Strauss implicitly refers the reader at the end of the Locke essay in *What Is Political Philosophy?* is the central part of that discussion, the consideration of the Aristotelian version of natural right. In Aristotle the doctrine is presented so briefly and so abstractly that there has been considerable disagreement over what it means ever since Aristotle's time. Strauss considers three interpretations of the Aristotelian doctrine: the Thomistic, the Averroistic, and his own conjecture of Aristotle's meaning. The discussion of the Averroists is thus the center of the center. We have already noted the Thomistic interpretation, which Strauss rejects as an interpretation of Aristotle, because Aristotle says "all natural right is changeable," whereas Aquinas makes only part of it changeable (*NRH*, 157). The Thomistic interpretation is geared to making Aristotle's dictum compatible with natural right understood in the Thomistic manner as natural law, for it allows changeable natural right to retain sufficient fixedness to have meaning as a binding mandate for all men and all times, i.e., to be conceivable as law. If we assume that Strauss is correct in rejecting Aquinas's reading of Aristotle, in itself that implies at most that on this point Aquinas disagrees with Aristotle more than he usually lets on. However, there are many other places where Aquinas deviates from "the philosopher," in some cases arguably improving on Aristotle's position.[6] But if Strauss is correct it also means that Aristotle cannot be enlisted as a support for Aquinas's interpretation of natural right as natural law.

At the opposite pole from Aquinas's interpretation is the Averroistic position, apparently the one of greatest importance for Strauss's Locke essay. The Averroists, including Marsilius (and Locke) among the Christians, notice, like Aquinas, a certain universality, or at least "the same broad rules of what constitutes justice . . . in all civil societies" (*NRH*, 158). These rules "specify the minimum requirements of society." Despite their universality, the Averroists see them as "conventional," because "civil society is incompatible with any immutable rules." But these rules, to be effective, must be presented by society "as universally valid," even though they are not. To be truly valid, the universal rules would have to come with many "qualifications," but because the rules do hold in their pure or unqualified form most of the time and because the citizens must not be encouraged to find or believe in exceptions to the rules as a matter of course, the rules do not contain the exceptions in their public expression. "The unqualified rules are not natural right but conventional right" (158; cf. 146, 147). Thus Strauss says in one place that "Marsilius lives as it were in another world than Thomas" (*HPP*, 276). Strauss sees the Averroistic interpretation of Aristotle's text to be no more valid than the Thomistic interpretation, however, "in so far as it implies the denial of natural right proper" (*NRH*, 159). Just as Aquinas loses one part of Aristotle's two-part doctrine on natural right, so the Averroists lose the other part. But the political philosophic question is, of course, not who or what position agrees with Aristotle, but which (if any) is true. In the context of the topic of the Locke essay, what is at stake is the truth or falsehood of the traditional natural law doctrine that Locke apparently affirms but actually doubts.

In connecting Locke to Averroes in *Natural Right and History*, Strauss attributes to Locke a much more negative stance toward the law of nature than he explicitly stated in the Locke essay in *What Is Political Philosophy?* Strauss claims to have brought out "how doubtful [Locke] was, from the beginning of his career, of the traditional natural law teaching" (*WIPP*, 218). The Averroists, explicitly called by Strauss "philosophers," who stand at the opposite pole from Thomism, can be expected to subject the traditional natural law doctrine to the "critique concerned exclusively with truth or falsehood" characteristic of political philosophy proper. Strauss implies that Locke is thus a stand-in for, or even a representative of, the premodern Averroistic philosophic critique of traditional natural law. This conclusion coheres with Strauss's observation at the end of his *Natural Right* chapter "Classic Natural Right" that the moderns reacted against traditional natural law on the basis of a "premise, which would have been acceptable to the classics" (*NRH*, 164).

In *Natural Right* Strauss discusses the traditional natural law in a very brief two pages. The main point of that short discussion is to account for the Thomistic deviations from the Platonic and Aristotelian versions of natural right. Unlike the Platonic version, the natural law doctrine has no doubts or reservations "regarding the basic harmony between natural right and civil society." Unlike the Aristotelian doctrine, the Thomist version has no doubts or reservations "regarding the immutable character of the fundamental propositions of natural laws" (*NRH*, 165). Strauss comments that "it is reasonable to assume that these profound changes were due to the influence of the belief in biblical revelation." The implications of that hypothesized dependence on revelation are far-reaching. "If this assumption should prove to be correct, one would be forced to wonder . . . whether the natural law as Thomas Aquinas understands it, is natural law strictly speaking, i.e., a law knowable to the unassisted human mind" (163). What is at stake is nothing less than the existence of the natural law as natural, and therefore as discernible by philosophy as opposed to theology (164). In other words, Strauss makes an assumption, a "reasonable assumption," about the natural law that explodes the natural law. But a "reasonable assumption," however reasonable, nonetheless remains an assumption and cannot be the basis for "a philosophic critique concerned exclusively with [the] . . . truth or falsehood" of philosophic doctrines. *Natural Right and History*, as we have noted earlier, remains a historical and not a fully philosophic book: As Strauss wrote of *Natural Right and History* in a private letter, "I agree then with your judgment that the value of my book consists rather in its historical than its philosophic aspects. . . . I myself regard the book as a preparation to an adequate philosophic discussion."[7]

Let us then hypothesize that the Locke essay completes, in effect, the discussion of natural law in *Natural Right* by fleshing out and providing support for the hypothesis in the earlier book that the natural law doctrine was illicitly dependent on revelation. That suggestion is at least supported if not confirmed by a comment Strauss made about the Averroists in a writing of a later date than the Locke essay. The Averroists were, according to Strauss, "those medieval Aristotelians, who as philosophers refused to make any concessions to revealed religion" (*SPPP*, 226). The Averroists rejected natural law; they made no concessions to revealed religion. Is the one the result of the other? So far as that is so, the essay on Locke, who is said to be an Averroist on the decisive issue, looks to be the place where the philosophic critique of traditional natural law as dependent on biblical revelation is presented.

On the surface, at least, neither Locke himself in *Essays*, nor Strauss in explicating Locke in *What Is Political Philosophy?*, explicitly makes the claim that traditional natural law depends on acceptance of revelation. But Strauss comes very close. Indeed, he acts like the pious ascetic of whom he speaks in the essay on Alfarabi in *What Is Political Philosophy?* The lesson he extracts from the story of that pious man is "that one can safely tell a very dangerous truth provided one tells it in the proper surroundings, for the public will interpret the absolutely unexpected speech in term of the customary and expected meaning of the surroundings rather than it will interpret the surroundings in terms of the dangerous character of the speech" (*WIPP*, 136). That lesson bears in particular on the practice of Plato, who "established for himself the character of a man who never explicitly and unambiguously says what he thinks about the highest themes" (137). With that reputation secure, Plato can then "sometimes ... say explicitly and unambiguously what he thought about the highest themes: his explicit and unambiguous utterances are not taken seriously" (137). However well the reputation imputed to Plato fits the Greek thinker, it surely fits Strauss well.

That tactic is on display when Strauss mentions, almost in passing, that Locke "follows," perhaps without knowing it, a claim made by Thomas Aquinas, "who says that it is not reason simply but reason informed by faith which dictates that God is to be loved and to be worshipped" (*WIPP*, 208). The connection of this bold claim to our question becomes clear if one notes that "love and worship" of God are dictates, indeed, "the first, the highest and the most weighty duties prescribed by natural law" according to Locke and, in slightly modified form, according to Aquinas as well (see *Summa Theologica* I–II Q94 A2, resp.; Q99). Aquinas's admission is damning, for it concedes that the most important content of the natural law is not in fact accessible without "faith," i.e., without a nonrational source of belief. Strauss has found an extremely authoritative witness in support of his "reasonable assumption" that the question of the truth or falsehood of the traditional natural law doctrine rests on whether it necessarily depends on an appeal to revelation.[8] Strauss explains Aquinas's problematic recourse to faith as a response to a "difficulty" to which Locke calls attention but which "was as well known in the middle ages as it is in modern times" (*WIPP*, 209). The difficulty to which Strauss adverts is the great variety of religious beliefs in the world, including much polytheism and atheism (208). That empirical fact implies that knowledge of the natural law and of propositions on which knowledge of natural law depends is insufficiently promulgated. Aquinas and Locke both hold that, like all binding law, the natural law must be sufficiently known or at least knowable by those (all humans) to whom it applies. That difficulty leads to alternative possibilities, either of which is fatal to natural law as such. Locke, Strauss suggests, saw the problem very clearly and used it in his critique, while Aquinas saw it and responded in a way that undermined his larger enterprise.

Strauss has Aquinas's own admission to validate his assumption, but in order to understand in greater depth Strauss's critique of Thomistic natural law one must return to the three "presuppositions" Locke identified as essential to the natural law. These correspond to three of the five elements of traditional natural law as identified by Strauss. The three are a natural demonstration of the existence of God, of his will for man (the content of the law), and of the immortality of the soul (the precondition for sanctions attached to the law of nature).

As should be clear already, Strauss approaches his critique in a very indirect manner—through the keyhole rather than through the front door as he once put it (*OT*, 236). He is especially indirect in his approach to the first "speculative doctrine" required to establish natural law. The key to Strauss's thinking on this important topic is his identification of two kinds of natural law in Locke's text—a natural law that cannot be transgressed, and a natural law that can be transgressed. Only the latter is natural law of the moral type that is relevant to his discussion of natural right in *Natural Right*. Locke plays on the ambiguity between these different types of natural law; he devotes his central proof for the existence of natural law to an argument that establishes the nontransgressible kind of law on the basis of observations and reasoning that Christians like Aquinas and pagan naturalists like Hippocrates share (*WIPP*, 203). This is the law Locke claims is recognized and obeyed by all (204). This law, which "governs all things," is responsible for "the orderly character of all natural things and actions . . . [and] may be said to have its source in nature rather than God." Strauss extracts from Locke the view that "in order to believe that man is subject to a law like all other beings, it is not necessary to reflect on God" (202). So the nontransgressible law of nature neither depends on nor contributes to a proof for the existence of God.

What about the moral law of nature? We have already seen that it does depend on the existence of God. Can reason establish the existence of a legislative God who could be the source of this law? Locke explicitly says yes, but Strauss shows him to have serious reservations about that, reservations that Strauss shares. In the central paragraph of the essay Strauss "note[s] that in demonstrating these two presuppositions of the knowledge of natural law [i.e., the 'existence of some wise and powerful artificer of all sensibly perceived things including man' and 'that God has a will as regards what one ought to do'], Locke presupposes the existence of natural law" (*WIPP*, 207). As part of the interpretation of Locke this observation brings out the circular or question-begging character of Locke's explicit argument. He seeks to prove the existence and content of natural law by proving the existence of God and God's will, assuming in doing so the very thing he is ultimately attempting to prove. Strauss cites two places in Locke where he does something like what Strauss says he does: Locke claims to have proved that there is a law of nature knowable by the light of nature before he has proved the propositions needed to establish God the legislator and his legislative will (*ELN*, 136, 146).

And Strauss gives us another angle on this problem when we recall an observation he made earlier: In the fifth paragraph of his essay Strauss reports on Locke's subtle claim not "that the existence of a God is evident to all men . . . but only that it is evident to all morally concerned men" (202). Locke made the recognition of "virtue or vice" the presupposition for those who find the existence of God to be "evident." Not only is Locke's argument viciously circular, as outlined above, but more significantly, it points toward the core of Strauss's "reasonable assumption" in *Natural Right and History*. The premise of the authoritativeness of moral "virtue or vice," understood in the authentically moral sense, i.e., not as instrumental to some nonmoral good, leads to the positing (or "proving") of God—as the source and support of morality thus understood. This argument will not do as a proof, for it takes as given that which cannot be taken as given and which requires the proof of God's existence as support, i.e., the unconditional or absolute validity of morality. But moral claims—from a philosophic perspective—can raise no such claims to a priori validity. Moral claims are not self-evident truths, as the variety of moral claims raised by human beings indicates. It is thus not possible for reason to establish the moral law as legislated by God, i.e., to establish that moral claims exist as natural law. Reason is not able to establish God as an intelligent, willing, morally concerned person, but only perhaps as the source of the order of necessary laws that constitute nature. Man does not have the capacity to establish by means of his natural faculties the existence of that morally concerned God who stands as the purported source of natural law. Man's knowledge, if it is truly knowledge, of that morally concerned God must thus come from God—reaching down, so to speak, and revealing himself to man. That is to say, knowledge of the natural law as natural law must depend on belief that God has so revealed himself; i.e., it must be "due to the influence of the belief in biblical revelation" (*NRH*, 163). And to repeat an earlier point: so far as the natural law depends on the God revealed in biblical revelation, it is not natural but supernatural. That in itself does not, of course, invalidate the law as divine law. Strauss's argument says nothing about the status of revelation and the revealing God. It merely reveals natural law to be an impossible synthesis of rational and revealed. It points once again to the "either-or" character of Strauss's thinking about the theological-political problem.

The Locke essay in *What Is Political Philosophy?* in effect completes or renders assertoric what was only a hypothetical argument against natural law in *Natural Right and History*. The same point might be made by following out what Strauss says about the two other "speculative principles" needed to establish the natural law: knowledge of God's will, and knowledge of immortality as the basis for knowledge of divine reward and punishment. Locke does not normally speak for Strauss, but the Averroistic Locke whom Strauss uncovers in *What Is Political Philosophy?* does speak for him, at least so far as he is a critic of the traditional doctrine of natural law.

Part III

Strauss in the Twentieth Century

CHAPTER NINE

Strauss's Practical Politics

From Weimar to America

C ritics have often decried Strauss's political attachments to the right. Some now go beyond accusing him of being a conservative critic of liberalism or of ostensibly having inspired the "neoconservative" foreign policies of the George W. Bush administration, and maintain that in the early 1930s Strauss openly sympathized with fascist imperialists, and even Nazis, and that he continued to advocate authoritarian politics, although more covertly, after he emigrated to the United States.[1]

In *The Truth about Leo Strauss* we responded to the charge that Strauss was the "mastermind" of the foreign policy of the Bush administration by showing that he did not favor imperialistic policies of either a liberal democratic Wilsonian or a more Machiavellian kind, and that he did not advocate the rule of a "philosophical elite." In this chapter we respond to Strauss's more extreme critics.

To show that Strauss was not a student or follower of Carl Schmitt, as some of these critics maintain, in the first part of this chapter we examine the review Strauss wrote of Schmitt's influential 1932 book *The Concept of the Political.* We argue that the critics' charges rest on a serious misreading of that review. And to disprove the claim that Strauss presented a Schmittian understanding of politics covertly in his later work, we contrast the "concept of the political" Strauss drew from his study of classical political philosophy with the Schmittian "concept" he had criticized in his review.

In the next part of this chapter we then examine the second and perhaps more serious source of the critics' charges, a letter that Strauss wrote to Karl Löwith shortly after Hitler came to power but that was published only in 2001. Rather than a profession of his own fascist political principles, we argue, the letter conveys Strauss's view of the political facts in Germany in May 1933 and the options open or closed to Jewish intellectuals at that time. Strauss explained his understanding of the political and intellectual circumstances in which he wrote the letter more fully in a talk he gave called "German Nihilism" in 1941.

Asked in the midst of World War II what was the true political doctrine, Strauss responded: "We shall not hesitate to answer: liberal democracy."[2] But he went on to caution Americans against an attempt to impose such a regime on Germany after the war, because he thought the Germans would not accept it. Why did Strauss favor liberal democracy where it could be established? In another talk that he wrote in the 1960s but that was not published until after he died in 1973, Strauss observed that the theoretical crises he had analyzed in modern political philosophy do not necessarily lead to a practical crisis. Although its theoretical foundation in modern political philosophy is defective, "liberal democracy ... derives powerful support from ... the premodern thought of our western tradition" ("TWM," 98). In the third and last part of this chapter we seek to identify the aspects of premodern Western tradition Strauss thought provided support for liberal democracy.

Strauss and Schmitt

Because some critics have argued that Strauss's "reactionary" politics were initially revealed in the review he wrote in 1932 of Carl Schmitt's *The Concept of the Political*, we begin our consideration of Strauss's practical politics by asking: how much did Carl Schmitt mean to Strauss? In a few words, we answer: at a certain time in his life, quite a lot; later and overall for his thinking in general, not very much.

When Strauss was young, unemployed, and just finding his own voice, Schmitt briefly did mean something to him. In 1932, when he was thirty-three, Strauss published a long review essay on Schmitt. In connection with that review there was some correspondence and even a personal meeting.[3] Among other things Strauss used his contact with Schmitt—older, far better established, already well known as a jurist and philosopher of law—to help him gain a fellowship in France and another in England to further his study of Hobbes, a thinker in whom both men were interested. To that end Strauss apparently sent Schmitt as much of his manuscript on Hobbes as he had completed at that time. Impressed with Strauss's essay on his book and with what Strauss had written on Hobbes, Schmitt recommended him to the Rockefeller Foundation. No doubt partly because of

Schmitt's letter, Strauss won the support of the foundation for his studies in France and England over the next two years.[4] Strauss was thus away from Germany when Hitler came to power in the spring of 1933, and he did not return until much later, after the war.

One claim often made—or perhaps better, insinuated—is that in July 1933, when he sought to enlist Schmitt's aid in securing a place in a proposed editorial project on the works of Hobbes, Strauss knew that Schmitt had joined the Nazi Party. This insinuation is then presented as evidence that Strauss had no objection to Schmitt the Nazi, and is used to support the broader claim that Strauss himself was not hostile to, perhaps was even friendly toward, the Nazi agenda. In fact, we have no direct evidence of what Strauss knew or didn't know of Schmitt's political associations. At the time Strauss was in Paris and apparently lacking detailed knowledge of events in the German academic world. From the evidence contained in letters between Strauss and his friend Jacob Klein, who was then still in Germany, Heinrich Meier concludes that "we have no evidence whatsoever for [the] assumption" that Strauss knew of Schmitt's party membership. Indeed, Meier concludes that "the exchange of letters with Jacob Klein suggests that Strauss knew nothing of the kind."[5] That conclusion, based on the evidence of the Klein correspondence and the fact that Strauss stopped writing to Schmitt when we know for certain that he had become aware of Schmitt's party membership, is far more plausible than the bare assumption that Strauss, living in a foreign country, knew of Schmitt's political party affiliation by July 1933.

John McCormick makes another unsupported and unsupportable claim about the Strauss-Schmitt connection when he asserts that the two are related as "master and student."[6] As our biographical sketch in chapter 1 indicates, this claim is certainly not true in the literal sense; Strauss never was a student of Schmitt. Nor is it true in a more extended sense of master and student. McCormick may have been impressed by the tone of one of Strauss's extant letters to Schmitt. Writing in March of 1932 Strauss expresses his gratitude for Schmitt's aid in acquiring the Rockefeller grant. Given Strauss's situation, and hope for further aid, such gratitude was perfectly understandable. But Strauss goes on: "Allow me, Professor, to submit that the interest that you have shown in my studies of Hobbes represents the most honorable and obliging corroboration of my scholarly work that has ever been bestowed upon me and that I could ever dream of."[7]

No doubt a strong statement, but not one that bespeaks a master-student relation. To understand it we must again consider the very different situations of the young Strauss and the well-established Schmitt. Not only was Strauss living a very precarious existence without a regular appointment, but he had so far published little, his only important publication being his 1930 book on Spinoza. Although that book was apparently well reviewed, Strauss was a relatively unrecognized—and unemployed—academic. To be recognized—and thereby validated by an academic luminary like Schmitt—would be gratifying (and encouraging) to anyone in Strauss's position.

But there is more to it than that. In his review of *The Concept of the Political* Strauss had been very critical of his so-called master. Both men recognized this feature of Strauss's essay. Schmitt referred to Strauss's essay as "very good," and also as "very critical of course."[8] At the conclusion of his second extant letter to Schmitt, containing further (postreview) reflections on possible confusions in Schmitt's book, Strauss remarks: "I close with the request that you take note of this supplement to my review with the same forbearance you show with respect to the review itself."[9] Strauss was thus particularly grateful and gratified that despite the critical character of his statement, Schmitt was favorably impressed with it and willing to engage with Strauss's criticism. In a word, the young Strauss was pleased to be taken seriously by the man he had made the target of his critique. How much greater is it to be taken seriously as a critic than as a flatterer. The premise of Strauss's extravagant original statement of gratitude was not the master-student relation that McCormick posits, but rather the author-critic relation that gave meaning to their interactions.

So when Strauss was young, Schmitt meant quite a lot to him. He gave Strauss much-needed material aid, as well as intellectual support and validation. But Strauss did not base his own later thought on principles he took from Schmitt. As a careful reading of his "Notes on Carl Schmitt, *The Concept of the Political*" shows, Strauss did not think that Schmitt had achieved what he sought in his book, a successful critique of liberalism. Nor was Strauss's own critique of early modern political philosophy based on, or the same as, Schmitt's critique of liberalism.

STRAUSS'S "NOTES ON CARL SCHMITT, *THE CONCEPT OF THE POLITICAL*"

Strauss begins his review by "noting" the explicitly polemical, present-oriented character of Schmitt's articulation of "the concept of the political." Schmitt wishes to overcome the negation of the political by modern liberalism and provide a new, firmer foundation for the state by bringing "the political" out of concealment. What makes him stand out among other critics of liberalism is his awareness that what is needed is to replace the "'astonishingly consistent ... systematics of liberal thought,' which is manifest within the inconsistency of liberal politics, by 'another system'" ("NCS," 85). Strauss thus finds Schmitt's work of particular interest because in contrast to the critics of liberalism who propose specific reforms, Schmitt sees that liberalism rests on a comprehensive understanding of the world that will have to be replaced by another equally comprehensive understanding if its faults are to be remedied. But Strauss does not think that Schmitt has succeeded in articulating the alternative that he seeks.

Strauss finds the critique of the liberal conception of culture *implied* by Schmitt's concept of the political especially noteworthy. That liberal notion of culture understands human life to be divided into a variety of "relatively independent domains," each of which is distinguished by a characteristic set of ultimate distinctions, e.g., in morals between good and bad, in aesthetics between beautiful and ugly, and in politics between friend and enemy. By denying that the political distinction is "equivalent and analogous" to the other distinctions, Strauss thinks that Schmitt implies a fundamental critique of the prevailing concept of culture (even though Schmitt himself does not present it). Such a critique would begin with the observation that "culture" is always the cultivation of nature. But, Strauss acknowledges, there are two ways of understanding this cultivation. The expression refers first to the development of natural predisposition (as in the ancient philosophical understanding of human virtue or excellence). However, "culture" can also refer to the conquest of nature (as in the work of modern philosophers like Bacon). Schmitt follows Hobbes in understanding "the status civilis in the sense of the specifically modern concept of culture ... as the opposite of the status naturalis," or the state of war ("NCS," 89). The state of war, which in Schmitt's terminology is the genuinely political, is according to Schmitt what underlies every state or political association. By his understanding of nature, Schmitt indicates his allegiance to the liberal perspective pioneered by Hobbes and not to the alternative understanding of culture and therewith of nature that Strauss wishes to restore.

Strauss points out that Schmitt differs from, indeed contradicts, Hobbes in maintaining that the state of war exists among groups—i.e., that war and/or identification of the enemy is an essentially public rather than private decision—whereas Hobbes argues that the state of nature is a state of war of individuals. However, since Hobbes admits that the state of war continues among nations after individuals have contracted to form their governments, Strauss does not think that this is the most important difference between Schmitt and Hobbes. The fundamental difference, nay opposition, lies between Schmitt's assertion that "it belongs to the essence of the political group that it can 'demand . . . from the members of its own nation the readiness to die'" and Hobbes's assertion of the right of every individual to the securing of his or her life so that "in battle he who deserts the ranks out of fear for his life acts 'only' dishonorably, but not unjustly (Lev. XXI)." Indeed, Strauss concludes, "Hobbes's foundation for the natural-right claim to the securing of life pure and simple sets the path to the whole system of human rights in the sense of liberalism" ("NCS," 91).

However, Strauss observes, there is a fundamental ambiguity in Schmitt's presentation of his concept of the political. At times Schmitt asserts that it does not matter whether one thinks "the political" opposition between friend and enemy is desirable or not; it is an undeniable fact.[10] But at other times Schmitt suggests that the liberal attempt to negate the political may indeed succeed. "If the political is ultimately threatened," Strauss comments, "the position of the political must ultimately be more than the recognition of the reality of the political, namely, [it must be] an espousal" ("NCS," 96).

On what ground, Strauss then asks, does Schmitt affirm the political? "Recognizing the possibility in principle of the 'world state' as a wholly apolitical 'partnership in consumption and production' of humanity united," Schmitt asks the Marxists who hope "that government of men over men will have become superfluous, because men will have become absolutely free," what these men will be free to do. The answer to that question, Schmitt sees, depends upon the assumptions one makes about human nature, whether one optimistically assumes that human beings will no longer be dangerous or that they will continue to be dangerous (and thus need to be ruled or dominated). But, Strauss notes, there is a further ambiguity in the definition of "evil." Schmitt observes that "the philosophers of statecraft of the seventeenth century . . . described men in the state of nature as 'evil' because they were 'like beasts' moved by their drives (hunger, cupidity, fear, jealousy)." But, Strauss points out, Hobbes described men in the state of nature as beasts, because he "understood man as by nature free, that is, without obligation" (and thus without sin); "for Hobbes, therefore, the fundamental political fact was natural right as the justified claim of the individual." Strauss thus concludes that "if one takes this approach, one cannot demur in principle against the proclamation of human rights as claims of the individuals upon the state . . . or against liberalism" ("NCS,"

99). If Schmitt wants to carry out the radical critique of liberalism he strives for, he has "to nullify 'the view of human evil as animal' and thus innocent, and return to the view of human evil as moral baseness; only in this way can Schmitt remain in harmony with himself if indeed 'the core of the political idea' is 'the morally demanding decision'" (99–100) as Schmitt declared in his book *Political Theology*.[11] In sum, Strauss suggests, it is a moral concern rather than Hobbes's concern with preservation that lies at the bottom of Schmitt's affirmation of the political as the friend-enemy distinction.[12]

Recognizing that Schmitt vacillates between a kind of "social scientific" or "realist" affirmation of the ineliminable and ubiquitous character of "the political," and his moral reaction against the possibility of the complete pacification of mankind, Strauss explains "what the affirmation of the political in disregard of the moral, the primacy of the political over the moral" would signify:

> Being political means being orientated to the "dire emergency." Therefore the affirmation of the political as such is the affirmation of fighting as such, wholly irrespective of what is being fought for.... He who affirms the political as such respects all who want to fight; he is just as tolerant as the liberals—but with the opposite intention: whereas the liberal respects and tolerates all "honest" convictions so long as they merely acknowledge the legal order, peace, as sacrosanct, he who affirms the political as such respects and tolerates all "serious" convictions, that is, all decisions oriented to the real possibility of war. Thus the affirmation of the political as such proves to be liberalism with the opposite polarity. ("NCS," 105)[13]

Even where he goes beyond or against Hobbes, Strauss concludes, Schmitt does not manage to escape liberalism. "The affirmation of the political as such can therefore not be other than merely the first word from Schmitt against liberalism. It can do no more than prepare the way for a radical critique of liberalism" (102–3).[14]

THE CRITICS

Commentators who argue that Strauss's politics are first revealed in his critique of Schmitt take this conclusion to mean that Strauss thought that Schmitt had prepared the way for his own radical critique. Nicholas Xenos begins his treatment of Strauss and Schmitt by observing that "on his own account, Leo Strauss's intellectual formation took a decisive turn in 1932 when he encountered Carl Schmitt's *The Concept of the Political*."[15] He asserts, moreover, that Strauss's review of Schmitt's book shows "the jibe

Hannah Arendt is reported to have directed at Strauss, noting 'the irony of the fact that a political party advocating views Strauss appreciated could have no place for a Jew like him,'" to be true.

Such a "jibe"—rather a tame way to describe an accusation as serious as the one reported—would seem to require some solid evidence to support it. It is remarkable how thin Xenos's evidence is for his claim regarding the supposed importance of Schmitt and the Nazis for Strauss. Xenos's assertion that "on his own account" Strauss attributed a "decisive turn" in his "intellectual formation" to his "encounter" with Schmitt no doubt refers to a comment by Strauss made in his 1965 autobiographical "Preface" to the English translation of his early book on Spinoza. That comment explained why he was including the translation of his "Notes" on Schmitt along with the Spinoza book. It is remarkable how different what Strauss actually said is from what Xenos has him saying. According to Strauss, the "change of orientation" in his thinking *"found its first expression"* in the essay on Schmitt (*LAM*, 257). He nowhere said that his encounter with Schmitt caused or instigated that change.

Strauss is quite clear in specifying what the "change of orientation" consisted in. "The present study [i.e., the Spinoza book] was based on the premise . . . that a return to pre-modern philosophy is impossible" (*LAM*, 257). The change announced in the Schmitt essay, then, is a new belief that a return to premodern philosophy *is possible*. On more than one occasion Strauss clarified what led to the change of orientation—and it was not Schmitt. The thinker who opened the way to Strauss's "new orientation" (as we noted earlier) was his friend Jacob Klein, for it was Klein who "was the first to understand the possibility which Heidegger had opened up without intending it: the possibility of a genuine return to classical philosophy, to the philosophy of Plato and Aristotle."[16]

Strauss never says that Schmitt was important to him in leading to the "turn" in his thinking, and Schmitt played a very small role in Strauss's intellectual life after 1933. After he wrote the "Notes" on Schmitt's *Concept of the Political* in 1932, he made only a passing reference to Schmitt in a public talk he gave in 1941, and another to Schmitt's judgment on Hobbes in the 1965 German edition of Strauss's Hobbes book.[17] He did not write anything further about Schmitt, and Schmitt has no role in his correspondence. In both respects Schmitt stands in contrast to Heidegger, with whom Strauss engaged in one form or another throughout his career.[18]

Strauss arranged for the printing of his essay on Schmitt in the 1965 reissue of the Spinoza book not because, as Jacob Schiff speculates, "Schmitt was clearly on [his] mind during the 1960's," but because what was on his mind was the shift in his philosophic orientation that led him in 1965 to speak of his mature disagreement with his youthful reading of Spinoza. "As a consequence of this [shift], I now read the *Theologico-political Treatise* differently than I read it when I was young. I understood Spinoza too literally because I did not read him literally enough" (*LAM*, 257). Strauss, in sum, was printing the Schmitt essay in 1965 not as a way of signaling the importance of Schmitt for his thinking, but as way of signaling and dating the shift in his own thinking.

Strauss's new orientation found expression in the Schmitt essay when he pointed out that the "critique of liberalism" by Schmitt "occurs in the horizon of liberalism." A proper critique of liberalism, which Schmitt did not achieve, would require "gaining a horizon beyond liberalism" ("NCS," 119). Given Strauss's understanding of Schmitt's failure and his understanding of what was truly required, it is quite impossible for Schmitt to have been responsible for Strauss's "decisive turn," for this was precisely a re-turn to premodern, and in particular to pre-Hobbesian, thought.[19]

Xenos, following McCormick, believes that Strauss was saying that Schmitt's critique failed because he did not understand Hobbes correctly. Whereas Schmitt understood human evil to be innocent evil, understanding Hobbes correctly, i.e., in terms of his fundamental "moral attitude" and not in terms of his surface "scientism," would allow one to see that Hobbes affirms that human evil is not innocent. McCormick and Xenos use this reading of Strauss's intentions in his confrontation with Schmitt and then in his Hobbes book to show that Strauss advocated authoritarian rule based on the cultivation of fear in the populace. According to Xenos, "Strauss's argument favors a return to a view of the human being as naturally evil, and not innocently so. . . . Properly understanding the evil nature of the human being should . . . lead to the more 'natural' response of authoritarian rule. . . . The necessity of dominion, of ruling human beings who are evil by nature, is primary."[20]

The only consideration that makes the McCormick-Xenos reading of the Schmitt essay and the Hobbes book at all understandable, though still not defensible, is that Strauss did not state explicitly what he meant by a "horizon beyond liberalism." In retrospect it should be clear that that horizon was the horizon of premodern or Socratic political philosophy. However, Strauss did make clear that what he was seeking could not be what McCormick and Xenos take it to be—a tougher version of Hobbes. In the last paragraph of his review Strauss wrote: "In such a horizon," i.e., the "horizon beyond liberalism," it is seen that "Hobbes completed the foundation of liberalism." The completion of the "critique of liberalism" cannot be performed on the basis of Hobbes, for, as Strauss says, Hobbes rightly understood supplies the "foundation of liberalism." Strauss believes that "a radical critique of liberalism is then possible only on the basis of an adequate understanding of Hobbes," an adequate understanding being one that brings out how Hobbes is not an alternative to liberalism but its founder. Such is the point indeed of Strauss's soon-to-follow Hobbes book. Strauss emphasizes Hobbes's break with traditional political philosophy and Hobbes's replacement of that by his own doctrine of the right of nature, the basis for the liberal principle of natural or human rights. One of the major points of the Hobbes book that McCormick and Xenos seem to miss is the critical stance Strauss takes toward Hobbes and his conviction that he had good reason to break with premodern political philosophy.[21]

How could intelligent and serious authors like McCormick and Xenos get Strauss so wrong that they attribute to him the opposite of the argument he is actually making? In part their errors are due to plain misreading, as when Xenos attributes to Strauss the claim that Schmitt led him to his "decisive turn." Such misreadings result, in turn, from the highly politicized environment in which much of the work on Strauss has been done. This is especially true of Xenos, who announces in the preface of his book his "polemical intent" to counteract the post-9/11 influence said to be wielded by "Straussians" in the Bush administration, an influence culminating in the invasion of Iraq in 2003. In our previous book, *The Truth about Leo Strauss*, we addressed these political charges and showed that the evidence advanced for them did not hold up when investigated. Ironically perhaps, given the political direction from which the charges came, the entire episode reminds of nothing so much as the larger episode of McCarthyism in the 1950s. Rumors, innuendo, guilt by association, strained claims of connections between Strauss and various policy makers, strained chains of connections between Strauss's thought and the widely decried policies of the Bush administration, long lists of "Straussians" in government — these were the stuff of the campaign against Strauss and the "Straussians."[22]

Xenos attempts to supplement that earlier wave of anti-Strauss literature by supplying evidence from Strauss's writings to uphold his position. Unlike most of the earlier writers in the genre, Xenos actually read some of Strauss's works, and he tries to build a case on the basis of Strauss's words. Having admitted that he began with a "polemical intent" based on his prior certainty that there was a "deeply reactionary substance [to] Strauss's own political position, one that had been formed in a spirit of counter-revolution against the forces of equality and social justice in Weimar Germany," Xenos discovered that it was more difficult to support his reading on the basis of Strauss's writings than he had expected.[23] He continues to think that "Strauss's writings are easy to figure out in the whole," but he finds them "frustratingly clumsy to untangle in the particular."[24] It was not easy to find in Strauss's writings the "deeply reactionary substance" that Xenos knew in advance of careful study must be there. Though he continued to be sure that the "real" core of Strauss's thought is "deeply reactionary," he was forced to admit that "there is always a quote available that says the opposite."[25] This unhappy fact led Xenos to "often tedious exegesis and convoluted lines of explication . . . in order to see what it is that lies behind the obfuscation,"[26] i.e., behind Strauss's failure to come out and say the things Xenos was sure Strauss believed.

There is, however, another reason that may partially explain, if not excuse, the misreadings of Strauss's works by critics like Xenos and McCormick. That is the difficulty posed by Strauss's distinctive manner of writing. We do not refer here to various devices of "esotericism" that Strauss is sometimes alleged to have employed. As we have shown in previous chapters, we believe that Strauss does at times write as he reads: he often counts paragraphs and notes and uses centers just as he says writers in the tradition did. We argued in our earlier book that Strauss employs these devices out of a kind of "pedagogical reserve" as well as a desire to demonstrate that one can write as he found authors in the tradition to have written (*TALS*, chap. 4). Contrary to what his enemies and many of his friends claim, these devices cannot be means of concealing his "true teachings," because in the context of *his* writing they have a different meaning than they had in the writings of a Maimonides or a Machiavelli. To take a striking example, according to Strauss, previous writers used central chapters or central items in lists to convey subtly their most important or most controversial thoughts, which they did not wish to present too openly. The center was appropriate for this because it is the least visible or most concealed part of a discourse: readers usually attend most closely to the beginnings and endings. However, for readers who seek to read Strauss as he read other authors, the center is not the least but one of the most obtrusive parts, because Strauss has made such a point of calling attention to its importance. He could not tell his readers to look to the center to find the hidden esoteric points in other texts and then expect to hide dangerous or problematic thoughts in the center of his own.

The manner of writing we have in mind is something quite different from Strauss's alleged esotericism. Even as early as his essay on Schmitt, Strauss demonstrates his commitment to "trying to understand an author as he understood himself."[27] Rather than standing outside the author and offering an interpretation of his words supported by quotations, Strauss attempts to replicate the thought of the author and present it in the author's own voice. As a result, Strauss's restatement of the thought of the thinker he is interpreting is often taken to be a statement of Strauss's own thought. So we see writers like Shadia Drury finding Machiavelli and Nietzsche and Heidegger or Thrasymachus in Strauss by mistaking his in persona presentation of their thought as his own. She and others thus attribute to Strauss the very eclectic, often contradictory views of the assembly of thinkers he has written on.

A variant of this phenomenon occurs in Xenos's interpretation of Strauss on Schmitt. The insight that Xenos believes gives the clue to understanding Strauss's politics in the 1970s as well as in 1932 is the following:

> In Strauss's judgment, Schmitt's critique of liberalism does not go far enough. It remains within the horizon of liberalism [because it is grounded in Schmitt's understanding of Hobbes]. To complete the critique it is necessary to go beyond that horizon, and for Strauss that means to go back behind it.[28]

Thus far Xenos is basically correct about Strauss's stance toward Schmitt. But a full understanding of Strauss's position depends on understanding what Xenos calls "going back behind" liberal thought. Xenos identifies Strauss's "effort" as one "to reconstitute the preliberal moral universe that Hobbes attempted to erase — and ultimately to resuscitate a preliberal notion of natural law."[29] And that preliberal view involves "a return to a view of the human being as naturally evil, and not innocently so." From here, Xenos reasons to Strauss's affirmation of "authoritarian rule" as "the more 'natural' response" to natural human evil. Xenos finds his reading confirmed by the supplementary letter Strauss wrote to Schmitt. In that letter Strauss calls attention to an ambivalence in Schmitt's book on how to characterize the difference between the political left and the political right. In one place Schmitt identifies the difference as one between international pacifism and bellicose nationalism, but later as between anarchism and authoritarianism.[30] Strauss writes to Schmitt both to call attention to this ambivalent and shifting formulation and to query the jurist on whether a certain line of thought that he (Strauss) has formulated captures Schmitt's underlying idea connecting these different formulations. He asks: "Does it accord with your understanding to explain the connection . . . as follows: The ultimate foundation of the Right is the principle of the natural evil of man; because man is by nature evil, he therefore needs *dominion*. But dominion can be established, that is, men can be unified only in a unity against—against other men."[31]

Here in a few words is the core of Xenos's interpretation of the politics and political philosophy of the young Strauss. The chief problem with Xenos's construction is that he is attributing to Strauss, as Strauss's own view, a conjecture Strauss is putting forward as a way to explain the ambivalence in Schmitt's book. This is not even a difficult case, as some are, when Strauss so blends his voice with that of the author he is interpreting that it is legitimately difficult to sort them out. But here Strauss introduces the whole conjecture with the query "does it accord with your understanding," i.e., do you understand things this way? That this is Strauss's reconstruction of what Schmitt thinks, or needs to, in order to present a consistent view is clear from the original "Notes." In describing Schmitt's "affirmation," i.e., normatively affirmative stance toward the political, Strauss asserts that "the task therefore arises—for the purposes of the radical critique of liberalism that Schmitt strives for—of nullifying the view of human evil as animal and thus of innocent evil and to return to the view of human evil as moral baseness; only in this way can Schmitt remain in harmony with himself if indeed the 'core of the political idea' is 'the morally demanding decision'" ("NCS," 110). Strauss has not endorsed any of these ideas as his own—not the idea of natural human evil and not the idea that the "core of the political" is the "morally demanding decision." All of these are Schmitt's affirmations, the logical structure of which Strauss is attempting to discern. As Meier points out, Strauss's challenge to Schmitt drives the latter to be more explicit about his grounding in Christian revelation, a grounding that gives him a way to speak of evil as anything but innocent. It is not clear to us that Strauss inferred Christian revelation rather than Hobbes to be the true foundation of Schmitt's thought; it is clear, however, that Strauss did not signal his own turn to Christian revelation and the notion of original sin in his critique of Schmitt.

STRAUSS'S UNDERSTANDING OF THE ORIGINAL "CONCEPT" OF THE POLITICAL

In order to determine the truth or falsity of modern philosophical concepts, Strauss argued in his essay "Political Philosophy and History," it is necessary to recapture the experiential basis and rationale of those concepts, first articulated by ancient political philosophers, which were adapted by medieval political philosophers to accommodate the world of revealed religion, and then further transformed by the moderns. The concepts Strauss had in mind included not only human nature and its potential for development or excellence, but also the basic kinds of regimes (monarchies, aristocracies, democracies, oligarchies, and tyrannies) and their goals (virtue, justice, liberty, equality, wealth and dominion).

By returning to the ancients Strauss thought he had recaptured the origin of a "concept of the political" radically different from those of both Hobbes and Schmitt. In *Natural Right and History* he summarized the classical understanding of what it is to be human as follows: "Man is by nature a social being. He is so constituted that he cannot live or live well, except by living with others. Since it is reason or speech that distinguishes him from other animals, and speech is communication, man is social in a more radical sense than any other social animal. . . . Love, affection, friendship, pity are as natural to him as concern with his own good and calculation of what is conducive to his own good" (*NRH*, 129). These "sociable" features of human nature are more primary than the enmity Schmitt posited as fundamental.

Classical political philosophers saw that, by virtue of our rationality, "human beings have a latitude of alternatives such as no other earthly being has." But these philosophers also thought that "the sense of latitude . . . is accompanied by a sense that the full and unrestrained exercise of that freedom is not right." They saw that human freedom was constrained in a number of different ways. First, they observed that a society designed to foster human perfection has to be kept together by mutual trust. Since trust presupposes acquaintance, a society dedicated to the pursuit of human excellence has to be small enough to permit mutual acquaintance and affection. And "if the society in which man can reach the perfection of his nature is necessarily a small and therefore closed society," they concluded, "the distinction of the human race into a number of independent groups is according to nature." But "this distinction is not natural in the sense that the members of one civil society are by nature different from the members of others" (*NRH*, 130–32). Cities do not grow like plants. They are not simply based on common descent.

The third and most fundamental reason human freedom is limited is that we are mixed, bodily creatures, constituted by nature so that we cannot achieve human perfection except by keeping down our lower impulses. We cannot rule our own bodies merely by persuasion. And "what is true of self-restraint . . . applies in principle to the restraint and coercion of others" (*NRH*, 130–32). Because human beings have to repress their violent passions in order to live together in peace, classical political philosophers thought, human societies, like the human soul, will always be characterized by a hierarchy of rulers and ruled. Political societies will, therefore, be characterized by ongoing controversies about who should rule.

Strauss may seem to sound a bit like Schmitt when he explains why his contemporaries no longer understand what is meant by *politeia* or "regime." "*Politeia* is ordinarily translated by 'constitution.' But when using the term 'constitution' in a political context, modern men almost inevitably mean a legal phenomenon, something like the fundamental law of the land." But, as the classical philosophers saw, laws have to be adopted, preserved, and administered by men. Regimes are thus defined, fundamentally, not by their laws but by the human type or types that a society regards as most respectable and worthy of admiration. All other things and activities are judged by whether they are embraced by or foster the development of the authoritative type or types, whether that be the common man, the priest, or the wealthy oligarch. Somewhat like Schmitt, therefore, classical political philosophers understood "the political" to be all-pervasive and to constitute a "way of life" rather than merely a set of laws and institutions (*NRH*, 136–37).

Strauss sounds even more like Schmitt when he observes that "the central significance of the phenomena called 'regimes' has become blurred. The reasons for this change are the same as those responsible for the fact that political history has ceded its former pre-eminence to social, cultural, economic, etc., history." This is the liberal conception of "culture," of which Strauss thought Schmitt's concept of the political implied a critique. As a result of the division of human life into state and society—and the consequent understanding of the powers of the "state" as limited—Strauss observes that "we are in the habit of speaking of 'civilizations' where the classics spoke of 'regimes.' . . . If we inquire how one can tell one civilization from another, we are informed that the most obvious and least misleading mark is the difference in artistic styles." But "societies do not go to war with one another on account of differences of artistic styles. Our orientation by civilization instead of by regimes, would seem to be due to peculiar estrangement from those life-and-death issues which move and animate societies and keep them together" (*NRH*, 138).

In contrast to Schmitt's view of the political, however, Strauss emphasizes that classical political philosophers did not think that societies are held together *merely* by the willingness of their members to risk their lives in order to defend their community from an external—or internal—threat. They thought that political associations are ordered and thus held together by a certain understanding of what is just or right. That understanding determines what type of person becomes authoritative, i.e., who rules. Strauss thus clarifies the difference between the classical understanding of politics that he wishes to revive and Schmitt's "concept of the political" when he observes that "a decent society will not go to war *except for a just cause*" (emphasis added). But, he acknowledges, what a generally decent society "will do during a war will depend to a certain extent on what the enemy— possibly an absolutely unscrupulous and savage enemy—forces it to do. There are no limits which can be defined in advance." Like Schmitt, Strauss recognizes that there may be an "extreme situation . . . in which the very existence or independence of a society is at stake." But he insists, in opposition to Schmitt, that "what cannot be decided in advance by universal rules, what can be decided in the critical moment by the most competent and most conscientious statesman on the spot, can be made visible as just, in retrospect, to all" (*NRH*, 160–61). Neither the actors nor the observers of political deeds should take their bearings or the standards by which they judge the necessity or morality of those deeds from the extreme situation in which the ordinary norms of decency, much less right, have to be violated. They must, on the contrary, judge those deeds or deviations in terms of ultimately just or unjust results. From Strauss's point of view, Schmitt was a follower of modern political philosophers like Machiavelli and Hobbes, who took their bearings from the extreme situation, rather than from the ordinary, decent, and right. And he thought that such an orientation had proved, both theoretically and practically, to be destructive of morality, justice, and moderate self-restraint.

Was Strauss a Fascist?

STRAUSS'S LETTER TO KARL LÖWITH IN MAY 1933

Xenos, McCormick, and others who made such strenuous efforts to connect Strauss to Schmitt were not interested in the merely scholarly issue of who influenced Strauss's developing thought. As should be clear from our discussion of Xenos, the driving force was an interest in Strauss's politics. Xenos wanted to vindicate the various efforts to connect Strauss to neoconservatism, George W. Bush, and the Iraq War. Others, like McCormick, wished to connect Strauss to authoritarian politics more generally.

For Xenos Strauss's essay on Schmitt was not the real tip-off about

Strauss's politics. That was supplied instead by a letter, published only in 2001, from Strauss to his longtime friend Karl Löwith. Dated May 19, 1933, the letter was written shortly after Hitler came to power. Strauss was, on that date, in Paris on the first of his Rockefeller grants. Xenos takes the letter to express a point of view Strauss arrived at in the early 1930s and that "remained constant thereafter." On coming to America, Xenos argues, Strauss muted, or rather concealed, his position under an exoteric "cloak."[32] This letter to Löwith supplies Xenos with an account of Strauss's "uncloaked" political views, which he then uses to decipher Strauss's texts where the uncloaked views do not appear so readily, requiring all that "tedious exegesis and convoluted explication" to bring to the surface what Xenos already knew to be there.

Xenos quotes the now infamous letter as follows: "That the Germany of the right does not tolerate us [Jews] absolutely does not follow from the principles of the right." On the contrary, "only from the principles of the right, from the fascist, authoritarian, *imperialist* principles, can one protest against the dreadful state of affairs." Xenos published an early version of the fuller argument he made in his 2008 book *Cloaked in Virtue* in an article in an electronic journal in the spring of 2004 that seems to have attracted little attention.[33] But two years later the letter was published in a law blog by Scott Horton, a Columbia University professor of law, and speculation about it then went mini-viral: the translation of the letter provoked forty-seven pages of commentary. Like some other early commentators Horton concluded, far more moderately than Xenos, that Strauss had been attracted to authoritarian, fascist ideas in the 1930s, but that he had later changed his mind.[34] Responding to a review of Eugene Sheppard's book on the early Strauss by Harvey C. Mansfield published in December 2009 in the *Claremont Review of Books*, Horton published another article in *Harper's*, in which he stated that he was not persuaded either by the Sheppard critique of Strauss or by the defense of Strauss by his students. Horton first quoted Mansfield's interpretation of the letter:

> The letter certainly confirms Strauss's disgust with the liberalism of Weimar Germany, a pitiful and cowardly liberalism unable to defend itself against the Nazis because it had abandoned its own fixed truths and absorbed much of the relativism of German nihilism. . . . Obviously this was not the case with all liberalism in 1933, for Strauss fled the Nazi enemy to France, then England, and finally to the United States—all liberal democracies and the last two, it turned out, not incurably infected with appease-

ment. In effect, Strauss's letter warns Löwith against putting his trust in the liberals (and Christians) of Germany, who had given false assurance of security to German Jews.[35]

But Horton then added his own gloss:

> Mansfield does an amazing job of projecting back to the first years of Strauss's emigration attitudes that he developed over a career of writing after he came to the United States. Essentially he's presenting Strauss as a dynamic new kind of liberal, who is prepared to act robustly (and militarily) to defend democratic institutions. This argument presents a strange contortion of liberalism, just as the main themes of neoconservatism present a departure from the traditional conservatism of the Anglo-American world. But it seriously distorts Strauss's attitude towards fascism at the time of emigration.[36]

Like Xenos, Horton was interested in maintaining the link between Strauss and the "neoconservative" foreign policy of the Bush administration. He thus concluded his article by reiterating his earlier judgment that Strauss had "clearly changed his attitudes as he came to see that the American project was not the unsustainable horror he first made it out to be. But," he also insisted, "much of Strauss's thinking and his thoughts about 'bolstering' American democracy go back to the Caesarism that was common coinage in the days of his university schooling. It clearly has been extremely influential. And not necessarily in a good way."[37]

In our 2006 book *The Truth about Leo Strauss*, we argued that Strauss was not the "mastermind" behind the war in Iraq. We did not address the Löwith letter, specifically, for two reasons: First, we were barely aware of it when writing the book (2003–4). We had seen Xenos's online article but had not paid much attention to the letter as reprinted there. Second, so far as we were aware of it, we were inclined to dismiss its importance for our task, the explication of Strauss's mature political thought. The letter dates from the early 1930s, well before Strauss intellectually became Strauss and well before he had experienced many of the events that would shape his political thoughts about the modern world and its possibilities. We will return to both of these themes below.

If for no other reason than the controversy it has spawned, the letter deserves address. We wish to place the letter in the somewhat broader context of Strauss's understanding of politics—practical politics—in the period between the world wars in Germany and after the war in the United States.

First, what should we make of the letter to Löwith? Should we take it to disclose Strauss's real, hidden, or not-so-hidden attachment to "fascism, authoritarianism, and imperialism," as Xenos takes it to be? We think not. One reason Xenos and some others find the letter so significant is implied in Xenos's title, with its emphasis on "cloaking" and "unveiling." In 1933, when he composed the letter, Strauss had not yet discovered the phenomenon of esotericism that has become his trademark methodological idea.[38] Giving weight to Strauss's own dictum that a thinker writes as he reads, Xenos and others conclude that the Strauss who writes after his discovery of esotericism writes esoterically, i.e., cloaks his unpopular or dangerous views in a politically acceptable rhetoric. The pre-esotericism letter is thus so revealing because it is the open version of his views, which Strauss went to great lengths to conceal or moderate later.

We have argued in *The Truth about Leo Strauss* that despite Strauss's dictum about reading and writing, one cannot so hastily conclude that Straus was esoteric, or a practitioner of the art of writing, in the way of, and for the reasons he attributed to, earlier writers in the philosophic tradition.[39] As we have argued above, we believe Xenos's interpretation of Strauss has been so much governed by his a priori notions of what Strauss "really thinks" that he badly misreads Strauss's texts.

We would preface our discussion of the Löwith letter and some of the other texts from the early 1940s with one general observation. Xenos and many others who take the letter very seriously look to it to find Strauss's true political principles or his "political understanding."[40] But the letter concerns a question of political practice, i.e., what should be done by certain individuals or kinds of human beings in a specific set of circumstances. It is not a statement, much less an explanation, of his principles. Indeed, in 1933, when Strauss wrote to Löwith, he had not yet worked out his mature understanding of the principles elaborated by the classics, much less their application to contemporary politics. He was immediately—one might even say, urgently—concerned about what members of the "German-Jewish intellectual proletariat," including himself and Löwith, should do after the Nazis' rise to power in Germany. These Jews could no longer honorably live, much less earn their bread, in the land where they had been born. To understand the significance of the letter, it is necessary to take account of the shared characteristics of the author and his addressee as well as the particular circumstances under which he wrote.

Strauss writes from Paris in the immediate wake of the ascent to power of the Hitler government. He begins the relevant part of the letter by complaining that he "will never *be able* to write other than in German," but goes on to say that despite that he cannot at that time return to Germany.

> I see no acceptable possibility of living under the swastika, i.e., under a symbol that says nothing more to me than: you and your ilk, you are *physei* [by nature] sub-humans and therefore justly pariahs. There is here only *one* solution. We must repeat to ourselves: we "men of science"—as our predecessors in the Arab Middle Ages called themselves—non habemus locum manentem, sed quaerimus . . . [we do not have a settled place, but we seek . . .]. And concerning that issue: the fact that new right-wing Germany does not tolerate us [Jews] says absolutely nothing against the principles of the right. To the contrary: only from the principles of the right, that is, from fascist, authoritarian and imperial principles, is it possible with propriety, that is, without resort to laughable and pitiful appeals to the *droits imprescriptibles de l'homme*, to protest against this shabby nuisance.[41]

Xenos's heavily excerpted version of the letter cloaks from his readers the structure of Strauss's thought here. Germany is unacceptable under Nazi rule, and Strauss explores first what is to become of him and men like him (fellow Jews? fellow Jewish intellectuals?), in a passage introduced by the sentence "there is *here* only one solution"; and then he considers what is to be with regard to Germany itself, introduced by the phrase "And concerning *that issue.*"

For himself and those like him the solution is, for the time being at least, the life of exile and wandering. At this time Strauss was scrambling to find foundation support abroad. He compares his situation to that of the "men of science" in the Arab Middle Ages; he is almost certainly thinking of Maimonides, a man of science who spent much of his life "wandering." It is worth noting that in retrospect Strauss appears to have much underestimated the threat posed by the Nazi regime. He refuses to return, not because he fears for his life or liberty, but because the regime is an affront to his sense of himself as both a human being and a Jew. Likewise, he refers to the Nazi regime as "a shabby nuisance"; he seems to have no suspicion of the brutality and horror the regime will become.

He also has no sense that the regime is permanent or irremovable. He is still seeking a way to "protest" against it. What can be done for Germany that might change the situation for the better? Of course, this is a bit of an academic question for Strauss at least, for he will not be there to work for change or to make a direct protest. Nonetheless, he speculates that the only solution for Germany must come from the right; a self-respecting Jew like

Strauss can support that option, for Nazi hatred of Jews is no inherent principle of the right per se. He most likely had in mind a Mussolini-like right, for in 1933 Mussolini had not pursued an anti-Jewish policy.

Both the communist/socialist left and the liberal democratic center had failed in Germany—what else did the Nazi ascent to power mean? Thus Strauss rules out appeal to the "rights of man." In the context, such an appeal would be "laughable and pitiful." The right—a particularly repellent form of the right—has triumphed in Germany, and Strauss believes that the only hope for displacing the Nazis is another right-wing movement, a movement marked by "fascist, authoritarian and imperial principles."[42] This is the line in the letter that has provoked the most outrage, along with his characterization of an appeal to the "inalienable rights of men" as "laughable and pitiful." That characterization cannot fail to pain readers who are themselves attached to the promulgation and preservation of such rights—like most liberal Americans. Strauss was not living in liberal America, however. He had been living and was talking about an appropriate protest in post–World War I Germany.

It was a principle of the mature Strauss that the politically good is always related to the politically possible. Aristotle gives advice on how to improve tyrannies when they are the only sorts of regime possible. The younger Strauss appears to be speaking in the same spirit. What is good in a given context is not necessarily what is good or desirable in itself but what is possible and better than the status quo. This is what it means to speak to a particular situation, rather than to speak of "principles."

Xenos and others, including Peter Minowitz, believe Strauss is speaking beyond the immediate situation in Germany. As Minowitz puts it, Strauss "conveys unmistakable sympathy for those principles" of the right that he commends as an alternative for Germany at the moment.[43] Perhaps that is so, but for reasons stated above, we do not believe that the evidence of this letter establishes that with any certainty. Taking proper account of the structure of the letter allows one to see that Strauss could recommend the right as the best, as the only nondiscredited option in the context, and still, in better circumstances, oppose the fascist right.

Reportedly Strauss's friend Hans Jonas commented that Strauss had temporarily supported Mussolini, suggesting that Strauss was friendly to the right, and not merely acting the Aristotelian political scientist.[44] Yet in assessing Strauss's statement we must view it with the eyes of 1933, and not with the wiser eyes of 1945 or 2014. On the basis of the experience that hindsight made possible, Strauss too came to think differently of fascism, as his regular, recurrent, persistent endorsement of liberal democracy as the best regime for our time and the regime most in accord with what the classics would recommend conveys to anyone who does not look at him with jaundiced eye and already formed preconceptions. Minowitz well brings out some of what comes to light when we look at Mussolini's fascist regime as it was seen in the early 1930s:

> Mussolini was a widely popular figure throughout the 1920's and at least half of the 1930's. In the United States, his "autobiography" was serialized in the 1928 *Saturday Evening Post*, and he was celebrated in magazines as diverse as the *New Republic, Commonweal,* and *Social Justice.* In a 1933 letter . . . President Roosevelt stated that he was "deeply impressed" by Mussolini's accomplishments; FDR elsewhere noted that he was "keeping in fairly close touch with that admirable Italian gentleman."[45]

In light of the failure of Weimar, it is not difficult to see how fascism might have been attractive even to bona fide democratic leaders like FDR. Liberal democracy had failed to cope with the economic dislocation and class conflict in Germany at that time; fascism promised at least a hope of class cooperation, and authoritarianism promised to bring order to societies that lacked but yearned for it. Almost certainly Strauss was to the right of FDR in the early 1930s, but there is nothing in his orientation toward the right then that necessarily closed his eyes to the developments of the later part of the century. The right revealed itself to be far worse than he had believed in 1933, and the liberal democracies proved themselves to be far better than they had appeared. Strauss drew the lessons from later experience, to say nothing of what he concluded from his deepening understanding of classical philosophy. The Löwith letter, certainly an interesting (if ambiguous) part of Strauss's biography, cannot be seen, as Xenos and many bloggers wish to see it, as the secret core of Strauss's mature political thought.

STRAUSS'S ANALYSIS OF THE SOURCES AND CHARACTER OF "GERMAN NIHILISM"

Having moved to liberal America, Strauss explained his understanding of the intellectual and political climate in postwar (World War I) Germany in a lecture he gave called "German Nihilism" on February 26, 1941, at the New School for Social Research.[46] Although that lecture was published in the spring 1999 issue of *Interpretation*, we have not seen many references to it in the internet exchanges about the Löwith letter (with the notable exception of the Mansfield review).[47]

In this lecture Strauss argued that National Socialism was the best-known species of a broader phenomenon that he and others called German nihilism. He tried to explain not only what it was but also how it arose and why it was preeminently a German phenomenon. According to Strauss, German nihilism consisted, at bottom, in a desire to destroy modern civilization. This desire arose out of German militarism and fed on a desire to see Germany rule the world, but the desire was neither simply destructive nor simply imperialistic in origin. It arose primarily out of a moral revulsion against the debased character of modern life.

Why had nihilism emerged particularly in Germany? "Civilization" had come relatively late to Germany, Strauss observed, but (*pace* Ralf Dahrendorf) Strauss did not think this fact was sufficient to explain the rise of German militarism, much less German nihilism.[48] "Civilization" had come equally late to the Slavonic nations, and they did not appear to be as militaristic as the Germans. For an explanation, Strauss thought it was necessary to look at the history of German civilization itself. "Germany reached the hey-day of her letters and her thought during the period from 1760 to 1830, i.e., *after* the elaboration of the ideal of *modern* civilization had been finished almost completely, and while a *revision* of that ideal, or a *reaction* to that ideal, took place." The problem was not merely that the ideal of "*modern* civilization" was of foreign, i.e., English and French, origin. The problem was the character or content of that ideal. Strauss recognized that "the meaning of that ideal is a highly controversial question." He nevertheless thought that one could

> define the tendency of the intellectual development which as it were exploded in the French Revolution, in the following terms: to lower the moral . . . claims, which previously had been made by all responsible teachers, but to take better care than those earlier teachers had done, for the putting into . . . political and legal practice, of the rules of human conduct. The way in which this was most effectually achieved, was the identification of morality with an attitude of claiming one's *rights*, or with enlightened self-interest. ("GN," 370–71)

Strauss did not think that the reaction of German thinkers to this lowering of moral and philosophical standards was successful, however, either in its original, nineteenth-century "idealist" or in its second, twentieth-century "nihilist" form. In opposing the identification of the morally good with the object of an enlightened self-interest, he observed, "German philosophers . . . insisted on self-*sacrifice* and self-*denial*; they insisted on it so much, that they were apt to forget the natural aim of man which is happiness." Because "the difference between the noble and the useful . . . is *most* visible in the case of one virtue, courage, . . . German philosophers . . . [such as] Fichte, Hegel, and Nietzsche succumbed to [the] temptation [to overstress the dignity of military virtue]" ("GN," 371).

Nineteenth-century German philosophy "conceived of itself as a *synthesis* of the premodern ideal and the ideal of the modern period." But, Strauss pointed out, the synthesis did not work.

> In the second half of the 19th century, it was overrun by Western positivism, the natural child of the enlightenment. Germany had been educated by her philosophers in contempt of Western philosophy . . . ; she now observed that the synthesis effected by her philosophers, of the pre-modern ideal and the modern ideal did not work; she saw no way out except to purify German thought completely from the influence of the ideas of modern civilization, and to return to the pre-modern ideal. National Socialism is the most famous, because the most vulgar, example of such a return to a premodern ideal. On its highest level [i.e., in Heidegger], it was a return to what may be called the pre-literary stage of philosophy, pre-Socratic philosophy. ("GN," 371–72)

Strauss indicated his own disagreement with and departure from this German philosophical tradition when he concluded, "On *all* levels, the premodern ideal was not a *real* pre-modern ideal, but a pre-modern ideal *as interpreted by* German idealists, i.e., interpreted with a polemic intention against the philosophy of the 17th and 18th century, and therefore distorted" ("GN," 372).[49]

Having been taught by their greatest thinkers that there is no virtue higher than courage, German youths in the early twentieth century saw their nation defeated in war and forced to adopt a form of government that proved patently ineffective. Strauss summarized his understanding of the character of post–World War I Germany and thus of the context in which he wrote the letter to Löwith as follows:

> No one could be satisfied with the post-war world. German liberal democracy of all descriptions seemed to many people to be absolutely unable to cope with the difficulties with which Germany was confronted. This created a profound prejudice, or confirmed a profound prejudice already in existence, against liberal democracy as such. ("GN," 359)

We see now why Strauss did not think it would be appropriate or effective to protest the rise of the Nazis in 1933 by appealing to liberal principles or the rights of man.

In post–World War I Germany, Strauss reported, there were "two articulate alternatives to liberal democracy.... One was simply reaction," i.e., an attempt to turn back the wheel of history. "The other alternative was more interesting." Its proponents "asserted that the conflicts inherent in the present situation would necessarily lead to a revolution, accompanying or following another World War—a rising of the proletariat and of the proletarianized strata of society which would usher in the withering away of the State, the classless society, the abolition of all exploitation and injustice, the era of final peace" ("GN," 359).

Critics who characterize Strauss as a conservative should take note of his critique of the first alternative. Objecting to Hermann Rauschning's characterization of National Socialism as "nihilistic" because it led to the "destruction of all traditional spiritual standards,"[50] Strauss commented:

> It is evident that not all traditional spiritual standards are, by their nature, beyond criticism and even rejection; we seek what is good, and not what we have inherited, to quote Aristotle. . . . I believe it is dangerous, if the opponents of National Socialism withdraw to a mere conservatism which defines its ultimate goal by a specific *tradition*. The temptation to fall back from an unimpressive present on an impressive past—and every past is as such impressive—is very great indeed. We ought not, however, cede to the temptation, if for no other reason, [than] *the* Western tradition is not so homogeneous as it may appear. . . . To mention one example out of many: the great tradition of which Voltaire is a representative, is hard to reconcile with the tradition of which Bellarmine is a representative, even if both traditions should be equally hostile to National Socialism. ("GN," 367)

Strauss also objected to Rauschning's reference to a "spiritual" tradition. He believed that "materialism is an error, but I have only to recall the names of Democritus and Hobbes in order to realize that materialism is *not* essentially nihilistic" (367).

It would not have been effective to protest the "shabby nuisance" that was Nazism with an appeal to the left any more than with an appeal to the liberal "rights of man," Strauss suggested, because German nihilism arose in reaction to the "more interesting" communist alternative. "The prospect of a pacified planet, without rulers and ruled, of a planetary society devoted to production and consumption only . . . was positively horrifying to quite a few very intelligent and very decent, if very young, Germans. . . . What to the communists appeared to be the fulfillment of *the* dream of mankind, appeared to those young Germans as the greatest debasement of humanity" ("GN," 360). We now see why Strauss thought that the only effective or suitable ground of protest against the Nazis would have to come from the right. The young Germans who were repelled by the debasing of human aspiration in the modern project needed to be shown another alternative. They were not.

Strauss thought that it was easy to locate "the fallacy committed by the young men in question. They simply took over the communist thesis that the proletarian revolution and proletarian dictatorship is necessary, if civilization is not to perish." But these young men took the "if" to signify a choice; they could bring about the destruction of civilization rather than accept the historical "inevitability" of pacification by means of what they called "irrational decision." These "adolescents were in need of teachers who could explain to them in articulate language the positive, and not merely destructive meaning of their aspirations." This is what Strauss believed could be offered by the classical tradition he was in process of rediscovering. "But the German youth believed [they had] found such teachers in a group of professors and writers who knowingly or ignorantly paved the way for Hitler (Spengler, Möller van den Bruck, Carl Schmitt, Ernst Jünger, Heidegger)" ("GN," 362). These authors all urged the supreme nobility of courage and berated the emptiness, if not vulgarity, of liberal bourgeois existence. "Only one answer [to the nihilist thesis] was given which was adequate and which would have impressed the young nihilists if they had heard it. It was not, however, given by a German and it was given in the year 1940 only," by Winston Churchill in what he "said after the defeat in Flanders about Britain's finest hour" ("GN," 363).

It is possible to seize victory out of seeming defeat. Strauss never accepted the thesis of historical inevitability. He thought that individual leaders could and should make a difference. Reporting on his own experience in postwar Germany in the 1965 preface to the English translation of *Spinoza's Critique of Religion*, Strauss observed that "the weakness of the Weimer Republic made certain its speedy destruction," but that weakness "did not make certain the victory of National Socialism. The victory of National Socialism became necessary in Germany for the same reason the victory of Communism had become necessary in Russia: the man who had by far the strongest will or single-mindedness, the greatest ruthlessness, daring, and power over his following, and the best judgment about the strength of various forces in the immediately relevant political field was the leader of the revolution" (*LAM*, 225). If a man like Churchill had arisen in Germany, instead of Hitler, history might have been different.

In a lecture he gave two years later, "The Re-education of the Axis Countries concerning the Jews," Strauss conceded that the philosophical education of the most promising young people in Germany for the last century had made the emergence of such an individual unlikely. Reversing a common sort of putdown of the English by German philosophers, Strauss pointed to the qualities of English life and culture that made a Churchill possible there and that helped inoculate Britain against the virus of nihilism.

> I believe that Nietzsche is substantially correct in asserting that *the* German tradition is very critical of the ideals of modern civilization, and those ideals are of *English* origin. He forgets however to add that the English almost always had the very un-German prudence and moderation . . . to conceive of the modern ideals as a reasonable adaptation of the old and eternal ideal of decency, of rule of law, and that liberty which is not license, to changed circumstances. This taking things easy, this muddling through, this crossing the bridge when one comes to it, may have done some harm to English thought, but it proved a blessing to English life. . . . Whatever may be wrong with the peculiarly modern ideal: the very Englishmen who originated it, were at the same time versed in the classical tradition, and the English always kept in store a substantial amount of necessary counterpoison. ("GN," 372)

Strauss therefore concluded: "In defending modern civilization against German nihilism, the English are defending the eternal principles of civilization." Strauss acknowledged that no one could tell what would be the outcome of the war, again expressing his opposition to any notion of historical inevitability.

> But this much is clear beyond any doubt: by choosing Hitler for their leader in the crucial moment, in which the question of who is to exercise planetary rule became the order of the day, the Germans ceased to have any *rightful* claim to be more than a provincial nation; it is the English, and not the Germans, who *deserve* to be and to *remain*, an *imperial* nation: for only

the English, and not the Germans, have understood that in order to *deserve* to exercise imperial rule, *regere imperio populos*, one must have learned for a very long time to spare the vanquished and to crush the arrogant. (373, quoting Virgil, *Aeneid* 853)

Alert readers will recognize the last phrase from the infamous 1933 letter and now understand its significance. It distinguishes rightful from cruel and violent rule.

STRAUSS'S EXPLICIT EMBRACE OF LIBERAL DEMOCRACY — WHERE IT IS POSSIBLE

When asked to speak on the prospects for "the re-education of the Axis countries concerning the Jews" at the annual meeting of the Conference on Jewish Relations on Sunday, November 17, 1943, Strauss once again expressed his pessimism about the possibility of establishing a liberal democracy in post–World War II Germany. He remembered "the argument of German students in the early 1920's: a country whose policies are *not* fettered by moral considerations is, other things being equal, twice as strong as a country whose policies are fettered by moral considerations." But he pointed out that "it is evident that this doctrine is subject to the test of sense-experience and hence that Nazi doctrine is a force only as long as Nazi strategy is successful. The victory of the Anglo-Saxon-Russian combination, if followed by a just and stern and stable peace, will be *the* refutation of the Nazi doctrine, and thus will uproot Nazi education. . . . No proof is as convincing, as education, as the demonstration *ad oculos*: once the greatest German blockheads, impervious to any rational argument and to any feeling of mercy, will have seen *with their own eyes* that no brutality however cunning, no cruelty however shameless can dispense them from the necessity of relying on their victims' *pity*, — once they have seen *this*, the decisive part of the re-educational process will have come to a successful conclusion."[51]

Strauss recognized that his auditors might well respond, "it is one thing for the Germans to realize that the Nazi doctrine was erroneous . . . ; [but] it is another thing for the Germans to discover the true doctrine and the right type of education. . . . We are then confronted with the question 'what is the true doctrine?'" Strauss responded: "*We shall not hesitate to answer: liberal democracy*" (emphasis added). But Strauss then asked, "will liberal democracy have any appeal to, any attraction for, the Germans? A German form of collectivism—perhaps an authoritarian regime of the bureaucracy based on a resuscitated authoritarian interpretation of Christianity perhaps—but not liberalism."[52] Strauss was, fortunately, proved wrong by events in his estimate of the receptivity of Germans to liberal democracy following the Second World War, but he was certainly consistent in stating his own view of their resistance to it. With regard to his supposed sponsorship of the U.S. war in Iraq, it is also important to emphasize the cautionary statement he gave of what Americans or others could accomplish in Germany. He stated without equivocation: "A form of government which is merely imposed by a victorious enemy will not last."[53]

The Powerful Premodern Support for Liberal Democracy

Strauss presented an especially succinct account of his understanding of the sources of the "crisis of liberal democracy" in a talk titled "The Three Waves of Modernity" that was published after his death. As we have seen in previous chapters, Strauss did not think that history as a whole had a necessary or inevitable direction. But he argued that there is a logical and in this sense necessary progression to modern thought. And in this talk Strauss drew the following "political conclusion" from that logical progression:

> The theory of liberal democracy, as well as communism, originated in the first and second waves of modernity; the political implication of the third wave proved to be fascism. Yet this undeniable fact does not permit us to return to the earlier forms of modern thought; the critique of modern rationalism or of the modern belief in reason by Nietzsche cannot be dismissed or forgotten. This is the deepest reason for the crisis of liberal democracy. ("TWM," 98)

However, as in his earlier talk "German Nihilism," so in his later talk "The Three Waves of Modernity," Strauss emphasized the difference between the defective theoretical foundation of modern liberal democracies and their practical political advantages. At the end of his analysis of "the three waves of modernity" he thus insisted:

> The theoretical crisis does not necessarily lead to a practical crisis, for the superiority of liberal democracy to communism, Stalinist or post-Stalinist, is obvious enough. And above all, liberal democracy, in contradistinction

to communism and fascism derives powerful support from a way of thinking which cannot be called modern at all: the premodern thought of our
western tradition. (98)

Perhaps because he thought that "the superiority of liberal democracy to
communism, Stalinist or post-Stalinist," was so obvious, Strauss did not
specify what exactly he thought the powerful "premodern" support for liberal democracy is. But reading his other works shows that he found three
aspects of the Western tradition particularly supportive of liberal democratic political institutions: the recognition of the limits of government
characteristic of classical political philosophy; the advocacy of a mixed
regime as the best form of government generally possible; and the recognition of the crucial role of education, both religious and liberal. Although
he argued that the theoretical foundations of modern liberal democracy
were faulty, Strauss thought that the practice was—or could be—generally
sound.[54]

WHY ALL GOVERNMENT SHOULD BE LIMITED

The first kind of support a "pre-modern" way of thinking provides for liberal democracy is a general argument showing that all political association,
power, or government is and ought to be limited. Strauss found such an
argument in the two primary and most famous works of classical political
philosophy, Plato's *Republic* and Aristotle's *Politics*. Both begin, as do many
modern political philosophies, with the observation that human beings
form communities because we are not self-sufficient as individuals. Human
beings thus band together, first, to preserve their lives; but having satisfied their basic needs, human beings seek a better, more satisfying way of
life. Because people differ in their natural capacities or talents, they benefit from specializing in what they do best through a division of labor and
exchanging the results. However, because people have different talents or
inclinations, once they satisfy their basic needs, they also tend to disagree
about what is most important in life. Conflicts thus arise not only with
other cities but also within the city itself. If the conflicts are to be resolved
justly, Plato and Aristotle agree, the decision as to who gets what—honors
as well as goods—needs to be made by someone who knows what is best
for human beings, both in general and in individual cases. It is not clear that
there is any such person, i.e., anyone who possesses the requisite knowledge of who can do what best by nature; but even if there were such a
person, it is even less clear that those to be ruled would agree to let some-

one else make all these decisions for them. As Plato argues in his *Statesman* (292d–301a), people are not apt to trust someone who claims to be wise with absolute power, and a wise person would not agree to rule, if he or she has to answer to the unwise. Indeed, it is not any more probable that a truly wise person would want to rule than that people will be willing to relinquish all forms of private property, abolish all distinctions between the sexes, and give their children over completely to the direction of the political authorities. As Plato shows in his *Republic*, it is extremely unlikely that a perfectly just regime will ever exist.[55] As Plato's Stranger argues in his *Laws* (757b–758a) and Aristotle shows in his *Politics* (1281b22–37, 1283a15–22), all actual regimes represent a kind of balance or compromise between the need for virtue—courage, wisdom, and trustworthiness—in rulers, on the one hand, and the need for the consent of the ruled, on the other. If the wise will not rule, rulers will of necessity be selected from the unwise; and it is clear that unwise rulers will need to be restrained by law and made accountable to the people they claim to be serving. To understand that the wise will not rule is, in other words, to understand that all political power is and ought to be limited.[56]

THE MIXED REGIME

The second way Strauss thought classical political philosophy provides support for modern liberal democracies is in the concept of the mixed regime as the best form of government generally possible. As he observes in his essay "Liberal Education and Responsibility,"

> The classics had no delusions regarding the probability of a genuine aristocracy [that is, the rule of the truly best or most virtuous members of a community] ever becoming actual. For all practical purposes the [classics] were satisfied with a regime in which the gentlemen share power with the people in such a way that the people elect the magistrates and the council from among the gentlemen and demand an account of them at the end of their term of office. A variation of this thought is the notion of the mixed regime, in which the gentlemen form the senate and the senate occupies the key position between the popular assembly and an elected or hereditary monarch as head of the armed forces of society. ("LER," 15)

And, Strauss emphasizes, "there is a direct connection between the notion of the mixed regime and modern republicanism" (15).

There are also important differences between ancient and modern republics, and in pointing out those differences Strauss indicates some of the advantages of the ancient conception of the mixed regime. "The modern doctrine starts from the natural equality of all men, and it leads therefore to the assertion that sovereignty belongs to the people" ("LER," 15). Modern republican government is thus made responsible to, and so at least potentially limited by, the sovereign people. But who or what is to limit the people and their use of sovereign power? That question points to an advantage of the ancient concept of the mixed republic over the modern republic. Rather than simply making governors answerable to the people they govern—which means in practice to the most powerful group in society and thus most often to the numerical majority—classical political philosophers saw the need to design and distribute offices so that the competing parts of a polity would have to work together to make decisions or laws for the whole. Rather than separating the legislative, executive, and judicial powers to make sure that government did what it was supposed to do, that is, to secure the rights of each and every citizen, classical political philosophers advocated a mixed regime in which deliberative, administrative, and judicial powers were shared by members of the two major economic classes (rich and poor) so that neither could use its political power to oppress the other. Because members of both classes would have to agree, the outcomes of both legislative and judicial deliberations would more closely approximate the common good than those of either a pure oligarchy or a pure democracy. Citizens might even learn to think more in terms of the common good than solely in the interest of their own particular party as a result of participating in such deliberations and needing to come to a mutually acceptable decision. There was, moreover, an even better kind of "mixed regime," which was often called an "aristocracy," because in it, at least some officials were elected on the basis of their virtue or merit. By honoring individual excellence, such "aristocratic polities" not only obtained the services of their best and most talented citizens but also encouraged individuals to develop their talents.

Classical political philosophers considered elections to be aristocratic institutions, because electing public officials involves a judgment of which person would be best. If citizens were truly equal, anyone would be as good as any other in performing any public function. For this reason ancient democracies selected all public officials, except generals, by lot. Strauss observes that the ancient democracies Plato and Aristotle criticized differed from modern democracies in two important respects. First, ancient democracies countenanced slavery; not all inhabitants, much less all human beings, were thought to be free and therefore equal. Second, in ancient democracies the rule of the people meant in effect, as it still does, the rule of the majority; but under conditions of scarcity, the majority were poor, and being poor, they were uneducated. As a result of the development of modern natural science, the shift from a primarily agrarian to a dominantly commercial-industrial economy, and popular enlightenment, modern democracies no longer constitute the rule of the uneducated and poor. Modern liberal democracies are characterized by large middle classes, whose children have the leisure to go to school and the freedom to choose their own occupations. Many more people have an opportunity not only to acquire the requisite education but also to become political leaders. In this way, Strauss points out, modern liberal democracies are much more just than older "aristocracies," which were, in fact, little better than oligarchies ("LER," 21). Indeed, he observes, modern democracy represents the aspiration to create a universal aristocracy, that is, a regime in which everyone is educated and has an opportunity to participate in public affairs.

LIBERAL EDUCATION AND RELIGION

Many skeptics have doubted that such a universal aristocracy is really possible. The third way in which Strauss suggests that a "pre-modern way of thinking" supports modern liberal democracy lies, therefore, in the emphasis it puts on education and its connection to excellence.

Although ancient and modern democracies differ in important respects, Strauss argues that they are both characterized—indeed, permeated—by what he calls "permissive egalitarianism." In the name of freedom, citizens of both ancient and modern democracies resist rule by others. The question thus arises of how they can be persuaded to rule themselves, to adopt just laws, and to obey those laws once adopted.

In the first stages of the development of modern liberal democracies, Strauss observes, the solution to this problem was sought "in the religious education of the people," that is, in an education, based on the Bible, that led people to regard themselves as responsible for both their actions and their thoughts to a God who would judge them ("LER," 15). (According to Strauss, "the premodern thought of our western tradition" thus supplies much of the content, as well as an emphasis on the necessity, of the education of citizens.) Strauss recognizes that both the content and the need for such a religious education have been under attack for centuries by the rationalizing thrust of modern political philosophy, which has sought to "conquer nature" (formerly understood to be the work of a divine Creator) in order to relieve man's estate. But he also suggests that in the age of nuclear weapons—to say nothing of genetic manipulation—the dangers of, and thus the need to limit or restrain, the attempt to "conquer nature" should be obvious to everyone.

Scriptural religion teaches the need not merely for personal and political but for "sacred" restraint. Early in his career Strauss began arguing that reason could not refute revelation (as modern philosophers like Spinoza claimed). Strauss soon realized, however, that his contention that revelation could not be disproved by reason, because the claims of revelation were not based on reason, justified all forms of irrationalism. Later he thus emphasized the extent to which the revelation-based moral teachings of the Bible correspond to the rationally based morality advocated by classical political philosophers. However, he also argued that instead of representing a "synthesis" of "reason and revelation," the Western tradition receives its vitality from the tension or conflict between them.[57] Strauss thus sought to revive "intellectual" or "philosophical" respect for the claims of religion at a time when most professional philosophers and many theologians were proclaiming the victory of "rationalization" and "secularization."

Strauss recognized, however, that the sort of education necessary to sustain a democratic republic extends beyond religion. Modern liberal democracies are representative democracies. As in ancient "aristocratic polities," the people of these modern republics elect those who will govern them and then hold their governors accountable. Because the individuals elected to office will not be perfectly wise, the advocates of both ancient and modern republics agreed, it is best for the law to rule. Whereas both public officials and sovereign peoples tend to act on the basis of their self-regarding passions if they are not restrained by laws, the law itself is general and impersonal. Laws do not make and administer themselves, however. It is important, therefore, to take account of the character, and thus of the education, of those who will make and administer the laws. Although the founders of modern republics advocated popular enlightenment, they recognized that the people who would occupy most public offices would continue to be drawn from the "professional" or "educated" classes. By making access to both education and public office open to people of humble origins, modern republicans created a society of "equal opportunity" that was more just than previous oligarchic "aristocratic" societies had been, precisely because it made possible the emergence and development of different natural talents rather than relying, in effect, on established distributions of wealth. In modern republics education tends to be "practical," however, which is to say, guided by materialistic concerns like income and status. Advocates of modern republican government like John Locke and John Stuart Mill thus saw the need to provide future governors or civil servants with a particular kind of "liberal" education not so immediately tied to considerations of occupation and income.

The notion of a "liberal education," Strauss reminds his readers, is also of ancient or "premodern" origin; it originally referred to the education suitable to a free man, that is, a man who did not have to work for a living. Such a liberal education was guided by a concern for beauty or nobility in contrast to mere utility. It included training in what we would call the fine arts for the sake of appreciation rather than performance, as well as training in military tactics for the sake of providing for the common defense. But it aimed, above all, at preparing those who would become rulers to deliberate about the broadest questions of politics and philosophy. Strauss observed that a tradition of liberal education still exists, at least in Britain and the United States, but that it is very much under pressure, if not attack, from the demand for specialization and the substitution of "method" for individual inspiration and genius. A liberal education now consists largely in the reading of the "classics" or "great books." But it remains important, because it reminds its recipients of what true human excellence is.

Strauss warns his readers not to expect too much from education, however. It is unreasonable to think that everyone will or should be liberally educated.

> Nor can we expect that the liberally educated will become a political power in their own right. For we cannot expect that liberal education will lead all who benefit from it to understand their civic responsibility in the same way or to agree politically. Karl Marx, the father of communism, and Friedrich Nietzsche, the stepgrandfather of fascism, were liberally educated on a level to which we cannot even hope to aspire. ("LER," 24)

Nevertheless, Strauss suggests, learning about their grandiose failures may

> make it easier for us . . . to understand again the old saying that wisdom cannot be separated from moderation and hence to understand that wisdom requires unhesitating loyalty to a decent constitution and even to the cause of constitutionalism. Moderation will protect us against the twin dangers of visionary expectations from politics and unmanly contempt for politics. (24)

Although he praises their superior justice, Strauss does not unambiguously endorse modern liberal democracies or republics. He does not, because the prevailing view is

> that democracy must become rule by the educated, and this goal will be achieved by universal education. But universal education presupposes that the economy of scarcity has given way to an economy of plenty. And the economy of plenty presupposes the emancipation of technology from moral and political control. ("WIPP," 37)

Strauss emphasizes that the essential difference between modern and premodern or classical views of democracy does not consist "in a difference regarding moral principle" or "a different understanding of justice: we, too, . . . think that it is just to give equal things to equal people and unequal things to people of unequal merit." According to Strauss, "*the difference between the classics and us with regard to democracy consists exclusively in a different estimate of the virtues of technology*." And he soberly warns that the classics' "implicit prophecy that the emancipation of technology . . . from moral and political control would lead to disaster or to the dehumanization of man has not yet been refuted" (37, emphasis added).

Strauss does not specify what the costs of trying to impose such moral and political control would be. Would we have to give up all the advantages of modern medicine? Would we have to relinquish the prosperity that has accompanied the development of commercial industrial societies and the more just social and political institutions that prosperity has made possible? These are the serious issues of today, with regard to which Strauss reminds his readers,

> we cannot reasonably expect that a fresh understanding of classical political philosophy will supply us with recipes for today's use. For the relative success of modern political philosophy has brought into being a kind of society wholly unknown to the classics, a kind of society to which the classical principles as stated and elaborated by the classics are not immediately applicable. Only we living today can possibly find a solution to the problems of today. (*CM*, 11)

In the meantime Strauss reminds his readers of the real and present advantages of living in a modern liberal democracy and of their obligations as individuals to take advantage of the freedoms such democracies provide. "We are not permitted to be flatterers of democracy," he urges, "precisely because we are friends and allies of democracy." However, "while we are not permitted to remain silent on the dangers to which democracy exposes itself as well as human excellence, we cannot forget the obvious fact that by giving freedom to all, democracy also gives freedom to those who care for human excellence. No one prevents us from cultivating our garden or from setting up outposts which may come to be regarded by many citizens as salutary to the republic and as deserving of giving to it its tone" ("LER," 24).

CHAPTER TEN

Strauss and His Contemporaries

In the previous chapter we argued that Strauss was never the "fascist, authoritarian, imperialist" his detractors have made him out to be while he was still in Germany. Nor did he teach such "principles" covertly after he emigrated to the United States. In this chapter we highlight the distinctive character of Strauss's response—both political and philosophical—to his difficult position as a Jewish student of philosophy in Weimar Germany by contrasting it with the responses of two other similarly situated individuals—Hannah Arendt and Emil Fackenheim.

Strauss, Arendt, and Fackenheim were all Jewish students of philosophy in Germany, Strauss and Arendt in the 1920s until the National Socialists came to power, Fackenheim in the 1930s. Because they were Jewish, they could not simply follow or adopt the exciting "new thinking" of the philosopher Martin Heidegger—especially after he publicly joined the Nazi party that called for the expulsion and, finally, the extermination of the Jews. Because they were students of philosophy, however, they could not simply dismiss Heidegger's thought on account of its horrible political consequences.

Their circumstances forced Strauss, Arendt, and Fackenheim to ask, first, what it means to be Jewish in the modern world. As we saw in chapter 4, Strauss arrived at an orthodox answer to that question (if not, as we shall soon see, by an orthodox route): to be Jewish means to repent and return to a life of pious obedience in a community constituted and ruled by the law of God. Arendt's experience of persecution as a Jew in the 1930s led her to see the importance of politics. But she concluded simply that Jews, like all other human beings, ought to have and exercise a right to form and become members of a state that would protect them. Like Strauss, Fackenheim thought that the Jews had a distinctive heritage that should be preserved, in part if only in part by the establishment of a Jewish state. In explicit opposition to Strauss, however, Fackenheim located that heritage in the lived experience or history of the people rather than their obedience to the law per se.

In order to preserve not merely their own people, but humanity as a whole and at its best, Strauss, Arendt, and Fackenheim also found it necessary to respond to the challenge posed by Heidegger's account of the necessary course and effects of the history of philosophy in the West. As we saw briefly in chapter 2, Strauss responded to the challenge posed by Heidegger by presenting another critical account of the history of philosophy to show that human life and thought are not necessarily or completely confined and defined historically. In contrast to Strauss, Arendt and Fackenheim both accepted Heidegger's contention that human life and thought are defined historically. The experience of the German concentration camps had persuaded both of them that human nature can be transformed. "Nature" could, therefore, no longer serve as a standard or foundation of right. Adopting Heidegger's general account of the history of philosophy and its deleterious effects on human life, Arendt argued against Heidegger that it was not "being" but the individuating and creative power of political action that had been forgotten and should now be recovered. Fackenheim also found Strauss's call for a revival of Socratic philosophy to be an inadequate response to the unprecedented crisis of our times. Confronted by the possible extinction of humanity, Fackenheim urged, philosophers should insist on the Kantian principle that no human being should be treated merely as a means and the Fichtean assertion that every citizen should act as if the destiny of his people depended upon him. In sum, whereas Strauss's response to Heidegger was primarily philosophical and historical, Arendt's was political, and Fackenheim's was moral.

Strauss: From "the Jewish Question" to Socrates
"THE JEWISH QUESTION"

Asked to give a lecture on "why we remain Jews" at the Hillel House at the University of Chicago on February 4, 1962, Strauss commented that the effective meaning of the question was whether Jews should strive to become so completely assimilated into modern American society that they would no longer constitute a recognizable group. He did not think that the inhabitants of any modern liberal or nonliberal regime would actually allow that. But, he insisted, even if Jews were completely tolerated without any discrimination, they should not forget or deny their own heritage.[1] "Why," Strauss asked, "should we, who have a heroic past behind and within us, which is not second to that of any other group anywhere on earth, deny or forget that past?" ("PR," 255).

The heroic character of his Jewish heritage did not make the meaning of that heritage unproblematic for Strauss, however. In one of his few autobiographical statements, Strauss reported that he had been "brought up in a conservative, even orthodox Jewish home somewhere in a rural district of Germany [Kirchhain (Hesse)]. The 'ceremonial' laws were rather strictly observed but there was very little Jewish knowledge."[2] At age seventeen he became a political Zionist.[3] As an adult, Strauss was never orthodox or observant.[4] He was, however, passionately concerned about recapturing and preserving the "Jewish knowledge" that had been lacking in his upbringing.

Strauss presented his understanding of the political and philosophical context in which he began to work in the autobiographical preface he added to the English translation of *Spinoza's Critique of Religion* in 1965. The persistence of private prejudice and discrimination against the Jews under the Weimar Republic led him to think that Jews would never be accepted as truly equal members of another state. To assert and protect their dignity as human beings, they would have to form their own state. As a youth, he thus became a political Zionist. Later he came to see that a secular "Jewish" liberal democracy would not be essentially different from any other liberal democracy. A distinctively Jewish state would have to be not only a "community of descent, of the blood" but "also a community of the mind." However, "the Jewish heritage presents itself not as a product of the human mind, but as divine gift, as divine revelation." Strauss thus concluded that political Zionism had to become "cultural Zionism" and that "cultural Zionism" had to become "religious Zionism," if and when it understood itself. But religious Zionism must "regard as blasphemous the notion of a human solution to the Jewish problem." Religious Zionists could see "the establishment of the state of Israel as the most important event in Jewish history since the completion of the Talmud." But a people who truly believed that their existence and salvation depended upon loving God could not regard the establishment of the state of Israel "as the arrival of the messianic age, of the redemption of Israel and of all men" (*LAM,* 229–30). The establishment of a Jewish state in Israel would benefit the Jewish people, but it would not and could not solve "the Jewish problem."

There was, however, "a Jewish problem which is humanly soluble." That was the problem confronted by a Jewish youth who had "severed his connection with the Jewish community in the expectation that he would thus become a normal member of a purely liberal or of a universal human society" and was perplexed when he found that there was no such society. That youth could return to "the community established by the Jewish faith and the Jewish way of life" (*LAM*, 231).

Some of his contemporaries objected that such a return would involve a sacrifice of their intellectual probity. But others assured them that the perceived conflict between religion, on the one hand, and science and history, on the other, was based on a misunderstanding of "revelation as a body of teachings and rules that could never become known to the unassisted human mind as true and binding." And this misunderstanding is "removed when the content of revelation is seen to be rational, which does not necessarily mean that everything hitherto thought to be revealed is rational" (*LAM*, 231). Strauss objected, however, that the claim that "the truth of traditional Judaism is the religion of reason, or the religion of reason is secularized Judaism" could be made for Christianity as well, "and however close secularized Judaism and secularized Christianity might come to each other, they are not identical, and as purely rational they ought to be identical." Even more problematic, "if the truth of Judaism is the religion of reason, then what was formerly believed to be revelation by the transcendent God must now be understood as the work of the human imagination in which human reason was effective to some extent." In other words, there is no reason not "to assert that God Himself is a product of the human mind" (*LAM*, 231–32).

Advocates of the "new thinking" like Martin Buber and Franz Rosenzweig thought they could overcome these problems by observing that such "rationalizing" interpretations of religion contradict not merely inherited opinions but present experience. God's revealing himself to Man is not known merely as a result of traditions going back to the remote past and thus merely believed. "It is the experience of an unequivocal command addressed to me here and now as distinguished from general laws or ideas which are always disputable and permitting of exceptions; only by surrendering to God's experienced call which calls for one's loving Him with all one's heart, with all one's soul, and with all one's might can one come to see the other human being as one's brother and love him as oneself." However, they also saw that because this is an "experience which every human being can have if he does not refuse himself to it, . . . the absolute experience will not lead back to Judaism . . . if it does not recognize itself in the Bible . . . , and if it is not linked up with considerations of how traditional Judaism understands itself and with meditations about the mysterious fate of the Jewish people" (*LAM*, 232–33).

Strauss observed, however, that in addition to showing that it was founded on present human experience and not mere hearsay or tradition and that an experience open to human beings as human beings could also be connected specifically to Jewish traditions, a "return to Judaism also requires today the overcoming of what one may call the perennial obstacle to the Jewish faith: of traditional philosophy, which is of Greek, pagan origin." As in the case of the youth worried about maintaining his intellectual probity, "respectable, impressive, or specious alternatives to the acceptance of revelation . . . have always presented themselves and still present themselves as based on what man knows by himself, by his reason" (*LAM*, 232–33).

The founder of the "new thinking," Franz Rosenzweig, thought that it was now possible to overcome the philosophical objections raised to the acceptance of revelation in the past, because "reason reached its perfection in Hegel's system; the essential limitations of Hegel's system show the essential limitations of reason and therewith the radical inadequacy of all rational objections to revelation" (*LAM*, 233). Reason cannot explain the absolutely loving God whom human beings experience; reason cannot, therefore, explain or encompass the whole. But there is no knowledge, strictly speaking, of anything, if there is no knowledge of the whole; all parts have to be understood as parts and thus in relation not only to each other but also to the whole. Previous philosophy, "the old thinking," did not start from the experience of God; it abstracted from such experience or excluded it. If this old philosophy was theistic, it was compelled, as in the works of René Descartes, to have recourse to demonstrations of the existence of God as a thinking or a thinking and willing being. The "new thinking," originated by Rosenzweig, "speaks of God, man, and the world as actually experienced, as realities irreducible to one another, whereas all traditional philosophy was reductionist" (233). Instead of reason's disproving revelation, Rosenzweig insisted, "revelation" in the form of this fundamental, irreducible experience of God, man, and the world is the foundation of all knowledge.

But Strauss observed that Rosenzweig's "new thinking" was "counteracted by another form of the new thinking . . . originated by Heidegger." And, although "it was obvious that Heidegger's new thinking led far away from any charity as well as from any humanity, . . . it could not be denied that he had a deeper understanding than Rosenzweig of what was implied in the insight or demand that the traditional philosophy which rested on Greek foundations must be superseded by a new thinking." Heidegger "would never have said as Rosenzweig did that 'we know in the most precise manner, we know it with the intuitional knowledge of experience, what God taken by Himself, what man taken by himself, what the world taken by itself "is""" (*LAM*, 233). On the contrary, as he showed in *Being and Time*, Heidegger saw the necessity of giving a much more detailed analysis of the structure and grounds of human "experience" in human "existence," both communal and individual, in order to uncover the temporal and thus historical character and grounds of human knowledge. Nor did Heidegger assume, "as Rosenzweig assumed, that we possess without further ado an adequate understanding of Greek philosophy, of the basic stratum of that old thinking which has to be overcome: with the questioning of traditional philosophy the traditional understanding of the tradition becomes questionable" (*LAM*, 234).

However, Strauss also thought that there was a contradiction at the heart of Heidegger's analysis of human existence in *Being and Time*. Heidegger's contention that human beings lived fundamentally in uncertainty, and hence in anxiety, presupposed the absence of a redeeming or saving god. His description of the "world" was, in other words, fundamentally atheistic. Yet Heidegger described the decisive characteristics of human existence in the obviously Christian terms of guilt, conscience, death, and anguish. He used these terms in a secularized, if not rationalized and hence derivative, nonbelieving manner, to be sure, but his use of them nevertheless indicated that he was describing human existence at a certain, post-Christian historical moment. He was not describing human existence per se.

Such considerations might have been taken to be reasons to adopt Rosenzweig's understanding of the new thinking. But Strauss saw two other obstacles, from a Jewish perspective, to adopting Rosenzweig's account of the Jewish experience. First, he insisted, "when speaking of the Jewish experience, one must start from what is primary or authoritative for the Jewish consciousness, and not from what is the primary condition of possibility of the Jewish experience." (This is the point with which Fackenheim later passionately disagrees. As Fackenheim sees it, the Torah will not survive if there are no people to follow it.) In order to recover an authentically and distinctively Jewish experience, Strauss argues that one must begin "from God's Law, the Torah, and not from the Jewish nation." As Maimonides and the other Jewish dogmatists of the Middle Ages pointed out: "if the Jewish nation did not originate the Torah, but is manifestly constituted by the Torah, it is necessarily preceded by the Torah, which was created prior to the world and for the sake of which the world was created." Rosenzweig makes the dogma of Israel's chosenness "the truly central thought of Judaism," because "he approaches Judaism from the point of view of Christianity, because he looks for a Jewish analogon to the Christian doctrine of the Christ." Strauss comments that "it is not necessary to emphasize that the same change would have been effected if the starting point had been mere secularist nationalism" (*LAM*, 237–38). In other, more blunt words, Strauss finds fundamentally the same problem with Rosenzweig's "new thinking" that he found in Zionism, i.e., it lost what was distinctive about Judaism.

"Rosenzweig never believed that his return to the biblical faith could be a return to the form in which that faith had expressed or understood itself in the past." He distinguished the historical question of "what the author of a biblical saying or a biblical story or the compilers of the canon meant" from "how the text affects the present-day believer." The first inquiry, if thought to be self-sufficient, was a part of the "old thinking" that understood things in terms of subjects and objects. The latter constitutes the "new thinking," which, like rationalizing liberalism, entails a selection from among the traditional beliefs and rules, even if the principle of selection differs somewhat. For example, Rosenzweig opposed the inclination of his orthodox contemporaries "to understand the Law in terms of prohibition, denial, refusal, and rejection, rather than in terms of command, liberation, granting, and transformation." But, Strauss objected, "it is not immediately clear . . . whether the orthodox austerity or sternness does not rest on a deeper understanding of the power of evil in man than Rosenzweig's at first glance more attractive view." More fundamentally, "Rosenzweig was unable simply to believe all biblical miracles." Strauss commented, "the orthodox Jew . . . would argue with Maimonides' *Treatise on the Resurrection of the Dead* that if God has created the world out of nothing and hence is omnipotent, there is no reason whatever for denying at any time any miracle vouched for by the word of God" (*LAM*, 238–39). In other words, Strauss suggested, there continued to be a greater tension between reason and revelation in Rosenzweig's thought that he seemed to admit.

Strauss himself thus took the path opened by Heidegger by seeking to recapture the original prephilosophical, "commonsense" human experience upon which all later philosophy and science, if not religion, were based. Like Heidegger, he thought it would be necessary to engage in some critical historical scholarship in order to unearth the original experience that had been covered over by the tradition. Concerned first, although not solely, with the fate of his own people (just as Heidegger was concerned first, but not solely, about the fate of the Germans), Strauss began with a critical study of Spinoza's *Theologico-Political Treatise*. Not only had that book contributed massively to the Enlightenment attack on revealed religion; it was also one of the first works to advocate the establishment of a liberal republic that would enable Jews to become full citizens.

Having concluded that modern Enlightenment thinkers like Spinoza had not been able to refute revelation with reason, as we showed in earlier chapters, Strauss began seeking a more satisfactory account of the relation between reason and revelation in the medieval Enlightenment of Maimonides. Strauss's study of Maimonides led him in turn to study the writings of Maimonides's teacher, the Islamic philosopher Alfarabi. And Strauss's study of Alfarabi showed him a new way of understanding Plato. Having discovered a way of reading Plato (as well as Xenophon and Aristotle) without the admixture of scriptural ideas introduced by the Christian scholastics, Strauss thought that he had recovered the experience or experiences in which philosophy—particularly political philosophy—originated. Armed with this new way of reading the ancient philosophers, Strauss felt himself equipped not merely to confront but to combat the "radical historicism" of Heidegger.

STRAUSS'S RESPONSE TO HEIDEGGER

Just as Strauss's own thought had developed and matured during World War II, so, Strauss saw, Heidegger's thought had changed, both politically and philosophically. The defeat of the Nazis had convinced Heidegger that "Nietzsche's hope for a united Europe ruling the planet . . . had proved to be a delusion. A world society controlled either by Washington or Moscow appeared to be approaching. For Heidegger it did not make a difference"[5] which was victorious, because he thought that "America and Soviet Russia are metaphysically the same."[6] In either case, it would mean,

> as Marx had predicted, . . . complete leveling and uniformity regardless of whether it is brought about by iron compulsion or by soapy advertisement of the output of mass production. It means unity of the human race on the lowest level, complete emptiness of life, self perpetuating routine without rhyme and reason; no leisure, no concentration, no elevation, no withdrawal, but work and recreation; no individuals and no peoples, but "lonely crowds." ("TL," 316)

Since "resolute" armed resistance had proved ineffective, Heidegger began to look for a different kind of "salvation" in the midst of the danger.[7] The task of what he now called "thought" in preparing for this salvation was twofold. The technology that threatened to make everything, including the human beings it was initially supposed to serve, into mere undifferentiated material or "standing reserve" to be transformed at will he now pronounced to be not merely rooted in, but a necessary outgrowth of, Western rationalism. Western rationalism was, in turn, a necessary outgrowth of Greek philosophy and its fundamental, if usually unrecognized, conception of Being as presence. To save humanity from the threat of technological extinction, it would be necessary to show that this old conception of Being was partial and, therefore, fallacious and so lay the grounds for the introduction of a new understanding of Being as ineluctable *Ereignis* (Event). Since the worldwide spread of technology was destroying all distinctions among things, Heidegger concluded, it would be necessary for "thought" to prepare for the emergence of a new god to disclose and define a new world.[8]

To counter the threat posed by the worldwide spread of technology, Strauss suggested, Heidegger's new god or religion would also have to be worldwide. Heidegger thus sought to initiate a dialogue between East and West. The East had an understanding of Being that did not lead to mastery, but despite its distinctive understanding of Being, the East was also threatened with extinction by the spread of technology. In order to have a dialogue—rather than a mere confrontation—between East and West, Heidegger recognized, it would be necessary to dig back into the roots of Western civilization to find a common ground. Because biblical religion was originally Middle Eastern, Strauss suggested, Heidegger might have attempted to find such a common ground on the basis of which to begin a discussion by trying to understand the Bible, not as the word of the universal god, but as a partial word, as Eastern, in the depths of our own Western tradition ("TL," 317). This was not, however, the tack Heidegger himself took.

Heidegger thought he could perceive the limits of the understanding of Being as presence that had first been announced in ancient Greece, because he lived at the time at which the possibilities of that understanding had been fully worked out and thus exhausted. He had analyzed the limitations of the Greek understanding of Being as presence in *Being and Time*. Only later did he come to see that his own recognition of the limitations of the Greek understanding belonged to and resulted from a working out over time of the consequences of the "oblivion of Being," which he more or less equated with the history of Western philosophy. That history had come to its end and completion in the modern technological realization of the truth that there is no necessary, inherent, enduring, or intelligible order— or Being—in the world. Both in his infamous speech as rector of the University of Freiburg in 1933 and in his unpublished *Beiträge*, Heidegger thus proclaimed the need for a new beginning. At that time he thought that the "new beginning" could be spearheaded by the Nazi party, which would, in turn, be informed by his thought. Quickly becoming disillusioned with the Nazis and retiring, in effect, from politics, Heidegger continued to work out his new understanding of the history of philosophy or Being in his lectures and writings. Because new understandings are "sent" or literally discovered, not made or created by human beings, Heidegger concluded, the most he and his contemporaries could do to prepare for a new dispensation was to point out the limitations of the old. To say that all understandings of Being and the world are historically limited is to say that all such views are partial; in revealing some of the truth of Being, such views also necessarily cover over other aspects. Because all particular things are and must be understood in terms of their context, Heidegger insisted from the beginning of his career until its end, human beings cannot understand anything if their thought does not have a historical horizon that delimits and so defines a kind of whole, the whole of what they see and can see at their particular time and place.

Even if Heidegger could justify his use of Christian categories in his first delineation of human existence and show that his claim to know that all thought is historically conditioned was not self-contradictory, Strauss pointed out, there was another fundamental problem with his new historically bounded and defined understanding of Being. Heidegger's insistence that Being could become known only in and through human beings meant, apparently, that there could be beings (e.g., the planets) without Being. (See *NRH*, 32.) In other words, Heidegger's account of human existence and understanding did not actually provide an account of the existence or intelligibility of the nonhuman cosmos. In his *Letter on Humanism*, Heidegger admitted that the analysis of human existence he had given in *Being and Time* was still too humanistic and hence traditional. But in trying to understand existence out of itself, Strauss charged, Heidegger's later thought remained fundamentally human in its scope or radius. It pointed out, correctly, that modern natural science is a human view and product, but it did not give an account of the existence of the nonhuman world or whole.

The reason Heidegger did not even try to present an account of the whole, Strauss suggested, was that Heidegger argued that "finitude" was the defining characteristic of human existence. He recognized, however, that finitude could be known and defined only in contrast to "infinity" ("TL," 313). Heidegger thus said, "ex nihil omne ens qua ens fit [out of nothing every being as being comes out]. This could remind one of the Biblical doctrine of creation [out of nothing]," Strauss commented, "but Heidegger has no place for the Creator-God" ("TL," 329).[9] Heidegger speaks of "Being" as "No-thing," because "Being is not a being. For precisely that reason Heidegger understands 'Being' to be fundamentally unknowable and hence 'mysterious.'"[10] We infer that there must be some cause for things as they are, but we define that cause or ground negatively, in terms of what it is not. According to Strauss, "*esse*, as Heidegger understands it, may be described crudely, superficially, and even misleadingly (but not altogether misleadingly) by saying that it is a synthesis of the Platonic ideas and the Biblical God: it is as impersonal as the Platonic ideas and as elusive as the Biblical God" ("TL," 316). Like Hegel's philosophy of history and Nietzsche's conception of the philosopher-legislator, Strauss thus concluded, Heidegger's radically historicist understanding of Being seeks to combine the two basic elements or poles of Western civilization—the essentially mysterious but somehow personal biblical God and the impersonal, rational Cause of ancient Greek philosophy. But these two elements are in fact fundamentally contradictory, incommensurable and incoherent.[11]

Strauss responded most fully and emphatically both to Heidegger's analysis of human existence and to the history of philosophy on which he later based his radical historicism in *Natural Right and History*. The title of Strauss's book reflected both the parallel and the differences between his thought and Heidegger's.[12] In *Being and Time* Heidegger wrote abstractly about "being"; in *Natural Right and History* Strauss spoke more concretely about nature. Heidegger argued that human existence is essentially temporal and historical. Strauss contended that it is essentially moral and political. "The 'experience of history' and the less ambiguous experience of the complexity of human affairs may blur, but they cannot extinguish, the evidence of those simple experiences regarding right and wrong which are at the bottom of the philosophic contention that there is a natural right. Historicism either ignores or else distorts these experiences" (*NRH*, 31–32).

In *Natural Right and History* Strauss criticized both Heidegger's claim that the truth of technology was available only in the twentieth century and the history of philosophy that Heidegger proposed to support that claim. First, he observed that a philosopher did not have to live in the twentieth

century in order to perceive the dangers inherent in a technology emanci-
pated from moral and political supervision. "Aristotle did not conceive of
a world state because he was absolutely certain that science is essentially
theoretical and that the liberation of technology from moral and political
control would lead to disastrous consequences." Since in the twentieth century we have seen that "uncontrolled progress of technology has made universal and perpetual tyranny a serious possibility," Strauss thought, "only a
rash man would say that Aristotle's view—that is, his answers to the questions of whether or not science is essentially theoretical and whether or not
technological progress is in need of strict moral or political control—has
been refuted" (*NRH*, 23).

Second, Strauss pointed out, the spread of technology did not mean
that the difference between the United States and the Soviet Union was
negligible. On the contrary, he concluded his essay "The Three Waves of
Modernity" by observing that "the superiority of liberal democracy to
communism, Stalinist or post-Stalinist, is obvious enough" ("TWM," 98).
To bolster the conviction of citizens of contemporary liberal democracies
that the principles of their governments and hence their way of life were
superior to those of their enemies, Strauss saw that it would be necessary
to meet and overturn the threat posed by the nihilist historicist argument
that denies that human beings have access to a transcendent, eternal truth
on the basis of which they can judge the goodness or badness of competing claims.[13]

Heidegger's contention that all thought is historically limited was based
on a history of philosophy, but, Strauss observed, this history had never been
submitted to critical analysis. Nietzsche and Heidegger both claimed that
there was an inexorable development from the emergence of rationalism in
ancient Greece to modern nihilism. Strauss's studies of the works of early
modern philosophers like Niccolò Machiavelli and Thomas Hobbes convinced him (and, Strauss hoped, would convince others) that these philosophers had knowingly and intentionally chosen to abandon the quest to find
the best possible, if highly unlikely, form of human existence in order to
achieve a better common life for more people more of the time. The change
from ancient to modern philosophy was not the result of any necessity, in
other words; it was a product of human choice or decision. The modern
reconceptualization of nature as the condition from which human beings
should move as far as possible as quickly as possible, rather than as the source
of a general standard whereby all claims about what is good and right could
be judged, had in the long run been the cause of the contemporary loss of

faith in the capacity of reason to provide human beings with guidance. As an alternative, Strauss thus tried by means of historical studies to recover an understanding of classical philosophy "as it understood itself." He did not attempt to show that classical philosophy was simply superior to modern philosophy. "Who can dare to say that Plato's doctrine of ideas as he intimated it, or Aristotle's doctrine of the *nous* that does nothing but think itself and is essentially related to the eternal visible universe, is the true teaching?" ("TL," 309). It would be sufficient, Strauss thought, to show that ancient and modern philosophers addressed the same fundamental problems.

Historicists claim they have discovered "a dimension of reality that had escaped classical thought, namely, the historical dimension." But "the question becomes inevitable whether what was hailed in the nineteenth century as a discovery was not, in fact, an invention, that is, an arbitrary interpretation of phenomena which had always been known and which had been interpreted much more adequately prior to the emergence of 'the historical consciousness'" (*NRH*, 33). Ancient writers like Thucydides and Xenophon knew about something they called history. That history was preeminently a record of political events. It did not have a necessary order or logic. It merely recorded a series of thereafters. "What we call History would be the succession or simultaneity of [Platonic] caves." In Plato's *Republic* "the [shadows reflected on the] ceilings [of the caves] are *nomōi* [by convention] which is understood in contradistinction to *phusei* [by nature]." In modernity, a new understanding of a kind of natural right emerged "which is based on the devaluation of nature; Hobbes' state of nature is the best known example." This devaluation of nature was a necessary but not sufficient condition for the emergence of a historical consciousness. "Nature" itself had to be reduced to a "conception" of nature or the world that varied from time to time as well as from place to place. From the earlier point of view, "history, the object of the historical consciousness, [thus becomes] a sequence of *nomoi*, *phusis* being understood as one *nomos* among many" ("TL," 326). Since neither modern natural science nor modern philosophy promises to provide human beings with knowledge of the whole, Strauss observes, we no longer talk about progress; we talk only about change. Under such circumstances, the older view of history might appear to be closer to the facts as we now see them than a philosophy that argues that these facts or *Weltanschauungen* have a necessary order. At the very least, by questioning the dominant understanding of our time, we can demonstrate in practice as well as in precept that human thought is not historically restricted in the way that Heidegger maintained.

Arendt: Rediscovering the Political

In contrast to Strauss, who was born into an orthodox Jewish family, became a Zionist as a youth, and spent much of his early academic career acquiring explicitly Jewish knowledge, Hannah Arendt was born into a secular Jewish family and pursued her philosophical education at Marburg, Freiburg, and Heidelberg under the tutelage of Heidegger, Husserl, and Karl Jaspers without evincing much interest or involvement in politics. All that changed in the 1930s when her friend, the German Zionist Kurt Blumenfeld, convinced her to do what she could to let the world know what was happening to the Jews in Germany, and she was arrested by the German police for collecting examples of anti-Semitic propaganda. She escaped from Germany by crossing the Czech border at night and began her eighteen years as a "stateless person." Arriving in New York in 1941, she began writing a column for the German-language Jewish newspaper *Aufbau*, in which she called for the creation of a "Jewish Army" to take the field with the Allies in the war against Hitler. The Jewish people would acquire a political voice, power, and freedom, she thought, only if they showed themselves willing to fight against a common enemy under their own flag. The experience of the Jews in twentieth-century Europe led her to repudiate the fiction of assimilation. She faulted European Jews for not organizing themselves as a political people, but allowing themselves to remain a vulnerable minority dependent upon state protection and the influence of a small set of Jewish plutocratic elites. She never became a Zionist, however, because she thought the movement had "tunnel vision."[14] Rather than emphasizing the particular identity or history of her people, as a result of her experience as a "stateless person" she adopted a more universalistic liberal-republican stance. Insisting on the importance of the "right to have rights," that is, the right of every human being to be a member of some organized political community, she advocated the formation of some kind of federal apparatus that would limit the idea and practice of national sovereignty so as to prevent any ethnic majority from denying the rights of a minority.[15]

TOTALITARIANISM: AN UNPRECEDENTED FORM OF TOTAL DOMINATION

Arendt's political concerns became theoretical when she began attempting to comprehend "the fact of Auschwitz" by identifying the political, cultural, and social factors that led to the establishment of the concentration and extermination camps in the heart of civilized Europe. She argued that these camps were the central and most distinctive institutions of an entirely new form of "totalitarian" government. These governments were novel and unprecedented in their use of terror. Unlike previous tyrannical and authoritarian regimes, totalitarian governments did not use terror merely strategically or tactically to quell dissent and break resistance. They used terror "systematically" to isolate and so alienate individuals from one another so that they could then be melded and molded into a formless mass, subject to complete, ideologically informed control. By destroying any public or social space for free movement or discourse, totalitarian governments stripped human beings of their capacity for spontaneous action and reduced them to subhuman "bundles of reflexes" subject to the supposedly objective, scientific laws of genetics or "race" in the case of the Nazis or to historically determined class conflict in the case of the Soviets. In sum, the camps constituted huge laboratory experiments in transforming essentially unpredictable individuals into raw material that could be molded and so made utterly predictable. And, she concluded even more provocatively, these experiments had succeeded. They had shown that human beings can be reduced to mere animals. That is, human nature can be changed or destroyed.[16]

REVIVING A GREEK UNDERSTANDING OF POLITICS

Arendt clearly did not accept Strauss's contention in *On Tyranny* (1949) that totalitarian regimes could best be understood as a new and more dangerous form of the ancient phenomenon of tyranny.[17] Like Strauss, she nevertheless came to think that it was necessary to take a fresh look at the origins of Western philosophy and politics in order to understand what had been forgotten and was therefore absent in contemporary life. The interpretation of that tradition that she presented in *The Human Condition* showed the influence of her onetime mentor, Heidegger; but as Dana Villa has shown, by reading the history of Western philosophy specifically with an eye to its relation to politics, Arendt fundamentally and creatively transformed Heidegger's thought.[18]

The threat to the preservation of humanity arose from the abolition of distinctions among individual human beings in mass society along with the power of modern technology to re-form everything. What was necessary, therefore, was to rediscover how human beings could distinguish themselves as individuals, instead of letting themselves be reduced to an undifferentiated mass.[19] From her studies of the ancient Greek origins of philosophy Arendt concluded that the *polis* was the place in which individuals had distinguished themselves by engaging in contests of speech. She thus sought to uncover and revive this ancient understanding of politics to counteract the modern threat. In contrast to the modern understanding of government as a means of securing human lives, liberties, and estates, i.e., goods that all human beings seek, the ancients had understood politics to be an activity undertaken for its own sake. Only those whose necessities were provided for by others could choose to engage in such a life. The life of political action was subsequently made subordinate to the rule of reason in the philosophy of Plato. Only with the rise of Christianity, however, had the *vita contemplativa* become generally more valued than the *vita activa*. Arendt maintained that Machiavelli was the last political theorist to assert the value of politics, with its striving for individual glory, against the contemplative model embraced by the Christians. When later theorists and practitioners turned back from the contemplation of eternal truths to the world, they made political activity subservient to the requirements of self-preservation and thus lost all sense of its human importance and fragility.

Arendt began her account of *The Human Condition* by reminding her readers of the distinction Aristotle draws at the beginning of his *Politics* between "activity" (political and philosophical), which is undertaken for its own sake, and "production," which is undertaken primarily by slaves in order to provide the necessities of life.[20] In the ancient *polis* "production" belonged to the "private" sphere of the household or *oikos*, the association devoted to accumulation of the goods and provision of the services necessary to sustain life. Only those free from the need to provide such necessities were able to enter and engage in public life, and only those who engaged in public debates were considered to be truly or fully human. Like everything associated merely with bodily preservation, "private" life was thought to be properly hidden.

Modern people, Arendt believed, no longer have a sense of the character and importance of "public" or distinctly political life, because public and private concerns have gradually been merged into the "social." After Rousseau, the private sphere came to be associated particularly with "intimacy" and affection, and the provision of necessary goods and services or "economics" became the chief concern of "public" business. Regarded merely as needy or even infinitely desirous animals, Arendt saw, human beings do not differ much from one another. The elevation of economic concerns to the top of the public agenda has thus been one of the major factors that have produced modern "mass" society and the condition for the emergence of totalitarian regimes.

Human beings distinguish themselves from each other as well as from other animals by means of their speech, not the labor or work by means of which they satisfy their needs and transform the world in which they find themselves. But Arendt did not simply endorse the Aristotelian definition of the human being as *zōon politikon* or *echon logon*, i.e., a political or rational animal, who actualizes its natural potential only by participating in public deliberations about what is good and bad, just and unjust, useful or useless. Following Heidegger, she objected to Aristotle's definition of the human species as a kind of being, a "what" rather than a "who." Human beings differ from all other animals inasmuch as each human being differs from all others from birth. Each has his or her own experience and perspective on the world. These differences become manifest only in speech, however, and human beings develop their ability to speak only in relation to others. We test the accuracy of our perceptions and conclusions about ourselves as well as about other things in the world by comparing them with the opinions of others who see the same things from a slightly different perspective. Arendt did not think, therefore, that we should follow Aristotle and talk about human "nature." Nor did she, like Strauss, attempt to revive an understanding of nature and "natural right." On the contrary, she emphasized, human life is thoroughly conditioned, and the conditions—like the *polis* or the various languages human beings speak—are products of human artifice.

Arendt thought that human beings develop and display their distinctive traits—both as individuals and as a species—only by engaging in what she called political "action," that is, by articulating and exchanging their views in public. But people do not necessarily or always establish and maintain the kinds of "public spaces" that make such action possible, even though the requirements for establishing the public space are relatively simple. A group of people need simply mark off the boundaries of a certain territory and establish a set of rules or laws that allow exchanges of opinions. The ancient Greeks established *poleis* when they acquired enough leisure to reflect on the evanescence of human life. The individuals who had persuaded others to follow them and their opinions wanted their preeminence and deeds to be remembered. Only a community that reproduced itself and so lasted beyond the lifetime of a single generation could promise such individuals that they could achieve immortal glory by living on in the memories of those who came later.

Arendt admits that actual historical examples of the kind of "action," i.e., public speech, that she calls "political" are rare. It occurred in Greek *poleis*, at the founding of the American republic, at the beginning of the French Revolution, in the first *soviets*, and at the outbreak of the Hungarian revolution.[21]

There are three reasons, Arendt suggests, why "politics" properly understood occurs so infrequently and tends to degenerate rather quickly into more utilitarian forms of action. First, the distinctive character of political "action" has rarely and, even then, incompletely been understood. Even the ancient Greeks and Romans were confused, as shown by the words they used to describe it. Unlike modern languages, Arendt observed, Greek and Latin have two words that mean "to act." The Greek verbs *archein* ("to begin," "to lead," finally "to rule") and *prattein* ("to pass through," "to achieve," "to finish") correspond to the two Latin verbs *agere* ("to set into motion," "to lead") and *gerere* (whose original meaning is "to bear"). The ancients thought that each action was divided into two parts, the beginning made by a single person and the achievement in which many could join. Over time, however, "the word[s] that originally designated only the second part of action, its achievement . . . became the accepted word[s] for action in general, whereas the words designating the beginning of action . . . came to mean chiefly 'to rule' and 'to lead.'"[22]

The second reason that the distinctive character of political action is easily misunderstood and consequently lost is that people want to see concrete results. Because each and every human being is different, the results of their interactions are essentially unpredictable. And because human beings are individually weak, they want to achieve security along with the order that makes exchanges of opinions possible. "Thus the role of the beginner and leader, who was a *primus inter pares* (in the case of Homer, a king among kings), changed into that of a ruler," who had the prerogative of giving commands to subjects who were obliged to obey them.[23]

Third, political action becomes identified with rule based on force, because everyone cannot take part in public debate, certainly not all of the time. Most people have been excluded from taking part in the decisions that determine much of the course of their lives by being forced to provide goods and services for those with the power to make the laws.

Although Arendt differs from Aristotle about both the natural basis and the content of "political" debate, her conception of the "political" finds a good deal of support in the *Politics*. In the first place, Aristotle observes (1255b20, 1259b1–5, 1277b7–10), political relations exist among equals. Since everyone cannot rule at once, fellow citizens rule and are ruled in turn. Second, Aristotle points out (1277b25–29), it is necessary to hold public office and make public decisions in order to demonstrate one's own practical wisdom or *phronēsis*. Third, Aristotle emphasizes (1254b3–5) that political rule occurs by means of *logos* (speech or reason). It does not rest on superior force like the power of a despot or master over his slaves.

Arendt probably chose not to cite Aristotle in her description of political "action" because he continues to speak in terms of "rule." He does not emphasize the importance of individuals' showing who they are by articulating their opinions in front of others. He suggests, moreover, that some people or parts of a political community will always rule others.[24] He thus not merely develops a taxonomy of regimes; he also investigates the grounds upon which the competing groups claim to rule justly and so, according to Strauss, shows the way in which political philosophy could arise directly out of political life.

Arendt's understanding of political "action" is also more egalitarian than Aristotle's. She does not recognize the existence of natural differences between slaves and masters or between men and women, nor does she suggest that political participation should be restricted on the basis of such differences. She has nevertheless been criticized for her "elitist conception of great action as being incomplete unless it is accompanied by great speech." Like Nietzsche, Sheldon Wolin observes, Arendt thought that the value and meaning of human life were determined by its highest examples.[25] Following Nietzsche, Arendt was, like Strauss, concerned above all to see that the conditions under which truly great individuals could emerge and flourish were not forgotten or destroyed.

It is, indeed, her "Nietzschean" concern about the importance of recognizing and preserving the individual differences that emerged in the contests (*agōn*) characteristic of the Greek *polis* that distinguishes her political thought most from that of her mentor, Heidegger.[26] Arendt took her understanding of distinctively human existence as an "open space" in which "truth" appears to those who exist "with others" in a shared "world" from her onetime teacher. By explicitly politicizing Heidegger's analysis of human existence, however, Arendt changed it significantly. Heidegger had emphasized the difference between a shared but "inauthentic" understanding of things, which gradually loses its basis in genuine insight and becomes ever more flat as it is repeated without thought in empty, everyday chatter, and the "authentic" insight individuals acquire into the fundamental uncertainty and nonnecessity of their own existence if they reflect on the basis of the underlying anxiety they feel. Such individuals have the option only of intentionally resolving to persist in the way of life of the people at the time and place in which they happen to have been born as a matter of their own choice rather than as the result of extrinsic accident. They do not have the power to change the fundamental character of their community or its dominant opinions. By emphasizing the differences among individuals that emerge in political debates, Arendt not only brought the description of a distinctively human existence closer to its origin in Aristotle's *Politics*. She also and more fundamentally emphasized the divisions within every people or polity and thus gave a more concrete account of the source of the "strife" Heidegger argued was responsible for creating the "open" space and the freedom that comes with it.[27] For Arendt public speech was capable not only of disclosing the truth, which revealed the distinctive character of each and every individual; it was also capable of creating a new public, more generally shared understanding of the world.

THE DIFFERENCE BETWEEN SOCRATIC POLITICAL PRACTICE AND PLATONIC PHILOSOPHY

Arendt followed Heidegger in arguing that Plato changed his readers' understanding of "truth" and the highest form of human existence, so that the original experience of both was gradually forgotten. But where Heidegger emphasized the change in the understanding of truth (from truth as disclosure [*a-letheia*] to truth as correctness [in the correspondence of idea to being]), Arendt emphasized the change in the understanding of the relation between politics and philosophy. She attributed the change not to Plato's reworking of the original understanding of *eidos* as shape or appearance, but to his reaction to a specific event—the trial and condemnation of Socrates.[28]

Arendt suggested that it was Socrates's failure not only to persuade his fellow Athenians that philosophy was beneficial to the city but also to convince his philosophical friends that political action was important that led Plato to turn away from the sphere of opinion and seek a more reliable, eternal truth upon which to base both politics and philosophy. "Platonic truth, even when *doxa* is not mentioned, is always understood as the very opposite of opinion." But Socrates's famous claim in the *Apology* that the Delphic oracle had declared him to be the wisest human being because he knew only that he did not know, meant not only that he had only opinions but also that he knew it. Socrates explicitly eschewed rhetorical speeches intended to persuade a multitude in order to engage in a dialectical conversation or dialogue with one other individual at a time, because he saw that such rhetorical speeches were not true acts of persuasion. They represented attempts to force one's own opinions on others by enacting them in law. "To Socrates, as to his fellow citizens, *doxa* was the formulation in speech of what *dokei moi*, that is, of what appears to me." For Socrates and his fellow Athenians "opinion" thus had the character of Heidegger's original "truth," although Arendt insisted, contra Heidegger, that this opinion or truth is different for every individual. This "truth" could, moreover, become manifest only in public. "The word *doxa* means not only opinion but also splendor and fame. As such, it is related to the political realm, which is the public sphere in which everybody can appear and show who he himself is." Although Socrates refused to speak in the public assembly unless required to do so by law, he did not retire into the private life of his own household (*oikos*). On the contrary, Socrates "moved in the marketplace, in the very midst of these *doxai*. . . . What Plato later called *dialegesthai*, Socrates himself called . . . the art of midwifery: he wanted to help others give birth to what they themselves thought . . . , to find the truth in their *doxa*."[29]

Socrates thus showed himself, according to Arendt, to be an individual who did not fit the previous understanding of a wise man (*sophos*) any more than he fit Plato's later conception of a philosopher-king. Unlike previous wise men, Socrates did not neglect human affairs in order to study cosmic or eternal truths. Recognizing that he did not possess knowledge, he went to the marketplace to test his own opinions in comparison with others'. Socrates's method rested on "a twofold conviction: every man has his own *doxa*, his own opening to the world," so that he can "not know beforehand" how things appear to others. "Just as nobody can know beforehand the other's *doxa*, so nobody can know by himself and without further effort the inherent truth of his own opinion."[30]

Socrates wanted to bring out the truth that everyone potentially possesses. Using his own metaphor of midwifery, we might say: "Socrates wanted to make the city more truthful by delivering each of the citizens of their truths. The method of doing this is *dialegesthai*, . . . but this dialectic brings forth truth *not* by destroying *doxa* or opinion, but on the contrary reveals *doxa* in its own truthfulness." The role of the philosopher, as represented by Socrates, "is not to rule the city but to be its 'gadfly,' not to tell philosophical truths but to make citizens more truthful."[31]

Unfortunately, Arendt observes, Socrates's fellow Athenians could not tell the difference between Socrates and his predecessors. Nor did they understand the way in which the kind of philosophy he practiced was politically useful. So they convicted him, and Plato concluded that persuasion was not a sufficient basis for politics or philosophy.

As a result, Plato and his successors lost two of Socrates's essential insights. One arose from the Delphic command to know thyself, which led the philosopher to examine both his own opinions and those of others. The second was that "it is better to be in disagreement with the whole world than, being one, to be in disagreement with myself." This experience of "being one," and yet able to talk to oneself as if one were two, is the basis not only of our ability to contradict ourselves but also of our fear of doing so. Someone who is not of one mind and thus vacillates or even opposes herself is not reliable. This experience of talking to oneself, as if one were two, is also the basis of friendship; and, as Aristotle saw, friendship rather than justice is the basis of political community. Only "because I am already two-in-one, at least when I try to think, can I experience a friend, to use Aristotle's definition, as an 'other self.'" A "friend understands how . . . the common world appears to the other." And "this kind of understanding—seeing the world (as we rather tritely say today) from the other fellow's point of view—is the political kind of insight *par excellence.*"[32]

In Arendt's account Plato distorted Socrates's insight into the essential plurality of human existence, which begins and is expressed in the dialogue we have with ourselves in attempting to understand who we are, by recasting the internal division we experience as a conflict between soul and body and insisting that the soul must rule. "To the philosopher, politics . . . became the field in which the elementary necessities of human life are taken care of."[33] Practical political activity thus came to be seen as far inferior to the contemplative life, and in modern times both practice and theory were devoted to providing the goods human beings need to survive. The Western philosophical tradition came to an end when Marx declared that labor was the source of all value and that technology would relieve human beings of the need to labor. Human life no longer had any distinctive purpose or meaning.

"To find a new political philosophy from which could come a new science of politics," Arendt thought, it would be necessary to regain the Socratic insight. "Solitude, or the thinking dialogue of the two-in-one, is an integral part of being and living together with others, and in this solitude the philosopher, too, cannot help but form opinions. . . . His distinction from his fellow citizens is not that he possesses any special truth from which the multitude is excluded, but that he remains always ready to endure the *pathos* of wonder and thereby avoids the dogmatism of mere opinion holders."[34]

HOW STRAUSS AND ARENDT DIFFERED IN CALLING FOR A
RETURN TO AN ANCIENT UNDERSTANDING OF POLITICS

Strauss shared Arendt's Nietzsche-inspired concern about the perpetuation of human greatness as well as her very anti-Nietzschean desire to revive a Socratic understanding of political philosophy. In a letter he wrote
to Karl Löwith in 1935 Strauss stated that "Nietzsche so dominated and be-
witched me between my 22nd and 30th years that I literally believed everything that I understood of him." By the time he wrote the letter, however,
Strauss had concluded that "Nietzsche himself became untrue to his intention to repeat antiquity, and did so as a result of his confinement within
modern presuppositions."[35]

Strauss had followed the path "which Heidegger had opened without
intending it: the possibility of a genuine return . . . to the philosophy of
Aristotle and of Plato."[36] But Strauss did not approach ancient politics and
philosophy on the basis of a fundamentally Heideggerian framework as
Arendt did. On the contrary, Strauss thought that he had obtained a fresh,
more original reading of ancient political philosophy by taking an untraditional path back to it. That path, as we have noted, led through medieval
Jewish and Islamic political philosophy, which differed in notable respects
from the Augustinian appropriation of Plato and the Thomistic appropriation of Aristotle that remained dominant not only in the early modern philosophical reactions against Christian scholastic theology but also in
the contemporary critiques of Plato put forward by Heidegger and Arendt.
Following Aristotle, this tradition emphasized the difference between the
eternally unchanging, purely intelligible "ideas" and the sensible world of
becoming and opinion in Plato's philosophy, and hence the difference between Plato and Socrates.

Strauss's view of the relation between Socrates and Plato was emphatically less traditional. He was no longer sure "that we can draw a clear line
between Socrates and Plato." He recognized that "there is traditional support for drawing such a clear line, above all in Aristotle." But, he observed,
"Aristotle's statements . . . no longer possess for us the authority that they
formerly possessed. . . . The clear distinction between Socrates and Plato is
based, not only on tradition, but on the results of modern historical criticism; yet these results are in the decisive respect hypothetical. The decisive
fact for us is that Plato as it were points away from himself to Socrates. If
we wish to understand Plato . . . we must take seriously . . . his deference to
Socrates. Plato points not only to Socrates' speeches but to his whole life, to

his fate as well" (*SPPP*, 168). And in his depiction of Socrates, Strauss concluded, Plato showed that the goodness of a philosophic way of life does not depend upon the possibility of human beings' attaining complete theoretical knowledge. It was possible, therefore, to revive Platonic political philosophy without insisting on or even affirming the truth of Aristotelian cosmology in the face of modern physics.

Like Arendt, Strauss emphasized that in Plato's *Apology* Socrates tells his Athenian jurors that the Delphic oracle declared him to be the wisest, because he knew that he did not know the most important things. (Knowing that one does not know is, of course, not knowing nothing; one has to know, among other things, what it is to know.) Socrates recognized that his fellow citizens might find his story about the oracle ironic. All he claimed to know on the basis of his own experience was that the "unexamined life is not worth living, but to make speeches every day about virtue and the other things about which you hear me conversing is the greatest good for a human being" (*Apology* 38a). Whether or not Socrates ever attained the knowledge he sought, Strauss concluded, Plato's presentation of his life represented the contention that philosophy is a way of life, is *the* form of human life that is by nature best. And if that claim could be made good, it would constitute a decisive response to Nietzsche and modern nihilism.

Instead of embodying the basic character of political action, as Arendt maintained, Strauss thought that Plato's depiction of Socrates's life and death showed why philosophers necessarily come into conflict with political authorities. Strauss nevertheless argued that Plato also showed that Socrates had been correct, as Cicero put it, to bring "philosophy down from the heavens" (*NRH*, 121). Philosophers seek knowledge of the whole. The philosopher himself, or more broadly humanity, is a particularly central or significant part of the whole, because human beings are the only parts that raise the question about the whole. The first commandment of the philosophic life thus becomes, "know thyself." Humanity exists first and foremost within social and political orders. To understand themselves, philosophers thus have to understand the social and political life of human beings, and how the life or questioning of the philosopher relates to this universal feature of human existence.

Nor did Strauss think that the trial and death of Socrates had led Plato (or any of his followers) to conclude that philosophers had to rule. In *On Tyranny* Strauss explained that like Socrates, "the philosopher must go to the marketplace in order to fish there for potential philosophers. His attempts to convert young men to the philosophic life will necessarily be regarded by the city as an attempt to corrupt the young. The philosopher is therefore forced to defend the cause of philosophy. He must therefore act upon the city or upon the ruler." But that does not mean "the philosopher must desire to determine or codetermine the politics of the city or of the rulers." On the contrary, "there is no necessary connection between the philosopher's indispensable philosophic politics and the efforts which he might or might not make to contribute toward the establishment of the best regime. For philosophy and philosophic education are possible in all kinds of more or less imperfect regimes" (*OT*, 205).

The fact that philosophers like Socrates did not seek to rule did not mean that they were not politically engaged and active. Like Arendt, Strauss insisted that "political activity" and rule are not synonymous. But where Arendt argued that Socrates's examinations of the opinions of his contemporaries were an expression and extension of the distinctively human capacity for "political action," Strauss insisted that Socrates was engaged in a certain kind of philosophical education. "If justice is taken in the larger sense according to which it consists in giving to each what is good for his soul, one must distinguish between the cases in which such giving is intrinsically attractive to the giver (these will be the cases of the potential philosophers) and those in which it is merely a duty or compulsory." If philosophers' overwhelming desire to acquire knowledge were taken into account, it would be clear that no philosophers would choose to spend their time attending to public business and hence, of necessity, give up the leisure necessary to pursue wisdom, their own greatest love. But that does not mean that they would not attempt to help their fellow citizens. "There is no reason why the philosopher should not engage in political activity out of that kind of love of one's own which is patriotism" (*CM*, 128). Although he understood the peak of human existence differently, Strauss agreed with Arendt in thinking that modern conditions threatened to make the achievement of this peak impossible. The combination of the universal principles characteristic of modern politics with the power of modern technology made it possible for rulers claiming to act on the basis of the "true philosophy," i.e., ruling ideology, to suppress and destroy philosophy as an open-minded quest for truth. When governments persecuted dissenters and critics in the past, Strauss observed, philosophers had simply gone underground or left the country. But if a government now acquired universal power and insisted that everyone under it subscribe to its "truth," there would be nowhere to flee (*OT*, 211). It was essential for the preservation of both human liberty and human dignity, therefore, to preserve a number of different nations with different regimes.

Like Arendt, Strauss thus emphasized the limitations of modern political philosophy and tried to revive an Aristotelian appreciation not only of the difference between theory and practice, but also of the autonomy and dignity of politics. By limiting politics to the preservation of life, liberty, and estate, Strauss argued, modern political philosophers had transformed government into a public means of achieving private, individual ends. The line they attempted to draw between "public" and "private" was not tenable, however. As Aristotle pointed out, the economy, social institutions, and character of individuals living in communities are decisively shaped by the government or "regime."

Strauss also faulted modern political philosophy for downplaying, if not altogether denying, the importance of individual leaders. As James Madison observed in *Federalist* 10, "enlightened statesmen will not always be at the helm." Modern philosophers thought that it would be better, therefore, to rely on institutions than on individuals. Recognizing that laws and institutions did not always have the intended effects, they found it necessary to look at the underlying, often unacknowledged, if not unconscious drives that impel human beings to act as they do. Political acts were thus reduced to reflections or results of subpolitical economic, social, or psychological needs.[37] In fact (and again in contrast to Arendt), Strauss suggested, it was impossible to explain either the rise of "totalitarian" regimes or the successful resistance by the Western democracies in World War II without reference to individual leaders. Just as it was impossible to explain the victory of National Socialism in Germany and Communism in Russia without referring to Hitler and Stalin, so the defense of the liberal democracies had depended upon the practical wisdom of Winston Churchill. One of the ways a philosopher could most help his people, Strauss urged, was to educate other potential political leaders.

Emil Fackenheim: Modern Judaism and Philosophy

Emil Fackenheim often stated that his own studies of Jewish thought received a decisive impetus and direction from reading Strauss's *Philosophie und Gesetz*.[38] Instead of treating Jewish thought as the subject matter of historical scholarship, as it was at the Hochschule für die Wissenschaft des Judentums in Berlin where Fackenheim went to study in 1935, Strauss asked whether the teachings of Maimonides or Spinoza or any other thinker he studied were true, and he thought that the only question worth asking. But Fackenheim did not pursue the path Strauss had taken back from Maimonides to his teacher Alfarabi, and from Alfarabi to studying classical political philosophy, because he accepted a fundamentally different understanding of truth as historically revealed.

Fackenheim accepted much of Strauss's analysis of the dilemma facing Jews in the modern world. He, too, saw that there was a fundamental antagonism between the modern Enlightenment, represented primarily by the work of Spinoza, and Jewish orthodoxy.[39] On the basis of the principles of the French Revolution, Fackenheim observed, Jews were offered the full rights of citizenship, first in France and later in Germany. They were able to accept and exercise the rights of citizenship, however, only if they gave up special privileges they had enjoyed (along with a great deal of oppression and discrimination) as Jews under the old regime, e.g., to decide criminal cases according to their own law in their own communities.[40] To become citizens of a liberal democracy, Jews thus had to become "men in general" who had a particular "Jewish" (Protestant-like) faith; they could no longer have their lives primarily defined by the Jewish law. Like Strauss, Fackenheim thought that Jews would not remain Jews if they did not retain an understanding of their distinctive character as God's chosen people; it was not sufficient for them to have the "right to have rights" as members of a political community, as Arendt thought. Both Strauss and Fackenheim regarded the establishment of the state of Israel as a blessing, but neither thought that it constituted a solution to "the Jewish question."

Although Strauss concluded that "the Jewish question" could not be "solved" on a collective level, he thought there might still be a solution for an individual. He could return to the community established by the Jewish faith and the Jewish way of life—*teshubah* (ordinarily rendered by "repentance") in the most comprehensive sense—by accepting as a matter of faith that the Bible is divinely inspired, that Moses was the writer of the Pentateuch, that the miracles recorded in the Bible have happened. But what if the individual was unable to believe that the Torah was the word of God? Intellectual probity appeared to forbid young Jews from sacrificing their intellects even for the sake of satisfying a vital need. Nietzsche's observation that "probity" was our last virtue showed Strauss that this attachment to the truth was the last vestige of a biblically rooted morality, and that, as Nietzsche showed, biblical morality has no foundation without belief in the God of the Bible. Having found that the post-Nietzschean "new thinking" of both the explicitly religious Rosenzweig and the atheistic Heidegger involved a problematic mixture of reason with revelation, Strauss first concluded that there was no alternative consonant with intellectual probity but a return to orthodoxy. But, he then observed, a return to orthodoxy was not possible unless Spinoza "was wrong in every respect." And, in an improved summary of his critique of Spinoza's critique of religion in the preface he wrote thirty years later, Strauss argued that Spinoza was not wrong in *every* respect. Spinoza understood the harsh political verities better than his modern critics. He also appreciated the superior excellence of a philosophical to a simply moral or political form of human existence. He erred insofar as he fundamentally grounded both his politics and his philosophy on an act of will. Instead of returning to orthodoxy, Strauss attempted to revive the ancient understanding of *political* philosophy, which did not base politics or philosophy on an act of faith or will. Rather than beginning either with an assertion of faith in an omniscient and omnipotent God or with a denial of the existence of such a God (as in modern political philosophy), classical political philosophy began simply with the question that is first and most urgent for all human beings—namely, how do we best live?

Fackenheim did not accept Strauss's definitions of either Jewish "orthodoxy" or the truth. According to Strauss, "orthodoxy" and thus the perpetuation and preservation of the core of Judaism consists in maintaining that the Torah is the word of God and, as such, is eternally true. Because the truth qua truth is eternal, there can be no essential change or adaptation of that truth in and through history. But, Fackenheim objected, such an understanding of the truth and hence Torah is fundamentally Platonic, and therefore not Jewish. Following Rosenzweig, Fackenheim insisted, Judaism is lived. Judaism does not consist merely in adhering to a set of propositions, doctrines, or laws. To be Jewish means to live with others in a covenant-based community explicitly in relation to what is essentially and always other and greater—in other words, in explicit relation to God. And, Fackenheim argued, what that means or requires changes in different historical circumstances.

In explicit opposition to Strauss, Fackenheim thus maintained: "Jewish religious self-understanding is itself historical: Jewish religious existence is *between* Creation (or Fall or Exodus) and the Messianic future."[41] Whatever their particular present circumstances, Jews thus look back to the past and forward to the future. The hope of future redemption is rooted or grounded in their perception of God's original and essential goodness.

Jews understand the existence of the world itself—Creation—to be the first and ongoing miracle. The continued existence of the universe, especially the birth of new generations, thus becomes an irrefutable, concrete evincing of God's inexplicable goodness. Although creatures or creations of God, human beings are not essentially and unqualifiedly good. The absolute difference between God and human as well as the absolute difference between the one true and many false gods remains.

In *To Mend the World*, the work he dedicated to the memory of Strauss, at least in part because it constituted a response to him, Fackenheim thus urged Jews to return to a modified form of Rosenzweig's "new thinking." He began his account of the "extremes of Jewish modernity, i.e., secularism and a postsecularist commitment to revelation" with a recapitulation of Strauss's critique of Spinoza.[42] In his *Theologico-Political Treatise* Spinoza became, in the words of Cohen, the "accuser of Judaism *par excellence* before an anti-Jewish world" in order to convince Christians as well as Jews to join together in a modern liberal state. In a "Machiavellian" argument, Spinoza made the "Old Testament . . . the scapegoat for everything he finds objectionable in actual Christianity." In other words, he blamed his own people and their holy writ in an attempt to reform the larger community's understanding of its own faith and politics so that it would accept the Jews as citizens, too, peacefully and equally.[43] (Cf. *LAM*, 244.) But, explicitly going beyond Strauss's analysis, Fackenheim observed that Spinoza was also the author of the *Ethics*, and it was the understanding of the possibility of a complete unity between the human mind and "God or Substance" that Spinoza announced there that made his thought fundamentally anti-Jewish.

> If "God or Substance" alone *is*, then all that ought to be already is, and the beginning of wisdom is neither fear nor hope—both geared to the future—but rather the transcendence of both, by means of the insight that everything actual or possible *other* than Substance already *is in* Substances. Thus with a single blow Spinoza disposes of Creation—the ultimate precondition of the revelation taught by his Jewish forefathers; redemption—its ultimate consequence; and hence he also disposes of revelation itself.[44]

Spinoza did not refute revelation, Strauss and Fackenheim agreed, so much as he denied or rejected its truth. Strauss and Fackenheim disagreed, however, about the reasons why Spinoza rejected revelation and the significance of the failure of his project. According to Strauss, Spinoza did not think that revelation was true; he thought, moreover, that *galut* Judaism had effeminized the Jews so that they had become victims of others. In order to defend themselves, the Jews needed a state. In contrast to Spinoza and Strauss, Fackenheim never understood "the Jewish problem" to be a political problem. For him the question had always been the truth of Judaism; and Spinoza denied the first of the two truths Fackenheim thought were fundamental to Judaism: first, that there is an irrevocable difference between man and God, and second, that there is only one true God. In contrast to Hegel, Spinoza might be said to have agreed that there is only one true God, but Spinoza's God was ultimately indistinguishable from the fundamental Being, Essence, or Substance of the pagan philosophers. Like Hegel, moreover, Fackenheim thought that the unity of mind and substance or God advocated by Spinoza was too abstract.[45]

Fackenheim thus endorsed Rosenzweig's response to Cohen's critique of Spinoza's philosophy as deeply unjust. Strauss had faulted Rosenzweig for accepting Spinoza's critique of orthodoxy. Fackenheim accepted Rosenzweig's critique in its own terms. Indeed, he thought, Rosenzweig could never have "become the greatest Jewish philosopher since Spinoza" if Rosenzweig had "attempted, along with a return to premodern Judaism, a return to the premodern world and its philosophy."[46] In other words, Rosenzweig would never have become the greatest Jewish philosopher since Spinoza, if Rosenzweig had followed the path of Leo Strauss!

The reason Fackenheim dismissed Strauss in favor of Rosenzweig becomes clear in two footnotes.[47] There, Fackenheim reports that in his talk "Why We Remain Jews" Strauss expressed his admiration for the Aleynu prayer, but stated that it would be inappropriate for him to repeat it, because he himself did not believe it. "Thus," Fackenheim noted, "the most powerful Jewish philosopher since Rosenzweig came to testify that the new thinking is intellectually inescapable."[48] If it was not possible for a Jewish philosopher to return to orthodoxy because he did not believe it, Fackenheim thought, that philosopher had no alternative but to continue to seek the truth in the historical experience of the Jewish people. Strauss had not embraced the "new thinking" because he thought Rosenzweig had substituted the existence of the Jewish people for that which defined and made that existence possible—the Torah. Fackenheim defended Rosenzweig's substitution on the ground that it alone made it possible for him to provide an "unfanatical," which is to say, nondogmatic and nonparticularistic, version of the truth of Judaism.

"This bold thinker did not hesitate to ascribe religious significance to the very existence of the Jewish people, quite apart from its beliefs, hopes, actions—simply by virtue of the fact that this people *is*." Fackenheim acknowledged that "Rosenzweig's turn to Jewish covenant was, of course, a return to a premodern doctrine." But, he emphasized, that turn was achieved "by a modern, post-Spinozist way of thinking. Premodern 'old' Jewish thinking accepted the covenant on the authority of the Torah, and was necessarily incompatible with the old Christian thinking whose authority is the Christian Scriptures. Spinoza's 'old' thinking refuted all premodern authorities and rejected (although it did not refute) each and every revelation." That is, it rejected all claims concerning miracles. Accepting Spinoza's "scientific" or "rational" critique of miracles, Rosenzweig could thus "reaffirm the Jewish revelation only by means of a shift from the centrality of the Torah *itself* to the centrality of an Israel *witnessing* to the Torah, a shift that removes the necessity of conflict between a 'new' Jewish and an equally new Christian *thinking*." Both the Jewish and the Christian forms of the "new thinking" were historical, even though the experiences to which the two forms of the "new thinking" referred were different. One belonged essentially to the Jewish people, whereas the other did not.[49]

According to Fackenheim, Rosenzweig had not collapsed the difference between Judaism and Christianity, as Strauss had charged. *The Star of Redemption* ended with an argument that Jews know that truth in their heart, received from birth like the heat of the sun, whereas Christians learn the truth by following its "rays" to their source. That is, Jews learn the truth as a result of their experience as members of the Jewish community, whereas Christians learn the truth theologically, by means of argument. Emphasizing the significance of the empirical existence of the people in contrast to their creed, Fackenheim pointed out that Jews are born Jews; anyone and everyone becomes a Christian through baptism.

As Strauss observed, Rosenzweig's "new thinking" grew out of and hence presupposed the failure of Hegel's system. But Fackenheim did not think Rosenzweig had simply taken over the three elements of the "old thinking"—God, man, and world—that Hegel had claimed to mediate. On the contrary, Rosenzweig had established a new relation of mutuality between God and man—and not man in general, but particular individuals and peoples. It was a love that was not yet consummated but that pointed to such a consummation in the future. The "old thinking" asked whether Creation is an arbitrary act extraneous to the divine Essence or whether it was a necessary part and result of God's activity. That is, did God create the world simply because he wished to do so, as a matter of his will, or did God create the world necessarily, because he was good and thus sought the good of the world and of man? Rosenzweig saw that a "transcendent"

God "who creates by a whim extraneous to his Essence would rival the Epicurean gods—pagan gods!—in 'apathy': He would be indifferent to the world." But "a God 'overflowing' into the world would be 'immanent' in it, thus robbing it of its independence." In contrast to both, Rosenzweig argued that "the 'far' God forever moving toward 'nearness' *creates an independent world and affirms it in its otherness. And only in a world thus affirmed can revelation take place.*" Fackenheim thought that Rosenzweig was correct in thinking that God's revealing himself to man is possible only if God remains separate from both man and world.[50] He admitted that the absolute experience of such a revelation cannot be verified—in itself or by its correspondence with a certain interpretation or way of life. It could only be witnessed to. But, he insisted, "the witnessing itself, however, must have empirical-historical facticity."[51]

And at this point Fackenheim thought that even Rosenzweig's explication of the meaning of revelation became incomplete. What if the Jewish people, the witnesses, were no longer to exist? Because Rosenzweig did not live to experience the Holocaust, he did not perceive the need to establish a Jewish state or to face the radical challenge of history. In the face of the Holocaust, Fackenheim joined Strauss in turning back to Spinoza's suggestion that the Jews needed to establish their own state. But in contrast to Strauss, he did not think that Spinoza had an adequate understanding of the reasons why such a step was necessary. According to Spinoza, "No one can ever so utterly transfer to another his power and, consequently, his rights as to cease to be a man; nor can there ever be a power so sovereign that it can carry out every possible wish." In our time, Fackenheim observed, the absolute and "most violent" tyranny Spinoza thought impossible has become actual. The *Muselmänner* whom Primo Levi had seen in the camps were "an anonymous mass . . . of non-men who march and labour in silence, the divine spark dead within them." Like Arendt, Fackenheim concluded that Nietzsche's "last man" had become a reality; "'human nature' after the Holocaust is not what it was before. Thus . . . historicity—whether a curse, a blessing, or something of both—emerges as inescapable."[52]

If historicity is inescapable, however, so is a confrontation with the thought of the thinker who insisted that not merely human existence but truth itself is radically historical. Could Rosenzweig's new Jewish thinking, suitably modified, stand up against the challenge of Heidegger? In *To Mend the World* Fackenheim sought to show that it could. "With regard to stern sobriety," Fackenheim conceded to Strauss, "it must seem that *Being and Time* surpasses the *Star of Redemption*."[53] Whereas Rosenzweig attempted

to show how Eternity enters into history, Heidegger emphasized and analyzed the finitude not only of man but also, in his later works, of Being itself.
But even though Heidegger argued that both human existence and Being
are essentially historical, Fackenheim pointed out, Heidegger's thought
remained remarkably lacking in reflections on the historical events of his
own time. When appointed rector of Freiburg University in 1933, Heidegger declared, "The Führer himself and he alone is German reality and its
law, today and henceforth."[54] Heidegger quickly became disillusioned with
the regime, and in a statement that was not published until after the war,
he complained:

> "World wars" and their "totality" are already consequences of the prior loss
> of Being. They press toward securing a constant form of using things up.
> Man himself is drawn into this process, and he no longer conceals the fact
> of being the most important raw material of all . . . ; he remains the subject
> of all using-up . . . in such a way that he lets his will be dissolved. . . . The
> moral outrage of those who do not yet know what is the case often aims at
> the arbitrariness and claim to dominance of the "leaders" [*Führer*].[55]

Abominable as Heidegger's political choices and sympathies were, Fackenheim did not fault him or his thought primarily for his brief association
with the Nazis—any more than did Strauss.[56] The problem with Heidegger's historical thinking was that it gave him no basis for distinguishing
between the nuclear bomb in Hiroshima (used against a nation that had
explicitly declared war on others) and the ovens at Auschwitz (whose victims had not stated a hostile intention, much less killed anyone else): for
him both were "technological" effects. For Heidegger, the United States,
the Soviet Union, and Nazi Germany all represented examples of the "technological frenzy" that was transforming everything, including the human
beings purportedly doing the transforming, into "standing reserve" to be
put to another use. The "truth" of this technological frenzy was the "oblivion" or nonnecessity of Being, order, or intelligibility. It could be and was
being disclosed to the human beings who opened their eyes or minds to
it. It could not be resisted, nor could or did it justify resistance. It did not
even explain the fact, much less the significance of the fact, that there were
people who did resist it—the Allies who successfully resisted and destroyed
the racist frenzy of the Nazis, in the first instance, but, even more importantly, the inmates of the camps who resisted the attempts to deny them
all human dignity.

Like Strauss, Fackenheim understood the Nazis to be a certain kind of modern "idealist" intent upon imposing their own will or "ideology" upon the world.[57] But like Heidegger and Arendt he also thought that their near-success showed that there is no natural order that withstands such nihilistic, willful attempts. For that reason, Fackenheim concluded, there can be no return to premodern thought. We have no alternative but to engage in a new kind of thought—newer, more original even than Rosenzweig's "new thinking." The Holocaust revealed an infinite capacity for evil in human beings. That capacity cannot be merely "understood" or comprehended, much less "transcended," without giving way to it. It must be resisted—first in thought, but then "in overt, flesh-and-blood action and life."[58]

Strauss did not pay sufficient attention to the horror of the Holocaust, Fackenheim suggested, because he insisted upon seeing the low in light of the high rather than the high in light of the low. The high should not be reduced to the low, Fackenheim agreed; but when the relation between God and man, as well as the very possibility of truth or a rational understanding of the world, had been ruptured, as it had been by the fact of the Holocaust, it was necessary to recognize the fact of the rupture, the break, or the abyss, in order to rebuild a bridge across it.[59] "Perhaps" it would be possible philosophically to "recover" what "once was" by showing that a rational understanding of the world is still possible, that it was not merely the fleeting experience (or dream) of men living in the past. "Perhaps the . . . recovery . . . [could arise] from a new reading of the old great texts of Western philosophy. . . . It may also find new meaning in the person and the teaching of Socrates."[60] But Fackenheim doubted the adequacy of what he took to be Strauss's response to the current crisis—both philosophical and political. He was convinced, instead, of the necessity of engaging in a philosophical inquiry into the meaning of the events of our time. "Socrates . . . was on trial for his life . . . for initiating the philosophical quest." But, Fackenheim observed, it was no longer necessary to initiate philosophical inquiry; it was necessary to perpetuate and apply it. Fackenheim thus thought that an otherwise unknown teacher of philosophy named Kurt Huber represented a better example of the role philosophy should play in the midst of the modern crisis. On trial for his life as a result of resisting the Nazis, Huber insisted that both the Kantian principle that no man must be regarded merely as a means, and the Fichtean assertion that each German should act as if the destiny of his nation depended upon his own acts as an individual and was, therefore, his responsibility, should be applied to people living in the twentieth century as well.

For Strauss, both Kant and Fichte helped constitute the revolutionary modern "idealism" that resulted in the elevation of the "idea of man" and his will. For Strauss, Socrates represented not merely the beginning of philosophy, understood primarily as a quest, but the recognition that underlies it. Socrates was the man who knew only that he did not know. He could not, therefore, deny or reject the truth of revelation. But he did not find revelation necessary in order to live a fully satisfying life. He sought to discover the truth on the basis of reason alone. Because he knew that he himself did not possess the requisite knowledge, he sought it. He was always willing to reopen the question or reconsider his previous opinions. He did not seek to impose his will on others or to show that human beings were and ought to be free from external restraint — natural or divine. The ancient form of rationalism represented by Socrates would not support the modern form of idealism that would rather will nothing than not will at all.[61] It could provide human beings with guidance concerning the best way to live.

CHAPTER ELEVEN

Strauss as Educator
The Great Books in the Modern World

"I own that education is in a sense the subject matter of my teaching and my research" ("LER," 9). So Leo Strauss stated in an essay on liberal education. Yet he wrote relatively little directly on the subject and in one place went to some lengths to speak of his "apprehension," of his "bewilderment," and to indicate with much hemming and hawing his reluctance to write explicitly on the subject when asked to do so for a conference sponsored by the Fund for Adult Education. Overcoming his apparent reluctance, he wrote the requested essay for the conference as a follow-up to his one other essay on the general subject of liberal education written the year before.

The two essays on liberal education, published in 1961 and 1962, were composed for particular occasions and particular audiences. The first was delivered as a commencement address at the Basic Program of Liberal Education for Adults at the University of Chicago. That address prompted the second essay, for the organizer of the conference on adult education requested Strauss to expand on some sentences of his first essay for a conference the following year.[1]

The essays were addressed, respectively, to an audience of adult graduates and to an audience of "professional educators" ("LER," 10). Strauss's way of addressing these two audiences differs markedly, as is visible even in his use of first-person pronouns. In the essay addressed to the graduates, Strauss employs first-person-plural pronouns (we, us, our) eighty-six times as opposed to the mere six times he uses first-person-singular pronouns (I, me, my). That is, he uses the first-person plural more than fourteen times as often as the first-person singular. This stands in marked contrast to the essay addressed to the professionals, where he uses the singular and plural forms an almost equal number of times (forty-one and forty-five, respectively). He distinguishes himself from his audience of professionals (as "I") *much* more often than he does from his audience of liberal arts program graduates. As he emphasizes in the latter address, "the teachers [in liberal arts education] themselves are pupils and must be pupils" ("WILE," 3). As such a teacher and thus as a fellow pupil Strauss shares much more with "the less experienced pupils" he is addressing than he does with the professionals, and so he can more readily speak to and of them as "we." Almost as striking as the relative distribution of singular and plural pronouns is the aggregate usage of all pronouns in the two addresses. The address to the professionals is roughly three times longer than the other (twenty-nine paragraphs to ten) but uses first-person pronouns fewer total times (eighty-six) than the much shorter address to the graduates (ninety-two times). In place of the personal pronouns of the shorter essay we find the impersonal pronoun "one" in the longer essay (three and twenty-one times, respectively).

Strauss signals with his use of pronouns how he stands toward his two audiences. Though a professional educator himself ("LER," 9), he identifies much less with those who claim to be the professionals than he does with the pupils. The difference between him as a teacher and the profession of teachers is indeed one of the subtle but pervasive themes of the essay. He is very different from them. He announces himself, for example, to be "almost solely concerned with the goal or end of education . . . and very little with its conditions and its how," the latter two, he implies, being the chief concerns of his audience (9). Although Strauss might consider it presumptuous to compare himself to Socrates, the situation he faces, as he presents it, is rather like that Socrates faced in Plato's *Protagoras*—a lone man of integrity in a room full of sophists—which may be why Strauss makes the following curious point in his opening paragraph: "I thought that it was my job, my responsibility, to do my best . . . with students wholly regardless of whether they are registered or not," i.e., regardless of whether they pay for instruction. Strauss is no sophist, for one of the distinguishing marks of sophists is that they teach for money. Thus Strauss illustrates a certain point in this address by adducing the example and teaching of Protagoras from Plato's dialogue of that name as one who "came to the democratic city of Athens in order to educate human beings, or *to teach for pay* . . . the political art" (12; emphasis added). Moreover, since he is attempting to sell his wares in democratic Athens, Protagoras must flatter the Athenians and accept or even cater to the premise of the democracy "that everyone is supposed to possess the political art somehow" (13). Strauss is careful to distinguish himself and his practice from that of the sophist: "We are not permitted to be flatterers of democracy" (24).

Strauss shares less with the professionals and therefore shares with them less of himself, as ironically evidenced by the much greater presence of "I" in his address to them. That impression is confirmed by his insistence at the outset of the address that he has not chosen his topic, that it was assigned or imposed on him, and that he does not even wholly understand the topic as given ("LER," 9). His address is in some important sense not voluntary; it is, if not exactly coerced, nonetheless not a presentation he chose for himself. The address to the graduates has nothing of that coerced or forced character, nothing of that alienation from his own topic that marks the address to the professionals. Indeed, he speaks to the graduates on the topic "What Is Liberal Education?," one of only two pieces in his entire corpus explicitly raising in its title *the* Socratic question, the "what is . . . ?" question. (Also see "WIPP," 1.) Strauss's two speeches on liberal education thus relate to each other as the two kinds of Platonic dialogues that Strauss identified—the voluntary and the involuntary (see *CM*, 59, 63).

"What Is Liberal Education?" addresses a topic Strauss apparently wishes on his own to address: it concerns a matter near and dear to him. "Liberal Education and Responsibility" addresses a topic that Strauss is less spontaneously eager to discuss but that he is somehow compelled to address. In Strauss's interpretation of the Platonic corpus perhaps the involuntary or coerced dialogue par excellence is the *Republic*. Would it be too much to say that this address is Strauss's *Republic* as well as his *Protagoras*?

As the example of the *Republic* shows, the involuntary dialogue is not in itself of lesser importance. Indeed it is not entirely the case that the topic of "Liberal Education and Responsibility" is alien to Strauss. As he tells it, he was asked to expand upon some sentences of his earlier address, i.e., to explain something he had already said in his spontaneous speech ("LER," 10). Moreover, it is difficult to say that the two addresses differ fundamentally when both culminate in the same recommendation for the practice of liberal education in our day—the study of the great books ("WILE," 6–7; "LER," 24).

Yet it would be a mistake to jettison the numerous indications that the addresses differ, despite their common advocacy of great books education. In order to understand Strauss's twofold intention let us begin with the statement he signals to be more fundamental—the shorter Socratic inquiry, "What Is Liberal Education?" Midway through that address Strauss identifies liberal education as "education to perfect gentlemanship, to human excellence"; "liberal education," he says, "consists in reminding ourselves of human greatness," which means attending to "Plato's suggestion that education in the highest sense is philosophy" ("WILE," 6). The highest theme, the theme of "What Is Liberal Education?," is education to or in light of philosophy as the peak of "human excellence," or "human greatness." Accordingly, in this speech Strauss makes one of the most extensive comments in his corpus on the nature and goodness of philosophy (6–8).

"Liberal Education and Responsibility" also touches on the relations between liberal education and philosophy. "In the light of philosophy, liberal education takes on a new meaning," i.e., new to the line of argument Strauss has been pursuing to this point, the classical understanding of liberal education as education for "gentlemen." In "the light of philosophy . . . liberal education, especially education in the liberal arts, comes to sight as a preparation for philosophy. This means that philosophy transcends gentlemanship," especially with regard to the virtues developed by and in the respective types of education ("LER," 13). At this point the second address looks as though it is making the same turn as the first address—to liberal education as philosophic education. But Strauss abruptly turns away from that theme "by assuming that the philosophers are not as such a constituent part of the city," and by from that point forward taking his bearings by the relation between liberal education and the city, thereby allowing him to fulfill his imposed obligation to speak of "liberal education and responsibility." Taking one's bearings by philosophy would not allow him to discharge that responsibility so well, for, as he emphasizes, the philosopher has only very limited responsibility to the city (14–15).

On both occasions Strauss addresses the topic of liberal education; on both occasions he promotes the cause of great-books education as the proper form of liberal education in our day. But in the one address he looks at liberal education in light of philosophy, in the other in light of the city or politics. The two speeches thus epitomize the themes of Strauss's life work—philosophy and politics—or they raise the "problem of political philosophy." That the address to the graduates corresponds to the "voluntary" Socratic conversation and the one to the educators to the involuntary or compelled Socratic dialogue now makes perfect sense. The two addresses together also reveal that liberal education lacks a single goal and a single method. The two together address the problem of liberal education today—the difference amounting, it seems, to a tension between liberal education as understood and practiced in the light of philosophy and liberal education as understood and practiced in the light of the political. Strauss's reflections on liberal education take the form of asking what that kind of education can contribute to the health or well-being of a human individual versus what it can contribute to the health or well-being of a political community. But since, he insists, philosophy transcends and is even in tension with the city, it cannot be the case that the twofold end of liberal education can readily be served by one educational practice. We would tentatively conclude, therefore, that the question posed by Strauss's writings on liberal education, as well as by his practice of liberal education, is how the tension or disproportion between the two goals of education can be negotiated or held together in one practice of education, and why that one practice is great-books education.

Philosophic Education and the Great Books

Why should education to philosophy or in light of philosophy be great-books education? Given the tendency within the contemporary study of philosophy to ignore or depreciate the history of philosophy, it is clear that those in charge of philosophic education in the modern university do not agree with Strauss. But these are authorities he would reject out of hand. Consider his comments on contemporary teachers of philosophy: they should no more be confused with philosophers than art historians should be confused with artists ("WILE," 7). Nonetheless, an authority for whom he has much greater respect, Plato, also does not present the education to philosophy as education in great books (cf. *Republic*, bk. 7).

Strauss presents three distinct arguments in favor of liberal education as great-books education. The three relate to each other dialectically. The first argument occurs in the very first paragraph of "What Is Liberal Education?," as an implication of his first proffered definition of liberal education as "education in culture or toward culture," where culture is understood on the model of agriculture, in this case as "the cultivation of the mind, the taking care and improving of the native faculties of the mind in accordance with the nature of the mind" ("WILE," 3). The cultivation of the mind is performed by teachers, the equivalent in this sphere to farmers in agriculture. But the teachers in turn are pupils, or have teachers until one reaches the very greatest minds, "who are not in turn pupils," but are the originators or greatest practitioners of the art of mind cultivation. Such great minds are rare and are met "only through the great books." Therefore, liberal education is defined as "studying with proper care the great books which the greatest minds have left behind" (3).

This definition of liberal education and accompanying defense of great-books education prove to be unsatisfactory, and Strauss announces very soon that he must "make a fresh start" ("WILE," 3). He provides a number of reasons for the need to begin anew, among which is that "the greatest minds do not all tell us the same things regarding the most important themes." That disagreement among the greatest minds is matched by the fact that there would appear to be not one but many types of "culture," a "variety of cultures." Strauss suggests that the difficulty may perhaps lie in our too-flexible notion of culture, according to which "any pattern of conduct common to any human group" is called a culture; to the extent that is so, the notion of education to "culture" can supply us no definite guidance for education.

A moment's reflection reveals that the difficulty with Strauss's first definition of liberal education goes deeper. It depends on the analogy between agriculture and education and implies that there is a natural end of human development as there is a natural end to the products of agriculture. It implies that in education we can unambiguously take our bearings by nature. But the facts of disagreements among "the greatest minds" and of the "variety of cultures" indicate that nature cannot so readily guide education as it can guide farming. Better and worse agriculture will produce better and worse crops of wheat, but no kind of agriculture will produce a crop of corn from seeds of wheat. But that is more or less the situation with mind culture: one model of a "greatest mind" will be a Plato, another a Heidegger. One sort of mind culture will produce a "culture of suburbia" and another "a culture of juvenile gangs" ("WILE," 3). One will produce an Athens, another a Maori tribe.

Strauss's initial definition of liberal education fails for at least the reason that it abstracts from convention and proceeds as if nature is all, or as if the nature of a human being is no more complex or problematic than the nature of an ear of corn. In response to the one-sidedness of his first definition Strauss tries another tack: liberal education somehow relates to modern democracy. This movement in the argument is meant to give an answer to the question "what can liberal education mean here and now?" ("WILE," 3). To ask about the "here and now" is to implicitly recognize what Strauss's first approach to the question ignored by taking for granted that liberal education takes its bearings by something timeless and uni-versal, "the nature of the mind" (3). "Here and now . . . liberal education is the counterpoison to mass culture" or "the necessary endeavor to found an aristocracy within democratic mass society" (4–5). Although modern democracy began in the hope of producing a "universal aristocracy," it seems rather to have produced "mass culture," a kind of culture marked by the dominance of mediocrity or less (5), belying those hopes that democ-racy would lead to the elevation of mankind. "Liberal education" serves as "counterpoison" to this kind of modern culture insofar as it "reminds those members of a mass democracy who have ears to hear, of human greatness" (5). Once again Strauss connects the idea of human greatness to the great books, for these are, as he said, products of the greatest minds. Proper study of the great books would indeed counter the mediocrity of mass society and contribute to the elevation of that society by reminding us of how much more can be aspired to than the normal run of intellectual achieve-ment and human depth achieved within mass culture.

Strauss's first definition of liberal education and his accompanying first defense of great-books education proceed on the basis of a very common notion of education as the development or perfection of natural human faculties. It looks at education as a means to individual self-development. The second set of definitions takes its bearings by another very common notion of the point of education—to serve social or political ends, to fit individuals to serve the common good. Strauss has folded into that basic idea several of his most characteristic themes: "society" as such is an ab-straction and one must rather think in terms of regime, or the ordering of authority within a society. The regime gives to the society its charac-ter. Concerned with the "here and now," Strauss limits his attention to the regime dominant today, modern democracy.

The dominance of mediocrity within modern democracy means that modern democracy needs something more than mass culture provides. Democracy, even as the home of mass culture, "requires in the long run qualities of an entirely different kind [from those typically produced within mass culture]: qualities of dedication, of concentration, of breadth, and of depth" ("WILE," 5). Liberal education, in this account, is required for the sake of the public good of modern democracy, i.e., as a requirement of regime maintenance. Liberal education as "counterpoison to mass culture," as an instrument for producing higher or more strenuous qualities, as a "re-minder of human greatness" supplies the transition to the third and last discussion of liberal education. Given that it is a transition to liberal education as preparation for philosophy, the transition is curiously made via appeal to the authority of Xenophon and Plato, and not on the basis of philosophy itself: the transition to philosophy must occur in the prephilosophic and therefore must occur nonphilosophically, i.e., via an appeal to authority.

The emergence of human greatness understood as philosophy seems to return to the initial definition of liberal education on the model of agriculture. That impression is correct insofar as the third treatment of liberal education returns to an individual perspective. But the impression of return to the first definition is mistaken, as can be seen if we notice what is missing from this third discussion. There is no mention of "culture" either in the sense of cultivation or in the sense of "any pattern of behavior" and belief. Where the first definition spoke very generally and vaguely of the end of education as "improving . . . the native faculties of the mind in accordance with the nature of the mind," the third speaks far more concretely of philosophy as that end.

The concreteness of Strauss's evocation of the end of education is not matched by the clarity of his discussion of that end. He is obscure and even apparently contradictory in what he says of this highest human activity. The difficulty of his discussion turns on two deep equivocations in the discussion. "Philosophy," he tells us, "is quest for wisdom or quest for knowledge regarding the most important, the highest, or the most comprehensive things." But the wisdom or knowledge sought in philosophy "is inaccessible to man." The conclusion he draws is "we cannot be philosophers . . . but we can love philosophy; we can try to philosophize" ("WILE," 7). The two equivocations occur right here. He seems to be using "philosophy" in two different senses—first, as the quest for wisdom, and second, as the achievement of wisdom. In the second sense we cannot be philosophers, but in the first sense we can try to philosophize. In the second sense there are no philosophers, but at the same time he tells us that the "philosophizing" that we can try to engage in "consists . . . in listening to the conversation between the great philosophers." These "great philosophers" existed and would then seem to be philosophers in the first sense, seekers after and lovers of wisdom, etc. A parallel equivocation occurs in Strauss's use of the pronoun "we" in this part of his address. After asserting the unavailability of wisdom per se, he concludes, "we cannot be philosophers," referring, apparently, to all human beings. In the immediate sequel, however, he seems to use "we" to refer to him and his audience, or to human beings of our time and place, for he emphasizes that the form of education in which we can engage is to listen "to the conversations between the great philosophers" ("WILE," 7).

Surely as careful a writer as Strauss is aware of the equivocations in his text. Let us try to sort out the various points raised in this puzzling discussion. First, he is bringing out the gap between the philosophic aspiration and the philosophic achievement, a theme he returns to many times in his corpus (e.g., "WIPP," 11, 38–40). That theme in turn leads to a most pressing problem—why philosophy, if philosophy is such a "Sisyphean" enterprise? (40). He will return to this question at the end of "What Is Liberal Education?"

Second, he is bringing out the particularly problematic character of philosophy in the "here and now," i.e., in modernity. This too is a common theme in his work. His general point could be stated as follows. Philosophy is always a difficult enterprise and a rare achievement. Although human beings are in a sense naturally ordered toward philosophy, much in them stands in the way. Few have the time or leisure for it, since most human lives are and must be devoted to the lower but far more urgent tasks of survival. Moreover, as social beings, humans live in communities held together by authoritative norms and myths. Much pressure exists in these societies, as we have previously noted, to maintain the authoritative norms, while philosophy requires intellectual questioning or challenging of all such norms. The moral pressure of society is thus arrayed against philosophy. Finally, that Sisyphean character of philosophy disappoints and hence discourages many from the pursuit. These are universal factors standing between human beings and philosophy.

There are other forces too that particularly afflict us moderns. For us it seems much harder to philosophize than it was, say, for individuals of Socrates's time. Thus Strauss says, "we cannot be philosophers" at the same time that he recommends to us the study of the philosophers of the past. What is not possible for us was possible for them. Strange to say, Strauss sees the very existence of a philosophic tradition as itself a barrier to philosophy. The tradition leads to a misunderstanding of the nature of philosophy: it makes us think that philosophy is doctrinal, systematic, and dogmatic, whereas it is not the articulation of doctrines but a way of living, and it is not systematic or dogmatic but zetetic. Moreover, as Strauss argues in *Natural Right and History*, the tradition preshapes our beginning points for thinking philosophically and thereby estranges us from the proper beginning points in pretheorized opinions or "common sense." One reason that it is much more difficult to philosophize today derives from the fact that unlike Socrates or Aristotle, we must struggle to find the starting points, for common opinion has been completely infected by residues of the philosophic tradition.

For us, study of the great books is the necessary propaedeutic to the recovery of philosophy. Particularly important is the conflict among the great thinkers, which invites or spurs us to attempt to judge among them, a task that pushes us toward philosophizing. Strauss notes more than once in "What Is Liberal Education?" the irony or even absurdity of the task liberal education poses: we who are probably lesser must judge those who are probably greater in intellect and depth.

The absurdity implicit in the task of liberal education in the here and now is obscured for us, Strauss suggests, by "a number of facile delusions," two of which he explicitly identifies. The first is the delusion of progress, the view that our modern point of view is superior to that of thinkers of the past and according to which judging among them is not very difficult, for the philosophic teaching closest to dominant opinion in our day is taken to be the most correct. Study of the great books under the reign of that view will never lead to philosophy or to serious engagement with the thought of the past.

Closely related is the relativist or historicist view that all thinkers are related to their times and situations in such a way that "none can be simply true" ("WILE," 7–8). This too cannot lead to philosophy or serious engagement. Both "delusions" are variants of the problem that most besets us moderns—the problem of history. The deepest problem we moderns face derives from our views of history or human historicity, views that are themselves the latest and most challenging products of the philosophic tradition itself. We moderns dwell, Strauss sometimes said, in a "cave beneath the cave" that Plato had spoken of in his *Republic*. Not only do we need to struggle to free ourselves from the illusions and restraints within the cave, but we must struggle to find our way back to the original cave so that we can struggle to free ourselves from it. Strauss's view of liberal education as education to philosophy thus finds us painted into a corner with no clear prospect that the paint will ever dry. We must have recourse to the tradition to find our way, but the tradition has closed off the means by which we could make good use of it.

Strauss, however, is more optimistic than he has to this point of his argument led us to expect him to be. In his closing paragraphs he addresses the two large problems of liberal education as the path to philosophy, the problem deriving from our modern situation and the problem deriving from the universal situation of philosophy as necessarily incomplete and frustrated in its aims. Our situation renders us particularly unable to fulfill our task of judging among the great books—and yet Strauss remarkably reverses his diagnosis. We must face our responsibility to judge in the face of our incompetence to do so, and of our delusional view that judging is either unnecessary or impossible.

> As it seems to me, the cause of this situation is that we have lost all simply authoritative traditions in which we could trust, the *nomos* which gave us authoritative guidance, because our immediate teachers and teachers' teachers believed in the possibility of a simply rational society. Each of us here is compelled to find his bearings by his own powers, however defective they may be. ("WILE," 8)

Philosophy is actually in some ways *more* evidently necessary for us now than it has been in the past precisely as a result of the work of the philosophic tradition, which heretofore appeared in Strauss's essay as a source of the occlusion of philosophy. The Enlightenment philosophers—the projectors of a "simply rational society" and the formulators of the delusion of progress—have quite unintentionally helped provide the basis for a return to philosophy in the destruction they wrought of *nomoi* that provided "authoritative guidance" for all previous societies and that constituted the chains that held us captive in the cave. Ironically, the cave beneath the cave provides the preconditions for freedom from the initial or "natural" cave. We have no authoritative guidance and thus are aware of our need to "find [our] bearings by [our] own powers, however defective these may be" (8). The destruction of all dogmas must therefore include the destruction of the historicist dogma as well. Such at least was the point Strauss made in one of the most common practices in his teaching: nearly every course began with a demonstration of the self-contradictory character of the historicist position, as prerequisite to opening the minds of his students to the possibility of that bold and even presumptuous act of judging that constitutes the step into philosophy.

Perhaps it should go without saying, but in affirming the possibility of philosophizing via the great books, Strauss is not implying that a nation of philosophers is possible. He has no illusion that the rational society sought by our predecessors is possible. The education into philosophy is for a few and has little likelihood of being transformative for society (cf. "LER," 24). As he emphasizes in "Liberal Education and Responsibility," "the city as city is more closed to philosophy than open to it" (15). "Philosophy can then only live side by side with the city" (14). That living side by side is particularly possible in modern democracy, for there is "the obvious fact that by giving freedom to all, democracy also gives freedom to those who care for human excellence. No one prevents us from cultivating our garden" (24). To cultivate one's own garden—that seems to be the philosophic vocation.

Thus our present paradoxical situation does not, contrary to first impressions, rule out liberal education as a path to philosophy. But what of the more universal problem of philosophy—its Sisyphean character? Here too Strauss is more hopeful than we might expect.

> We cannot exert our understanding without from time to time understanding something of importance; and this act of understanding may be accompanied by the awareness of our understanding, by the understanding of understanding, by *noesis noeseos*, and this is so high, so pure, so noble an experience that Aristotle could ascribe it to his God. ("WILE," 8)

Although philosophy may not be able to achieve its goal of wisdom, Strauss in an uncharacteristically poetic passage indicates its goodness despite its limits. The conscious experience of understanding, of progress in knowing, is enough, enough to make us aware "of the dignity of the mind, . . . the true ground of the dignity of man and therewith the goodness of the world, whether we understand it as created or as uncreated, which is the home of man because it is the home of the human mind" (8). Philosophy may not be capable of settling the question of the created versus the eternal world, but it can settle a yet more fundamental question—what is the place of man and man's mind within the whole? These pleasures and the insight into the correspondence of man and world make philosophy a life worth living, and the basic experience of understanding is open to many if not all, for the experience of understanding is not limited to the "greatest minds."

Strauss emphasizes that it is the act of understanding more than the particular content understood that matters. "This experience [of understanding] is entirely independent of whether what we understand primarily is pleasing or displeasing, fair or ugly" ("WILE," 8). It is in the spirit of that claim that we must understand Strauss's parting words: "Liberal education supplies us with experience in things beautiful" (9).

Liberal Education and Modern Democracy

The organizers of the conference at which Strauss delivered the talk "Liberal Education and Responsibility" charged him to expand his comments on liberal education as a means "to found an aristocracy within democratic mass society" ("LER," 10). The organizers perhaps noticed what we have briefly adverted to. One of the three perspectives from which Strauss views liberal education in his first address is the political. In that perspective liberal education was identified as the "counterpoison" to the mass culture of modern democracy, a function it serves by reminding of human greatness in a context in which such reminders are necessary in order to maintain democracy. However, perhaps on account of time constraints, Strauss no sooner introduced the idea of human greatness than he slid away from the political function of liberal education to its role as road to philosophy. Since his topic in the first lecture was the Socratic question "what is liberal education?," it is understandable that he was eager to ascend to the highest aim or purpose of liberal education, philosophy. But in rushing so quickly to philosophy, he almost completely slighted the political theme he had raised.

Partly because of the prodding of the organizers, Strauss was compelled to address the relation between liberal education and responsibility, a concern, he makes clear at the opening of his essay, that is strictly moral and political, for "responsibility," he concludes, was a substitute for more directly moral phenomena, such as "duty," "conscience," or "virtue" ("LER," 10). But whatever that substitution means—Strauss seems to claim not to know—"responsibility" remains a political-moral phenomenon. His assigned task thus pushed him to put liberal education in a completely different light from that of his first address.

Strauss's second address is much longer than the first and covers a much wider array of topics. It covers more but does not go as deep: although it raises the issue of philosophy and liberal education, it is not nearly so revealing about the nature of the philosophic life. The scope of the second essay is so great that in it Strauss moves from liberal education in its "original political meaning" to "the prospects for liberal education within mass democracy" ("LER," 10, 24; "WILE," 4).

Originally, liberal education was the education suited to "a man who behaved in a manner becoming a free man," that is to say, education for those not subject to the necessities imposed by slavery or by earning a living. It was education for men who could live a life good for its own sake and without being subject to external necessities ("LER," 10–11). The original liberal education is not primarily bookish education, although it contains some bookish elements. "It consists above all in the formation of character and taste. The fountains of that education are poets," not philosophers. But it largely consists in "experiential learning" based on "familiar intercourse with older or more experienced gentlemen." Original liberal education "requires leisure" and is therefore "the preserve of a certain kind of wealthy people" (11). It is emphatically not based on commitment to the proposition that "all men are created equal" (15). The original liberal education is geared to men who are to rule their societies (11–12). Thus, it definitely relates to "responsibility," the assigned topic of Strauss's paper: this education "not only fosters civic responsibility: it is even required for the exercise of civic responsibility" (13).

These gentlemen—aristocrats as it were—have two main pursuits or activities: politics, to which Strauss has devoted much of his attention, and philosophy, to which he turns in the tenth paragraph. But the philosophy with which the gentlemen concern themselves is not philosophy "understood strictly"; it is rather "what is now called intellectual interests" ("LER," 13). However, philosophy in the strict sense is relevant to understanding the situation and nature of the gentlemen, and therewith the liberal education they receive. There is both an important discontinuity and an important continuity between them and the philosophers. Philosophy is higher than gentlemanship. "The gentleman's virtue is not entirely the same as the philosopher's virtue," for they have different ends and goods, captured well enough in the characteristically political life of the gentleman and the apolitical life of the philosopher (13). "According to classical philosophy, the end of the philosophers is radically different from the end or ends . . . [of] the nonphilosophers" (19–20). Since they have different ends, the education they receive is perforce different or at least has different aims. So far as liberal education is education toward gentlemanship, it is governed by the fact that "the gentleman accepts on trust certain most weighty things"—the fundamental moral, political, and theological beliefs of the gentlemanly class—"which for the philosopher are the themes of investigation and of questioning" (13). Although Strauss does not dwell on it, this difference is immense and necessarily affects the character of liberal education "all the way down." Education that "accepts on trust" or even inculcates those "weighty things" and education that encourages the questioning or even challenging of those "weighty things" are two very different practices indeed. But since the young do not come prelabeled as gentleman or philosopher, the serious question immediately arises: how does one combine in one educational practice these two different—opposite—educational regimes? In his essays on liberal education Strauss does not explicitly address that decisive question, but his well-known answer concerns that kind of speaking and writing that says different things to different people.

Despite the great difference between the virtue of the gentleman and that of the philosopher, Strauss makes the perhaps surprising claim that "the gentleman's virtue is a reflection of the philosopher's virtue; one may say it is its political reflection" ("LER," 14). The basis of this extraordinarily important claim lies in the feature of the gentleman's moral orientation that Strauss emphasizes on several occasions: "The gentlemen regard virtue as choice worthy for its own sake, whereas the others praise virtue as a means for acquiring wealth and honor. The gentlemen and the others disagree, then, as regards the end of man or the highest good; they disagree regarding first principles" (19–20). But the philosopher agrees with the gentlemen relative to the nongentlemen: there is a human activity choiceworthy for its own sake and not "as a means for acquiring wealth and honor." The philosophers, as Strauss sees it, are entirely correct in their judgment, while the gentlemen have but a "reflected," i.e., distorted, view, but they nonetheless embody the crucial claim that allows the gentlemen to elevate their entire society when they are sufficiently prominent in it, the claim of a good beyond the lower goods of survival, pleasure, wealth, and honor, the claim that there is a good or ground of moral judgment, the noble, beyond the merely instrumental (cf. 20).

The relation of liberal education to politics changed considerably in modern times, setting the particular political task of liberal education in the here and now. These changes resulted from changes in both political life and education ("LER," 15, 19). Strauss speaks of three moments in the evolving relation between politics and liberal education in the modern era. Modern politics in all three moments differs from earlier politics in that it affirms "the natural equality of all men, and it leads therefore to the assertion that sovereignty belongs to the people" (15). There can be no question then of the gentlemen or the philosophers ruling in their own right. But originally at least, modern politics was marked by the distinction "between the sovereign and the government," which meant that though the people were sovereign, they did not need to rule (15). Indeed, the early moderns generally accepted an arrangement according to which elites, who were responsible to the people, ruled (15–16). The people, who held an ultimate power under this arrangement, were to be formed by a religious education "based on the Bible," whereby each was to come to "regard himself as responsible for his actions and for his thoughts to a God who would judge him" (15–16). There was no thought of a universal enlightenment. The elites in turn would be prepared for their task via liberal education, which in the case of classic early moderns like Locke still had many echoes of classical liberal education. It was to be "education in 'good breeding,'" based in large part on classical literature and modern political philosophy (16).

But as modernity progressed, this solution did not hold. "The enlightenment was destined to become universal enlightenment" ("LER," 20). The relatively clear distinction between popular sovereignty and government was blurred as the norm of ever more democratic governance spread (15). While the ideal of enlightenment spread, the felt need for special liberal education receded—"the only thing which can be held to be unqualifiedly good is . . . a good intention, and of good intentions everyone is as capable as everyone else, wholly independently of education." Indeed, education may be a disadvantage: "the voice of nature or of the moral law speaks in [the uneducated] perhaps more clearly and more decidedly than in the sophisticated who may have sophisticated away their conscience" (22).

We now live in a third phase marked by "tension between the ethos of democracy and the ethos of technocracy," a tension that apparently replaces the earlier tension between the city and philosophy. Our situation is the ultimate result of the various innovations introduced by modern philosophy. In one of his most pregnant formulations Strauss identifies the genesis of modern philosophy in the identification of "the end of philosophy . . . with the end which is capable of being actually pursued by all men," or "more precisely," in the subordination of philosophy to the end "capable of being actually pursued by all men." Most men—the nonphilosophers and the nongentlemen—pursue preservation, wealth, and honor. The new aim of philosophy can be captured in the Baconian formula, "the relief of man's estate" ("LER," 20; cf. chapter 7).

With the collapse of the distinction of ends between the philosopher and the nonphilosopher comes the collapse of the distinction between the gentlemen and the nongentlemen. All human beings and all human aims are now assimilated to the latter class. Philosophy became a means to power and thus becomes technologized. Morality becomes instrumentalized as merely the rules best suited to achieving the nonmoral goods ("LER," 20–21).

The advanced stages of these various processes leave us with a mass democracy—ever-larger political societies governed by or responsible to the masses—and the authority of science, which leads to a new conception of education and our present situation. Science has had two particularly potent effects in addition to the large increase in power put in the hands of modern humanity. On the one hand, science pronounced itself unable to produce "rational knowledge of 'values,' that is, . . . science or reason is incompetent to distinguish between good and evil ends" ("LER," 22). This amounts to positivism, which Strauss often identifies as one of the elements of the "crisis of our times." The other development sponsored by the triumph of modern science is the growth of specialization, which produces individuals, according to the now-familiar adage, who know more and more about less and less. Our predicament, in a word, is that we have ever-increasing power and ever-weaker resources for controlling it and putting it to good use, in part because no one has broad enough vision to see the whole landscape and in part because we are increasingly unable to say what the good ends are.

Liberal education is of importance in this context; it is needed to overcome the narrowness of specialization and the aimlessness promoted by current thinking about "values." Strauss is not particularly optimistic that liberal education can fill the needs of the day, however. The universities are dominated by the very intellectual trends that need to be countered. Under conditions of mass democracy "the insufficiently educated are bound to have an unreasonably strong influence on education" ("LER," 23). It is thus difficult to find the lever by which education can be moved to counter the present situation.

So far as there is hope, it lies in liberal education understood as great-books education ("LER," 24). We must, of course, recall Strauss's warnings in "What Is Liberal Education?" about the modern delusions that will prevent us from deriving any benefit from the great books. To the warnings about historicism of the first essay must be joined the warnings about positivism in this essay. So long as either science or history leads to the dismissal of value questions, great books will neither lead to political good nor prepare the way for philosophy. Thus in Strauss's own educational practice the critique of positivism and historicism almost inevitably prefaced every inquiry into political philosophy. Strauss sometimes seemed obsessive about these twin demons, but as he saw it, they are the threshold barriers that must be overcome if liberal education is to be of any value.

The great books of the past are particularly useful in providing the broadening and deepening required in our age of technocracy and democratism because they were produced by men of particular intellect and humanity. They were produced by thinkers not themselves under the sway of technocratic specialization and democratic willfulness. Strauss does not expect liberal education, even when pursued well, to have an indoctrinating effect of any sort. "We cannot expect that liberal education will lead all who benefit from it to understand their civic responsibility in the same way or to agree politically" ("LER," 24). He cites the examples of Marx and Nietzsche, two extraordinarily liberally educated individuals, who disagreed with each other as much as possible politically. The political aim of liberal education today is not the inculcation of one or another political ideology but rather the fostering of political moderation, a moderation that stays away from both the extreme of "visionary expectations from politics" and the opposite extreme of "unmanly contempt for politics" (24). In its political or moral bearing liberal education is not to promote the tending of one's own garden and is to encourage moderation rather than mania.

The theme so prominent in Strauss's first essay—the conflict and disagreement among the great thinkers—must be in part the basis for his hopes that liberal education will promote moderation. That disagreement, which we are so incompetent to adjudicate, discourages hasty and one-sided conclusions. It fosters the kind of moderation that sees a point in various alternatives, and thus hesitates to put all its eggs in any one basket or alternative. Strauss, writing not too long after the horrors of World War II and in the midst of the Cold War, also counts on our experience of "the grandiose failures" of the political regimes that less moderate projectors like Marx and Nietzsche fathered or grandfathered ("LER," 24). The chief political lesson Strauss hopes liberal education can impart is that "wisdom requires unhesitating loyalty to a decent constitution and even to the cause of constitutionalism" (24). He attempts to reproduce within modernity the effect of liberal education in premodernity: "thus it may again become true that all liberally educated men will be politically moderate men" (24). Nonetheless, he cautions, the most we can expect are "palliatives," not "cures" (25).

Strauss championed liberal education in the great books as especially valuable in the context of the modern situation of technocracy and democratism. Those possessed of technical knowledge certainly contribute essential skills to our modern kind of life. Society as we know it could not survive without them. Yet there are definite limitations to the technocrat's competence. Strauss was always impressed with Max Weber's analysis of the narrowness, the shallowness of vision, and the lack of heart of the bureaucratic and technical classes. Important as they are, they lack the personal character or knowledge to rule a society. Great-books education was,

Strauss hoped, an avenue by which a class of persons better suited to supply the leadership needed in society, the modern equivalents of the gentlemen of whom he often spoke, could be educated. The technically trained tend to have a notion of the ends of action entirely bound up with their technical specialty, or they defer to the idea that the preferences of the people ought to supply the content of the ends, while they would supply the technical means to the achievement of those ends. Strauss thought that great-books education would help develop a leadership stratum that would think better, i.e., more deeply and broadly, than the technocrats and bureaucrats. The great books were not written under the spell of positivism or historicism, and thus they engaged in full-bodied discourse about ends, just the sort of broadening the leaders of our kind of society need. After reading and thinking hard about Aristotle and Spinoza and Kant, individuals would not be likely to concur that the point of political life is merely the maximization of "safety, income, and deference," as a famous social scientist once put it. Nor would they likely agree that rational choice theory as now practiced captures the core of human action and can provide a guide to genuinely rational decisions.

Strauss's Educational Practice

As is now clear, liberal education understood in light of philosophy and liberal education understood in light of politics and morality point in two different, if not simply conflicting, directions. Strauss leaves us with the conundrum of how to combine those two ways into one educational practice. As it happens, we probably know more about Strauss as a teacher than we do about many other historical political philosophers. From some time in the late 1950s until the end of his career, Strauss's classes were audiotaped, and the transcripts from these tapes are now or soon will be available on the website of the Leo Strauss Center (http://leostrausscenter.uchicago.edu). Moreover, several of Strauss's students have left reminiscences of him as a teacher, many of which are also available on the Strauss Center website.

Almost all his courses were graduate seminars—although they were not the small-group experiences one thinks of when one thinks of seminars. At the University of Chicago in the 1960s he had perhaps fifty students in the average seminar, which thus had to meet in a regular classroom, not a seminar room. Not all fifty persons in the room were ordinary registered students, for many were older students writing dissertations, or even beyond the dissertation stage; some were walk-ins from outside the university. As Strauss said in his essay on liberal education, he never turned away nonpaying students.

His seminars were all conducted in the same way. They ordinarily covered only one text. In one stretch in the mid-1960s he taught Grotius; individual dialogues of Plato (*Gorgias, Protagoras, Meno, Apology,* and *Crito*); Aristotle's *Politics,* Kant's historical essays, Hegel's *Philosophy of History,* Nietzsche's *Beyond Good and Evil* and *Genealogy of Morals* (an exceptional two books), and Montesquieu's *Spirit of the Laws* and *Persian Letters* spread over two quarters. He taught a full range of texts from across the history of political philosophy, focusing a bit on areas of current interest to him, but also making it a practice to teach on a regular basis basic texts that he thought the graduate students needed to know.

He ran his seminars in a hybrid Germanic-American manner. He divided the text to be considered into as many segments as there were class sessions and assigned the segments to the registered students. Each class period began with the presentation of a student paper—a strict twenty-minute limit on the papers—followed by an on-the-spot commentary on the paper by Strauss. He then turned to a more or less systematic treatment of the text for the day. He was careful to get through the entire assignment, which meant that for some of the longer texts he skipped across the material, while for some, like the shorter Platonic dialogues, he was able to proceed almost line by line. Occasionally he paused to deliver something more akin to a minilecture, providing more of an overview than the passage-by-passage treatment allowed. In his later years he had a reader who read aloud the passages Strauss wished to comment on. Strauss combined this German mode of comment with a more American, discussion-centered format. Some of the transcripts are remarkable for how much lively discussion Strauss provoked and how open he was to learning from the students. Although he always had great authority in the classroom, he also encouraged students to contribute by calling attention to passages that puzzled him or that raised issues in need of airing. He was courteous in an old-world sort of way and always treated students with respect and encouragement. He could be critical of student presentations but never presented his criticisms harshly. He was not the sort of teacher who reduced his students to tears.

But of course no description of the externals of his procedures or of the atmosphere of his classroom can explain how his practice of teaching related to his understanding of the task of liberal education in our day. Perhaps most obviously, Strauss provided the great-books education for which he called—he taught the works of "the greatest minds." He taught them in such a way as to bring the great texts to the fore. A Strauss class was not about him, not about his particular philosophic or political views. He faded into the background and tried so far as he could to let or help the thinkers speak to his listeners. In his writings and in his classroom teaching Strauss entered into the thought of the thinker and presented the thinker in the thinker's voice so far as he could, whether he, Strauss, agreed with that thinker or not. Occasionally, but only occasionally, he commented on the thought from his own point of view, but he found it more important to help modern readers understand the authors as they understood themselves than to judge them in the facile ways modern readers are prone to. His classroom style thus does not strictly conform to the task he laid out in "What Is Liberal Education?" that we must judge among the great thinkers. It is not that he ever put the question of the truth of the thought aside, but he exemplified for students the idea that one had to understand a thinker properly before one could judge him. The foregrounding of understanding the thinkers adequately by learning how to read them "with the proper care" is one of the ways in which Strauss combined in one pedagogy the two different ends of liberal education.

Another way in which he acted on his notions of liberal education is his aforementioned and nearly universal practice in both the classroom and his writings of critiquing positivism and historicism. Nearly every course began with some version of this critique, a part both of liberal education toward philosophy and education toward moderate and decent politics. Moreover, a large part of the substantive emphasis of his teaching was directed against historicism. Strauss attempted to show that the doctrine that even the greatest thinkers' minds merely reflected "their times" was false and that the appearance that lent that assumption plausibility was largely an artifact of the "art of writing" philosophers of the past employed. For various reasons they presented themselves as much more in harmony with reigning opinion of their times than they actually were. Strauss's attempt to respond to historicist claims at this empirical level led to some of the very controversial readings of the philosophers that he produced.

Strauss's activity as a teacher was not, of course, exhausted in the classroom. His many books were also acts of teaching, and he was always conscious of the difference between what was appropriate to the classroom and what was appropriate to the book. When teaching Hegel, for example, he pointed to the much greater accessibility of Hegel's lectures compared with his books. The same certainly holds for Strauss as well. The books clearly go deeper and are far more challenging than his classroom proceedings. But there is a great continuity between his classroom teaching and his scholarly works as well. The best way to characterize that continuity, we believe, is in terms of what we have elsewhere called pedagogical reserve. That reserve is perhaps the chief means by which Strauss holds together the two dimensions of liberal education in his own pedagogical practice. We are referring to that aspect of Strauss's writing and speaking that often leads readers and critics to attribute to Strauss the kind of esoteric writing he attributes to some of the thinkers in the tradition. It is certain that Strauss withholds much in his communication. He sometimes withholds conclusions—what he thinks follows from arguments he is presenting. He sometimes withholds parts of the argument but gives us his conclusions. He sometimes scatters his points through his writing, requiring of the reader an effort to put the points together on his or her own. The omissions, the scatterings, his subtle qualifications of points, the often difficult-to-penetrate structures of his writings are best understood, we think, as invitations to those more philosophically inclined to go deeper with him. Both in the classroom and in his books Strauss was a teacher who proceeded by offering such invitations. He certainly offered something to those who did not often take up these invitations—they came away with some sound and certainly very interesting intellectual history. They came away with the firm message Strauss emphasized in his second essay on liberal education, the desirability of political and moral moderation, and the misguided character of the modern thinking that took its bearings from positivism or historicism. Those who took up his invitations came away with more—but not really different. Pedagogical reserve is not another name for "noble lying," as some of Strauss's recent critics have charged. He really believed in the value of political moderation; he really believed that positivism and historicism were misguided guides to understanding human thought. Strauss was, in sum, a man who practiced liberal arts education as he preached it.

CHAPTER TWELVE

Straussians

M ore than most thinkers of the twentieth century, Leo Strauss polarized his audience. One was either for him or against him, influenced by him or repelled by him. Thus has arisen the phenomenon, nearly unique among the century's academic thinkers, of a recognized group of "followers," called "Straussians." Where and when the label arose, and what, exactly, it means, are uncertain. It seems originally to have been invented by the opponents of Strauss and applied to individuals who had studied with or were manifestly influenced by him. Over time, and somewhat reluctantly, the label appears to have been accepted by many if not all of those to whom it has been applied.

In the early twenty-first century, especially in the moment near the beginning of the Iraq War of 2003, the Straussian label leaped across the fire line separating the academic world and the world of politics and became attached to a group of political figures identified with the neoconservative movement and the Bush administration. Strauss was said to be the "guru" or the intellectual father of the neoconservatives and, somehow, thirty years after his death, the inspiration for the Iraq War. Most striking about the wildfire of accusation and denunciation of the political "Straussians" was how ill informed and irresponsible this outburst of "Straussian hunting" was. Some Bush policymakers, but nowhere near as many as those called "Straussians," had had some contact with Strauss or students of Strauss. But even with regard to them, no real connection between their political action and the thought of Strauss was ever established. These "Straussians" have about as much to do with Leo Strauss as owners of Levis, or admirers of the soundtrack of the film *2001*. They will henceforward be ignored (*TALS*, esp. 1–20, 261–67).

As originally applied, the label "Straussian" referred to a group of academics and was meant to designate them as uncommonly dedicated to following the doctrines of one individual. It was originally a label proposed in a spirit of enmity because it was intended to suggest, at the extreme, something like a cult, or, more moderately, a group with a unified set of views, which views were decidedly not those of mainstream academics in the fields of political science or philosophy. It was meant, in other words, to designate an "unorthodox orthodoxy."

That original attribution of unity of outlook has since given way to recognition, by those within and by many without the "Straussian" world, that no such unity exists. The so-called Straussians have broken into different, sometimes warring, camps and to a discerning eye embody less unity of viewpoint than, say, rational choice theorists or international relations realists in political science.

Indeed, it is now a question, as it always was, whether there is any real content to the label "Straussian." At first, it could plausibly be applied to the students of Strauss, a direct biographical criterion of belonging. Now, forty years after Strauss's death, with the entry of many of Strauss's ideas into the mainstream, and with the attenuated chains of filiation that arise from the existence of students of students, and even of students of students of students of Strauss, the number of those who might be identified in some way or another with Strauss has increased greatly, while the content of what they share has dropped dramatically. Given the variety of alleged "Straussians," it is a serious question whether the label has any real content or meaning. As our recent survey of the "Straussians" concluded:

> Contrary to what is often said, those who have followed [Strauss] are far from single-minded in what they take from him, except perhaps for some threshold or methodological commitments. That philosophy is important, that political philosophy is a viable enterprise, that philosophic texts must be read in a particularly attentive manner, that the distinction between ancients and moderns means something (although just what remains contested in Straussian circles)—these propositions are what individuals known as Straussians mostly agree about. (*TALS*, 267)

To this list of common characteristics must be added, we suppose, a self-conscious admiration of and orientation toward but by no means comprehensive agreement with Strauss himself. A "Straussian" for our purposes, then, is one who works to a degree that cannot be entirely specified within a framework of Strauss's questions and chief concepts, and, if the scholar in question is concerned with textual studies, deploys Strauss's methods of close reading.

According to these very loose criteria, the number of "Straussians" is quite large, and the studies they pursue extremely diverse and varied in character.[1] The number and the diversity of subjects make it impossible to canvass or catalogue the universe of "Straussians." The principle of selection to be followed here is to focus on some of the major lines of cleavage discernible among the "Straussians." Those are often spoken of in terms of East and West Coast and even Midwest Straussians. This classification serves some rough and ready purposes, but it is probably more revealing to identify the actual substantive disagreements among the Straussians. There are, of course, disagreements on how to read Plato's *Phaedrus*, or how to read Locke; disagreements over whether the Supreme Court is a good or bad political institution—a myriad of disagreements of that sort. We propose to focus, however, on a series of disagreements that cut closer to the core of Strauss's own thinking, because they play off the various meanings of "the problem of political philosophy" and its solutions as Strauss developed them. The disagreements in question center on certain puzzles or now-familiar ambiguities in Strauss's thinking. The two most fundamental puzzles are: (1) what is the status of religion, or the problem of Athens and Jerusalem, and (2) what is the status of morality, or the problem of Plato and Aristotle.

On Religion

Strauss is well known for having advanced interpretations of some philosophers, particularly early modern philosophers, as essentially antireligious, or at best tolerant of religion as civil religion, i.e., as a social institution useful for procuring good order in society. This position is then often attributed to Strauss as well.

There is much evidence to suggest that this is a misattribution, however. In his early book *Spinoza's Critique of Religion* Strauss brings out the antireligious character of Spinoza's thinking, in particular his claim that he can supply a successful rationalist critique of biblical revelation. The chief point of Strauss's book, however, is to deny that Spinoza did or could succeed at that critique. He does not agree with the early moderns about religion.

Moreover, in a rather late statement (1964), Strauss described his early work as devoted to the "theological-political problem" or the question of "the extent to which the critique of orthodox—Jewish and Christian—

theology deserved to be victorious." In raising the question in this way he clearly is not taking for granted that the critique deserved to be victorious. Significantly, he concluded by affirming that "the theological-political problem has since remained *the* theme of my studies."[2]

How Strauss himself meant to answer questions about religion has proved to be puzzling, however. Perhaps most striking is his insistence, contrary to the explicit doctrine of much of the tradition, that philosophy and revelation are altogether different and irreconcilable, to such a degree that no synthesis of the sort championed by, for example, Thomas Aquinas is possible. It is, Strauss insists, reason *or* revelation, not both.

Posing the philosophy-revelation issue as an either/or raises a whole further set of problems, however. Strauss also insisted that philosophy, properly understood, i.e., Socratically understood, was knowledge that one did not know, that is, that one did not know the whole. Philosophy is the quest for knowledge of the whole, but this knowledge is not attainable. Lacking knowledge of the whole, Strauss argued, philosophy cannot refute the *possibility* of revelation. It cannot establish comprehensive knowledge of the whole such that it could demonstrate that there is no room for a mysterious revealing God as the source of that whole. Similarly, revelation can no more refute the possibility or even rightfulness of philosophy than philosophy can refute revelation. The one can "refute" the other only by assuming in advance the favored answer.

It is, therefore, not evident that one should opt for revelation, but it is also not evident that one should opt for philosophy. However, this state of things is particularly problematic for philosophy, for philosophy is the effort to take one's bearings by what is evident. To rest on the inevident, Strauss seems to say, is fatal to the enterprise and life of philosophy. The failure of revelation to rest on evident foundations is not fatal for it, because revelation has no such demand to fulfill. Given this line of reasoning, it seems especially difficult to affirm the philosophical life, but this is nonetheless precisely what Strauss does.

Strauss's position can apparently be stated in a yet more concise way, in the form of three propositions, or even a syllogism of sorts.

PROPOSITION 1: In order to be a rationally defensible pursuit, philosophy must be able to refute revelation in a non-question-begging way.

PROPOSITION 2: Philosophy cannot refute revelation.

PROPOSITION 3: Philosophy is a rationally defensible pursuit.

It is evident that there is a problem of some sort in holding those three propositions together, so it should be no surprise that one of the great divisions among the Straussians has arisen over the question of how to understand Strauss on the status of religion.[3] Although they differ greatly among themselves, the Straussians follow a common strategy in attempting to resolve Strauss's puzzle. All in effect claim that Strauss denied one of the three propositions. But they disagree over which proposition to reject, producing four large alternatives, with some variants, among Straussians on the status of religion: *rationalists*, who believe that philosophy can indeed refute the claims of revelation; *decisionists*, who deny that philosophy, as Strauss saw it, can refute revelation, and thus claim that Strauss arbitrarily or only exoterically decided for philosophy; *zetetics*, who argue that Strauss persisted in his view that the possibility of revelation could not be refuted by philosophy but who also maintain that Strauss had worked out a way to rationally justify the choice of the philosophic life without that refutation; finally, there are *faith-based Straussians*, who believe that Strauss's position on the relation between faith and reason opens the way for faith or even compels it.

The most outspoken of the Straussian rationalists is Heinrich Meier, whose book *Leo Strauss and the Theologico-Political Problem* purports to present Strauss's resolution to the problem, a resolution that, according to Meier, disposes of the claims of revealed religion of all kinds. Meier takes particularly seriously Strauss's claim that the theological-political problem was the abiding theme of his life work. He takes that to mean that Strauss recovered a notion of philosophy not as a set of doctrines, but as a way of life devoted to rational inquiry and rational understanding. Philosophy is thus obliged to bring itself before the bar of reason and ask whether the philosophic life is itself defensible. The justification of philosophy must occur in dialogue with or against the chief alternative, or "the most powerful objection to philosophy."[4] He quotes Strauss's affirmation that "the Bible . . . offers the only challenge to the claims of philosophy which can reasonably be made."[5] The two claims—the claim of philosophy that the true human good or happiness "consists in free investigation or insight" and the claim of the Bible that man's good or happiness "consists in obedience to God"—stand as the two most serious claims facing a human being.[6] "No alternative," says Strauss, "is more fundamental than the alternative: human guidance or divine guidance. Tertium non datum."[7]

Meier emphasizes the tension within Strauss's thinking between the first two propositions above. He realizes that Strauss cannot draw the conclusion contained in proposition 3 unless Strauss can achieve what proposition 2 says cannot be achieved. Meier disregards Strauss's many affirmations of proposition 2:

> In order to counteract the avoidance of the most important question [the either/or of philosophy or obedience to God], the question of the right or the best life, Strauss not only makes the challenge posed by faith in revelation as strong as he possibly can. He also occasionally makes it stronger than it actually is, or . . . he allows the position of philosophy to appear weaker than it proves to be on closer examination.[8]

Meier in effect dismisses proposition 2 as a kind of rhetoric.

He feels confident that he can do that, for he believes he has found the refutation of revelation that Strauss worked out and left in some unpublished notes for a lecture he delivered at a theological seminary in 1948. Strauss's notes take up about one printed page. Meier devotes an illuminating chapter of his book to expanding these notes. That chapter presents the core of rationalist Straussianism.

The notes present a "genealogy" of the idea of the revealing God, and of what he reveals. As explicated by Meier it is a dazzling explanation, which does indeed give us a theory of revelation. Starting from the fact of the need for human social or political existence and therefore of law, Strauss (as read by Meier) explains the coming to be of the idea of the biblical God and the main tenets of his revelation. That is, Strauss's analysis reveals religion and the God of religion to be in service to the needs of political society.

Although the substance of Strauss's genealogy as Meier describes it certainly differs from that of, say, Freud, Hobbes, or any number of others who have developed genealogies of the religious phenomena, yet the *type* of explanation is just the same. Given this fact one wonders whether Strauss himself would endorse Meier's form of rationalism. He surely was aware of genealogical accounts, and his general response to such accounts would seem to apply to this one as well. A genealogy is an attempt to explain by natural causes what appears or claims to be the result of supernatural causes, of a miracle. Strauss asserts quite vehemently, however, that "there is . . . only one way of disposing of the possibility of revelation or miracles: one must prove that God is in no way mysterious, or that we have adequate knowledge of the essence of God."[9] Strauss's genealogy does not even presume to supply such knowledge of the divine essence, or, as he elsewhere demands, knowledge of the whole such that there could be no room in it for the mysterious creating, revealing God whose ways are not man's ways.

Thus many Straussians do not accept Meier's restatement of the Athens-Jerusalem issue. Meier quotes but does not take literally an important programmatic statement by Strauss in the notes for his lecture "Reason and Revelation": "The starting point of philosophic explanation of *revelation* would therefore be the fact that the foundation of belief in revelation is the belief in the central importance of morality."[10] Indeed, Strauss's genealogy takes the "central importance of morality" as its central thought, but note that Strauss speaks of the "philosophic *explanation* of revelation," not the philosophic *refutation* of revelation.[11] Philosophy as the enterprise of explaining phenomena rationally must attempt to explain revelation, or purported revelation, along with many other phenomena of the natural and the human world. So long as philosophy cannot disprove the possibility of revelation by a superhuman or miraculous event, every explanation it supplies of alleged revelation as a natural event is hypothetical or question-begging. Thinkers who begin from the premise of revelation can equally give an "explanation" of philosophy as a way of life: "philosophy is self-deification: philosophy has its root in *pride*."[12] This, too, is a question-begging or hypothetical explanation, but it has as much power in principle as Strauss's genealogy. Philosophy as philosophy must attempt such an explanation, and must be able on its own terms to mount a successful explanation, but Strauss points out that such explanations, in particular genealogies of all kinds, are incapable of supplying a refutation.

Another example of the rationalist approach to the religion issue in Strauss is Thomas Pangle's ambitious book *Political Philosophy and the God of Abraham*.[13] His topic is the opening chapters of Genesis as construed through the lens of political philosophy. A proper understanding of this book requires locating it within the context of Strauss's grappling with "the theological-political problem." We are led to place it in the Straussian context in part because the book is marked by a certain opaqueness of intention. Pangle is not clear in identifying his aim or his assessment of his accomplishment in the whole or in many of its parts. Strauss's treatment of the theological-political problem can help tease out of the book Pangle's aims and his sense of his achievements.

The question is: which of the typical Straussian positions, if any, does Pangle adhere to? It might seem at first glance that he adheres to none of them. He frequently states an aim far more modest than resolving Strauss's paradoxical syllogism. Most commonly he gives the following sense of his aims and achievements: The shallow thinking of today has lost sight of what both philosophy and revelation stand for. This is especially due to the intentional privatizing, flattening, and simplifying of the issues by early modern philosophers, who sought to defeat revelation by trivializing it. Thus, the first task is to recapture Strauss's notion of the real tension—even opposition—between the life of philosophy and the life of faith. The farthest aim of the book, Pangle sometimes suggests, is to reawaken a richer, fuller understanding of both reason and revelation. The result is to be a mutual enrichment of both rather than a partisanship for either.

But there are other indications in the book that point to a more ambitious goal. Clearer than any explicit statement in *Political Philosophy and the God of Abraham* is a passage in another Pangle book, *Leo Strauss: An Introduction to His Thought and Intellectual Legacy.* Here Pangle says about some efforts to escape "the Straussian problematic" that these may well "spring from a failure to appreciate what was for Strauss the heart of the matter. *That heart is the challenge posed by revelation, and the Socratic dialectical investigation of justice and nobility as the key to meeting that challenge.*"[14] If the effort to set Pangle's book in a Straussian context is correct, then this passage can be especially helpful, for it gives us Pangle's estimate of where Strauss himself came out on the theological-political problem.

To translate this passage into the language of our three propositions, we take Pangle to be saying here that he believes Strauss rejected proposition 2 and thereby adhered to the rationalist position. He says the *heart* of Strauss's enterprise is the effort to explain the challenge posed to philosophy by revelation *and* to demonstrate the philosophical response to the challenge in the Socratic dialectical inquiry into justice and nobility. Although this latter statement has its ambiguities, we read it to mean that Pangle sees Strauss to have revealed *the* response to the challenge of revelation, i.e., to have established the rational case for philosophy over and against the claims of revelation.

In the light of this identification by Pangle of what he takes Strauss's aim and achievement to be, we lean to the hypothesis that Pangle is engaged in the enterprise of attempting to present, somewhat more explicitly and certainly at greater length than Strauss, an account of what he takes to be Strauss's resolution of the "theological-political problem," what Pangle has called "the heart" of the matter. The key to the structure of Pangle's book, and thus to the articulation of its main themes, comes early when Pangle speaks of the classical medieval rationalists, whose perspective he explicitly commits himself to recapturing. According to Pangle, these authors—men like Alfarabi and Maimonides—identified two questions most in need of pursuing: first, the question of creation and the divine attributes; and second, the meaning of divine law and right as delivered in prophecy, that is, the "principles of justice and nobility underlying and animating the divine law, and also animating the providence and prophecy that bring this law from God to humanity."[15] The second question was, in the view of the medieval rationalists he aspires to emulate, "most decisive." From the point of view of orthodox theology this may seem an odd claim, for it implies that the questions of theology proper (e.g., the divine attributes) are less decisive than what we might call political theology. This implies in turn that for the medieval rationalists as Pangle understands them, *the* decisive issues are those that overlap with political philosophy and not those that belong to metaphysics or theology proper. However this may be, the identification of the two central issues of medieval rationalism sheds light on the structure of Pangle's book, for it divides according to these two topics.

The first main section—on creation and divine attributes—contains three main themes especially worthy of note. First, Pangle presses the question, does Genesis affirm creation ex nihilo? He strikingly brings out an odd fact—theological tradition regularly says yes, but the text of Genesis is not so clear. By itself it may better support a different reading. In an interesting and learned discussion, Pangle traces the emergence of the ex nihilo thesis, which much postdates the text of Genesis and seems to be the result of a confrontation with Greek philosophy. Pangle's conclusion: the ex nihilo thesis, though not in the text and not appearing for a long while, is *nonetheless* the real presupposition of the text. The thesis about ex nihilo creation and an omnipotent God is posited because it is necessary in order to ground something more fundamental.

The more fundamental thing is the unconditionality of moral demands, the affirmation of obedience to the divine law as *the* one thing needful. What is at stake is God's mastery over nature. Is there matter preexisting creation, which might be independent of and resistant to God? Ex nihilo creation says no. And since matter is entirely subordinate to God, the resurrection of the body or immortality is in principle possible, which is connected to the unconditionality of moral demands. So Pangle concludes or suggests the conclusion that the omnipotent God is an inference from the moral insight, i.e., the subject matter of the second question is prior to and more fundamental than the subject of the first question.

Nonetheless, Pangle brings out in his discussion of the divine attributes certain tensions or even contradictions in the concept of God thus derived. Perhaps the most interesting of them is this: "There seems to be a tension within the concept of creation or omnipotence, inasmuch as the concept includes both unneedy or wholly self-sufficient will and, on the other hand, divine love, justice, and mercy."[16] This is a claim rich with implications, but let us focus on what is most important in the context of Pangle's discussion—the omnipotent God and the ex nihilo creation as the presuppositions for the moral demands of obedience. The moral concern that drives conceptualizing about God leads to a God who is in danger of going beyond morality, beyond action, and therefore beyond creating. The God needed for a moral function no longer can fulfill a moral function.

The discussion of creation and divine attributes thus indicates why Pangle considers the moral and political topics of the second question to be more fundamental. Therefore, the "decisive" things in the Bible are precisely those on which the Bible most obviously overlaps with the topics of political philosophy, making Pangle's juxtaposition possible and plausible. But can he go beyond a "compare and contrast" treatment? Can he establish the superior truth of one of the treatments of the moral and political themes? On this question, he provides the following: "The Bible thus presupposes, as what is to be explained or accounted for, a foundation in universal experience, a foundation shared with philosophy." Pangle quotes Strauss to specify what this foundation is: "what one may call the phenomenal world, the given whole, the whole which is permanently given, as permanently as are human beings." The quotation goes on: "All human thought, even all thought human or divine, which is meant to be understood by human beings willy-nilly begins with this whole." But, Pangle continues, "[t]o be sure, this universally experienced whole is given a specific and controversial (if lucid) articulation by the Bible, and that specific articulation is a consequence of the revelation of the radically mysterious origin of the whole in the unfolding act of divine creation."[17]

There is, Pangle affirms, a "foundation in *universal* experience" from which all human thinking of all sorts begins. That experience has sufficient content to provide some fixed or nearly fixed points for thinking, but is not so determinate as to be complete and self-explanatory. The "universal experience" is a matter for wonder, or even for awe. There have been several human efforts to make sense of the universal experience, the two most interesting of which are Socratic philosophy and the Bible. Both are attempts to make sense of the given "whole" or intimation of the whole. The question, then, as Pangle sees it, is simple to ask (though difficult to answer): which is more adequate as an interpretation/explanation/explication of the "universal experience"? The body of his book is the attempt to answer that question. His answer is that the Socratic or political philosophic explication is superior.

The general point, leaving out the details, is this: the Bible and Socratic philosophy are both attempts to do the same thing—to make sense of the "given," of the intimations we have of the whole. They thus have two significant commonalities: a common starting point in the "universal experience," and a common aim, to make the best sense of it. Thus there is in fact a common ground for comparing them: which of them achieves the common aim more successfully? Philosophy does, for it presents a more self-consistent account, more in accord with the common experience.

A full assessment of Pangle's achievement would require a detailed consideration of his claim that political philosophy gives a better account of the "universal experience." But we limit ourselves to discussing briefly the most decisive issue. Strauss said that neither philosophy nor revelation can refute the other in a non-question-begging way. The question, then, is, does Pangle's account of God and justice escape the vicious circle Strauss pointed to? It is difficult to conclude that it does. Does not Pangle's account of the genesis of the God of Genesis already, like Meier's, take for granted the legitimacy of a genetic account? Does it not also take for granted the authority of the criteria of rationality when it finds contradictions in the God-idea thus generated? Is it not deeply question-begging to say that the Bible is a humanly generated attempt, like philosophy, to make sense of the universal experience? Although Pangle's hypothesis is interesting and in its way powerful, can it ever be more than a hypothesis? To interpret the Bible in this manner is already to assume the validity of the rationalist way, but that is precisely what is at stake. Moreover, to conclude that one or the other manner of explicating this universal experience supplies a more adequate account is to accept in advance the criteria of rational explanation as the supreme authority. But this too is to beg the relevant questions. To apply standards of adequacy, i.e., to ask which can account for more of the "data" in a consistent and noncontradictory way, is to begin with the criteria of rational inquiry, which are just what are disputed by the revelatory account, in Strauss's version at least. It should be no surprise then that not all Straussians accept the rationalist solution.

All the other sorts of Straussians except the rationalists thus affirm (at least on Strauss's behalf) proposition 2. The decisionist Straussians like Stanley Rosen and Laurence Lampert conclude from the conjunction of propositions 1 and 2 that proposition 3 cannot be true. Thus, they say,

Strauss is ultimately a skeptic about philosophy, not only in the sense of the zetetic skepticism that he always admitted to, but in a much deeper sense. The choice for philosophy is itself arbitrary or the product of a mere ungrounded act of will. Strauss is, on this account, a decisionist. Lampert takes this thought in the direction of maintaining that Strauss is at bottom a Nietzschean — human life is an act of will performed on a tightrope over an abyss. Strauss endorses philosophy, thinks Lampert, but in the Nietzschean sense of philosophy as legislation of values.[18]

Lampert's Strauss is a timid Nietzschean, however. Lampert's Strauss differs greatly from the Strauss most readers meet on the pages of his books. The Strauss we normally see is one who objects to the very term "values," much less who claims to "legislate values." Lampert's Strauss is too timid to legislate values in the open as Nietzsche did, so he reverts in public to the view that philosophers discover rather than create truth. Lampert surmises that Strauss knows better but is afraid to shed his Clark Kent everydayness to step forth as the Superman he could be.

Stanley Rosen endorses a variant of this view, but if anything he is more radical than Lampert. Like Lampert, Rosen asserts the impossibility of Strauss's accepting proposition 3. Strauss arbitrarily decides for philosophy. But Rosen does not dismiss proposition 1 as Lampert does. His Strauss is therefore a decisionist with a bad conscience, or a decisionist who cannot believe in his own decision. Thus, at the end of the day, his Strauss does not, cannot believe in philosophy. The Straussian teaching of the possibility and goodness of philosophy, Rosen concludes, is exoteric doctrine, persisted in by Strauss to keep other human beings from despairing of their situation out of despair for the truth. Strauss's "noble lie" is philosophy.[19]

In some respects Rosen's Strauss is truer to the surface of Strauss's writings than Lampert's, because he takes seriously Strauss's proposition 1 while Lampert merely ignores it or attributes it to Strauss's timidity. But in other respects it is much further from the Strauss of the Strauss corpus, for no theme is more prominent in Strauss than philosophy itself, and Lampert, far better than Rosen, gives an account of Strauss that keeps the commitment to philosophy at the center.

Like the decisionists, faith-based Straussians also take seriously Strauss's insistence on the limits of philosophy, i.e., on philosophy as uncompletable quest for wisdom, rather than as wisdom itself. They take especially seriously his insistence that philosophy shows its limits in its inability to refute the possibility of revelation. There are two subgroups of "faithful" Straus-

sians, one associated with so-called West Coast Straussians (as the rationalist position is loosely associated with East Coast Straussians), and one a
rather separate grouping.

Like almost everything associated with West Coast Straussians, this
branch of the faith-based group owes its main inspiration to Harry V.
Jaffa, who, in his earliest scholarly work, a book called *Thomism and Aristotelianism*, wrote like an "orthodox" Straussian in insisting on the wide
distance that separated Thomas Aquinas's and Aristotle's moral philosophies.[20] Later on, Jaffa moved in a quite different direction, toward reconciliation of philosophy and the Bible, a reconciliation made possible by the
very limitation of philosophy that Strauss always emphasized. "Does not
philosophy—confidence in the ultimate significance of reason—depend on
an act of faith as much as belief in the God of the Bible?"[21] Jaffa is looking
at the same aspect of Strauss's thinking as the decisionists, the inability to
fully establish proposition 3. He sees that as an opening toward the reconciliation of reason and faith.

One of the most interesting adumbrations of the West Coast faith-based
option is Susan Orr's *Jerusalem and Athens*, a book-length commentary on
Strauss's essay "Jerusalem and Athens."[22] Like many of the close readers
of Strauss, she finds him to be practicing a special and surprising kind of
rhetoric in this essay and elsewhere. Strauss's rhetoric makes him "appear
more impious on the surface than he is upon deeper examination."[23] It is
the reverse of the rhetoric Strauss usually uncovered in philosophers of the
past, who had a more pious veneer than the depth of their thought supported. Why would Strauss practice this reverse rhetoric? Because, according to Orr, the "orthodoxies" of our day are different: "atheism *had* become
the reigning academic fashion."[24] Strauss, thinks Orr, wants to "draw the
reader into discovering the Bible only after he has sufficiently disarmed him
by allowing him to hold on to his prejudices, at least temporarily." Having
hooked his reader with his secular rhetoric, Strauss can then show how
Genesis "provides a comprehensive account of the whole." More than that,
he shows that Genesis "can even be understood as a rebuke to philosophy."[25] She wavers between arguing that Strauss is essentially neutral or
evenhanded in his presentation of Jerusalem and Athens, and that "he tips
the scales . . . towards Jerusalem." Her last word indeed is this: "Strauss's
exegetical defense [comes] to the aid of the God of Abraham, Isaac, and
Jacob. Such an endeavor is undertaken with pious intention and pious results."[26] In the last analysis Orr gently aligns Strauss with Jerusalem. Like

the decisionists, she rejects proposition 3, but unlike them, she takes very seriously the path that Strauss always holds up as *the* alternative to philosophy, biblical revelation.

Not even all the faith-based Straussians, much less all the other sorts, are satisfied with this solution, however. The other wing of the faith-based camp has more filiation with the East Coast Straussians, but has decisively broken with them as well. It has taken a more oppositionist stance toward Strauss himself, for it does not accept Orr's conclusion that Strauss sides with Jerusalem over Athens, or Jaffa's various attempts at making Strauss into a synthesizer of the Thomistic type.

This second group of faith-based Straussians are serious critics as well as followers of Strauss. As Ralph Hancock concludes one of his essays: "And so, without for a moment forgetting our immense debt to Leo Strauss's unsurpassed elucidation of the political-philosophical problem, we must forsake once and for all his 'final solution,' and rediscover or find other ways to think the good of thinking together with the good of humanity."[27] Hancock's declaration of independence from Strauss confirms the point that Strauss made about the centrality of morality for the faithful. Hancock and the others in his camp "actually find human beings and their concerns (as expressed in politics, religion, art) interesting, perhaps even loveable."[28] They suspect that Strauss does not. Most important, Strauss does not give sufficient weight to the connection between the moral and the sacred or the holy. All forms of human life, including, or perhaps especially, philosophy, must recognize "the authority of something above oneself, even if one cannot fully—perhaps can hardly begin—to articulate the nature of this authority." The Straussian philosopher, however, recognizes no such authority, but aims and claims to achieve autonomy or full self-sufficiency.[29]

The faith-based Straussians thus break with Strauss, but do so in dialogue with him and in part via the path he has set forth. They rely heavily on his demonstration both of the nature of modernity (as, they say, inherently atheistic) and of its failures, moral, political, and philosophic. They accept Strauss's explanation of the self-unraveling dialectic of modernity, whereby the movement from Machiavelli's innovation of a new kind of philosophy to Heidegger's declaration of the end of philosophy is a necessary development.

The faith-based Straussians take seriously Strauss's three propositions, and unlike Rosen do not suspect him of insincerity or exotericism in affirming proposition 3. They even more strongly reject the rationalist position. They rely on Strauss's case against philosophy's ability to refute revelation:

Strauss has shown that revelation cannot be dismissed. They also emphasize Strauss's invocation of the erotic, i.e., of the recognition of incompleteness and the striving for completeness in the eternal in the souls of human
beings, a striving to which modern philosophy is blind.

Where they most emphatically take issue with Strauss is on the adequacy
of the philosophic life as the fulfillment of that erotic striving. In this they
remind one more than a little of Augustine, but they find their way back
to Augustine via Strauss's own depiction of the philosophic life. Strauss's
rendition of the philosophic life, as opposed, say, to the Neoplatonic version with which Augustine was most familiar, brings out on its own the
severe limitations of the philosophic life. It is quest for knowledge of the
whole, but the chief discovery of Straussian Socratic philosophy is that such
knowledge is in principle unattainable. Moreover, the Socratic philosopher
is tied to society and other human beings, to the normal ways and concerns
of ordinary persons, because the Socratic "way of opinion" requires the philosopher to begin from and remain ever in contact with "the city." As Peter
Lawler summarizes the faith-based Straussian position: they dissent "from
both Strauss and Straussians by doubting that philosophy can truthfully
liberate a human being, even the greatest thinkers, from their natural orientation toward morality and God." Thus, while the faithful Straussians
are open to and, one presumes, committed to revelation, they claim to rest
their case on an "anthropology" that points toward, if it does not fully get
them to, the morality and divinity affirmed in revelation.[30]

In the final analysis, the faith-based position is surprisingly similar to
the theological position Strauss described in his 1948 lecture "Reason
and Revelation." Its exponents charge Strauss with the same pridefulness,
self-deification, and illusory self-sufficiency that Strauss identified as the
standard theological case against philosophy.[31] Relevant to these post-
Straussian believers is Strauss's demonstration that that traditional theological position certainly does not amount to a refutation of philosophy,
for it is question-begging.

In 1948 Strauss developed responses to all these criticisms. Perhaps most
pertinent is this:

Take Pascal's famous argument of the misery of man without God, i.e., without the God of Abraham, Isaac, and Jacob, an argument which is meant to
be conclusive "*par nature.*" This argument does not in any way refute Plato's
thesis that the philosopher, as exemplified by Socrates in particular, lives on
the islands of the blessed.[32]

That is to say, the admitted limitations of the philosopher's achievement do not destroy the fullness and satisfactoriness of the philosophic life, as witnessed by the testimony of those who have lived and observed that life.

The zetetic or Socratic Straussians deny proposition 1. They notice that Strauss posits proposition 1 only when he is presenting the modern philosophic position or "present day argument," as in his oft-quoted statement of the position in "Progress or Return?," or the "social science position," as in his chapter on Max Weber in *Natural Right and History*.[33] The demand that philosophy refute revelation to secure its own enterprise is said by the Socratic Straussians to be a demand not of classical or Socratic philosophy, but only of modern philosophy. They maintain that the rationalists and decisionists, in particular, fail to take account of the recurring distinction Strauss draws between Socratic and modern philosophy vis-à-vis the problem of revelation. The moderns do indeed come to decisionism, but, according to Strauss, the Socratics do not, because their case for philosophy does not depend on a refutation of revelation. This is one of the important reasons for Strauss's call for a "return to the ancients."

Strauss's clearest and fullest statement of the case is worth quoting. In a paragraph starting out as an explication of the thinker Yehuda Halevi, a great defender of orthodoxy, Strauss speaks of "the philosopher who refuses assent to revelation." Such refusal amounts to rejection of revelation, which is "unwarranted if revelation is not disproved." That is to say, "the philosopher, when confronted with revelation, *seems* to be compelled to contradict the very idea of philosophy by rejecting without sufficient grounds" ("PR," 296; emphasis added).

But Strauss shows that there is a "philosophic reply" to this argument by the sophisticated orthodox like Halevi:

> The question of utmost urgency, the question which does not permit suspense [of judgment], is the question of how one should live. Now this question is settled for Socrates by the fact that he is a philosopher. As a philosopher he knows that we are ignorant of the most important things. The ignorance, the evident fact of this ignorance, evidently proves that quest for knowledge of the most important things is the most important thing for us. ("PR," 296)

Strauss's conclusion is significantly framed in language that directly responds to the orthodox position to which he is replying, a position that proposition 1 actually attributes to him. "Philosophy is then evidently the right way of life." It is the right way of life precisely because the question of the right way of life is the most urgent question and there is no evident answer given to the question. Most urgent, then, is the quest for the answer to that question, and philosophy is just that quest. It is, as Strauss emphasizes in this context, a "way of life" and not a set of doctrines, for what is "evident" is the rightfulness of the quest, not any given conclusions. Philosophy is the "right way of life," Socrates and the Socratics conclude, despite the fact that Socratic ignorance is unable to refute the possibility of revelation.

This solution to Strauss's puzzle about religion leaves the answer to one crucial question unsettled: if "the way of Socrates" establishes philosophy as the right way of life, does this imply that following revelation is never equally electable?

On Morality

Strauss's first puzzle implicates one of his best-known polarities—Jerusalem and Athens. The second puzzle implicates another polarity in his thinking, one that is much less recognized: Plato versus Aristotle. Normally Strauss treats the classical thinkers as more or less agreeing in their understanding of natural right and philosophy. But implicitly, and at least in one place, as we have seen, very explicitly, he insists on a distinction between Plato (or Socrates) and Aristotle. Socrates invented or discovered political philosophy, but Aristotle invented political science, i.e., a discipline supplying knowledge of political matters, which is "one discipline among a number of disciplines" (*CM*, 25). Aristotle's political science articulated the political as a closed and autonomous sphere, with prudence as its governing principle. Socrates and Plato saw no such sphere. The "discovery" that allowed Aristotle to treat the political in this way is, according to Strauss, the Aristotelian affirmation of "moral virtue," i.e., the claim that "just and noble deeds" are "choiceworthy for their own sake."[34]

Despite this large and important difference between the Socratic and the Aristotelian, Strauss commends both founders to his readers. Thus in his "Epilogue" to a book critical of "the new science of politics" Strauss urges political scientists to adopt or take their bearings by Aristotelian political science. But he is even better known for his championing of Socrates, or of Plato and Xenophon, our two main sources for understanding Socrates.

The group often known as East Coast Straussians gravitate most strongly to Strauss's Platonic pole. The so-called West Coast Straussians gravitate to the Aristotelian pole, although many Straussians adhere to the Aristotelian alternative without any particular connection to West Coast Straussianism. The issue between Platonic Straussians and Aristotelian Straussians is not, however, whether they have particular allegiance to one or the other of the Greek thinkers, but rather how they understand the status of morality and politics, especially in relation to philosophy. Thus, paradoxically, there are Platonic Straussians who look to Aristotle (read "Platonically") as their guide, just as there are Aristotelian Straussians who read Plato in an Aristotelian way. And, of course, to be a Platonist or an Aristotelian Straussian does not require that one focus one's attention or write on either of these two philosophers at all.

ARISTOTELIAN STRAUSSIANS

Aristotelian Straussians are in many ways much closer in their political philosophy to standard readings of the classical philosophers than are other Straussians. An early and outstanding version of the Aristotelian Straussian position was presented by one of Strauss's first students, Harry V. Jaffa, who studied with Strauss at the New School for Social Research not long after Strauss arrived there. Jaffa has been a major figure in Straussian circles from the beginning, being the founder of West Coast Straussianism and one of the first to develop a Straussian approach to the study of American politics (*TALS*, 217–27). He is probably best known for his two books on Abraham Lincoln, *Crisis of the House Divided* and *A New Birth of Freedom*, both devoted to developing an Aristotelian-Straussian understanding of Lincoln and the American regime.[35]

Jaffa's two books on Lincoln, published some forty years apart, both contain despite important modifications an underlying Aristotelian-Straussianism as their central point. In his earlier *Crisis of the House Divided* Jaffa argued that Lincoln came on the scene of American politics not merely to counter the pernicious doctrine of unlimited popular sovereignty sponsored by his opponent Stephen Douglas, but to counter, reform, and elevate the principles of the American regime as bequeathed by the American founders. The founders had adopted the modern principles of Locke (and behind him of Hobbes) in constructing their regime, and that flaw at the outset threatened the integrity, success, and very existence of the American experiment by the 1850s. The crisis of the house divided was a crisis over *the* American principle, the principle of equality. The regime based on this principle proved remarkably vulnerable to the beguilements of the institution of slavery, either directly, as in the "slavery as positive good" ideology, or indirectly, as in Douglas's idea that one group of people had a right to vote on whether another group of people could be enslaved. The American regime, Jaffa's Lincoln saw, was in danger of becoming attached to the "might makes right" doctrines of Plato's Thrasymachus or Callicles. Jaffa thought this danger was not merely adventitious. Following Strauss, he saw the problem to reside in the deficient modern principle embodied in the American political order. According to those principles, the standard of right, natural rights, was nothing but the Hobbesian doctrine of right as based on the strongest passion, the fear of death, or the desire for preservation. Such a doctrine lacks all nobility, and does not even secure the equality and right it aims to secure, for it contains no genuinely moral restraint. If one group can get away with enslaving another group, then this Hobbesian doctrine has little to say against it.[36]

The solution to which Jaffa appealed was an Aristotelianization of the regime. Lincoln's greatness resided not merely in his reaffirmation of the principle of equality in such a form as to stand unequivocally against slavery and in favor of government by consent, or government of, by, and for the people. More than that, Lincoln reconceived the good of equality in Aristotelian terms. Those terms involved affirming the deeper truth of human inequality: some human beings belong to "the tribe of the eagle" and are indeed "better" and deserve to rule. Such, in effect, was Aristotle's argument in book 3 of his *Politics*. But the true greatness of a man is a moral greatness, superiority in virtue. The peak of moral virtue, as Jaffa presents the Aristotelian-Lincoln position, is magnanimity—the great-souled man who, in his greatness and virtue, is beyond the concern for honor and power. The great-souled man is truly superior but has no interest in asserting his superiority. The theoretical truth, then, is inequality because of the differential achievement of virtue or excellence, but the practical or political truth is equality, for the truly excellent man will not raise claims to honor and rule, and those who do raise such claims are not truly excellent.[37]

Forty years later in *A New Birth of Freedom*, Jaffa has transformed many elements of his story, but the Aristotelianism of his position remains constant. Here, however, he carries his Aristotelianism deeper into the founding: the founders themselves were Aristotelians, as perhaps was Locke himself. Lincoln did not improve on the founders but instead reaffirmed their position. Even though Lincoln, Jefferson, and Locke emphasized doctrines that seem the opposite of, or at least very different from, Aristotle's, Jaffa expends considerable energy establishing how, on Aristotelian grounds, they might arrive at such doctrines as are affirmed in the Declaration of

Independence. The aim of this account is very similar to that of the earlier account in *Crisis*: to show that the American regime was originally, or after Lincoln reinterpreted it, aimed at the noble and just, i.e., at virtue as understood by Aristotle. Jaffa's political science, in other words, is a version of the Aristotelian political science Strauss recommended; it takes its bearings by the Aristotelian-Straussian orientation around moral virtue. Jaffa has devoted his considerable polemical skills to defending this doctrine against liberals, other conservatives, and most vehemently, other Straussians.

Another extremely thoughtful version of Aristotelian Straussianism, which focuses more directly on Aristotle himself, is Mary Nichols's *Citizens and Statesmen*.[38] Nichols is no West Coast Straussian, but instead was a student of Joseph Cropsey, a man very close to Strauss personally and his literary executor.

Nichols's book on Aristotle is explicitly addressed against the Platonic-Straussian reading of Aristotle and political life. Her study shares the spirit of Aristide Tessitore's comment about Aristotle:

> Unlike Plato, Aristotle gives greater scope to the kind of moral and political excellence constrained by the vicissitudes of political life. Indeed, he maintains that ethical virtue possesses a certain kind of self-sufficiency, qualified to be sure, and is characterized by the high and admirable standard of reflectiveness found in the individual who embodies practical wisdom. Aristotle invests the non-philosophic way of life with unplatonic seriousness.[39]

Like Jaffa, Nichols sees Aristotle as supplying a way to reconcile democracy and aristocracy, the claims of freedom (and equality) and the claims of virtue (excellence). More explicitly than Jaffa, however, she probes the issue that tends to divide the Platonic from the Aristotelian Straussians, that is, the issue of philosophy. If philosophy is the highest human possibility, as Strauss and the Straussians tend to hold, and if philosophy is in inexorable tension with the city, i.e., with political life, as Strauss and the Straussians aver, then political life cannot be the locus of the good life in any simple or straightforward way. If philosophy is the highest or best human life, what is the status of morality and justice? And what is the status of political life itself?

As opposed to the Platonic Straussians, who, as we shall see, tend to emphasize or even exacerbate the differences and tensions among these three things, Nichols sees in Aristotle a comprehensive and successful reconciliation of the three that Plato himself could not effect. Nichols locates her study between two alternative positions: the democratic view, which finds grounds for "participatory democracy" in Aristotle's theory, and the aristocratic view, which sees Aristotle's politics as satisfying (or suited only) to the "well-bred gentlemen" or the "few" who "are capable of such fulfillment."[40] At the extreme end of the aristocrats she locates the Platonic-Straussian position that "views the value of politics, finally, less as a fulfillment of human nature than as a means of fostering the conditions in which the philosophic—and hence apolitical—virtue of the few [philosophers] can flourish."[41] While acknowledging some truth in the democratic and aristocratic views as well as the extreme Platonic-Straussian view, she finds all three partial and incomplete. The truth about human nature according to Aristotle is that "human beings realize their freedom—and fulfill their highest natural capacities—through the activities of citizens and statesmen." Aristotle brings out "the connection between the freedom the democrats seek through political participation and the virtue that aristocrats seek through elite rule."[42] His model of "polity," a combination or variety of combinations of the many and the few, is the basis for the existence in theory and practice of that "connection" or comprehensive presentation of the human political good.[43] She clearly affirms the reality of moral virtue as described by Strauss as the basis of Aristotle's "discovery" of political science.

Philosophy nonetheless finds its place in Nichols's version of Aristotelian Straussianism. The philosopher is paradigmatically the political philosopher, not the apolitical contemplative. Aristotle's activity as a political philosopher is the model; it is at once a participation in ruling and being ruled, and a form of the "rational" life that is the political life. The relationship among the democratic concern with freedom, the aristocratic concern with virtue, and the philosophic concern with thinking and understanding is one of continuity, not diremption. "*Politikē* [political science] is both the means to self-knowledge and the activity that best expresses it."[44]

PLATONIC STRAUSSIANS

Many Straussians belong in the Platonic-Straussian category, but perhaps those who have carried this line of thought furthest are Seth Benardete and the circle around him. There are, of course, many others, including most of those known as East Coast Straussians. The Platonic Straussians are far from affirming the comprehensive harmony that Nichols identifies as characteristic of true political philosophy. Benardete is perhaps the most radical spokesman for Platonic Straussianism. Unlike many of Strauss's other students, who were members of political science or philosophy departments, Benardete was a classicist, renowned for his extraordinary expertise in the Greek language. He was also the author of a large number of books and articles on topics in Greek poetry and philosophy.

Benardete clearly saw his own work on Plato as having its roots in Strauss's "rediscovery" of Plato, a rediscovery Benardete thought was as fundamental as Alfarabi's rediscovery of philosophy in the tenth century.[45] Benardete finds the original "rediscoverer" of philosophy, however, to have been Socrates, as presented by Plato.[46] That first rediscovery, which was at the same time the discovery of political philosophy, or the overcoming of the "false start of philosophy," was called by Socrates in *Phaedo* his "second sailing." That kind of Socratic philosophy is what Benardete saw Strauss to be practicing; it is also how he identified his own works, as his interpretation of Plato's *Republic*, titled *Socrates' Second Sailing*, illustrates.[47]

The idea of the "second sailing" is central to Benardete's understanding of Plato's philosophy and forms the basis for his often brilliant and always difficult interpretive studies of the dialogues. Every dialogue, when read Benardete-like, that is, when read in the full appreciation of the interaction of argument and action, induces in the reader the Socratic experience of the second sailing, that is, the emergence of "an entirely new argument . . . that could never have been expected from the argument on the written page."[48] That emergence comes with "revolutionary unexpectedness" and involves a "turnaround" in what the reader sees in the dialogue. It is not too much to say that Benardete sets the dialogues on their heads, in that he discovers meanings in them almost opposite to what their surface appears to be presenting. The surface argument always fails, he argues, and metamorphoses into something quite different. His revolutionary readings of Plato are clearly descendants of Strauss's own remarkable and controversial readings. Benardete takes Strauss's tendency to unorthodox readings (as measured against the standard scholarly literature) of classical texts and radicalizes it. Benardete is the master of paradox and reversal.

A particularly revealing case in point, which is also highly revealing of Benardete's treatment of the puzzle about morality, is his interpretation of Plato's *Gorgias*. That dialogue is an especially hard test case for the general line that Strauss takes on Plato. Rather than depreciating or even dismissing moral virtue as mere "vulgar" or "political" virtue, Socrates argues in *Gorgias* that "it is better to suffer injustice than to do it." Socrates's interlocutors, worldly men one and all, have a hard time believing that Socrates is serious about this thesis. So does Benardete.

In the introduction to his study of *Gorgias* Benardete announces that

"Socrates . . . is not out to defend morality but to understand 'so-called rhetoric.'"[49] The radicalness of Benardete's interpretation stands out when we place it in the context of the more standard reading of the dialogue. In *Gorgias*, Socrates has conversations with three men—the famous rhetorician Gorgias; a student of Gorgias, now a professor of the subject himself, Polus; and a young Athenian aspiring politician, Callicles, who has also studied rhetoric with Gorgias. In appearance, the discussion finds Socrates pitted against a man who is at best indifferent to justice (Gorgias), a friend to tyranny (Polus), and a defender of injustice (Callicles). In that context Socrates rises to the defense of justice and promotes the very strong thesis that it is better to suffer injustice than to do it. That is how the dialogue is usually read.

Benardete turns all this almost on its head. The rhetoricians are not champions of injustice; Socrates is not a champion of justice. (It is not that Socrates is a champion of injustice, but he is a champion of philosophy, i.e., of his knowledge of ignorance.) The morality that the rhetoricians champion (somewhat contrary to their own self-understanding) is the position that Socrates brings to explicitness in his moral formula "it is better to suffer injustice than to do it." The rhetoricians, Benardete argues, are moralists, and rhetoric as such depends on moralism. Socrates does not defend this moralism in *Gorgias* but supplies a critique of it. The critique is needed because moralism is the form of dogmatism that stands in the way of philosophy as genuinely open-minded inquiry into the truth of being. Socrates's critique does not have a practical aim, e.g., to overturn public morality, but is solely oriented toward opening up the philosophic life for those capable of it.

The deeper ground for the claims Benardete raises in his interpretation of *Gorgias* is contained in the *Republic* as he reads it. The *Republic*, he maintains, is the attempt to "postulate . . . utopia's reality," an attempt necessary to ground "morality" as "based on the absoluteness of the will," i.e., the attempt to show how morality can be an end "in itself."[50] It is a positing meant to reveal the nature of justice, not to effectuate justice. Therefore, the *Republic* is not only, as Strauss taught, a critique of political idealism and the utopian desire for perfect justice, but a critique of justice or moral virtue as such (*CM*, 65, 138). As Benardete says, "the 'idea' of justice . . . is the delusion of thumos," i.e., of the spirited part of the soul. The centerpiece of Benardete's interpretation of the *Republic*, perhaps of all of his thinking, is his analysis of the "thumoeidetic," the term Socrates uses in the *Republic* to refer to the spirited part of the soul. It is, Benardete points out, an odd term, for it combines the word *thymos* (spirit, heart) with the root for the word *eidos*, one of the terms Plato uses in developing his famous doctrine of the ideas. In a subtle analysis of the brief discussion of the thumoeidetic in book 4 of the *Republic* Benardete attributes to Plato (and apparently accepts as his own) the view that the thumoeidetic, i.e., a nonrational part of the soul, is the source of both the stable intellectual (eidetic) structures human beings, particularly philosophers, posit in their quest to understand, and the understanding of the human soul as capable of morality and thus under moral injunctions.[51] The structures developed by the thumoeidetic are, in effect, the results of the "first sailing." The "second sailing," which necessarily begins with the opinions and moral-intellectual structures of the "first sailing," necessarily but subtly has the character of a deconstruction of those "given" structures. Genuine philosophy is, indeed, deeply and thoroughly in tension with the city, which is constituted precisely through the moral idealism produced by the thumoeidetic. Philosophy, according to this version of Platonic Straussianism, is thus very far from affirming moral virtue, the discovery or affirmation of which formed, according to Strauss, the basis for Aristotle's political science.

This version of Platonic Straussianism is also very far from affirming the kind of harmony among morality (the just and the noble), politics, and philosophy that Nichols defends, as is visible in Michael Davis's book on Aristotle's *Politics*.[52]

Unlike Benardete and Jaffa, Davis never studied with Strauss; the largest influence on him has been his friendship with Seth Benardete, who is, for him, "the full embodiment . . . of the philosophic life."[53] One need look no farther than the introduction to his *The Politics of Philosophy* to see how different his grasp of the political in relation to both morality and philosophy is from that of Nichols. Where she treats the moral virtues as largely unproblematic, Davis sees multiple tensions:

> The *Nicomachean Ethics* as a whole is the working out of the problematic nature of human virtue and so of human nature itself first within the particular virtues themselves and then in relations among the particular virtues that culminate in this tension between the godlike self-sufficiency of pride and the acknowledged mutual dependence of justice. The problem is then worked through in terms of the tension between the whole of moral virtue, understood as the correct disposition of our appetites, and appears again within intellectual virtue itself in the tension between *sophia* [wisdom] and *phronesis* [prudence].[54]

The dualisms reproduced at every level of Aristotle's presentation can find no "third" in which they are reconciled.[55] Davis's Aristotle is not a thinker of harmonies as is Nichols's.

The particular character of Davis's interpretative method comes out in his analysis of nearly every book of the *Politics*. Where Nichols attempts to supply an overall and coherent account of the argument, following for the most part Aristotle's own presentation, Davis instead begins with puzzles, anomalies, oddities in the Aristotelian text. Although he does not use the language of Benardete, Davis treats the surface of the text, what most readers focus on, as elements of the "first sailing," and the oddities that pop up every now and again as the clues to get to the real core. Thus book 5 of the *Politics*, which appears to be about revolution, turns out to be about *eros*. The significant point of departure for understanding book 2 of the *Politics* is not so much the substance of what Aristotle has to say in criticism of his predecessors, but the fact that the book is obtrusively divided and subdivided into units of three, for Aristotle criticized one of his predecessors, Hippodamus, for doing that very thing in his plans for political reform.

For Davis, then, moral virtue, about the coherence of which he has doubts, does not provide the ground or orienting principle for understanding politics as an autonomous or self-enclosed sphere, but philosophy itself is the model, pattern, and core of political life and provides the "solution" to the political problem so far as there is one. This is not to say, however, that Davis accepts the kind of diminution of the tension between politics and philosophy that Nichols does. That tension is central and if anything intensified by Davis's attempt to demonstrate "that the connection between politics and philosophy is much deeper than is ordinarily understood."[56]

His treatment of book 1 of the *Politics* is indicative of the Benardete-like reversals he effects. Book 1, it seems to most readers, is meant by Aristotle to establish the thesis that the *polis* (the political association) and therewith political life is natural, and "that we who are by nature political can for that reason live naturally, and so, happily, within a political order." Aristotle, according to Davis, is no more defending that thesis than Plato, according to Benardete, is arguing that "it is better to suffer injustice than to do it." What Aristotle does show in the *Politics* is "the problematic character of [the] claim that it is [natural]."[57] Davis shows that it is problematic in multiple senses. On the one hand, the *polis* is held to be the natural end for the lesser and prior human associations, which are themselves said to be natural. The basic unit of the *polis* is the household, which consists, according to

Aristotle, of father-husband, wife-mother, children, and slaves. Given the natural sexual force that brings man and woman together and the natural process that brings children, it is not implausible to affirm these relations as natural.

But what about slavery? Aristotle, Davis maintains, is driven to his notions about natural slaves in order to salvage the surface thesis that the household, of which the slave is an integral part, is natural, a minimal prerequisite to the thesis that the *polis* is natural. The attempt to establish the naturalness of slavery in turn drives Aristotle to formulate what Davis calls a doctrine of "strong teleology," i.e., the claim that natural entities have ends not only within their own class of being (e.g., for a man to be a *good* man), but across classes, or in relation to something like a "great chain of being." Lower beings are naturally ordered toward the good of higher beings. Thus some men are slaves for the sake of other (higher) men. But this notion of teleology threatens the integrity of all classes and points toward a rigid hierarchy and subordination of all to the one best, which is incompatible with the nature of politics and the generic character of classes. Davis concludes that the point of the discussion of natural slaves is to show how problematic the notion of the naturalness of the *polis* is, and how problematic the conception of nature to which one would have to appeal in order to make good the claims about natural slaves. It is an argument meant to undercut the thesis Aristotle is purportedly defending in book 1. To see the problem with the "first sailing" notion of naturalness is the point of the "second sailing" argument. Davis emerges, then, with a very Platonic reading of Aristotle and political life. It is not natural; it does not rest on the centrality of the moral virtues; it does not abolish the tensions between the human good, philosophy, and the political life.

We have given the barest sketch here of Davis's argument, as we have of the others we have discussed. More than that, we have discussed only a few of the Straussians who can be located in terms of the two sets of puzzles that serve to distinguish many of the different groups of Straussians from each other, to say nothing of the fact that we have said nothing at all about the very large number of Straussians whose work cannot plausibly be related to these two puzzles. What is perhaps most striking at the end of this brief survey is how diverse the Straussians are. Strauss himself worried that schools were dangerous things for philosophy in that dogmas and other substitutes for thinking took root in such schools (*OT*, 194–96). Although Straussian circles are not immune to these vices, it would be fair to say that intellectual vigor and disagreement are more apparent in them than hardening of the intellectual arteries. This result is largely the outcome of Strauss's way of presenting his thought. To the chagrin of the professionals, he left much unsaid. He left ambiguities and puzzles. His aim was not to transform the world but to understand it, and to encourage the young, the ones he called "the puppies of the race," toward philosophy. The vibrant disagreements among the so-called Straussians are testimony to the degree to which he succeeded in not inspiring a set of dogmas and orthodoxies that straitjacket those who, loosely, follow him.

Strauss's Project

Reviving Socratic Political Philosophy

L eo Strauss was born into a world in crisis. While that crisis became apparent to him as a young Jew in Germany first and most obviously in politics, his studies led him to see that the crisis extended to religion, morality, philosophy, and science, i.e., to human life and knowledge as a whole. It was no longer clear that any of the greatest achievements of Western civilization had a firm foundation. The outbreak of World War II convinced many others that the future of Western civilization as a whole was at stake.

Although the danger was great, Strauss also came to believe, the crisis in Western civilization constituted a great opportunity. As a result of the radical critiques of Western rationalism by Nietzsche and then by Heidegger, his friend Jacob Klein had persuaded Strauss that it was possible to read the canonical works of the Western philosophical tradition afresh, unfettered by long-accepted interpretations of them.

Following out this "opportunity" led Strauss to his lifelong project—the restoration of Socratic philosophy, which, he maintained, correctly understood is political philosophy in the original and still valid sense. Political philosophy, however, is no straightforward thing. The most perspicuous way to capture its complexity is to note that Socratic philosophy, taking seriously the "human things" and engaging dialectically with opinion, propels the philosopher into a deeply ambiguous relationship with ordinary human life as lived in the city. That leads to the multifaceted "problem of political philosophy," which Strauss made the center of his lifework, and which we have attempted to elucidate in this book.

Socratic philosophy, unlike the pre-Socratic variety as parodied in Aristophanes's *Clouds*, is thoroughly aware of its dependence on the city, and therefore for self-interested reasons if no others, cannot be indifferent to the well-being of the human communities in which it is practiced. Thus Socrates defends himself before the city of Athens in Plato's *Apology* as one who has, at some personal expense, spent much of his life exhorting his fellow Athenians to virtue, as a way of making Athens as good as it can be. As he says in that speech, it would be most foolish for him to do what his accusers say he does—attempt to corrupt the young. It would be foolish, because he, like all other citizens, has a personal stake in the city in general, and it is to his advantage for his associates in particular to be good citizens. When the young men who listen to him question others go home and imitate Socrates by interrogating their fathers, and their fathers prove unable to answer their sons' questions, the fathers may get angry at Socrates. But, Plato's Socrates suggests, these fathers do not understand the difference between Socrates's interrogations of individuals concerning their opinions about the noble and good and the pre-Socratic philosophical investigations of nature that undermined traditional beliefs in the gods. By going to his fellow citizens individually and asking them why they fear death and seek ever more honor and wealth, Socrates attempts to make them both braver and more law-abiding. By serving in the army and abiding by the law himself, he supports his own speeches with deeds. The Socratic philosopher is, in a word, public-spirited. As Plato and Aristotle both suggest, he serves as "umpire" of the competing claims made by the different elements in the cities with an eye to reconciling them; and so he gives advice to leaders of all the different kinds of regimes about how to make their regimes better.

Strauss was not much given to offering political advice, nor did he spend much time admonishing his fellows to be more virtuous. His public-spirited activity took the form of attempting to counter the two widespread doctrines, positivism and historicism, that he thought undermined the West's self-confidence in its historic commitment to liberty and rationalism. Since he saw both positivism and historicism as results of modern philosophy in its turn away from Socratic rationalism, he sought to show not only why modern political philosophy led, logically and inexorably, to these undesirable results, but also that a return to a Socratic understanding and practice of philosophy was possible. His entire effort to reconceive the Western tradition and reopen the case for classical political philosophy is thus part of a public-spirited activity intended to revive belief in human freedom and rationality.

Strauss hardly ever got political in the narrower sense. He did not endorse candidates or say much about policy issues, unlike, say, the Martin

Heidegger of the 1930s or the Jacques Derrida of the 1980s. One exception was his loud and clear anticommunism. He made a theoretical case against the modern form of tyranny in his debate with Alexandre Kojève in *On Tyranny*; and, perhaps following the example of Socrates in urging his fellow Athenians to be virtuous, he exhorted his fellow Americans on several occasions to remain firm in opposition to communism. His critiques of positivism and historicism must be seen in this context as well as in the more theoretical context in which he often framed them, because he thought these doctrines encouraged the kind of flaccid relativism that undercut the will to stand up to dangers.

What Strauss wanted his fellow citizens to stand up for is subject to much misunderstanding. Modern liberal democracy, Strauss argued, was the historical consequence of the early or first wave of modern political philosophy. Since Strauss is well known for finding fault with this kind of philosophy, many readers have concluded that he must, openly or secretly, oppose modern liberal democracy as well. We found unpersuasive the claims of some writers to have "discovered" that Strauss was "really" a hard-core right-winger, hostile to liberalism and to democracy, and friendly to imperialism, war, drastic forms of political inequality, and even unspeakable monstrosities like National Socialism. Such cases are built on the basis of a few statements by the young Strauss, as if comments regarding a particular horrendous political situation are the key to his views about all situations. Or they are built on the thought that as the products of an alleged practitioner of esotericism, Strauss's texts are fair game for extravagant "interpretation," which finds the absence of explicit support for a position in or on the lines of his writings to be adequate basis for attributing that position to Strauss "between the lines."

These "interpreters" of Strauss miss his real point. Socratic political philosophy supplies the basis for an embrace not of modern pathologies but of constitutionalism, rule of law, political and moral moderation—all features that Strauss found in liberal democracy at its best. Thus Strauss's political philosophy led him to endorse modern liberal democracy as the best option available in the modern world. Like Alexis de Tocqueville he identified himself as a "friend" of democracy, but refused, he said, to be its flatterer. That is, he was not so much a partisan of liberal democracy as many of his fellow citizens were. He thought that modern democracy was different from, and better in some ways than, the ancient democracies the classical writers tended to depreciate, because of modern science and technology. These make possible a level of wealth and education that obviates many of the features of ancient democracy that the classics decried. Modern societies are thus "more just" in important ways. However, his recovery of classical political philosophy also led him to have some reservations about modern democracy. Of these, there were two in particular. First, while not as apocalyptic about it as Heidegger, Strauss shared something of the latter's misgivings about the release of the technological genie from the bottle of scientific knowledge. The unleashing of all this power for "the relief of man's estate" could lead, Strauss feared, to the destruction of man's estate. He considered the jury to be still out on whether technology's effects were truly beneficial in the long run (*NRH*, 23; *TM*, 298–99).

Strauss's second major misgiving about modern liberal democracy derived from his familiar emphasis on the "lowering of sights" that constituted the modern project. He was influenced by Nietzsche's depiction of the "last men," who seek no more than petty contentment and whose lives center on modest pleasures, entertainment, and conformism. His response was to remind his readers of the loftier moral and intellectual aspirations that found voice in the classical writings of Plato, Xenophon, and Aristotle. He attempted especially to remind the intelligent, ambitious young of the philosophic life as a life worthy of their aspirations and to show them that it was possible to live such a philosophic life as a private individual in a liberal democracy.

One response to the problem of political philosophy is the public-spirited philosopher, a valid and even necessary part of the philosophic life, for the problematic status of philosophy in the city means that philosophy must make a case for itself, for its value to the citizens. But the problem of political philosophy has another face that Socrates in his defense speech emphasizes somewhat less than his "gadfly" role of serving the common good by "stinging" his fellows to virtue. Socrates not only exhorts his fellows but also questions them, most especially about moral issues like justice, courage, and the noble. In so questioning, the philosopher falls into a confrontational or even an antipathetic relation to ordinary citizens so far as they are attached to opinions that Socrates shows they do not understand and cannot support with reasons. This is a problem, indeed, for both the philosopher and the community. The solution, to which Strauss devoted a great deal of his attention, is the particular kind of rhetoric a Socratic philosopher employs. The philosopher must say different things to different people, and the Socratics found ways to do this. One way to capture this aspect of the problem of political philosophy is to note that the philosopher must find a way to combine in one speech act a moderation of expression addressed to the public at large and an indication of thoughts addressed to potential philosophers.

As Strauss saw it, the classics "solved" the multilayered problem of political philosophy in one way, and the moderns solved it in quite a different way. Starting with Machiavelli, the moderns sought to make the case for philosophy in the city in terms of its usefulness to the *demos*. Instead of taking its bearings from the highest human type, the true philosopher, and the civic reflection of that highest type, the gentleman, modern political philosophy appealed to what all human beings seek and thus took its bearings from what all or most human beings share, the passions. Along the way the original idea of philosophy was lost, and eventually philosophy itself was jettisoned. The conclusion of the modern effort to solve the problem of political philosophy was a position that threatened both the goods of political health, as Strauss thought was visible in the persistent dangers of hitherto unprecedented kinds of tyranny, and the highest good of human life, philosophy. On the basis of that analysis, it is no wonder that Strauss found modern political philosophy on the whole less satisfactory than the classical sort.

As an émigré to the United States, Strauss attempted to persuade the victorious peoples (as well as the defeated) that the crisis had not ended with the war. On the contrary, it was perpetuated by two pervasive schools of thought: positivism, which perpetuated the crisis in religion and morality by declaring that all such beliefs were mere "value judgments"; and historicism, which maintained that all "knowledge" was determined by, and so limited to, its context.

Strauss did not restrict himself to trying to awaken his contemporaries from their complacency, however. He tried to respond to the substance or causes of the crisis by finding new foundations for both morality and rational inquiry in the Western tradition itself.

Ironically, in light of the frequently voiced accusation that he sought to free a philosophically trained elite from all moral or political restraints, Strauss thought that he found not merely one but two different bases for morality in the Western tradition. The first was in human reason. Reason shows that the rules of morality, generally speaking, specify the requirements for maintaining a human community, and that communities are, in turn, required to preserve the lives and well-being of both individuals and the species. There is, in other words, a rational foundation for "citizen" morality, although unlike the Kantian categorical imperative, it is not morality for its own sake. In contemporary terms that Strauss did not use, this rationalist morality is consequentialist rather than deontological. Moral regulations are justified because they are necessary if human beings are to survive, much less prosper.

Strauss thought that a second, purer form of morality was to be found in Aristotle and even more in Scripture: "the Bible sets forth the demands of morality and religion in their purest and most intransigent form" (*TM*, 133). These demands are grounded not on rational argument but on faith in the one omniscient, omnipotent God, who will be what he will be, and whose will is revealed most clearly in his commands and his fulfillments of his promises.

What makes Strauss's argument controversial is his contention that these two sources of the Western tradition, reason and revelation, exist in tension with one another. Revelation excludes philosophy, because it teaches that wisdom begins in fear of the Lord and culminates in the demand that he alone be loved unqualifiedly. Neither God's wisdom nor his goodness can be questioned. He asks human beings to act on the basis of good intentions and to have righteous hearts. To justify its questioning of all authoritative opinions, philosophy has to try to refute revelation. But, Strauss regularly reminded his readers, revelation cannot be disproved by reason because revelation is based not on reason but on faith. Strauss also recognized, however, that the inability of reason to refute revelation would not convince any unbeliever to believe in it or its necessity.[1] Theologians might point to the despair needy human beings experience in the absence of a saving God; but, Strauss observed, there are other philosophic explanations of the experience of human finitude or insufficiency (including Heidegger's "being-toward-death"), guilt, and conscience. And, most important, there is Socrates's testimony that he lived a fully satisfying human life even though he did not claim to possess a rational account of the whole or to have the support of a loving and merciful God. For Strauss, the importance of the inability of philosophers to provide a rational account of the whole that would exclude the possibility of revelation was to remind them of the true nature of their activity: it consists in a search for wisdom, not the possession thereof.

By returning to a Socratic understanding of philosophy as a way of life, Strauss thought that he had also found a rational basis for the life of inquiry. Even though philosophers would probably never acquire knowledge of the whole, their lives were not tragic, nor were their efforts Sisyphean. They could take pleasure in the knowledge they were able to acquire, even if it was only partial and, therefore, provisional. True knowledge has to consist in knowledge of the whole, because the knowledge we think we have of any part might look different in light of knowledge we acquire of another part or of the whole itself. Strauss thought that knowledge of the whole had eluded and would continue to elude the philosophers who sought it. In "What Is Political Philosophy?" he explained:

> The knowledge which we possess is characterized by a fundamental dualism which has never been overcome. At one pole we find knowledge of homogeneity: above all in arithmetic, but also in the other branches of mathematics, and derivatively in all productive arts or crafts. At the opposite pole we find knowledge of heterogeneity, and in particular of heterogeneous ends; the highest form of this kind of knowledge is the art of the statesman and of the educator. ("WIPP," 39)

Impressed by the achievements of modern natural science, many contemporary philosophers and social scientists seek knowledge of the reductive, mathematical kind, even of human beings. Strauss argued, on the contrary, that knowledge of the ends of human life is superior to the kind of knowledge we acquire through mathematics.

> Knowledge of the ends of human life ... is knowledge of what makes human life complete or whole; it is therefore knowledge of a whole. Knowledge of the ends of man implies knowledge of the human soul; and the human soul is the only part of the whole which is open to the whole and therefore more akin to the whole than anything else is. (39)

But, Strauss acknowledged, "this knowledge — the political art in the highest sense — is not knowledge of *the* whole" (39).

The search for knowledge itself can be justified only in terms of human ends or goals. Following Nietzsche and Heidegger, Strauss saw that "science" cannot answer the question, why science? Science is a human activity. To explain why human beings engage — or should engage — in it, one must, implicitly if not explicitly, presuppose some understanding of what is good for human beings. Socratic philosophy, philosophy as a way of life, is justified, precisely because it recognizes the necessity of asking what is good for human beings as the first and most urgent question. In pursuing the answer to this question, it does not begin from an act of faith or will.

Because Socratic political philosophy begins with the question that is first for us, as human beings, it has to begin by distinguishing human beings from other sorts of beings. Socrates understood the recognition of essential differences among the kinds of being implied by his characteristic "what is . . . ?" question to be a return to "common sense," according to Xenophon, because even though "the roots of the whole are hidden, the whole manifestly consists of heterogeneous parts." In contrast to both pre-Socratic philosophy and modern natural science, Socrates observed, ordinary human beings register differences they perceive among various kinds of things in the opinions they have about the good and the bad, the noble and the base. Socrates thus famously turned to investigate those opinions in order to discover what is truly good and noble. Because these opinions are contradictory, he was forced to ascend from the realm of opinion or law to nature. But, Strauss emphasizes, Socrates did so cautiously. He recognized the necessity of showing the need for such an ascent "by a lucid, comprehensive, and sound argument which starts from the 'common sense' embodied in the accepted opinions and transcends them." As a result, he remained "chiefly, if not exclusively, concerned with the human things: with what is by nature right and noble." "In its original form," Strauss concluded, "political philosophy broadly understood is the core of philosophy or rather 'the first philosophy.'" But, he emphasized, "it also remains true that human wisdom is knowledge of ignorance: there is no knowledge of the whole but only knowledge of parts, hence only partial knowledge of parts, hence no unqualified transcending, even by the wisest man as such, of the sphere of opinion" (*CM*, 19–20).

In order to show that a return to Socratic political philosophy was both possible and desirable, Strauss had to challenge the traditional understanding of the history of philosophy in which the criticisms later philosophers made of earlier thinkers were taken to show that earlier thought was not tenable.[2] The signal importance of the thought of Martin Heidegger for Strauss was that it made a fresh reading of that history possible for the first time in many centuries. As we have attempted to show in chapters 3–8, Strauss thus gave extremely novel and highly controversial readings of the canonical works constituting the entire history of Western philosophy—ancient, medieval, and modern. As we pointed out in the prologue, however, the understated character of his presentation of many of his novel readings of canonical texts has resulted in their having often been dismissed as mere summaries, if not clearly wrongheaded interpretations—precisely because his readings are so untraditional.[3] By entering into the thought of the author in question, Strauss makes it extremely difficult for a reader to determine exactly what Strauss himself is claiming and why. Our chapters on Strauss's readings of specific ancient and modern political philosophers have, therefore, been primarily explications of Strauss's thought in which we have tried to show what he is claiming, on what basis, and why his claims are controversial.

Because Strauss makes it so difficult to separate his own thoughts from those of the philosophers he is explicating, we are not convinced that we have always or completely succeeded in explicating Strauss's thought. Nor are we convinced that Strauss's novel readings of the work of canonical philosophers are simply correct. In concluding, we would therefore like to point out some of the questions we found unanswered and that we think should be raised about Strauss's arguments.

In the case of Plato, for example, Strauss dismisses the so-called "theory of the ideas" that most commentators, following Aristotle, have taken to be the core of his philosophy.[4] Strauss accentuates Plato's emphasis on Socrates—that is, on the way of life rather than the doctrines or specific arguments Plato attributes to Socrates in the dialogues. (We do not mean to suggest that Strauss ignores the arguments, but that, as the title of his book *The Argument and Action of Plato's "Laws"* indicates, he insists on reading the arguments in light of the "action" or drama, especially as the arguments are directed ad hominem to specific individuals.) In his interpretation of the *Republic* Strauss points out that the way in which Socrates and the brothers seek to define justice by looking at the origin of a city does not conform to the way Socrates usually insists his characteristic question about what something is must be answered, i.e., in terms of its participation in an unchanging idea. Strauss concludes that Plato shows that the city, which is clearly not an eternally unchanging or even purely natural kind of being, can be known, because its limits can be known.[5] To be knowable is *not*, on Strauss's showing, to participate in an Idea. In his lectures called "The Problem of Socrates" Strauss suggests that Socrates, as presented in the works of Xenophon and Plato, could inquire into "the human things" generally, and discover what "the political" is specifically, because his insight into the noetic heterogeneity of things allowed him to see that different kinds of "things," the human and the nonhuman, had to be investigated in different ways. It was, therefore, possible to acquire partial or provisional knowledge about a part of the whole, especially that part closest and most immediately of interest to us as human beings, without possessing complete knowledge of the whole. Since the recognition of noetic heterogeneity Strauss finds in the thought of all the classical political philosophers (Socrates, Plato, Xenophon, Aristotle, and Cicero) does not appear to correspond to the doctrine of the "ideas" in any of the forms in which Socrates presents such an argument in the dialogues, we are led to ask what the basis of the insight into this "noetic" heterogeneity is. Strauss makes it clear that it consists in a return to the "surface" or "commonsense" understanding of things, but he does not draw out the specific connections or show very precisely what the "noetic" character or basis of the heterogeneity human beings undeniably perceive in the world is.

Likewise, in the only analysis Strauss published of Aristotle's thought, in contrast to "classical political philosophy" more generally, he first suggests that Aristotle's political science was founded on his teleological view of nature. That is a widely accepted traditional view based on Aristotle's declaration in the first book of the *Politics* that human beings are directed by nature to politics; and Aristotle's understanding of politics is often summarily dismissed by modern readers for precisely that reason. Strauss emphasizes, however, that Aristotle's political science is not theoretical. The highest political virtue, according to Aristotle, is prudence. Prudence requires knowledge of the ends of human life in order to determine the best means to those ends, but in his *Ethics* Aristotle suggests that such knowledge is available to human beings without theoretical knowledge. A conception of moral virtue as choiceworthy in itself, and not a teleological notion of nature more generally, thus becomes the ground of politics. Because prudence requires taking moral virtue as the end of action, in discussing politics Aristotle takes the perspective of the involved actor rather than the disinterested theoretical observer. Aristotle's political science shows itself to be a clarification of the prescientific or "commonsensical" experience on which all science is based. It corresponds to that version of political philosophy that arises directly out of political life. That experience shows us that human beings are inclined to live in political communities because they are inclined to seek happiness. But, Aristotle observes, all human beings do not live in political communities; some live in tribes. Nor do all—or even most—achieve happiness. The reason, Aristotle shows, is that nature does not fully provide for human needs, as he first suggests; on the contrary, nature enslaves human beings in a variety of ways. Aristotle thus points to, although he does not embrace, the modern conclusion that human beings need to conquer nature, not despite but especially because he suggests that moral excellence and human happiness are, or ought to be, available to all.

The difference between Strauss's reading of Aristotle's *Politics* and the readings of other scholars is indicated most clearly by the centrality Strauss attributes in Aristotle to the question of "regime" and to the corresponding disagreements about which sorts of human beings should rule (as opposed to Aristotle's initial declaration concerning the naturalness of the *polis*). Different regimes foster different virtues. *The* highest, *the* natural end of human existence, according to Aristotle, is, moreover, the life of philosophy, which is possible only for a few. But, we are thus led to ask, can an understanding of philosophy as theoretical contemplation of an eternal intelligible order be separated from Aristotle's ostensibly teleological understanding of nature? As Strauss himself observes in *Natural Right and History*, it is ultimately impossible to understand human nature (as opposed to "the human things") in isolation from nature as a whole. It is extremely difficult to determine, in the end, whether and, if so, how Strauss thinks an Aristotelian understanding of political practice can be made compatible with an understanding of the nature of the universe derived from modern physics.

Strauss's most distinctive and controversial thesis, about "persecution and the art of writing," is based primarily on his novel readings of medieval Islamic and Jewish philosophers like Alfarabi and Maimonides. Although these philosophers appear to be trying to reconcile revelation in the form of law with Aristotelian philosophy, Strauss argues, they were, in fact, "Averroists" who recognized the fundamental conflict between philosophy and revealed law. In order to avoid persecution, he suggests, these authors employed an "art of writing" through which they presented their thought as if they agreed with the dominant opinions (laws) of their societies and conveyed their heterodox views by means of subtle hints, including contradictions and slightly changed restatements or repetitions. However, if the results of "reading between the lines" in the texts of these authors can never be proved to be correct, as Strauss explicitly admits, because the whole point of an author's employing "the art of writing" is to escape the censors by repeating and endorsing authoritative opinions more frequently than he questions them, we have to ask just how much credence should be placed in the discovery of their "secret teachings." We have argued that purported applications of Strauss's method of reading other philosophers to his own works have produced gross misreadings. But we are also led to ask whether Strauss's rereading of the works of classical political philosophers in light of the conflict between philosophy and law with which the medieval Islamic and Jewish philosophers were explicitly concerned does not distort the thought of those ancient philosophers who were not aware of and did not explicitly address scriptural revelation.

In examining Strauss's indications of the way in which Aristotle's discovery of moral virtue made it possible for his philosophy to be combined with Scripture in Christianity and Strauss's further contention that this combination constituted the necessary but not sufficient condition for the emergence of modernity, we applied to Strauss's own work Strauss's maxim that an author indicates the way in which he writes by the way in which he reads others. In analyzing his essay on Aristotle in the *City and Man*, as well as in his essays on Marsilius and Machiavelli in the *History of Political Philosophy* and his essay on Locke in *What Is Political Philosophy?*, we counted paragraphs. We also carefully examined his restatements of his own arguments in previous works in order to identify the subtle changes or developments. In one case we have concluded at the end of a long analysis of Strauss's reexamination of the grounds of his own interpretation of Locke that he indicated the lines of his own critique of natural law in the critique he attributes to Locke. In his essay on Marsilius, we found evidence that Strauss thought that the combination of Aristotelian philosophy with scriptural morality in Christianity constituted a necessary but not sufficient condition for the emergence of modernity. Marsilius was not merely an Aristotelian in his political philosophy and a Christian in his political theology; according to Strauss, he was an "Averroist" who did not think that philosophy should make any compromise with revealed religion. But, Strauss argues, Marsilius's attempt to reform both politics and the church by separating them did not produce modernity. That required Machiavelli's "anti-theological" ire or passion. By tracing the differences in Strauss's three major statements on Machiavelli, first in *What Is Political Philosophy?*, then in *Thoughts on Machiavelli*, and, finally and most fully, in the chapter he wrote on Machiavelli in the *History of Political Philosophy*, we concluded that Strauss thought that Machiavelli had changed the character of philosophy itself by making it a servant of popular ends.

Strauss's contention that Machiavelli was a philosopher is controversial in itself; Machiavelli appears and is usually taken to be concerned solely with politics. Strauss responds to this objection by observing that we should have learned from Socrates that "the human things" are the key to all things, that is, by suggesting that Machiavelli was a kind of Socratic philosopher.[6] In suggesting that Machiavelli was a kind of Socratic, Strauss reads Machiavelli, not surprisingly, in light of his own understanding of the true and original character of philosophy and the tension he sees between the requirements of a good political order and unconstrained inquiry. But did Machiavelli understand himself to be a Socratic? Did he think that a life of philosophy is superior to a life of politics?[7] Did Strauss understand Machiavelli, as Strauss admonishes his readers they should try to understand every philosopher, as Machiavelli understood himself? Or did Strauss put his own critique of Christianity and its effects on both politics and philosophy into the mouth of the infamous "teacher of evil"? In other words, did Strauss use Machiavelli the same way we have argued that he used Locke?

Our finding that Strauss used Locke as the spokesman for his own view of natural law may well surprise many readers. Strauss presents himself from the beginning to the end of his career as a critic of modern liberal political philosophy; and Locke is the modern liberal political philosopher par excellence. Strauss has often been accused of being a covert (or perhaps not so covert) Machiavellian. But, we have attempted to show, Strauss did not think that Machiavelli's amoral political thought was internally consistent, because Machiavelli could not explain or account for his own activity. And although Machiavelli sought to have an effect on politics by changing popular opinion, Strauss thought, his amoral political thought was not popularly palatable. It had to be combined with the doctrine of natural rights developed by early modern political philosophers like Hobbes and Locke in order to become widely accepted. And it was Locke, moreover, who succeeded in making the "lowering of sights" that occurred in early modern philosophy accepted by presenting its positive results in primarily economic and popular rather than military and politically coercive form. By making Locke his spokesman in revealing the problems with the traditional understanding of natural law, did Strauss accept more of the modern critique of ancient political philosophy than is usually thought?

In the essay he devoted to education, which he said could be considered to be the subject matter of both his teaching and his research, Strauss suggested that students of philosophy today needed to put the canonical philosophers in dialogue with one another. He attempted to do so by opposing the ancients to the moderns, advocates of reason in opposition to spokesmen for revelation, and poets like Aristophanes in opposition to philosophers like Plato. In trying to present the position or arguments of each author as he understood himself, Strauss often seems to disappear in the specific studies he presents of the works of various philosophers, the way Plato remains almost invisible in the background of the conversations he relates. It thus becomes difficult to determine precisely what Strauss thought about the enduring questions or problems he sees the different philosophers address and attempt to settle in conflicting ways. It is, indeed, difficult even to determine exactly what he thought those problems were.

As we show in the last chapter of this book, close and devoted students of Strauss have disagreed about the character of political philosophy, as he presented and practiced it. Their different responses correspond to the two different sources of political philosophy as, we have argued, Strauss understood it.

Our point in reviewing some of the findings of this book is not merely to summarize them for the reader. We wish to highlight what is truly controversial and worthy of study in Strauss's work. Strauss's understanding of philosophy was emphatically antidoctrinal. It was no accident, therefore, that he wrote in the way that he did. Like Plato, Strauss invited his readers to consider the arguments, the many opposed and contradictory arguments philosophers in the past offered for their varied conclusions, because the results of those arguments have been melded in an untenable if not thoughtless way in the opinions we have inherited. Like Plato, Strauss thus invited his readers to take part in the philosophic conversation and to think through the arguments for themselves.

Notes

PROLOGUE

1. Eugene Sheppard, *Leo Strauss and the Politics of Exile* (Waltham, MA: Brandeis University Press, 2006), 108–9.

2. On the difference between the analytic approach to philosophy and Strauss's understanding of it, see Steven B. Smith, "Philosophy as a Way of Life: The Case of Leo Strauss," *Review of Politics* 71, no. 1 (2009): 37–39.

3. For a lucid account of Strauss on the "fundamental alternatives," see Victor Gourevitch, "The Problem of Natural Right and the Fundamental Alternatives in *Natural Right and History*," in *The Crisis of Liberal Democracy: A Straussian Perspective*, ed. Kenneth Deutsch and Walter Soffer (Albany: State University of New York Press, 1987), 30–47.

4. E.g., Laurence Lampert, "Strauss's Recovery of Esotericism," in *The Cambridge Companion to Leo Strauss*, ed. Steven B. Smith (Cambridge: Cambridge University Press, 2009), 63–92.

5. Consider Strauss, "On a Forgotten Kind of Writing," in *WIPP*, 223, 231–32.

6. Leo Strauss, "On Plato's *Apology of Socrates* and *Crito*," in *SPPP*, 38.

7. Leo Strauss, "Preface to *Hobbes Politische Wissenschaft*," in *JPCM*, 453.

CHAPTER ONE

1. Leo Strauss, preface to *Spinoza's Critique of Religion* (New York: Schocken Books, 1965), repr. in *LAM*, 224–59, and *JPCM*, 137–80; Leo Strauss, *Early Writings (1921–1923)*, ed. Michael Zank (Albany: State University of New York Press, 2002); and Jerry Muller, "Leo Strauss: The Political Philosopher as a Young Zionist," *Jewish Social Studies: History, Culture, Society*, n.s., 17, no. 1 (2010): 88–115.

2. Letter to Karl Löwith, 23 June 1935, in *Gesammelte Schriften*, ed. Heinrich Meier, vol. 3 (Stuttgart: Metzler Verlag, 2001), 648–50.

3. Steven B. Smith, "Leo Strauss: The Outlines of a Life," in *The Cambridge Companion to Leo Strauss*, ed. Smith (New York: Cambridge University Press, 2009), 13–40.

4. It is a matter of some controversy whether Strauss attended the Davos debate. Eugene Sheppard, *Leo Strauss and the Politics of Exile*, 39–40, speculates that he may have. Sheppard also compiles the most detailed evidence we have of Heidegger's effect on the young Strauss (35–41).

5. See Leo Strauss, "An Unspoken Prologue," in *JPCM*, 449–52, and Jacob Klein, *Greek Mathematics and the Origins of Modern Algebra*, trans. Eva Brann (Cambridge, MA: MIT Press, 1968).

6. Letter to Karl Löwith, 19 May 1933, in *Gesammelte Schriften*, 3:624–25. See also Susan Shell, "'To Spare the Vanquished and Crush the Arrogant': Leo Strauss's Lecture on 'German Nihilism,'" in Smith, *Cambridge Companion to Leo Strauss*, 171–92.

7. Leo Strauss, "German Nihilism," *Interpretation* 26, no. 3 (1999): 352–78, and "TWM."

8. William Galston, "Leo Strauss's Qualified Embrace of Liberal Democracy," in Smith, *Cambridge Companion to Leo Strauss*, 193–214; Sheppard, *Leo Strauss and the Politics of Exile*, 91; *TALS*, 74–79.

9. See Steven B. Smith, *Reading Leo Strauss: Politics, Philosophy, Judaism* (Chicago: University of Chicago Press, 2006), 112–13.

10. Leo Strauss, "Introduction to Political Philosophy," lecture 1 (6 January 1965). A transcript of the lecture series is available at http://leostrausscenter.uchicago.edu/audio -transcripts.

11. Strauss observes in passing that Comte's claim about the questions raised has been refuted by modern biology, but that his thesis that science addresses the question of how rather than why has nonetheless survived.

12. In this respect, Strauss comments, contemporary positivists are truer descendants of Descartes, who introduced the notion that everything must be doubted and all knowledge rationally reconstructed.

13. Georg Simmel, *Einleitung in die Moralwissenschaft*, 2 vols. (Berlin: W. Hertz, 1892–93), 1:232, translated and quoted by Strauss, "Introduction to Political Philosophy," lecture 3 (13 January 1965).

14. On Weber, see Strauss's chapter on positivism in *NRH*, 35–80. Also see Nasser Behnegar, *Leo Strauss, Max Weber, and the Scientific Study of Politics* (Chicago: University of Chicago Press, 2003); Behnegar, "Strauss and Social Science," in Smith, *Cambridge Companion to Leo Strauss*, 215–240; and Robert Eden, "Why Wasn't Weber a Nihilist?," in *The Crisis of Liberal Democracy: A Straussian Perspective*, ed. Kenneth L. Deutsch and Walter Soffer (Albany: State University of New York Press), 212–42.

15. Behnegar, "Strauss and Social Science," 216–17.

16. "WIPP," 18–19; "Introduction to Political Philosophy," lecture 3; "Epilogue," *LAM*, 220.

17. "Introduction to Political Philosophy," lecture 4 (18 January 1965).

18. The example is adapted from Alasdair MacIntyre, *After Virtue* (Notre Dame, IN: University of Notre Dame Press, 1984), 57–58.

19. Strauss incorporates many of the arguments and some of the same examples he gave in his critique of Weber in *NRH* into these lectures.

20. Arnold Brecht, *Political Theory: The Foundations of Twentieth-Century Political Thought* (Princeton: Princeton University Press, 1959), 262–65. Emphasis in the original.

21. "Introduction to Political Philosophy," lecture 5 (20 January 1965).

22. In fact, Nagel quoted from Strauss's "The Social Science of Max Weber," *Measure* 2 (1951): 211–14. The same arguments are to be found, however, in *NRH*, 50–53.

23. Ernest Nagel, *The Structure of Science: Problems in the Logic of Scientific Explanation* (New York: Harcourt, Brace & World, 1961), 491.

24. Ibid., 324. Strauss quotes from this work in "Introduction to Political Philosophy," lecture 5.

CHAPTER TWO

1. As mentioned, Strauss first published this essay in 1949, in the well-known and highly respected *Journal of the History of Ideas*, before he published *Persecution and the Art of Writing* in 1952 and *Natural Right and History* in 1953. It is, therefore, surprising that none of Strauss's critics even refers to this essay. These critics include conservatives such as Claes G. Ryn ("Leo Strauss and History: The Philosopher as Conspirator," *Humanitas* 18, nos. 1 and 2 [2005]: 31–58) and Paul Edward Gottfried (*The Search for Historical Meaning: Hegel and the Postwar American Right* [DeKalb: Northern Illinois University Press, 1986]); "historicists" such as Quentin Skinner ("Meaning and Understanding in the History of Ideas," *History and Theory* 8, no. 1 [1969]: 3–53); and more recent commentators such as Rafael Major ("The Cambridge School and Leo Strauss: Texts and Context of American Political Science," *Political Research Quarterly* 58, no. 3 [2005]: 477–85) and Ian Ward ("Helping the Dead Speak: Leo Strauss, Quentin Skinner and the Arts of Interpretation in Political Thought," *Polity* 41, no. 2 [2009]: 235–55), who try to show that Strauss and Skinner are closer to each other than they think.

2. Paragraph numbers in this chapter are to "PPH."

3. Strauss seems to be referring to Aristotle's famous statement in the *Poetics* (1451b6–7) that poetry is more philosophical than history, because it depicts types rather than particular instantiations, but the "traditional" view is, of course, not limited to Aristotle. One of the notable characteristics of this particular essay, in contrast to many of the essays in *WIPP*, is that in this essay Strauss rarely associates particular arguments with particular philosophers or locates their origin in particular works.

4. Strauss thus agrees with Skinner ("Meaning and Understanding," 53) about one of the main political and philosophic functions of historical studies; but that function does not require or depend upon the "historicist" claim that all political thought is tied to the particular time and place in which it was first expressed.

5. Strauss would appear here to be referring particularly to the work of Machiavelli, who urged his readers to study ancient history, but not ancient philosophy. More broadly see his discussion of the emergence of history as relevant for philosophy in *PPH*, 44–58.

6. In claiming that "Strauss's way of dealing with the problem of history indicates that some of the most important ideas of modern philosophy are largely unknown to him" and that Strauss's "reductionist construct 'historicism' . . . precludes attention to the philosophically crucial idea of *synthesis*," Ryn ("Leo Strauss and History," 36) ignores Strauss's response to the Hegelian and other secularized versions of a purported "synthesis" between the Greek and scriptural roots of Western civilization in "PR."

7. Strauss indicates some of the grounds of the latter assumption in his account of the "modern solutions" in "What Is Political Philosophy?" when he observes that "the second wave of modernity," which includes both German idealistic philosophy and romanticisms of all kinds, "consisted in the first place in a return from the world of modernity to pre-modern ways of thinking. Rousseau returned from the world of finance, from what he was the first to call the world of the *bourgeois*, to the world of virtue and the city, to the world of the *citoyen*. Kant returned from Descartes' and Locke's notion of ideas to the Platonic notion. Hegel returned from the philosophy of reflection to the 'higher vitality' of Plato and Aristotle. And romanticism as a whole is primarily a movement of return to the origins. Yet in all these cases, the return to pre-modern thought was only the initial step of a movement which led, consciously or unconsciously, to a much more radical form of modernity" ("WIPP," 50). These partial returns to premodern thought led to more radical forms of modernity, Strauss

suggests, because the return in all cases took place on the basis of modern principles. For example, he observes that "Rousseau returned from the modern state as it had developed by his time to the classical city. *But he interpreted the classical city in light of Hobbes's scheme*" (50; emphasis added). And later, "The right order may have been as loftily conceived by Hegel as it was by Plato, which one may doubt. It certainly was thought by Hegel to be established in the Machiavellian way, not the Platonic way; it was thought to be established in a manner which contradicts the right order itself" (54). In his letter to Karl Löwith in 1935 Strauss reported that he had broken with Nietzsche, because he did not think that Nietzsche had succeeded in recapturing the ancient view of human excellence, a failure due to Nietzsche's inability to free himself sufficiently from modern concepts and concerns ("Correspondence of Karl Löwith and Leo Strauss," *Independent Journal of Philosophy*, nos. 5 and 6 [1988]: 183). The question arises therefore whether and how Strauss's comments about restorations and modifications apply to his own effort of restoration.

8. In a related context Strauss referred to Edmund Burke. See *NRH*, 294–323.

9. Ryn, "Leo Strauss and History," accuses Strauss of this kind of abstraction, partly on the basis of Strauss's critique of Burke in *NRH*, 294–323. Paul Gottfried, "Strauss and the Straussians," *Humanitas* 18, nos. 1 and 2 (2005): 26–30, and *Leo Strauss and the Conservative Movement in America* (Cambridge: Cambridge University Press, 2010), also maintains that Strauss's criticism of Burke shows that he is not a true conservative.

10. Skinner, "Meaning and Understanding," 45–46. In emphasizing the commonality between Skinner's argument that it is necessary to study history because "some writers voluntarily . . . convey their meaning with deliberate obliqueness," and Strauss's argument in *Persecution and the Art of Writing* that "many authors deliberately engage in the 'metaphoric' practice of 'writing between the lines,'" Major ("Cambridge School and Leo Strauss," 480–81) misses the performative element of Skinner's argument that makes Skinner look at past authors solely in terms of their possible effect on their contemporaries, given current opinions and circumstances, and not in terms of their intended effects on posterity, as Strauss does. Both Nathan Tarcov, "Quentin Skinner's Method and Machiavelli's *Prince*," *Ethics* 92, no. 4 (1982): 692–709, and Michael Zuckert, *Launching Liberalism* (Lawrence: University Press of Kansas, 2002), 57–81, emphasize this difference and its effects on the way that Skinner and Strauss, respectively, interpret texts.

11. J. G. A. Pocock, "The History of Political Thought: A Methodological Enquiry," in *Philosophy, Politics and Society*, 2nd ser., ed. P. Laslett and W. C. Runciman (Oxford: Basil Blackwell, 1962), 184–85; Pocock, *Politics, Language and Time* (London: Methuen, 1972); Pocock, "Verbalizing a Political Act: Toward a Politics of Speech," *Political Theory* 1, no. 1 (1973): 35–41; Pocock, *The Machiavellian Moment* (Baltimore: Johns Hopkins University Press, 1975), viii, 3–5, 57–58, 83–84. See also David Boucher, "Language, Politics and Paradigms: Pocock and the Study of Political Thought," *Polity* 17, no. 4 (1985): 761–76.

12. Strauss takes the example from R. G. Collingwood, *An Autobiography* (Oxford: Oxford University Press, 1939), 59–62. He agrees with Collingwood that *polis* is not the same thing as a modern "state" or "city," and should not be translated by "state" or "city-state." He suggests that "commonwealth" may be the nearest equivalent. See *CM*, 30; Strauss, "Introduction to Political Philosophy," lectures 4, 6, 7, and 10.

13. Strauss is probably thinking, first and foremost, of Jean-Jacques Rousseau.

14. One could so interpret Xenophon's *Education of Cyrus*.

15. M. Zuckert, *Launching Liberalism*, 57–81.

16. Strauss quotes A. D. Lindsay, *The Modern Democratic State* (New York: Oxford University Press, 1943), 1:45.

17. Strauss seems here to have what he later (*NRH*, 26–29) calls "radical historicism," or Heidegger, in mind (see Strauss to Kojève, 26 June 1950, *OT*, 251). At times, e.g., in "The Age of the World View" (in *The Question concerning Technology and Other Essays*, trans. William Lovitt [New York: Harper and Row, 1977], 115–54), Heidegger appears, like other historicists such as Collingwood, to argue that the questions change from era to era. For example, in this essay Heidegger suggests that the ancients asked *why* whereas the moderns ask *how*. Both in *Being and Time* and in his later work, however, Heidegger argues that the "truth" disclosed by the entire history of Western philosophy has been limited by its original experience and definition of "Being" as presence. By arguing that "Being" is, in fact, temporal, and thus that "Being" is fundamentally historical, Heidegger claims to have disclosed the limitations of previous philosophy and so to have opened the possibility of a "new beginning" for which he calls in both his infamous *Rektoratsrede* and the posthumously published *Beiträge zur Philosophie*. In contrast to less philosophically rigorous historicists, Strauss argues in a later essay, Heidegger did not confront the possibility that all ages are not equal with regard to the disclosure of truth; but like Hegel, Marx, and Nietzsche before him, Heidegger argued (and had to argue) that the truth about the historical character of the disclosure of the truth had become evident only at his time (Leo Strauss, "Philosophy as Rigorous Science and Political Philosophy," in *SPPP*, 29–37).

18. For a thorough examination of this thesis, see Arthur Melzer, "Esotericism and the Critique of Historicism," *American Political Science Review* 100, no. 2 (2006): 280.

19. That was the reason Strauss suggested earlier in his essay that we need to recapture a sense of the original meaning of the *polis*, even though there are no longer any *poleis* to be observed directly, in order to understand what we still mean by "politics" or "the political."

20. "PPH," 75; G. W. F. Hegel, *The Phenomenology of Mind*, trans. J. B. Baillie, 2nd ed. (London: Allen and Unwin, 1931), 94. For a more precise analysis Strauss refers his readers to Jacob Klein, *Greek Mathematical Thought and the Origin of Algebra*, trans. Eva Brann (Cambridge, MA: MIT Press, 1968).

21. Stanley Rosen, a former student of Strauss, challenges both Strauss and Strauss's teacher Edmund Husserl by arguing that there is no such thing as a "natural consciousness" (Stanley Rosen, *The Elusiveness of the Ordinary: Studies in the Possibility of Philosophy* [New Haven, CT: Yale University Press, 2002], 54–93, 135–58).

22. Consider Husserl's idea of "sedimentation" as in *The Crisis of European Sciences and Transcendental Phenomenological Philosophy* (Evanston IL: Northwestern University Press, 1970), 361.

23. Strauss to Löwith, in "Correspondence," 183.

24. Strauss gave the talks that constitute "Progress or Return?" three years after he first published "PPH," the same year he presented his Walgreen lectures (1949), which he later published as *NRH* in 1953. See the editor's note in *An Introduction to Political Philosophy: Ten Essays by Leo Strauss*, ed. Hilail Gildin (Detroit: Wayne State University Press, 1989), 248.

25. Strauss did not name a particular proponent of the "radical historicist" thesis in *NRH*. But in his letter to Kojève of 26 June 1950 he wrote, "I have once again been dealing with Historicism, that is to say, with Heidegger, the only radical historicist" (*OT*, 251).

26. Richard Velkley, *Heidegger, Strauss, and the Premises of Philosophy* (Chicago: University of Chicago Press, 2011), emphasizes the themes that Strauss and Heidegger share that other commentators have either denied or ignored.

27. See Catherine H. Zuckert, "Martin Heidegger: His Politics and His Philosophy," *Political Theory* 18, no. 1 (1990): 51–79.

28. According to Strauss, Alfarabi and Maimonides followed Plato in presenting philosophy as a way of life in such an explicitly political framework (*PAW*, 9).

29. Strauss also systematically addressed this issue in his essay "On a Forgotten Kind of Writing," in *WIPP*, 221–32. See also David Janssens, "Fishing for Philosophers: Strauss's Restatement on the Art of Writing," in *Leo Strauss's Defense of the Philosophic Life: Reading "What Is Political Philosophy?,"* ed. Rafael Major (Chicago: University of Chicago Press, 2013), 173–90.

30. Melzer, "Esotericism," 279, 284–86, 290.

31. Cf. Skinner, "Meaning and Understanding," 4–7.

32. Leo Strauss and Hans-Georg Gadamer, "Correspondence concerning *Wahrheit und Methode*," *Independent Journal of Philosophy* 2 (1978): 5–6.

33. See Thomas Pangle, *Leo Strauss: An Introduction to His Thought and Intellectual Legacy* (Baltimore, MD: Johns Hopkins University Press, 2006), 58.

34. Leo Strauss, "Farabi's *Plato*," in *Louis Ginzberg: Jubilee Volume*, ed. Saul Lieberman et al. (New York: American Academy for Jewish Research, 1945), 364, 371–72; *PAW*, 13.

35. For a fuller discussion of historical testimony on the practice of esoteric writing, see Melzer, "Esotericism," 280–81, and J. Judd Owen, "John Toland and Leo Strauss on Esoteric Writing," in *Recovering Reason: Essays in Honor of Thomas L. Pangle*, ed. Timothy Burns (Lanham, MD: Lexington Books, 2010), 209–22.

36. In "Correspondence concerning *Wahrheit und Methode*," Strauss denied that he had a general theory of interpretation like the one Gadamer had put forth.

37. Strauss cites Cicero, *Orator* 15.50 and *De oratore* 2.77.313, in *PAW*, 185.

38. Strauss thus begins his essay "How to Begin to Study *The Guide of the Perplexed*" with an outline of the chapter headings that contrasts markedly with Maimonides's own explicit organization of the book (*LAM*, 140–42).

39. On the basis of his suggestion that an author often reveals the way he himself writes in the way he reads the works of others, many commentators have concluded that Strauss himself writes esoterically (e.g., Pangle, *Leo Strauss: An Introduction to His Thought and Intellectual Legacy*; Smith, *Reading Leo Strauss*; Shadia Drury, *The Political Ideas of Leo Strauss* [New York: St. Martin's, 1988]). As we see in the case of Spinoza, however, Strauss did not think that all authors should necessarily be read the same way they read others.

40. See Smith, *Reading Leo Strauss*, 126.

41. Consider Melzer, "Esotericism," 280: Strauss's claims about esotericism "open up a Pandora's box of interpretive difficulties."

CHAPTER THREE

1. For a biographical account of Strauss's early contacts with Heidegger, see Sheppard, *Leo Strauss and the Politics of Exile*, 35–40.

2. See Smith, *Reading Leo Strauss*, 109.

3. Velkley, *Heidegger, Strauss, and the Premises of Philosophy*, 67, quoting Leo Strauss, "The Living Issues of German Postwar Philosophy," in Heinrich Meier, *Leo Strauss and the Theologico-Political Problem* (Cambridge: Cambridge University Press, 2006), 137.

4. Smith, *Reading Leo Strauss*, 114, 122.

5. See ibid., 115.

6. See ibid., 116.

7. *NRH*, 79; Leo Strauss, introduction to *HPP*, 2; Velkley, *Heidegger, Strauss, and the Premises of Philosophy*, 15.

8. On Husserlian aspects of Strauss's thought, see Stanley Rosen, "Leo Strauss and the Problem of the Modern," in Smith, *Cambridge Companion to Leo Strauss*, 120–21. Also Hwa Yol Jung, "Two Critics of Scientism: Reflections on Leo Strauss's Encounter with Heidegger and Husserl," *Independent Journal of Philosophy* 2 (1978): 81–88.

9. See Friedrich Nietzsche, *Thus Spoke Zarathustra* I, §15 "On the Thousand and One Goals."

10. For developments of Strauss's theme, see Seth Benardete, *The Bow and the Lyre* (Lanham, MD: Rowman & Littlefield, 1997), 86, and David Janssens, "The Philosopher's Ancient Clothes: Leo Strauss on Philosophy and Poetry," in *Modernity and What Has Been Lost*, ed. Paweł Armada and Arkadiusz Górnisiewicz (South Bend, IN: St. Augustine's Press, 2011).

11. Aristophanes, *Clouds* 368, 428, 815–35, in *Four Texts on Socrates*, trans. Thomas G. West and Grace Starry West (Ithaca: Cornell University Press, 1984).

12. *NRH*, 93; see also Velkley, *Heidegger, Strauss, and the Premises of Philosophy*, 15.

13. See Leo Strauss, "The Problem of Socrates: Five Lectures," in *RCPR*, 133.

14. Catherine H. Zuckert, *Plato's Philosophers* (Chicago: University of Chicago Press, 2009), 8–13.

15. Aristophanes, *Clouds* 576–94; *SA*, 19, 46.

16. Leo Strauss, *On Plato's "Symposium,"* ed. Seth Benardete (Chicago: University of Chicago Press, 2001), 95–96, 120; see Velkley, *Heidegger, Strauss, and the Premises of Philosophy*, 152.

17. Aristophanes, *Clouds* 1475–1511. In his study of Plato's *Apology of Socrates*, Strauss greatly emphasized the theme in Socrates's defense speech of the "old accusers," that is, that Socrates was being tried by the city in 399 mostly on the basis of old prejudices that can be traced back to Aristophanes's rendition of the philosopher in *Clouds*. The accusers and the jurors did not understand or appreciate sufficiently the turn Socrates had made many years before away from the kind of pre-Socratic philosophizing satirized in *Clouds* (*SPPP*, 39–41, 50).

18. Aristophanes, *Clouds* 205–16.

19. Ibid., 1420–31.

20. Leo Strauss, "On Classical Political Philosophy," in *WIPP*, 78–94; originally published in *Social Research* 12, no. 1 (1945): 98–117.

21. Nathan Tarcov, "Leo Strauss's 'On Classical Political Philosophy,'" in Major, *Leo Strauss's Defense of the Philosophic Life*, 65.

22. E.g., Karl Popper, *The Open Society and Its Enemies* (London: Routledge, 1945); Terence Irwin, *Plato's Ethics* (New York: Oxford University Press, 1995); C. D. C. Reeve, *Philosopher-Kings* (Princeton: Princeton University Press, 1988).

23. See Rosen, "Leo Strauss and the Problem of the Modern," 123–24.

24. Tarcov smartly calls attention to Strauss's unusual and emphatic use of "I say" in this passage. "Leo Strauss's 'On Classical Political Philosophy,'" in Major, *Leo Strauss's Defense of the Philosophic Life*, 76.

25. Niccolò Machiavelli, *The Prince*, chap. 15.

CHAPTER FOUR

1. "PR," 249–310. The editor notes that "the first two parts of this essay were published in *Modern Judaism* 1 (1981): 17–45 and represent an edited version of two of the three lectures Leo Strauss delivered at the Hillel House, University of Chicago, in November 1952. Part three, the third lecture, was published as 'The Mutual Influence of Theology and Philosophy' in *The Independent Journal of Philosophy* 3 (1979): 111–18. The text of the original lec-

ture was edited slightly to bring it into line with a published Hebrew translation (in *Iyyun: Hebrew Philosophical Quarterly* 5, no. 1 1954)" (248).

2. See also "Jerusalem and Athens," *SPPP*, 168.

3. Even a philosopher like Socrates who claimed to know only that he did not know the most important things took comfort, if not pride, in the "human" wisdom he had attained. See "PR," 278; Plato, *Apology of Socrates* 20d–e, 38a.

4. Strauss thus begins his lecture to an audience at the Hillel House by appealing to the Jewish notion of "return." "Return is the translation for the Hebrew word *t'shuvah*. T'shuvah has an ordinary and an emphatic meaning. Its emphatic meaning is rendered in English by 'repentance.' Repentance is return, meaning the return from the wrong way to the right one. This implies that we were once on the right way before we turned to the wrong way" ("PR," 249). As in the autobiographical preface to the English translation of *The Political Philosophy of Hobbes* he wrote more than a decade later (see chap. 10 of this book for a fuller analysis), Strauss first addresses the problem as it specifically confronts Jews. However, he rather quickly shows that neither the "crisis of Western civilization" as he understands it nor the response he advocates is simply, solely, or even primarily Jewish.

5. The end of the quotation is not made clear in "PR," but is in *JPCM*, 97.

6. Because each of the three "waves" of modernity Strauss identifies in his essay "The Three Waves of Modernity" begins with an attempt to recapture ancient virtue, Frederick G. Lawrence ("Leo Strauss and the Fourth Wave of Modernity," in *Leo Strauss and Judaism*, ed. David Novak [Lanham, MD: Rowman & Littlefield, 1996], 111–30) argues that Strauss's own work constitutes a "fourth wave" that brings even greater dangers of nihilism. Strauss's notion of return, with its rejection of historicism, is meant to forestall just such an outcome.

7. Daniel Tanguay, *Leo Strauss: An Intellectual Biography* (New Haven: Yale University Press, 2007), 109–22.

8. E.g., John Yolton, "Locke on the Law of Nature," *Philosophical Review* 67, no. 4 (1958): 477–98; John Dunn, *The Political Thought of John Locke* (Cambridge: Cambridge University Press, 1968); Martin Seliger, *The Liberal Politics of John Locke* (New York: Praeger, 1969).

9. Strauss traces the development of this thought both in *NRH* and "TWM."

10. The difficulty is to be found basically in the contradiction between Nietzsche's proclamations that the will to power is the truth of all things at all times and that the will to power is merely the interpretation of one individual living at this time (see *Beyond Good and Evil*, 1.5–7). That "interpretation" is nevertheless intended to change the way other human beings understand their own lives. Heidegger famously explores the difficulties in Nietzsche's teaching in his lectures in *Nietzsche*, ed. David Farrell Krell, 4 vols. (San Francisco: Harper & Row, 1979–87), and "The Word of Nietzsche: 'God Is Dead,'" in *The Question concerning Technology and Other Essays*, trans. William Lovitt (New York: Harper & Row, 1977), 53–114.

11. As we noted in chapter 3, Strauss argues that Machiavelli "lowered the sights" (or goals) of modern political philosophy in reaction to the utopian demands of the combination of classical rationalism and biblical morality in Christianity, which by elevating the "theological virtues" of faith, hope, and charity had, in fact, legitimated unprecedented forms of cruelty and tyranny. In *TM*, 31, Strauss pointed out that in the two books Machiavelli said contained everything he knew, he did not mention the soul, devil, or afterlife. Later modern political philosophers reintroduced more "idealistic" elements. But if modern political philosophy culminated in an essentially historical understanding of human life, it culminated in an understanding of human life, not merely as always changing, but with-

out any particular order of "becoming" as in the ancient notion of cycles. Classical political philosophers recognized the limitations of human nature, but they suggested that at least some human beings had access to something eternal in the intelligible order of things. Or, as Strauss tended more modestly to put it, philosophers like Socrates recognized that there was a question whether there was such an order. They did not deny its existence outright. As Heidegger pointed out in "The Question concerning Technology," the modern attempt to master or remake nature entailed a denial that anything has a necessary character or order that cannot be changed, i.e., that there is anything eternal. To embrace such a view of the world, Strauss saw, was to deny the erotic desire all human beings display to achieve some kind of immortality, according to Diotima in Plato's *Symposium*, the highest form of which is philosophy.

12. Having published a critical study of *Spinoza's Critique of Religion* in 1930, Strauss had turned to a study of the "medieval Enlightenment" in *Philosophy and Law* (originally published in German in 1935).

13. Strauss first developed this argument in Leo Strauss, *Philosophy and Law: Contributions to the Understanding of Maimonides and His Predecessors*, trans. Eve Adler (Albany: State University of New York Press, 1995).

14. *PAW*, 42–48; *LAM*, 145–49. For a good introduction to Strauss's view of Maimonides, see Hillel Fradkin, "A Word Fitly Spoken: The Interpretation of Maimonides and the Legacy of Leo Strauss," in *Leo Strauss and Judaism: Jerusalem and Athens Critically Revisited*, ed. David Novak (Lanham, MD: Rowman and Littlefield, 1996), 55–86; and for a more traditional, nonesoteric reading, see Kenneth Seeskin, "Maimonides' Conception of Philosophy," in *Leo Strauss and Judaism*, 87–110.

15. "The Law also forbids one to study the books of idolaters on idolatry, for the first intention of the Law as a whole is to destroy every vestige of idolatry; and yet Maimonides, as he openly admits and even emphasizes, has studied all the available idolatrous books of this kind with the utmost thoroughness. . . . Above all, the Law forbids one to seek for the reasons of the commandments; yet Maimonides devotes almost twenty-six chapters of the *Guide* to such seeking (III 26; cf. II 25). All these irregularities have one and the same justification . . . to uphold or to fulfill the Law (I Introd. and III Introd.). Still, in the most important case he does not, strictly speaking, transgress the Law, for his written explanation of the secrets of the Law is not a public but a secret explanation. The secrecy is achieved in three ways. First, every word of the *Guide* is chosen with exceeding care; since very few men are able or willing to read with exceeding care, most men will fail to perceive the secret teaching. Second, Maimonides deliberately contradicts himself, and if a man declares both that *a* is *b* and that *a* is not *b*, he cannot be said to declare anything. Lastly, the 'chapter headings' of the secret teaching are not presented in an orderly fashion, but are scattered throughout the book" (*LAM*, 143–44). See also *PAW*, 54, and Tanguay, *Leo Strauss: An Intellectual Biography*, 69–73.

16. By confining his own discussion to the text leading up to Maimonides's discussion of the difference between the adherents of the law and the philosophers with regard to the question as to whether the world was created or is eternal, Strauss himself may be said to be adhering to the law in a way analogous to the way he argues Maimonides did. See also Smith, *Reading Leo Strauss*, 38–40.

17. Strauss elaborates: "If the world, or more precisely the sphere, is created, it is indeed self-evident that it was created by some agent, but it does not necessarily follow that the creator is one, let alone absolutely simple, and that he is incorporeal." That is the reason, presumably, that Maimonides declared the arguments of the Kalam to be sophistical. "On

the other hand, if the sphere is eternal, it follows, as Aristotle has shown, that God is and is incorporeal; but on this assumption the angels or separate intelligences, each of which is the mover of one of the many spheres, are as eternal as God (cf. I 71, II 2 and 6). It is therefore a question whether monotheism strictly understood is demonstrable" (*LAM*, 181).

18. In an earlier discussion of Maimonides's analysis of the attributes of God, Strauss concludes, "if we did not know that God is absolutely perfect, we would ascribe we know not what to what we do not know, in ascribing to Him 'being,' or we would ascribe nothing to nothing; we certainly would not know what we were talking about.... God's perfection is an unfathomable abyss. Thus we understand why the doctrine in question, in spite of its philosophic origin, can be regarded as the indeed unbiblical but nevertheless appropriate expression of the biblical principle, namely, of the biblical teaching regarding the hidden God who created the world out of nothing, not in order to increase the good—for since He is the complete good, the good cannot be increased by His actions—but without any ground, in absolute freedom, and whose essence is therefore indicated by 'Will,' rather than by 'Wisdom' (III 13)" (*LAM*, 177).

19. In his Jewish book on the "true science" of the Law (*Mishneh Torah*), Strauss emphasized, "the nonidentity of the teaching of the philosophers as a whole and the thirteen roots of the Law as a whole are the first word and the last word of Maimonides" (*LAM*, 145).

20. Leo Strauss, "Maimonides' Statement on Political Science," in *WIPP*, 155–69; Strauss, "Note on Maimonides' *Treatise on the Art of Logic*," in *SPPP*, 208–9. The three "notes" on different works of Maimonides were the only parts of this posthumously published collection of essays that Strauss had not already published elsewhere.

21. Joshua Parens, "Strauss on Maimonides' Secretive Political Science," in Major, *Leo Strauss's Defense of the Philosophic Life*, 121–24, presents a similar reading of this passage.

22. Strauss was more open in his letters. On 20 January 1938 he wrote Jacob Klein that Maimonides had "a truly free mind," and on 16 February that "Maim. was *absolutely* not a Jew in his belief" (in *Gesammelte Schriften*, ed. Meier, 3:545, 549). On 20 May 1949 Strauss wrote to Julius Guttman that "Maimonides was a 'philosopher' in a far more radical sense than is usually assumed today" (quoted in Meier, *Leo Strauss and the Theologico-Political Problem*, 23n).

23. "In the *Guide* Maimonides had considerably mitigated the opposition between philosophy and Judaism in regard to particular providence.... One may find a trace of this intention in a rather casual remark that he makes in the *Letter on Astrology*.... We lost our kingdom since our fathers sinned by turning to astrology, i.e., to idolatry, and neglected the art of war and conquest" (*SPPP*, 207).

24. Tanguay, *Leo Strauss: An Intellectual Biography*, 80–94.

25. In his *Treatise on Logic* Maimonides thus appears to have followed Alfarabi in identifying happiness as the end of politics, as opposed to ethics, which is dedicated to the acquisition of virtue. See *WIPP*, 157.

26. *PAW*, 15. In his essay "How Farabi Read Plato's *Laws*" (in *WIPP*, 134–54), Strauss points out many other examples of ways in which Alfarabi inserted discussions that are not to be found in Plato's dialogue and ignored topics or whole parts (like the discussion of piety in book 10) that are, in what appears at first glance to be merely a boring "summary." In claiming that Strauss availed himself of the same "immunity of the commentator" in relating his own views through the mouths of Thrasymachus, Machiavelli, and Nietzsche, Shadia Drury (*Political Ideas of Leo Strauss*) fails to show the way in which Strauss's accounts of these thinkers obviously contradict what they say or wrote. See David Lewis Schaefer,

"Shadia Drury's Critique of Leo Strauss," *Political Science Reviewer* 23 (1994): 80–127; *TALS*; and Peter Minowitz, *Straussophobia: Defending Leo Strauss and Straussians against Shadia Drury and Other Accusers* (Lanham, MD: Lexington Books, 2009), for more complete responses to her claims.

27. In his "Restatement on Xenophon's *Hiero*," Strauss ironically points out: "Syntheses effect miracles. Kojève's or Hegel's synthesis of classical and Biblical morality effects the miracle of producing an amazingly lax morality out of two moralities both of which made very strict demands on self-restraint" (*OT*, 191).

28. We present a similar analysis of the reasons Strauss exposed the techniques of the kind of esoteric writing these philosophers practiced in *TALS*, 120–54.

29. Strauss explicitly recognizes that Socrates is an exception to this general statement. "PR," 277.

30. According to Sharon Portnoff, *Reason and Revelation before Historicism* (Toronto: University of Toronto Press, 2011), 155–57, 209–10, Strauss thought that because reason and revelation both recognize that being is essentially mysterious, they "come within hailing distance" of one another and so define a "theoretic realm in which reason and revelation may coexist" (156). By positing such a shared "theoretic realm" she then reduces the question of the relation between reason and revelation to a "practical choice." However, the two lines of thought that Strauss saw coming into hailing distance of one another in the text she cites ("Why We Remain Jews," *JPCM*, 328–29) are modern natural science with its belief in infinite progress and revelation. As we have seen, Strauss thought that the modern notion of progress, based to a considerable extent on modern natural science, had borrowed its fundamental concept from revelation in an unacknowledged, unjustified, and unjustifiable way. He explicitly follows Maimonides in arguing that "reason" or Greek philosophy and "revelation" or Torah are fundamentally incompatible at a theoretical level and, therefore, at a practical level as well.

31. In "How to Begin to Study *The Guide of the Perplexed*," Strauss observes that Maimonides did not dispose of the Platonic possibility. But in "Jerusalem and Athens" (in *SPPP*, 165–66), Strauss himself argues that the demiurge in the *Timaeus* is the closest ancient Greek figure to the biblical god; he is good and he makes the cosmos. But the demiurge follows the models of the eternal ideas, i.e., he does not create out of nothing.

32. Smith, *Reading Leo Strauss*, 17.

33. In chapter 12 below we outline Strauss's case for a rationally defensible choice of the way of reason.

34. Strauss presents his reading of Genesis, so briefly sketched here, as well as the evidence for it more fully in "Jerusalem and Athens" (*SPPP*, 151–63) and in Leo Strauss, "On the Interpretation of Genesis," in *JPCM*, 359–76.

35. E.g., *Philosophy and Law*, 29–38; "PR," 305, 308–9.

36. Meier, *Leo Strauss and the Theologico-Political Problem*, 5.

37. Leora Batnitzky, "Leo Strauss and the 'Theologico-Political Predicament,'" in Smith, *Cambridge Companion to Leo Strauss*, 41–62, also emphasizes the different epistemological foundations of reason and revelation, according to Strauss.

38. Ernest L. Fortin, "Rational Theologians and Irrational Philosophers: A Straussian Perspective," in *Classical Christianity and the Political Order: Reflections on the Theologico-Political Problem*, ed. J. Brian Benestad (Lanham, MD: Rowman and Littlefield, 1996), 295.

39. "Philosophy as such is nothing but genuine awareness of the problems. . . . It is impossible to think about these problems without becoming inclined toward a solution. . . .

Yet as long as there is no wisdom but only quest for wisdom, the evidence of all solutions is necessarily smaller than the evidence of the problems" (*OT*, 196).

40. See *WIPP*, 92–94, for Strauss's definition of "political philosophy" and for the reasons why he could give a book containing essays on medieval and modern philosophers as well as ancient the title *Studies in Platonic Political Philosophy*.

CHAPTER FIVE

1. Leo Strauss, "Quelques remarques sur la science politique de Maïmonide et de Farabi," *Revue des Etudes Juives* 100 (1936): 1–37 ("Some Remarks on the Political Science of Maimonides and Farabi," trans. Robert Bartlett, *Interpretation* 18, no. 1 [1990]: 4–17); Strauss, *Philosophy and Law*; Strauss, "Farabi's *Plato*."

2. E.g., Martin Heidegger, "Plato's Doctrine of Truth," trans. John Barlow, in *Philosophy in the Twentieth Century*, ed. William Barrett and Henry D. Aiden (New York: Random House, 1962), 3:251.

3. Alfarabi, *The Philosophy of Plato and Aristotle*, trans. Muhsin Mahdi (Ithaca: Cornell University Press, 2001).

4. Tanguay, *Leo Strauss*, 80–84, calls this Strauss's "Farabian Turn." As Thomas L. Pangle points out in his introduction to *SPPP*, 2–3, Strauss's discounting of the doctrine of the ideas or the knowledge philosophers purportedly need to acquire is the most unusual element of his reading, not merely of the *Republic*, but of Plato's works as a whole. In his essay "On Plato's *Republic*" in *The City and Man*, Strauss observed: "No one has ever succeeded in giving a satisfactory or clear account of this doctrine. It is possible however to define rather precisely the central difficulty" (*CM*, 119). Strauss did not state the source of his explanation of that difficulty—the existence of the ideas separate from the things which participate somehow in them—but he gave basically the same critique Aristotle had in his *Metaphysics*.

5. *SPPP*, 38–88. Strauss also wrote, although he himself did not publish, an essay on Plato's *Euthyphro*, in which he concluded that Socrates was guilty as charged, i.e., he did not believe in the gods of the city. This essay is included in *RCPR* (187–206), a collection of Strauss's unpublished writings put together by Thomas L. Pangle. Because Strauss wrote essays on the first three of the four dialogues usually thought to depict the trial and death of Socrates, it is a striking fact that Strauss never wrote on *Phaedo*, the dialogue in which Socrates states that he must make a second apology to his friends, and in which he defends not only his hypothesis about the ideas but also the immortality of the soul.

6. *LAM*, 65–75. First published in the third volume of *Mélanges Louis Massignon* (Damascus: Institut français de Damas, 1957), "How Fārābī Read Plato's *Laws*" was included by Strauss in *WIPP* (134–54).

7. Underlining the extent to which he was breaking with the received understanding of the history of philosophy, in his commentaries on Plato Strauss concentrated on the dialogues and rarely addressed other commentators or interpreters. Three notable exceptions were his lengthy review of *Plato's Theory of Man* by John Wild, "On a New Interpretation of Plato's Political Philosophy," *Social Research* 13, no. 3 (1946): 326–67, which he never reprinted; his review of *The Liberal Temper in Greek Politics* by Eric Havelock, *Review of Metaphysics* 12, no. 3 (1959): 390–439, included in *LAM*, 26–64; and a parenthetical comment on an error made by Glenn Morrow and a reference to E. B. England's *Laws of Plato* (London: Longmans, Green, 1921), 167, at *AAPL*, 44.

8. Both in his own initial remarks on the character of Alfarabi's writing in *PAW*, 10–37, and in his later "Correspondence concerning *Wahrheit und Methode*" with Hans-Georg Gadamer (5–12), Strauss insisted that each author must be read in his own terms. Plato and

Alfarabi wrote at very different times and thus under quite different conditions; they also wrote their works in very different forms. To note the most obvious differences, Alfarabi wrote explicitly in light of scriptural revelation and the religious wars provoked by different versions or beliefs about the content and character of that revelation; Plato did not. Alfarabi also wrote treatises and commentaries, whereas Plato wrote dialogues. Strauss also wrote under different circumstances, at a time when a series of the world's greatest philosophers—Hegel, Marx, Nietzsche, and Heidegger—had all declared, if for somewhat different reasons, that philosophy had come to an end. Strauss was trying to revive philosophy by returning to its origin in Plato and giving those origins a fresh reading. See Strauss, "Philosophy as a Rigorous Science and Political Philosophy," in *SPPP*, 29–37; "An Introduction to Existentialism," in *RCPR*, 27–46; Catherine H. Zuckert, *Postmodern Platos: Nietzsche, Heidegger, Gadamer, Strauss, Derrida* (Chicago: University of Chicago Press, 1996).

9. In his later works Strauss rarely refers to Plato's letters. He never mentions the Second Letter. In "On a New Interpretation of Plato's Political Philosophy," he does remind his readers that Plato says that he wrote nothing, he simply reported the sayings of a Socrates made young and beautiful or noble. Strauss refers to the Seventh Letter in *CM*, 63, in a footnote pointing out the differences between the discussion in the *Republic* and subsequent historical attempts to overthrow the Athenian democracy. But he never discusses Plato's account of the problematic results of his own political involvement.

10. "The Platonic dialogue shows us much more clearly than an Epistle Dedicatory could, in what manner the teaching conveyed through the work is adapted by the main speaker to his particular audience and therewith how that teaching would have to be restated in order to be valid beyond the particular situation of the conversation in question" (*CM*, 54).

11. Strauss points out that the two, and only two, aspects of the dialogues that can unquestionably be attributed to Plato himself are the titles and the selection of the conversations to be depicted (*CM*, 56–57). Insofar as the dialogues are works of art, moreover, rather than products of nature or random conjunction, they are products of intention, which abstracts from chance (*CM*, 60).

12. Strauss thus corrects the tendency to associate Socrates with the Thirty Tyrants, because of his association with Critias and Charmides (e.g., Indra Kagis McEwen, *Socrates' Ancestor* [Cambridge, MA: MIT Press, 1993], 97). As Strauss pointed out in his review of John Wild's book, "On a New Interpretation of Plato's Political Philosophy," neither Plato nor his Socrates was a member of a political party, nor can their arguments properly be used to support one.

13. If we look back at Xenophon's account of Socrates's conversation with Glaucon in the *Memorabilia* (3.8), we discover that it is very different from that of the *Republic*. Whereas Xenophon's Socrates questions Glaucon in order to shame him into admitting that he knows nothing about politics and has therefore nothing of value to offer the Athenian people, Plato's Socrates gives his companions a lesson in "self-control regarding the pleasures, and even the needs, of the body" by substituting the conversation about justice, a feast of thought in which he conjures up "many grand and perplexing sights" like the city in speech and his famous images of the divided line and the cave for the dinner they were initially promised. This dual lesson in moderation—both physical and intellectual or political—constitutes the action of the dialogue. Both of Socrates's students thus show him teaching continence as the precondition for wisdom, but Plato's Socrates is much less austere. He gives his readers an indication of the sort of intellectual pleasure that, Xenophon's Socrates explained to Antiphon, produced his continence regarding bodily things. To do

so, he has to become something of a poet himself by presenting his interlocutor with "grand sights" or images.

14. Strauss later comments, "Socrates' procedure in the *Republic* can perhaps be explained as follows: there is a particularly close connection between justice and the city and while there is surely an idea of justice, there is perhaps no idea of the city. . . . The eternal and unchangeable ideas are distinguished from the particular things which come into being and perish. . . . Perhaps the city belongs so radically to the sphere of becoming that there cannot be an idea of the city. Aristotle says that Plato recognized ideas only of natural beings. . . . Yet if there is a strict parallel between the city and the human individual, the city would seem to be a natural being" (*CM*, 92–93).

15. Strauss's student Seth Benardete emphasizes that difference in the reading of the *Republic* he gives in Benardete, *Socrates' Second Sailing* (Chicago: University of Chicago Press, 1989).

16. Although these guardians are also said to be experts in one military art, Strauss pointed out, they, unlike the other citizens, are explicitly admitted not only to have but also to need a dual nature, containing two opposed drives or tendencies. The proposition that each human being is designed by nature to do one and only one thing is thus shown to be, at best, only partially true. Only when the city thus becomes divided into two potentially opposed factions, one armed and one unarmed, does its organization become political, properly speaking; only now are there rulers and ruled. Strauss did not agree with Hans-Georg Gadamer, "Plato and the Poets," in *Dialogue and Dialectic*, trans. P. Christopher Smith (New Haven: Yale University Press, 1980), 54–56, however, that the political is the historical. On the contrary, he pointed out, the premise of the description of the inferior regimes in book 8 is that the best regime was once actual. The inferior regimes are decayed versions; there is no notion of progress gradually achieved over time (*CM*, 129).

17. Strauss's use of the qualifying clause "what Adeimantus calls theology" (*CM*, 98) suggests he does not think Socrates or Plato would call "theology" anything that did not begin with the question, what is god?

18. "Somewhat later in the conversation Socrates suggests that justice is a specifically human virtue (392a3–c3), perhaps because justice is rooted in the fact that every human being lacks self-sufficiency and hence is ordered toward the city (369b5–7) and therefore that man is essentially 'erotic' whereas the gods are self-sufficient and hence free from *eros*. *Eros* and justice would thus seem to have the same root" (*CM*, 99–100). For this reason in book 10 of the *Nicomachean Ethics* (1178b10–15) Aristotle declares that, being self-sufficient, the gods have no need for justice. The existence of Socrates's gods would not seem to depend upon human beings' believing in them.

19. Both Socrates and Strauss seem to ignore or abstract from international relations. Does the city not need to deal justly with other cities? As Socrates suggests in explaining, first, why guardians become necessary and then why they must be carefully educated, the city that does not restrict its citizens' desires to what they need to survive will have to take things from others unjustly. The relations of a just city with others will be limited, therefore, to defense. Will a city that contains a sufficient number of people and variety of trades to provide for the necessities be large enough to defend itself from others? It is not clear. (In Plato's *Laws* the Athenian Stranger thus suggests a good city needs to be founded in an isolated but sufficiently fertile place.) The need for defense itself raises a problem, moreover. When the city asks some of its citizens to give their lives in its defense, it subordinates the good of the individual to the good of the rest. But such a subordination of the good of one to the good or advantage of others was the definition of injustice, according to the exchange

between Thrasymachus and Socrates in book 1. The problem associated with defense points to the reasons Socrates has to abstract from the body or concerns with bodily preservation in the parallel he proceeds to draw between the individual and the city.

20. "A provisional consideration of the soul seems to . . . [show that it] contains desire, spiritedness or anger, and reason, just as the city consists of the money-makers, the warriors, and the rulers" (*CM*, 109–10).

21. Like Hans-Georg Gadamer, "Plato's Educational State," *Dialogue and Dialectic*, 86–87, Strauss observes how strange it is that the answer to the question "what is justice?" should be given less than halfway through the dialogue. Like everything else in the dialogue, he argues, this anomaly reflects the political context or setting. Unlike philosophical inquiries, political questions have a certain urgency; they have to be answered, somehow, now. Since the answer Socrates gives here is defective, the difference between the apparently doctrinaire character of the *Republic* and the clearly elenctic dialogues is more apparent than real (*CM*, 105–6).

22. The parallel Socrates draws between the city and the soul is defective, not merely because it results in a problematic abstraction from the body; it also produces a distorted view of the character and relation of the parts of the human soul. "It is very plausible that those who uphold the city against foreign and domestic enemies and who have received a music education should be more highly respected than those who lack public responsibility as well as music education," Strauss observes. "But it is much less plausible that spiritedness as such should be higher in rank than desire as such." Just as "spiritedness" encompasses a "large variety of phenomena ranging from the most noble indignation about injustice . . . to the anger of a spoiled child who resents being deprived of anything," so desire includes "*eros*, which ranges in its healthy forms from the longing for immortality through offspring . . . to the longing for immortality through participation by knowledge in the things which are unchangeable in every respect" (*CM*, 110). Socrates can maintain that spiritedness is unqualifiedly higher and more reasonable than desire only by abstracting from *eros*.

23. *RCPR*, 159; Seth Benardete, "Leo Strauss' *The City and Man*," *Political Science Reviewer* 8 (Fall 1978): 9.

24. In his "Restatement on Xenophon's *Hiero*," Strauss observed that the "defense of philosophy before the tribunal of the city was achieved by Plato with a resounding success (Plutarch, *Nicias* ch. 23). . . . One sometimes wonders whether it has not been too successful" (*OT*, 206). In *PAW*, 34–37, he suggested that philosophers in the past had concealed parts of their thought not merely to avoid persecution or simply to act in a socially responsible manner by not challenging salutary opinions. They also sought to guide young, potential philosophers "step by step from the popular views which are indispensable for all practical and political purposes to the truth which is merely and purely theoretical . . . by certain obtrusively enigmatic features in the presentation of the popular teaching." Referring explicitly to Plato's *Symposium*, Strauss concluded that "the works of the great writers of the past are very beautiful even from without. And yet their visible beauty is sheer ugliness, compared with the beauty of those hidden treasures which disclose themselves only after very long, never easy, but always pleasant work." In *TALS* we called this third function of "the art of writing" "pedagogical reserve" (136).

25. According to Strauss, there is an important difference between Aristophanes's "female" utopia and Socrates's "corrected version," headed by philosopher-kings, which is "altogether of male origin." Aristophanes's utopia is egalitarian, whereas the *Republic* is an aristocracy. Cf. *SA*, 282; *CM*, 114.

26. Whereas Strauss maintains that the "fiction" is the possibility of establishing the city

in speech in fact, in *How Philosophy Became Socratic: A Study of Plato's "Protagoras," "Charmides," and "Republic"* (Chicago: University of Chicago Press, 2010), Laurence Lampert contends that the "noble lie" Socrates propagates in the *Republic* is the new "religion" of the "ideas" with which he convinces Plato's brothers that they are philosophers who deserve to rule.

27. As Strauss points out with regard to the final "proof" of its immortality, one cannot know what the order or good of the soul is without knowing what the soul is. But like the question "what is god?," the question "what is soul?" is not raised in this or any other of Plato's dialogues. Strauss indicates the reasons these questions are not asked in his analysis of *Minos*, the Platonic dialogue in which Socrates explicitly raises one of the questions Xenophon's Socrates did not, "what is law?" In that dialogue, Socrates utterly dismisses consent as an ingredient of law, which he defines solely as the dictate of the divine intellect. Most laws are, we realize, mixtures, as Plato's two philosophical "strangers" teach. So, we believe, are the concepts of "soul" and "god" mixtures—of life with intellect in the case of soul, and in the case of God, as Strauss himself shows in his analysis of Maimonides's arguments concerning the attributes of God in his *Guide*, agency that can punish injustice with intellect that can produce order. There is, in other words, no simple or adequate answer to the "what is . . . ?" question in these cases. To show that there is no soul or god per se would have pernicious effects on salutary popular opinions. The unanswerability of these three questions is an expression, however, of the noetic heterogeneity of the whole. Cf. *LAM*, 65–75.

28. Plato, *Apology* 38a.

29. Myles F. Burnyeat, "Sphinx without a Secret," *New York Review of Books*, May 30, 1985, 30–36. G. R. F. Ferrari, "Strauss's Plato," *Arion* 5, no. 2 (1997): 36–63, provides a detailed response to Burnyeat's critique.

30. Thomas C. Brickhouse and Nicholas D. Smith present such a view in *Plato's Socrates* (New York: Oxford, 1994).

31. As Alfarabi pointed out, Plato's Socrates converses only with members of the elite, if not the highest elite.

32. The reason Socrates says he does not propose exile is that "in any other city . . . he would have the same troubles as in Athens. The young men would listen to his speeches; if he were to chase them away, they would persuade their elders to expel him; if he would not chase them away, their fathers and other relatives would" (*Apology* 37d–e; *SPPP*, 50). But, as Socrates reminded his audience in his first speech, he had survived in Athens for seventy years. As Strauss pointed out in his introduction to *AAPL*, the conjunction between the reasons "the laws" give in *Crito* why Socrates should not run away with the setting of the *Laws* suggests the philosopher could have gone anonymously to Crete and continued philosophizing there, if he had been younger.

33. In presenting reasons why he should not escape to safety after he had been convicted in *Crito*, Strauss pointed out, Socrates does not mention either the soul or philosophy—considerations both he and the Athenian Stranger argue should take precedence over concerns not only about one's bodily self-preservation but also about one's forebears, one of the grounds "the laws" give for his obligation to obey. The reasons "the laws" give correspond to Kriton's, but not to Socrates's own concerns. (In referring to "Kriton" rather than Crito, we follow Strauss's practice in this essay.)

34. In *Hermeneutics as Politics* (New York: Oxford University Press, 1987), 123, Stanley Rosen wonders why Strauss said in his discussion of Plato in *CM*, 61, that the dialogues are only "slightly" more akin to comedy than to tragedy. Here we have one reason: in the *Apology of Socrates*, Plato seems to many readers to present a tragedy. The conflict between politics

and philosophy appears comic only "from some perspectives." (In his analysis of Aristophanes Strauss pointed out that a comedy cannot depict a death, because it is too serious.) There is, however, something comic about Socrates's presentation of himself as a tragic hero. He does not "seem to notice the slight incongruity of comparing his dying in ripe old age with Achilleus' dying young" (*SPPP*, 44).

35. "Deeds are more trustworthy than speeches: Socrates did stay in prison, he chose to stay, he had a logos telling him to stay. But is this logos identical with the logos by which he persuades Kriton? We have indicated why this is not likely. . . . Kriton is concerned above all with what the people of Athens will say if he has not helped Socrates to escape from prison: what Socrates tells Kriton, Kriton can and will tell the people" (*SPPP*, 66). In *Birth of Tragedy*, sec. 13, Nietzsche also suggested that Socrates orchestrated his own death. See M. Zuckert, "Rationalism and Political Responsibility: Just Speech and Just Deed," *Polity* 17 (1984): 271–97.

36. In Plato's *Meno*, Socrates is shown to outrage Anytus by arguing that outstanding Athenian statesmen like Pericles have failed to educate even their own sons. In Xenophon's *Apology to the Jury*, Socrates makes a snide prediction about the future of Anytus's own son. In Xenophon's *Symposium*, Lykon is shown to be so enamored of his son that he sees little else.

37. E.g., Hans-Georg Gadamer, *The Idea of the Good in Platonic-Aristotelian Philosophy*, trans. P. Christopher Smith (New Haven: Yale University Press, 1988), 46–62.

38. Most scholarly discussions treat the *daimonion* in terms of the difference (or not) between the religious and rational bases of Socrates's actions: e.g., Mark McPherran, *The Religion of Socrates* (University Park: Pennsylvania State University Press, 1996); Nicholas D. Smith and Paul B. Woodruff, eds., *Reason and Religion in Socratic Philosophy* (Oxford: Oxford University Press, 2000); and Pierre Destrée and Nicholas D. Smith, *Socrates' Divine Sign: Religion, Practice and Value in Socratic Philosophy* (Kelowna, BC: Academic Printing and Publishing, 2005). They do not, like Strauss, treat the *daimonion* as a covert excuse.

39. Readers are reminded of the positive aspect of that *daimonion* or of Socrates's *eros*— his desire to associate with young men as well as his ability to attract them to him—when Kleinias goes immediately to Socrates's side, to which after a short deliberation the sophists also go. Although the authenticity of *Theages* is questioned, Strauss points out, Plato shows the same relation between the *daimonion* and Socrates's *eros* in this dialogue that Xenophon did (*SPPP*, 46–47). In Plato's *Symposium* 216c–219c Alkibiades suggests that Socrates only pretends to be attracted to young men; his purported *eros* is really a way of attracting them to him so that he can guide, if not dominate, their lives.

40. In contrast to Xenophon's Socrates in his *Oeconomicus*, Strauss emphasizes, Plato's hero does not want to spend even an afternoon telling a foolish young man how to become *kalos k'agathos*, conventionally understood.

41. Socrates responds to Dionysodoros's critique of the doctrine that beautiful things "participate" in the beautiful and yet are different from the beautiful-in-itself with an eristic argument concerning the same and the different that reminds of one of Plato's other philosophical spokesmen, the Eleatic Stranger, who suggests in the *Sophist* that we define everything according to its similarities and differences with others.

42. For a good introduction, see Mark Blitz, "Strauss's *Laws*," *Political Science Reviewer* 20 (Spring 1991): 186–222.

43. In the *Politics*, Strauss reminded his readers, Aristotle calls the Stranger Socrates. Plato's greatest student did not see any significant difference between Socrates and the Athenian Stranger.

44. Cf. *AAPL*, 2; *WIPP*, 154: just as Strauss observed that "Fārābī invented Platonic speeches . . . with ease" (*WIPP*, 154), so he suggested that "Plato invented . . . Socratic and other stories" (*AAPL*, 2).

45. Alfarabi points to such an opposition, Strauss observed, by remaining altogether silent about philosophy in his *Summary of Plato's "Laws"* and by attributing the *Laws* to Socrates in his *Philosophy of Plato*, but not mentioning law as the subject of the dialogue. "It is as if Fārābī had interpreted the absence of Socrates from the *Laws* to mean that Socrates has nothing to do with laws, and as if he had tried to express this interpretation by suggesting that if *per impossibile* the *Laws* were Socratic, they would not deal with laws" (*WIPP*, 153).

46. In "How Fārābī Read Plato's *Laws*," Strauss concluded that "Socrates' silence about laws . . . must be understood in the light of the implicit distinction [made in section 30 of Alfarabi's *Philosophy of Plato*] between the way of Socrates and the way of Plato" (*WIPP*, 153).

47. Alfarabi's failure to use the word "philosophy" in his *Summary* "must be understood in light of the implicit distinction . . . between the way of Socrates and the way of Plato. The way of Plato emerges through a correction of the way of Socrates. The way of Socrates is intransigent: it demands of the philosopher an open break with the accepted opinions. The way of Plato combines the way of Socrates, which is appropriate for the philosopher's relations to the elite, with the way of Thrasymachus, which is appropriate for the philosopher's relations to the vulgar. The way of Plato demands therefore judicious conformity with the accepted opinions. If we consider the connection, stated in the *Summary*, between the vulgar and the laws, we arrive at the conclusion that the appreciation or legitimation of laws becomes possible by virtue of Plato's correction of the way of Socrates" (*WIPP*, 153). In the note Strauss appended to this statement, he observed, "The first half of the *Philosophy of Plato* ends with 'Socrates'; the second half ends with 'their laws,' i.e., the laws of the Athenians."

48. In taking Strauss's comment on Alfarabi's "pious ascetic" to be an endorsement of "noble" lying, Shadia Drury fails to note Strauss's own conclusion that the ascetic lied "in deed," and that his lying was justified only by the requirement of his own self-preservation. Cf. *Political Ideas of Leo Strauss*, xi, 14, with *TALS*, 116–20.

49. In his account of Alfarabi's reading (*WIPP*, 148–50), Strauss pointed out that, although the gods are frequently mentioned in his *Summary* in contrast to their complete absence in his *Philosophy of Plato*, they are not mentioned in Alfarabi's account of book 6 (although they appear both in Plato's text and in Strauss's).

50. *Laws* 709e–710d; *AAPL*, 56–57. Commentators like Drury who take such restatements by Strauss of the positions taken by Plato's characters as Strauss's own endorsement of the advantages of combining philosophy with tyranny (or philosophers' seeking to obtain absolute power) fail to notice Strauss's insistence that philosophers in Plato (and according to Strauss) will not seek rule. Cf. *OT*, 202, and *TALS*, 158–66.

51. In other words, the argument of the *Laws* does not abstract from body the way the argument of the *Republic* does. This is the reason that the regime of the *Republic* is said in *Laws* book 5 to be best, but to be suitable only for gods or demigods and not for human beings. In the *Laws* citizens are allowed to have private property and to select specific individuals to marry. Inequalities in wealth are strictly limited, however; members of the two sexes are treated as equally as possible; and family life is subject to a good deal of public supervision. The city is ruled, moreover, by a "Nocturnal Council" of wise old men who choose young men to join their secret deliberations and so to become educated. As Aristotle observes in *Politics* 1265a1, the institutions of the *Laws* finally become hard to distinguish from those of the *Republic*.

52. Strauss emphasizes his own agreement with this analysis when he reiterates "the necessity . . . of diluting true proportionate equality which for us is always the political right" (*AAPL*, 180).

53. This moderation is the quality Nietzsche lacked in contrast to Plato, according to Strauss (*SPPP*, 174, 183, 191). It is, we might venture to suggest, the distinguishing quality of the political philosopher qua political philosopher. *Sōphrosunē* is also the only "cardinal" virtue Socrates does not claim himself in Plato's *Apology*. But, as Xenophon shows, at his trial Socrates wanted to provoke the Athenians to condemn him; he was not trying to persuade them to live with him in peace.

54. Although he teaches that citizens must be led to honor their souls, second only to the gods, and to believe that, as the source of motion, soul is prior to matter and so presumably to believe in the gods as well, the Athenian does not, any more than Socrates, raise or answer the questions "what is soul?" or "what is god?"

55. The obfuscation is not accidental, however. The Athenian explicitly argues that the successful legislator must convince his people that the laws he has drafted just now have been in effect from ancient times. Because *nomos* consists of a kind of opinion, it never has or can have the status of knowledge and will not, therefore, be able to answer philosophical questions or critiques. It has the same defect, in other words, that Socrates attributes to writing in general in *Phaedrus*.

56. Cf. *SPPP*, 42–43. In his essay "On Plato's *Apology of Socrates* and *Crito*" Strauss argued that Socrates shows "the primary charge concerns his corruption of the young and that the other three charges [concerning his impiety] are pure inventions thought out in order to give some plausibility to the corruption charge" (*SPPP*, 41).

57. Strauss indicated the extent to which *thymos* has been abstracted from in the *Laws* by rarely using the word in his summaries. Thomas Pangle lists more than seventy-seven instances in which the word "spiritedness," "spirit," or *thymos* occurs in the index to his translation, *The Laws of Plato* (Chicago: University of Chicago Press, 1988), 560. But Strauss used the English translation of *thymos*, "spirit," only twice—once in his account of the need for human beings to be both gentle and spirited in his presentation of the discussion of the soul in book 5 (*AAPL*, 68), and second in his commentary on book 10 (*AAPL*, 141, 143), where he pointed out that, having urged his interlocutors that they need to try to persuade atheists of the existence of the gods without spirited anger, the Athenian then found it necessary to arouse Kleinias's spirit. The Athenian's speech had apparently smothered the passion that led "fathers" like Kleinias to persecute Socrates. Strauss used the Greek word only in his account of book 11 (*AAPL*, 167), when he observed that the Athenian's critique of "the kind of madness that comes from a bad nature and training of spiritedness (*thymos*)" led the Athenian by "logographic necessity" to talk about "evil-speaking," ridicule, and hence comedy—a reference, no doubt, to Aristophanes, who warned Socrates about the danger he might encounter if he aroused the spirited opposition of the fathers by teaching their sons to be impious. Observing that comedy, although not necessarily tragedy, would be allowed in the city, Strauss concluded by noting that "what one ought to stress is the corresponding devaluation of *thymos* (cf. 888a2–6)."

58. Victor Gourevitch, "Philosophy and Politics, I," *Review of Metaphysics* 22, no. 1 (1968): 60–61.

CHAPTER SIX

1. G. E. M. Anscombe, "Modern Moral Philosophy," *Philosophy* 33, no. 124 (1958): 1–19; Alasdair MacIntyre, *After Virtue* (Notre Dame, IN: University of Notre Dame Press, 1984).

2. John Finnis, *Natural Law and Natural Rights* (Oxford: Oxford University Press, 1980); Joseph Raz, *The Morality of Freedom* (Oxford: Oxford University Press, 1988).

3. Leo Strauss, *Xenophon's Socratic Discourse: An Interpretation of the Oeconomicus* (Ithaca, NY: Cornell University Press, 1970); Leo Strauss, *Xenophon's Socrates* (Ithaca NY: Cornell University Press, 1972).

4. For parallels, see also Leo Strauss, "On Classical Political Philosophy," in *WIPP*, 78–94; "TWM."

5. *WIPP*, 27–55.

6. For a fuller discussion, see *TALS*, 49–57.

7. For another and more explicit account of the problems with Aristotelian moral virtue, see Strauss, "On Classical Political Philosophy," 89–90.

CHAPTER SEVEN

1. Nor could Strauss have referred to another time or set of circumstances. Marsilius was born within a few years of Aquinas's death.

CHAPTER EIGHT

1. Paul Sigmund, editor's introduction to *The Selected Political Writings of John Locke* (New York: Norton, 2005), xxvii.

2. See also, e.g., John Yolton, "Strauss on Locke's Law of Nature," in *Selected Political Writings*, 281.

3. Leo Strauss, "Locke's Doctrine of Natural Law," *American Political Science Review* 52, no. 2 (1958): 490–501.

4. Leo Strauss, "The Political Philosophy of John Locke," lecture 5 (20 January 1958). A transcript of the lecture series is available at http://leostrausscenter.uchicago.edu/audio -transcripts.

5. Sigmund, introduction to *Selected Political Writings*, xxvii.

6. See Mary Keys, *Aquinas, Aristotle, and the Promise of the Common Good* (Cambridge: Cambridge University Press, 2008).

7. Leo Strauss, "Letter to Helmut Kuhn," *Independent Journal of Philosophy* 2 (1978): 23–26.

8. One aspect of Strauss's discussion of Alfarabi might seem to ill fit Strauss's own deployment of the "Platonic" tactic of unobtrusively speaking on matters of a "dangerous character." "Danger" of course is contextual, and it may describe situations other than physical threat. The "danger" in Strauss's presenting an open refutation of Thomistic natural law derives from the fact that Strauss regularly identifies Catholics and Catholic "social science" as a key ally in his opposition to positivism (*NRH*, 2). Of course, Strauss does not see opposing Catholic philosophy as dangerous in the sense of personally threatening, nor does he go to very great lengths to conceal his real reservations about it, as is visible in the *NRH* discussion of Aquinas.

CHAPTER NINE

1. E.g., John McCormick, "Fear, Technology, and the State: Carl Schmitt, Leo Strauss, and the Revival of Hobbes in Weimar and National Socialist Germany," *Political Theory* 22, no. 41 (1994): 619–52; Nicholas Xenos, *Cloaked in Virtue: Unveiling Leo Strauss* ((New York: Routledge, 2008); William H. F. Altman, *The German Stranger: Leo Strauss and National Socialism* (Lanham, MD: Lexington Books, 2010). Paul Gottfried, *Leo Strauss and the Conservative Movement in America* (Cambridge: Cambridge University Press, 2012), dismisses the

claims of Strauss's left critics that he was a fascist. Indeed, according to Gottfried, Strauss was no "true conservative." He was a "Cold War liberal" who spent his adult life trying to dissuade others from sharing his own youthful obsession with Nietzsche and Heidegger. Gottfried nevertheless decries Strauss's influence on some of the neoconservatives who shaped the Bush foreign policy.

2. Both Strauss's answer to the question and his caution are to be found in a talk he was asked to give at the New School on 7 November 1943, "The Re-education of Axis Countries concerning the Jews," reprinted in *Review of Politics* 73, no. 4 (2007): 532 ff.

3. Meier, *Carl Schmitt and Leo Strauss*, 123–28, reprints three letters from Strauss to Schmitt.

4. See Strauss's letter to Schmitt of 10 July 1933, in ibid., 127.

5. Ibid., xviii.

6. McCormick, "Fear, Technology, and the State," 619, 628.

7. Strauss to Schmitt, 13 March 1932, in Meier, *Carl Schmitt and Leo Strauss*, 123.

8. Schmitt to Ludwig Feuchtwanger, 10 June 1935, in ibid., 8n7.

9. Strauss to Schmitt, 4 September 1932, in ibid., 126.

10. In his "social-scientific" or "Weberian" mode, Strauss notes, Schmitt asserts that "applied to the political, *all* ideals are nothing but 'abstractions,' *all* 'normative prescriptions' nothing but 'fictions.' For the political is constituted by reference 'to the real possibility of physical killing' of men by men: and 'there is no rational purpose, no norm however correct, no program however exemplary, no social ideal however beautiful, no legitimacy or legality that can justify men's killing one another for its own sake'" (ibid., 93).

11. *Pace* Jacob Schiff, "From Anti-liberal to Untimely Liberal: Leo Strauss' Two Critiques of Liberalism," *Philosophy and Social Criticism* 36, no. 2 (2010): 157–81, Strauss does not himself endorse theological grounds; he merely specifies what would be necessary to make Schmitt's arguments in his two books consistent with one another.

12. Relevant here is Meier's extension of Strauss's point to the claim that Schmitt's affirmation ultimately rests on a theological claim. As Meier emphasizes, that is not obvious in Schmitt's book, nor does Strauss explicitly raise the point in his essay.

13. It could be noted that Strauss's analysis of Schmitt shares much with his much later interpretation of Weber in *NRH*.

14. As Heinrich Meier has argued, Schmitt went on to define his position in more explicitly theological terms as a battle against the atheistic, anarchist, technocratic enemy. (In doing so, he thus continued to define his position primarily in terms of opposition to an enemy. He also continued to align himself with "realist" political theorists like Machiavelli and Hobbes.)

15. Xenos, *Cloaked in Virtue*, 53.

16. Strauss, "An Unspoken Prologue," in *JPCM*, 450.

17. Leo Strauss, "German Nihilism," *Interpretation* 26, no. 3 (1999): 353–78 (with corrections by Wiebke Meier in *Interpretation* 28, no. 2 [2000]: 33–34); Leo Strauss, *Hobbes' politische Wissenschaft* (Neuwied: Hermann Luchterhand, 1965).

18. On Heidegger in Strauss's correspondence, see Velkley, *Heidegger, Strauss, and the Premises of Philosophy*.

19. David Janssens, "A Change of Orientation: Leo Strauss's 'Comments' on Carl Schmitt Revisited," *Interpretation* 33, no. 1 (2005): 93–104, gives a detailed analysis of Strauss's review to show how his later orientation toward classical political philosophy is already present.

20. Xenos, *Cloaked in Virtue*, 57, 58.

21. See *PPH*, chap. 8, for a strong critique of Hobbes's break with the preceding political

philosophic tradition. For an exposition of this critique, see Devin Stauffer, "Reopening the Quarrel between the Ancients and the Moderns: Leo Strauss's Critique of Hobbes's 'New Political Science,'" *American Political Science Review* 101, no. 2 (2007): 223–33.

22. See *TALS*, prologue and conclusion.

23. Xenos, *Cloaked in Virtue*, xi.

24. Ibid.

25. Ibid.

26. Ibid.

27. See chapter 2.

28. Xenos, *Cloaked in Virtue*, 57.

29. Ibid.

30. Ibid, 58.

31. "NCS," 125; quoted in Xenos, *Cloaked in Virtue*, 28.

32. Xenos, *Cloaked in Virtue*, xvii.

33. Nicholas Xenos, "Leo Strauss and Rhetoric of the War on Terror," *Logos* 3, no. 2 (2004): 3.

34. Scott Horton, "The Letter," *Balkinization* (blog), http://balkin.blogspot.com/2006 /07/letter_16.html. Also see Sheppard, *Leo Strauss and the Politics of Exile*, 54–67.

35. Horton, "Will the Real Leo Strauss Please Stand Up?," *No Comment* (blog), *Harper's Magazine*, January 21, 2008, http://harpers.org/blog/2008/01/will-the-real-leo-strauss-please -stand-up/.

36. Ibid.

37. Ibid.

38. See especially the letters written to Jacob Klein included in Strauss, *Gesammelte Schriften*, 3:455–605.

39. See *TALS*, chap. 4.

40. Xenos, *Cloaked in Virtue*, xviii.

41. Translation by Minowitz, *Straussophobia*, 155. We have used his more accurate translation rather than that of Xenos.

42. A note on the translation: the word Xenos has rendered "imperialist" and italicized as if for greater emphasis is actually in the German text *imperialen*. This is not the German word for "imperialist"—that would be *imperialistische*. Strauss has used the word *imperialen*, an inflected and thus somewhat Germanified version of an English word or a Germanified version of a Latin word, and has it italicized (or underlined) because it is a borrowed word in a German text. Xenos's rendition gives a quite misleading impression of what Strauss is saying, for the word *imperial* in English, with its echoes of the Latin *imperium* (rule), need not refer to imperialism, as Xenos has it. Consider the use of the phrase by the American founders—they would institute an "empire of liberty."

43. Minowitz, *Straussophobia*, 184; Xenos, *Cloaked in Virtue*, 149n55.

44. Xenos, *Cloaked in Virtue*, 149n55; Minowitz, *Straussophobia*, 184.

45. Minowitz, *Straussophobia*, 184.

46. According to Susan Shell, "Strauss's audience consisted of fellow members of the General Seminar, a group of distinguished scholars, most of them refugees, whose common topic that year was 'Experiences of the Second World War'" ("'To Spare the Vanquished and Crush the Arrogant,'" 173).

47. In his blog *Democratic Individuality* (entry of August 11, 2009, http://democratic -individuality.blogspot.com/2009/08/leo-strauss-courage-to-destroy.html), Alan Gilbert

refers to an article by William H. F. Altman, "Leo Strauss on 'German Nihilism': Learning the Art of Writing," *Journal of the History of Ideas* 68, no. 4 (2007): 587–612. Although Strauss claims to be revealing the roots of "German nihilism" in the first part of his lecture and contrasts German imperialism negatively with its British counterpart in the third part, Altman argues that Strauss's "secret teaching" is to be found in the center of the talk when Strauss explicitly presents the position of the young German nihilists and not his own. Like Xenos, Altman maintains that Strauss does not mean what he says, because he is engaged in "secret teaching." Altman thinks that Strauss is engaged in "secret teaching" because he published his essay "Persecution and the Art of Writing" in 1941, the year he gave this talk. Assuming his conclusion, Altman contends that Strauss had to engage in secret teaching because he feared persecution as a nihilist in liberal America. That was the reason, Altman suggests, that Strauss did not publish the talk (as if he published every other talk he gave). Like Xenos and McCormick, Altman takes the position that Strauss explicitly attributed to others, in this case, to young German nihilists, to be Strauss's own. Like Xenos and McCormick, Altman maintains that Strauss was still adhering to the principles of the right he had endorsed in the May 1933 letter to Löwith, even though Strauss explicitly concluded that, as a matter of right, Britain should defeat Hitler's Germany. Altman finds it significant that Strauss does not endorse Britain explicitly as a liberal democracy. Altman apparently does not mention that although Britain held an empire, her government in 1941 was neither fascist nor authoritarian.

48. Ralf Dahrendorf, *Gesellschaft und Demokratie in Deutschland* (Munich: R. Piper, 1968).

49. Both in this lecture and in his restatement of the point in *WIPP*, Strauss insists that Nietzsche was not directly responsible for and would not have welcomed the "vulgar" form of German nihilism. Nevertheless, Strauss insisted that Nietzsche's influence was an important factor contributing to its emergence.

50. Hermann Rauschning, *The Revolution of Nihilism: Warning to the West* (New York: Longmans, Green, 1939). According to Shell ("'To Spare the Vanquished and Crush the Arrogant,'" 173), "Rauschning was a former Nazi who criticized the movement from the standpoint of a disillusioned conservative nationalist." His text had recently been translated into English and was the assigned text for the seminar.

51. Strauss, "Re-education of Axis Countries concerning the Jews," 532.

52. Ibid., 532–33. The reasons Strauss gives for his pessimistic judgment concerning the possibility of establishing a liberal democracy in post–World War II Germany in his lecture echo his description of political conditions in post–World War I Germany in "German Nihilism": "Where are the roots, in German soil, of liberal democracy? Of course, there is a tradition of German liberal democracy—but we have to add, a tradition of political *inefficiency* of German liberal democracy. It came to power only once: after Germany's defeat in the last war. Seven years later, long before the economic world crisis, it was already doomed: the election of Hindenburg to the presidency of the Reich in 1925, and, more visibly, the demonstrations in the streets of the German cities after the election, showed to everyone who did not deliberately blind himself, where Germany was going. Nothing really *known* permits us to indulge the hope that the politically efficient part of the German people has changed their minds as regards liberal democracy" (533).

53. Strauss, "Re-education of Axis Countries concerning the Jews," 533.

54. On Strauss's grounds for supporting liberal democracy, one should also consult Galston, "Leo Strauss's Qualified Embrace of Liberal Democracy," 171–92.

55. See *CM*, 127, on the impossibility of the just city, and 138, where Strauss refers to Cicero's observation that "the *Republic* does not bring to light the best possible regime but rather the nature of political things" in *De republica* 2.52. See also chapter 5 above.

56. By showing the limits of politics, Strauss argues, "the *Republic* supplies the most magnificent cure ever devised for every form of political ambition" (*CM*, 65).

57. "PR" and chapter 4 above.

CHAPTER TEN

1. The lecture has been published in *JPCM*, 311–56.

2. "A Giving of Accounts: Jacob Klein and Leo Strauss," *The College* 22, no. 1 (April 1970): 1–5, reprinted in *JPCM*, 459–60.

3. On Strauss's Zionism, see Michael Zank, *Leo Strauss: The Early Writings (1921–1932)* (Albany: State University of New York Press, 2002), 3–23. Jerry Muller, "Leo Strauss as a Young Zionist," *Jewish Social Studies* 17, no. 1 (2010): 97–98 and 112, points out, however, that Zank's attribution to Strauss of an identification with the Blau-Weiss is not warranted by Strauss's explicit statements or by the tenor of his writings.

4. Letter to Gerhard Krüger, 19 August 1932, in *Gesammelte Schriften*, 2:xxviin34.

5. Strauss gave a lecture titled "Existentialism" at the Hillel House at the University of Chicago in 1956. The typescript from the Strauss archives has been slightly edited and published as "TL." A more seriously edited version of the lecture can be found in *RCPR*, 27–46. The quotation is from "TL," 307.

6. Martin Heidegger, *Introduction to Metaphysics*, trans. Ralph Mannheim (New Haven: Yale University Press, 1959), 37–38.

7. See Martin Heidegger, "The Question concerning Technology" and "The Turning," in *The Question Concerning Technology and Other Essays*, trans. William Lovitt (New York: Harper, 1977), 3–49.

8. Martin Heidegger, *What Is Called Thinking?*, trans. J. Glenn Gray (New York: Harper, 1968); "The Spiegel Interview," in *Martin Heidegger and National Socialism: Questions and Answers*, ed. Gunther Neske and Emil Kettering (New York: Paragon House, 1990), 61–62.

9. Quotation from "The Problem of Socrates," the second of the two lectures published in "TL," at 329.

10. Velkley, *Heidegger, Strauss, and the Premises of Philosophy*, emphasizes the commonality between Heidegger and Strauss insofar as they both argue that human knowledge is limited, because the whole is unknowable. Heidegger and Strauss come to this conclusion, however, for very different reasons. According to Heidegger, Being is hidden by the disclosure of the beings that Being makes possible. According to Strauss, Being is intelligible only as differentiated into beings (*NRH*, 123–25), but the different kinds of beings (homogeneous and heterogeneous) are not commensurable (*WIPP*, 39–41).

11. As Strauss argued in "Jerusalem and Athens," in *SPPP*, 147–73, and "PR." See chapter 4 above for a more detailed account of his reasoning.

12. Cf. Steven B. Smith, "Destruktion or Recovery?," *Review of Metaphysics* 51 (December 1997): 374.

13. Gregory B. Smith, "The Post-Modern Leo Strauss?," *History of European Ideas* 19, no. 1 (1994): 192, also emphasizes Strauss's fervent defense of liberal democracy in contrast to Heidegger's continued insistence on the "inner truth and greatness of National Socialism."

14. Dana Villa, "Hannah Arendt, 1906–1975," *Review of Politics* 71, no. 1 (2009): 20–26; Elisabeth Young-Bruehl, *Hannah Arendt: For Love of the World* (New Haven: Yale University

Press, 1982); Hannah Arendt, *The Jewish Writings*, ed. Jerome Kohn and Ronald H. Feldman (New York: Schocken Books, 2007).

15. Hannah Arendt, *The Origins of Totalitarianism* (New York: Harcourt Brace, 1973), 296–97.

16. Ibid., part 3.

17. Strauss did not deny that modern "totalitarian" governments differed from classical tyrannies in their use of modern technology and ideology. But he did maintain, for reasons he lays out in his essay "Political Philosophy and History," that it is necessary to unearth the classical roots of concepts like "tyranny" in order to see the way in which they have been covered over and transformed in modern political philosophy.

18. Dana Villa, *Arendt and Heidegger: The Fate of the Political* (Princeton: Princeton University Press, 1996).

19. In chapter 11 we will see that Strauss thought that liberal education offered the best response to the problem of mass culture, although admittedly a partial one.

20. Hannah Arendt, *The Human Condition* (Chicago: University of Chicago Press, 1958), 22–78.

21. For the modern examples, see Hannah Arendt, *On Revolution* (London: Penguin Books, 1963).

22. Arendt, *Human Condition*, 189.

23. Ibid., 169.

24. On the inaccuracy of Arendt's description of the ancient *polis* and her "flat-footed" readings of Plato, see J. Peter Euben, "Arendt's Hellenism," in *The Cambridge Companion to Hannah Arendt*, ed. Dana Villa (Cambridge: Cambridge University Press, 2000), 151–52.

25. Sheldon Wolin, *Politics and Vision* (Princeton: Princeton University Press, 2004), 455–56.

26. See Villa, *Arendt and Heidegger*, 171–240.

27. Heidegger, *Introduction to Metaphysics*, 152, 163–64, 191.

28. Hannah Arendt, "Philosophy and Politics," *Social Research* 57, no. 1 (1990): 81; Heidegger, "Plato's Doctrine of Truth," 251–70.

29. Arendt, "Philosophy and Politics," 81.

30. Ibid.

31. Ibid.

32. Ibid., 83–84.

33. Ibid., 101–2.

34. Ibid., 103, 101.

35. Löwith and Strauss, "Correspondence," 183–84.

36. Strauss, "Unspoken Prologue," in *JPCM*, 1.

37. Cf. Strauss, "An Epilogue," in *LAM*; Arendt, *Human Condition*, 22–78.

38. E.g., in a lecture delivered on 26 March 1985, at the Faculty House of the Claremont Colleges, first published in *Claremont Review of Books* 4 (1985): 21–23, repr. in *Jewish Philosophers and Jewish Philosophy*, ed. Michael L. Morgan (Bloomington: Indiana University Press, 1996), 97–105.

39. Emil L. Fackenheim, *Encounters between Judaism and Modern Philosophy: A Preface to Future Jewish Thought* (New York: Basic Books, 1973), 4.

40. See Lynn Hunt, ed., *The French Revolution and Human Rights* (New York: St. Martin's, 1996), 93–101.

41. Fackenheim, *Encounters between Judaism and Modern Philosophy*, 87.

42. Emil L. Fackenheim, *To Mend the World: Foundations of Post-Holocaust Jewish Thought* (Bloomington: Indiana University Press, 1994), 23.

43. Ibid., 38–45. See also Leo Strauss, "How to Study Spinoza's *Theologico-Political Treatise*," in *PAW*, 142 ff.

44. Fackenheim, *To Mend the World*, 51.

45. "Hegel . . . blames him for being an 'acosmist' (who saves God but loses the world, and hence man as well)" (ibid., 51).

46. Ibid., 61.

47. Ibid., 89n, 264n.

48. Ibid., 89n.

49. Ibid., 81.

50. Ibid., 75.

51. Ibid., 79.

52. Ibid., 99.

53. Ibid., 149.

54. Ibid., 167–68.

55. Ibid., 180.

56. Cf. Strauss, "Philosophy as Rigorous Science and Political Philosophy," in *SPPP*, 30.

57. Fackenheim, *To Mend the World*, 183 ff.

58. Ibid.

59. Cf. ibid., 183 ff.

60. Ibid., 262–63.

61. See Friedrich Nietzsche, *Genealogy of Morals*, III, §1, quoted by Martin Heidegger in "The Word of Nietzsche: 'God Is Dead,'" in *The Question Concerning Technology and Other Essays*, 79.

CHAPTER ELEVEN

1. Walter Nicgorski, "Leo Strauss and Liberal Education," *Interpretation* 13, no. 3 (1985): 233.

CHAPTER TWELVE

1. See, for example, Thomas Pangle, *Leo Strauss: An Introduction to His Thought and Intellectual Legacy*, 89–127; John Murley, *Leo Strauss and His Legacy: A Bibliography* (Lanham, MD: Lexington Books, 2005).

2. Strauss, *Hobbes' politische Wissenschaft*, quoted in Meier, *Leo Strauss and the Theologico-Political Problem*, 4.

3. Meier, *Leo Strauss and the Theologico-Political Problem*, 3.

4. Ibid, xiii. Cf. Thomas Pangle, *Political Philosophy and the God of Abraham* (Baltimore: Johns Hopkins University Press, 2003).

5. Meier, *Leo Strauss and the Theologico-Political Problem*, 6.

6. Ibid.

7. Strauss, "Reason and Revelation," in Meier, *Leo Strauss and the Theologico-Political Problem*, 149.

8. Meier, *Leo Strauss and the Theologico-Political Problem*, 16.

9. Ibid, 154.

10. Ibid, 165.

11. Ibid. Emphasis added.

12. Ibid, 163.

13. Pangle, *Political Philosophy and the God of Abraham*.

14. Pangle, *Leo Strauss: An Introduction to His Thought and Intellectual Legacy*, 13; emphasis added.

15. Pangle, *Political Philosophy and the God of Abraham*, 13.

16. Pangle, *Leo Strauss: An Introduction to His Thought and Intellectual Legacy*, 57.

17. Ibid.

18. Laurence Lampert, *Leo Strauss and Nietzsche* (Chicago: University of Chicago Press, 1996).

19. Rosen, *Elusiveness of the Ordinary*, 135–58.

20. Harry V. Jaffa, *Thomism and Aristotelianism* (Westport, CT: Greenwood, 1979).

21. Harry V. Jaffa, "Leo Strauss, the Bible, and Political Philosophy," in *Leo Strauss: Political Philosopher and Jewish Thinker*, ed. Kenneth L. Deutsch and Walter Nicgorski (Lanham, MD: Rowman and Littlefield, 1995), 199–200.

22. Susan Orr, *Jerusalem and Athens: Reason and Revelation in the Works of Leo Strauss* (Lanham, MD: Rowman and Littlefield, 1995).

23. Ibid, 149.

24. Ibid, 150.

25. Ibid, 151.

26. Ibid, 158.

27. Ralph C. Hancock, "What Was Political Philosophy? Or: The Straussian Philosopher and His Other," *Political Science Reviewer* 36 (2007): 39.

28. Ibid.

29. Ibid, 38.

30. Peter Lawler, "Strauss, Straussians, and Faith-Based Students of Strauss," *Political Science Reviewer* 36 (2007): 12.

31. See Marc D. Guerra, "Leo Strauss and the Recovery of the Theologico-Political Problem," *Political Science Reviewer* 36 (2007): 75n81.

32. Strauss, "Reason and Revelation," 161.

33. "PR," 298; *NRH*, 35–80; *TALS*, 149–54; Guerra, "Strauss and the Recovery of the Theologico-Political Problem," 67.

34. *CM*, 27. See chapter 6 above.

35. Harry V. Jaffa, *Crisis of the House Divided* (Seattle: University of Washington Press, 1973); Jaffa, *A New Birth of Freedom* (Lanham, MD: Rowman and Littlefield, 2000).

36. Herbert Storing, "Slavery and the Moral Foundations of the American Republic," in *Toward a More Perfect Union: Writings of Herbert Storing*, ed. Joseph M. Bessette (Washington, DC: AEI Press, 1995), 131–50.

37. Jaffa, *Crisis of the House Divided*, 183–232.

38. Mary Nichols, *Citizens and Statesmen* (Lanham, MD: Rowman and Littlefield, 1992).

39. Aristide Tessitore, *Reading Aristotle's "Ethics": Virtue, Rhetoric, and Political Philosophy* (Albany: State University of New York Press, 1996), 119.

40. Nichols, *Citizens and Statesmen*, 2–3.

41. Ibid, 4.

42. Ibid, 1.

43. Ibid, 85–125.

44. Ibid, 167.

45. Seth Benardete, *The Argument of the Action: Essays on Greek Poetry and Philosophy* (Chicago: University of Chicago Press, 2000), 407.

46. Ibid, 408.

47. Ibid.; Seth Benardete, *Socrates' Second Sailing: On Plato's "Republic"* (Chicago: University of Chicago Press, 1989).

48. Ronna Burger and Michael Davis, editors' introduction to Benardete, *Argument of the Action*, xi.

49. Seth Benardete, *The Rhetoric of Morality and Philosophy: Plato's "Gorgias" and "Phaedrus"* (Chicago: University of Chicago Press, 1991), 1.

50. Seth Benardete, "Leo Strauss's *The City and Man*," *Political Science Reviewer* 8 (1978): 11.

51. Benardete, *Socrates' Second Sailing*, 91–102.

52. Michael Davis, *The Politics of Philosophy* (Lanham, MD: Rowman and Littlefield, 1996).

53. Michael Davis, *Wonderlust* (South Bend, IN: St. Augustine's Press, 2006), 131.

54. Davis, *Politics of Philosophy*, 5.

55. Ibid.

56. Ibid, xii; cf. *Wonderlust*, 131–55.

57. Davis, *Politics of Philosophy*, 29.

CONCLUSION

1. "Reason and Revelation," 142.

2. E.g., Charles Larmore, "The Secret Philosophy of Leo Strauss," in *The Morals of Modernity* (Cambridge: Cambridge University Press, 1996), 65–76.

3. E.g., Terence Irwin, review of *Xenophon's Socrates*, by Leo Strauss, *Philosophical Review* 83, no. 3 (1974): 409–13; Burnyeat, "Sphinx without a Secret."

4. Aristotle, *Metaphysics* 987a29–988a17; *SPPP*, 168. See above, chapter 5.

5. *CM*, 92–93, 138; see above, chapter 5.

6. The suggestion is ironic, because Strauss emphasizes that the ancient political philosopher upon whom Machiavelli most often draws is Xenophon, but in citing Xenophon, Strauss observes, Machiavelli refers only to his admiration for Cyrus and remains completely silent about Xenophon's admiration for Socrates. See *TM*, 288–98.

7. Machiavelli's well-known persistent attempts to seek employment from the Medici would appear to speak against such a conclusion.

Index